The Role of Interest
in Learning and Development

The Role of Interest
in Learning and Development

Edited by

K. Ann Renninger
Swarthmore College

Suzanne Hidi
Ontario Institute for Studies in Education

Andreas Krapp
Universität der Bundeswehr—Munich

LEA LAWRENCE ERLBAUM ASSOCIATES, PUBLISHERS
1992   Hillsdale, New Jersey   Hove and London

Lawrence Erlbaum Associates, Inc., Publishers
365 Broadway
Hillsdale, New Jersey 07642

Library of Congress Cataloging-in-Publication Data

The Role of interest in learning and development / edited by K. Ann
    Renninger, Suzanne Hidi, Andreas Krapp.
        p.   cm.
    Includes bibliographical references (p.) and index.
    ISBN 0-8058-0718-7
    1. Interest (Psychology)   2. Learning, Psychology of.
I. Renninger, K. Ann.   II. Hidi, Suzanne.   III. Krapp, Andreas.
LB1065.R57   1992
370.15′23 — dc20   92-2865
                                                                        CIP

Printed in the United States of America
10 9 8 7 6 5 4 3 2

Contents

List of Tables

List of Figures

Preface

The impetus for this volume stems from an extended lunch during the 1988 Meetings of the American Educational Research Association in New Orleans. We, the editors and some of the authors of chapters in this book, were discussing the emerging "interest" in interest research and its importance as a critical bridge between cognitive and affective issues in both learning and development. It was clear to us that interest research provided a way to focus the increasing concern of educators and psychologists for studying the individual in context, examining affective variables as opposed to purely structural features of text, analyzing the interrelationship of cognitive and social development, understanding practical applications of theories of motivation, and recog-nizing the importance of developmental psychology for the study of learning. We discussed the need for a forum in which those studying interest might share their work with others, and decided to compile a book about recent theoretical and empirical contributions to this field. Lawrence Erlbaum Associates agreed to publish this book.

It was acknowledged at the outset that each of the contributing authors would offer a unique perspective on understanding interest and its effects on learning and development. Despite a long tradition of interest-related research in both psychology and education, the more recent work in this area could only be described as an emerging phenomenon—no two researchers were really working with exactly the same sets of questions. In fact, as editors we were not in particular agreement with each other about what interest was, although we all agreed that interest was important and that we needed to continue to talk with each other in order to understand how the questions we were each addressing were in fact related or complementary.

Our work had only just begun, however. A particular feature of the book is its emphasis on theory-driven research. It is commonly acknowledged that Europeans are more rigorously trained in theory and those from North America are more versed in empiricism. In inviting authors to contribute to this volume, we asked each to contribute a chapter articulating his or her own understanding of interest, clearly stating a theoretical perspective as well as appropriate findings from the author's own program of research on interest. As editors, we have worked with each of the authors to incorporate both theoretical considerations and empirical research into the chapters. Yet with three editors in three different geographical locations, and only one whose native language is English, additional editorial assistance to provide continuity across chapters was needed especially with respect to language usage. Here Valerie Anderson was of unparalleled help. She tackled ten of the chapters with a critical and unyielding eye, making valuable additions and editorial suggestions that have resulted in a more comprehensible text. For several chapters she is clearly a ghost co-author. We are indebted to her for her contributions to these chapters and thus to the volume as a whole.

Others to whom we owe many thanks include Steve Adams, who translated the German authors' chapters into English, and John McLaren, who provided technical assistance and back-up statistical consultations during the process of reading and editing the chapters in their various incarnations. Finally, we would like to acknowledge the hard work, commitment to perfection, and sense of humor of Sarah S. Fought, who prepared the manuscript as camera-ready copy.

K. Ann Renninger
Suzanne Hidi
Andreas Krapp

Foreword

Researchers who investigate learning and comprehension processes quickly discover that interest is a very potent factor in their studies. We all have excellent intuitions about what is interesting and why, but the task of providing an explicit scientific account for these intuitions and for the role of interest in learning is a difficult one, and one that has not received as much attention as it deserves. The present book represents a major step in the scientific study of interest and interestingness.

Like many other common-sense terms that scientific psychology deals with, interest is a useful but slippery concept. It is useful in everyday communication, but it is a difficult concept to define precisely. The papers in the present volume go a long way toward clarifying the domain of interest by making distinctions that are not observed in the everyday use of the term, but are crucial for its scientific use.

The kinds of questions that are raised here may be introduced by an example. Suppose I am invited to give a colloquium talk somewhere. I would like to make the talk interesting. A myriad of questions arise at this point. Why should I have to make the talk interesting—after all, it is about my research, my life's work, which to me is the most interesting thing there is! But the talk has to interest other people. Somehow I have to build bridges to topics my listeners are interested in. Somehow I have to present my material in an interesting way. A well-chosen anecdote may be fine to relax the audience, but my real goal is to inform the audience about the research which I have to report, to interest them in what I have to say by the way I say it.

It is a problem that has many dimensions. So far, the research in this area has concentrated on distinguishing these dimensions and on asking how a person's interests or an object's interestingness affect comprehension and learning. In addition, researchers are beginning to ask more analytic questions about the mechanisms by which interest effects are generated, as well as how interest itself arises. It seems quite clear at this point that there will be no simple answers (in the sense that interest can have all kinds of effects and sources, depending on the psychological and situational context), and that for a thorough understanding of interest, detailed process theories will have to be developed that explicate the interactions involved. It is a worthwhile, a promising, and a very interesting task that awaits the continued effort of psychological and educational researchers!

Walter Kintsch

GENERAL QUESTIONS IN THE STUDY OF INTEREST

1 Interest, Learning, and Development

Andreas Krapp
Universität der Bundeswehr – Munich

Suzanne Hidi
Ontario Institute for Studies in Education

K. Ann Renninger
Swarthmore College

Over the last few decades, theory and research on learning and development has shifted from discrete and largely passive models of individual functioning to models that include the individual's goals and intentions, knowledge about the self and environment, ability to develop and change optimal strategies of action, etc. Whether this represents a paradigmatic revolution, in the sense of Kuhn (1967), or is a metatheoretical consideration (Valsiner, this volume), there is no doubt that modern thinking about learning and development has been heavily based on, and to some extent restricted by, cognitive psychology.

As a result, an enormous number of new ideas, concepts, models, and theories about how the cognitive system functions, how new information is selected, stored, and organized, and how these concepts relate to both school-based and informal learning has been developed (e.g., Anderson, 1976; Kintsch & Van Dijk, 1978; Rumelhart, 1977; Van Dijk & Kintsch, 1983). There is no doubt that this research has expanded our knowledge of learning and development significantly. On the other hand, its theoretical shortcomings also have been recognized recently by more and more researchers (e.g., Bransford, 1979; Brown, 1982; Brown, Collins, & Duguid, 1989; Hidi & Baird, 1986; Hidi, Baird, & Hildyard, 1982; Jenkins, 1979; Mandl, Stein, & Trabasso, 1984; Mandler, 1975; Sorrentino & Higgins, 1986; cf. Clark & Fiske, 1982; Csikszentmihalyi, 1988; Snow & Farr, 1987; Van Dijk & Kintsch, 1983). Perhaps the most

3

important aspect of these critiques is that cognitive theories lack an adequate conceptualization of the impact of motivational and emotional factors in learning. This is at least true with respect to educationally important questions about how individual preferences, values, and goals are integrated into the process of cognitive functioning.

In the past, assumptions about the role of interest and its implications for meaningful learning have played an important role in both psychology and education. As early as the beginning of the 19th century, Herbart (1806/1965) developed a theory of interest based on philosophical and psychological considerations. By the beginning of the 20th century, some of the more important thinkers were grappling with the relation between interest and learning (e.g., Baldwin, 1897, 1906, 1907; Claparède, 1909; Dewey, 1913; James, 1912; Kerschensteiner, 1926; Rubinstein, 1935/1958; Thorndike, 1935; for a summary, cf. Arnold, 1906; Berlyne, 1949; Lunk, 1926, 1927).

Following this surge of interest in interest, however, there was a noticeable decline in research devoted to the topic. There are at least two reasons for this: first, the conceptualizations of interest were many and varied, and second, the development of more discrete research approaches (and theories) appeared to render a concept of interest superfluous. As a result, many investigators (frequently under the influence of Behaviorism) chose either to sharply limit the interest concept so that their measures would yield unambiguous results (e.g., vocational interest), or to avoid the interest concept entirely. Research questions that were related to interest—although sometimes the term interest was not used—typically focused on a single aspect of interest. Examples of such a single focus include research on attention (Eysenck, 1982), curiosity (Berlyne, 1960), emotion (Izard, 1977) attitude (Evans, 1971), value orientation (Allport, Vernon, & Lindzay, 1960), and motivation—especially achievement motivation (Atkinson & Raynor, 1974; Heckhausen, 1980,) intrinsic motivation (Day, 1981; Deci, 1975; Deci & Ryan, 1985), and flow (Csikszentmihalyi, 1975 Csikszentmihalyi & Csikszentmihalyi, 1988, 1990; Larson, 1988). Nevertheless, empirical research into the relation between interest and learning in some areas continued throughout this period, and, as it became more and more clear that modern theories do not adequately account for all the important aspects of the traditional concept of interest (Krapp, 1988, 1989b; Krapp & Schiefele, 1986; Prenzel, 1988), researchers have shown a renewed interest in "interest" as an explanatory construct.

Hence, various areas of research have witnessed a renaissance of the interest concept. There has been a relatively large number of new empirical studies concerned with both the influence of interest on learning and development and the origin and transformation of interests (cf. Hidi, 1990; Hidi, Baird, & Hildyard, 1982; Krapp, 1989a; Renninger, 1984, 1989, 1990; Renninger & Leckrone, 1991; Renninger & Wozniak, 1985; Schiefele, Winteler, & Krapp, 1988). This rejuvenation of interest research exhibits a variety of different interest concepts that do not lend themselves to direct comparison with one another. Rather they represent different perspectives and questions about learning and development. These concepts, however, do relate to one another in that they address complementary yet different aspects of phenomena. Up to now, the research on interest has had two foci: (a) the influence of individual interests as content- or topic-specific preferences for particular object domains, and (b) the effect of interestingness (i.e., those environmental factors found in the learning situation or material) that trigger a situation-specific interest in the learner.

THE CONCEPT OF INTEREST

Interest can be conceptualized in a variety of ways, each of which reflects the theoretical orientation of the research questions being asked and methods being used. In spite of their differences, common to most of this work is the assumption that interest is a phenomenon that emerges from an individual's interaction with his or her environment. This idea is variously referred to as the person–object relation (Fink, 1991; Prenzel, Krapp, & Schiefele, 1986), as person–stimulus interaction (Hidi, 1990; Hidi & Baird, 1986, 1988), and as an interdependence of the individual and a class of objects, tasks, events, or ideas within a larger social milieu (Renninger, 1984, 1987, 1989, 1990; Renninger & Leckrone, 1991; Renninger & Wozniak, 1985).

Although most investigators acknowledge that interest always originates in some form of person–environment interaction, researchers assign differing significance to the two components. Specifically, there have been two distinct areas of focus. One body of research has emphasized variations in individual or personal interests, including their origins and their effects, with special emphasis being given to the effect of interest on some categories of cognitive performance, such as learning. Another group of investigators has concentrated more on the specific characteristics of any learning environment that captures the interest of many individuals (e.g., interestingness of a text). Interest as a psychological state, and situation-specific factors that bring about interest, then, reflect two distinct research approaches for investigating the role of interest in learning and development (Hidi, 1990; Hidi & Baird, 1988; Renninger, 1990).

In addition to largely determining how the topic of interest has been researched, these two views of interest also correspond to the way in which interest as a psychological state is identified. Individual interests are always specific to individuals. Generally, researchers liken them to dispositions that develop over time. Individual interests are considered to be relatively stable and are usually associated with increased knowledge, positive emotions, and increased reference value. Situational interests, on the other hand, are generated by certain stimulus characteristics (e.g., life themes, novelty) and tend to be shared among individuals. Because this type of interest may be evoked suddenly by something in the environment, it often has only a short-term effect and marginal influence on the subject's knowledge and reference system. It may, however, have a more permanent effect and serve as the basis for the emergence of individual interests.

Individual Interest. In modern psychology, particularly in an applied domain such as counseling, theories and measurement of vocational interests have found wide application (Allehoff, 1985; Holland, 1985; Kay, 1982; Walsh & Osipow, 1986).[1] Holland's "Vocational Preference Inventory" (VPI), for example, is based on a classification scheme with six personality types, each of which is associated with a clear preference for career activities: realistic, investigative, artistic, social, enterprising, and conventional. The concept of interest as a vocationally relevant disposition is closely related to concepts of attitude in social psychology. In fact, some authors go so far as to define interest as attitude (cf. Evans, 1971; Gardner, 1975).

In addition to both dispositional theories of applied psychology and attitude theories of social psychology, interest concepts based on theories of action have become more and more common (Oppenheimer & Valsiner, 1991). This approach conceptualizes a person's interest-oriented actions to result from a multi-level process of action regulation (Fink, 1991). From this perspective, interests represent personality-specific

---

[1] The contributions to the present volume do not address the concept of vocational interest.

orientations, reference valuations, or an awareness of possibilities for action. Interests provide important categories for action goals in these situations, where one is free to do as one pleases (reference value aspect). In addition, the effects of previous interest-oriented actions in the form of emotional reactions, differentiated structures of knowledge pertaining to the object domain (declarative knowledge), and knowledge of possible forms of engagement involving the object of interest (procedural knowledge) are all aspects of interest engagement.

For any individual, his or her interests have personal significance. The German "person–object theory of interest" (Fink, 1991; Krapp & Fink, this volume; Prenzel, Krapp, & Schiefele, 1986), for example, postulates a long-term relation between the person and a class of interest objects that are often integrated into the reference value system of a person and are basic components of his or her self-concept. Renninger (1989, 1990; Renninger & Leckrone, 1991), on the other hand, takes a more cognitively oriented approach to interest and specifies that such a relation between an individual and a class of objects (events, ideas, etc.) includes both stored knowledge and stored value but is not something of which the person is necessarily metacognitively aware. Rather, she suggests that interest as a psychological state influences the individual's subsequent activity.

There are at least two different ways in which individual interest can be conceptualized: individual interest as disposition and individual interest as actualized state. Dispositional interests are relatively enduring characteristics or general orientations to action. For example, theoretical models and empirical studies designed to explain and predict academic achievement often use measures of dispositional interest in particular content areas as predictors. This use is based on the assumption that such interests endure over the long term; interest is thought to influence learning not only in some cases, but in many or even all situations in which the learner has the opportunity for voluntary engagement.

Process-oriented theories and studies of the conditions of learning are usually less concerned with the dispositional aspect of individual interest. They devote more attention to the concrete, actualized form of individual interest. Interest can be said to "show itself" in particular psychological states, such as focused, prolonged, relatively effortless attention, all of which are accompanied by feelings of pleasure and concentration (actualized individual interest).

Such actualized interest is believed to arise out of an interaction between internal and external conditions. According to Hidi and Baird (1986, 1988), two sources are involved: the person, with his or her characteristics, attitudes, and general orientations, and the situation, which contains the special stimuli and conditions for an interested engagement. However, it should be noted that the situation-specific sources that can elicit interest include not only the characteristics of the object of interest (e.g., the content of a text), but other factors as well, such as the instructional design that fosters interest. Likewise, a person's social relationships (e.g., peers, teachers, role models) can influence the emergence of interest.

Differences among authors regarding interest as a personal characteristic stem from different conceptualizations of the individual and of the nature of task involvement. Most conceptualizations, however, include notions of knowledge and/or reference value and refer to a person's interaction with a *specific* class of tasks, objects, events, or ideas. Such specificity distinguishes individual interests from other psychological concepts such as intrinsic motivation, attention, arousal, curiosity and exploration.

Situational Interest. Situational interest is used to describe interest that is generated primarily by certain conditions and/or concrete objects (e.g., texts, film) in the environment. Like individual interest, situational interest can be described from the perspective of either the cause, the conditions that induce interest, or the perspective of the person who is interested.

Research directed at the conditions that elicit interest (interestingness) has concentrated on text. The passages studied have been thought to be of general interest to people, although they might be tailored to the general interests of a particular age or other groups. Viewed from this perspective, situational interest is not unique to the individual but tends to be common across individuals. This type of situational interest, which Hidi and Baird (1988) called *text-based interest,* includes phenomena that might occur only once, or repeatedly. Examples of this type of interest are the way in which individuals react to seductive details (see chapters by Garner, Brown, Sanders, & Menke; and Wade, this volume), surprise-ending stories (Iran–Nejad, 1987, this volume), and interesting sentences in text (e.g., Anderson, 1982; Anderson, Mason, & Shirey, 1984; Shirey, this volume).

Conceptually, situational interest is similar but not identical to the concepts of curiosity and exploration (Berlyne, 1960; Görlitz & Wohlwill, 1987; Voss & Keller, 1983). Berlyne (1960, 1974), for example, argued that certain structural stimulus characteristics, such as novelty, surprisingness, complexity, and ambiguity (collative variables), lead to motivational states, marked by uncertainty and conflict, which result in curiosity and exploratory behavior. He further suggested that physiological arousal is the mediating variable between collative variables and individual performance. He maintained that these variables have arousal potential; that is, they can affect the level of arousal.

Optimal arousal is presumed to lead to optimal human performance. If arousal is too low, one seeks stimulation in order to raise the arousal level; if it reaches uncomfortably high levels, one seeks arousal reduction. In both cases, the individual manifests an increased willingness to engage in exploratory behavior. Berlyne and others have distinguished between specific and diversive curiosity, or exploration, both of which contribute to the maintenance of an optimal level of physiological arousal. It is important to note that both types of curiosity are attributed to the collative stimulus properties of an object in the person's field of experience.

Both situational interest and specific curiosity are, in some ways, motivational states that encourage a person to interact with the environment in order to acquire new information. In addition, situational interest and specific curiosity are strongly influenced by environmental factors, some of which are common to both (e.g., novelty). Although the two concepts are clearly similar, Hidi and Anderson (this volume) suggest a number of points on which the concepts differ, the most important of which are: (a) situational interest can be elicited not only by collative variables, but by content-specific text characteristics, and (b) situational interest may develop into relatively enduring individual interests.

Relations Between the Various Concepts of Interest. As seen in Figure 1.1, three major points of view are reflected in interest research: (1) interest as a characteristic of the person, (2) interest as a characteristic of the learning environment, and (3) interest as a psychological state. Both individual interest, in the sense of relatively stable preferences, and interestingness can bring about experiences and psychological states in an individual that are generally referred to as interest. Typical characteristics of this state might include increased attention, greater concentration, pleasant feelings of applied effort, and increased willingness to learn, although the extent to which these characteristics are generated by interest remains an open question.

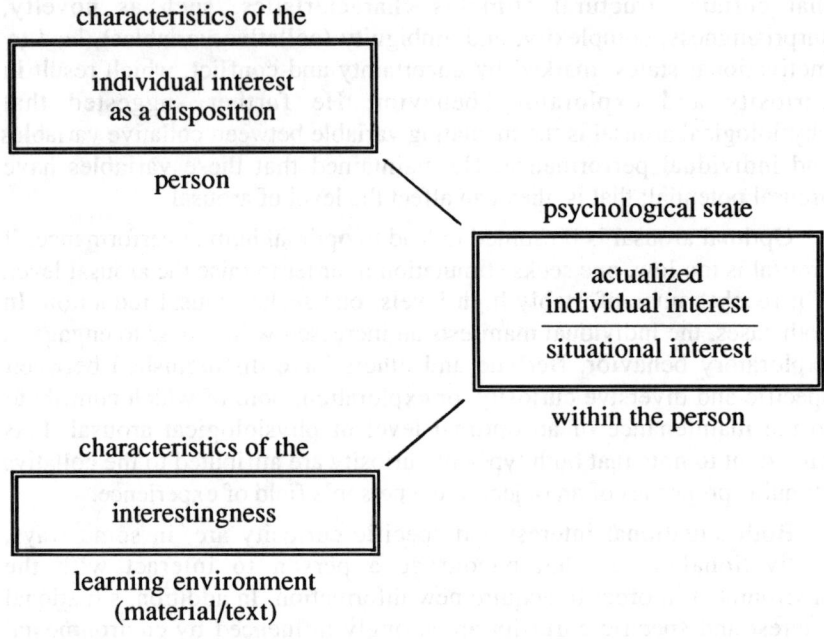

Fig. 1.1. Three approaches to interest research

Given that the theoretical interpretation and/or the operationalization of the interest concept varies from author to author largely as a function of research questions, we suggest for now that the states of interest brought about by external stimuli be separated in theory and terminology from those generated by individual interest. Although the state of interest, in the sense of an actualized individual interest, seems closely related to the experiential state of situational interest, it has not been demonstrated that the psychological processes and the effects of the two states are identical, or even comparable.

INTEREST AND LEARNING

Educational research concerns itself first and foremost with the question of how interest affects learning. More specific versions of this question vary, depending on whether the researcher is investigating the influence of individual interests or situational interests. In any case, interest has typically been studied as an independent variable, and dependent variables have been some aspect of learning, operationalized either as a feature of an acquired cognitive structure (e.g., knowledge) or as an evaluation of achievement based on learning outcomes (e.g., grades). Some investigations have analyzed the causes or mechanisms of these interest effects. For example, they have examined the effects of more generalized learning conditions, such as learning strategies or the cognitive and affective processes involved in learning (e.g., attention).

Figure 1.2 provides a classification scheme for these studies. Empirical work is first classified by independent variable, that is, the ways in which interest has been conceptualized theoretically and measured empirically. In most of these studies interest is conceptualized in terms of individual or situational interest. The second classification shows the ways in which the dependent variables, the interest effects, have been measured. Correlational and predictive studies are typically designed to rely on measures of evaluated outcomes, such as test results and/or grades. More recent studies have been designed to measure achievement more precisely, for example, by examining subjects' cognitive representation of a text. Some studies have also been designed to analyze the effects of interest on cognitive and emotional processes in that data are gathered while the learning process is going on (e.g., nature and extent of elaborations, level of attention, intensity of flow experience).

The classification scheme depicted in Figure 1.2 identifies five fields of interest research: the relation between individual interest and academic achievement, the relation between individual interest and the structure of acquired knowledge, the relation between situational interest and academic achievement, the influence of situational interest in text-based learning, and the explanation of the interest effect. Empirical research within each of these fields seems to have evolved independently, and the exchange of ideas, methods, and results among them has been limited.

The Relation Between Individual Interest and Academic Achievement (Field 1). Most empirical studies of the relation between interest and academic achievement typically have been designed to use correlational methods to explain the observed variance in achievement. Individuals' interests have been measured with formal or informal tests, or by simply asking subjects about their preferences for particular topics.

INDEPENDENT VARIABLE	DEPENDENT VARIABLE		
	learning achievement		learning process
interest	evaluated outcome (e.g. test scores, grades, GPA)	cognitive structure (e.g. knowledge representation)	mediating variables (e.g. learning strategy, attention
interest as characteristic of the person: individual interest	field 1	field 2	field 5
interest as result of interestingness: situational interest	field 3	field 4	

Fig. 1.2. Five fields of research in the analysis of the relation between interest and learning

Some of these studies have been designed to predict academic achievement. These efforts are based on the assumption that a combination of cognitive (intelligence) and noncognitive (interest) factors can be used to accurately predict future achievement (Evans, 1971; Lavin, 1965; Super, 1960; Todt, 1978). Schiefele, Krapp, and Winteler (this volume) report findings from a meta-analysis of prediction studies, which show that across all school types, grade levels, and subjects, the best (average) correlative estimate of the interest–achievement relation is approximately .30. This relation, however, appears to be a function of gender, school subject, and age/grade level. Specifically, subject matter-related interests show a greater influence on the grades of males than on those of females. There also seems to be a stronger relation between interest and academic achievement at higher grade levels.

Information pertaining to the prognostic power of interest measurements is relevant to academic counseling, to college admission decisions, and to other matters related to students' academic futures. The problems of prediction-based decisions illustrate why researchers of these topics have conceptualized interests as a personality characteristic. Only dispositions, in the sense of stable value orientations, attitudes, or characteristics, lend themselves to long-term prediction (Friedman & Willis, 1983; Krapp, 1979; Schwarz, 1971).

The Relation Between Individual Interest and the Structure of Acquired Knowledge (Field 2). Most studies of the relation between individual interests and knowledge structures have focused on learning through the reading of texts. Assessment of learning has been based on both quantitative and qualitative characteristics of text comprehension, such as the number of words correctly recognized or remembered, and the type and quality of answers given to content-related questions. Most of these studies show overwhelming effects of interest that remain observable even after controlling for important factors such as previous knowledge, intelligence, and text readability. Research has also indicated that interest effects on text comprehension might be more pronounced in terms of qualitative criteria than in terms of quantitative criteria (e.g., Fransson, 1977; Hidi, 1990; Schiefele, 1988; and chapters by Hidi & Anderson; and Schiefele, in this volume).

The Relation Between Situational Interest and Academic Achievement (Field 3). Both naive and formal theories of instruction might suggest that classroom instruction and materials that are interesting play a large role in determining learning achievement (Hofer, 1986; Todt, 1985b; Travers, 1978). It is assumed that there is a relation between the interestingness of text, its connectedness to the material covered, and the grades and later success of the student. Whereas this assumption appears implicitly or explicitly in both research and practice, it is interesting that there seem to be no studies that have directly investigated this relation. Some researchers, however, have touched on this issue indirectly. For example, studies have demonstrated that girls are less affected by and receive poorer grades when engaging in interesting instruction in science than boys (Lehrke, 1988; Lehrke, Hoffmann, & Gardner, 1985). In an effort to explore this effect, Kubli (1987) studied the factors that contributed to the interestingness of physics, and then made suggestions for using these findings to adjust the instructional setting for girls. For example, he suggested that girls could become more interested if physics problems were linked to social or everyday problem situations. Similar points have been made by Tobias (1978, 1990) with respect to students learning in both mathematics and science.

The Influence of Situational Interest in Text-Based Learning (Field 4). Research on interestingness and situational interest focuses on the role of certain text characteristics in text-based learning (Hidi, 1989, 1990; Hidi & Baird, 1988). The research methodology has usually involved the following steps. First, the stimulus text under investigation is rated for interestingness. Second, subjects perform some kind of cognitive operation (e.g., reading) with the rated stimulus. Finally, the relation between the rated interestingness and performance is determined.

The empirical research on interestingness and text-based learning has been summarized by Hidi and Baird (1986), Hidi (1990), and Schiefele (1988). Studies involving texts have shown that the following characteristics seem to foster interest: character identification, novelty, life themes, imagery value, and intensity of action (Anderson, Shirey, Wilson, & Fielding, 1987; Hidi & Baird, 1983, 1988). The overall findings also clearly show that interesting texts motivate people to read, influence comprehension, and tend to result in quantitatively and qualitatively superior learning. However, some researchers have argued that interesting text segments do not always have positive effects on learning (Garner, Gillingham, & White, 1989; Garner et al., this volume; Hidi, Baird, & Hildyard, 1982). In fact, Garner et al. (1989; see also Garner et al., and Wade, this volume) demonstrated that interesting but unimportant information, referred to as seductive details, might interfere with the learning of important ideas.

Explanation of Interest Effect (Field 5). Research into the effect of interest on learning and achievement consistently shows that individual and situational interest both have an important role in learning. However, what this role is and how it can be explained remain open questions. According to Krapp (1989b), explanatory variables for the interest effect can be described as reflecting different levels of analysis. Thus, on the one hand, explanations are sought at the level of general motivational and cognitive orientation, whereas the specific cognitive and affective processes that accompany the learning activity reflect another level.

One explanation for the relation between interest and academic achievement relates its effects to motivational orientations (Dweck, 1985) and/or learning strategies. Dweck and her colleagues (e.g., Dweck, 1985; Dweck & Leggett, 1988; Elliott & Dweck, 1988) distinguish motivational orientations on the basis of the predominant type of achievement goals: "learning goals," those that aim at developing personal competence (mastery orientation); and "performance goals," those that are aimed at winning recognition from others. In reviewing recent research, Lepper (1988) concluded that a motivational orientation characterized by a willingness to engage in an activity for its own sake and an inner certainty that one is the initiator of the activity leads to comparably more differentiated and original knowledge structures among high school and college students.

Closely related to motivational orientation is the students' preferred type of learning strategy. Entwistle and colleagues (e.g., Entwistle & Ramsden, 1983), who distinguish between deep-processing strategies and surface-level strategies, argue that, in the former case, the learner attempts to see subject matter from different angles, establish diverse relationships, recognize problems, and solve difficulties on his or her own. In the latter case, the learner is satisfied to memorize facts, and prefers those aspects of subject matter that lend themselves to this. Findings from Entwistle and Ramsden (1983), Nolen (1988), and Schiefele (1989) indicate that interest-oriented learning corresponds to the deep-processing orientation. Thus, high-interest subjects are more likely to process a text by using more elaborations, establishing more cross references, and valuing the long lasting acquisition of basic knowledge than are the low-interest subjects. In this way, high-interest subjects build up a qualitatively superior representation of a text and are more able to recall basic components of it at a later point.

In contrast to the number of discussions of interest and motivation, there are relatively few discussions of the relation between interest and cognition. Much of this work has been undertaken by Renninger (this volume). Renninger and Wozniak (1985), for example, reported that interest influenced the likelihood that young children would shift attention to, recognize, and recall play objects that were identified objects of interest more frequently than other, equally available play objects. Building on these findings, Renninger's subsequent studies have addressed the role of interest in the students' access to and processing of information (see Renninger, this volume).

On a slightly different tack, a discussion of the specific characteristics of the interest–attention relation has ensued among researchers of situational interest. This discussion addresses the issue of resource allocation. A common assumption about the role of attention in learning is that the capacity of the information-processing system is limited. From this perspective, it is expected that attention must be focused on an object for longer periods of time to allow for cognitive processing (Csikszentmihalyi, 1988; Garner, Gillingham, & White, 1989). Anderson et al. (1984; Shirey & Reynolds, 1988; Shirey, this volume) hypothesized that a reader pays more attention to the interesting portions of a text and thus focuses for a longer period of time on interesting passages. Recently, however, questions have been raised about this hypothesis. Hidi (1990) used Kahnemann's (1973) work to suggest that interest results in spontaneous rather than conscious, selective allocation of attention and, therefore, might result in learning that requires less cognitive capacity and less cognitive effort. This thesis is supported by numerous empirical findings that have been reviewed by Hidi (1990; Hidi & Anderson; and Iran–Nejad, this volume). Clearly, further work is required to clarify when interest may involve more prolonged and/or less effortful processing. In addition, research into the specific relation between interest and other affective variables such as flow (cf. Csikszentmihalyi, 1984, 1988; Csikszentmihalyi & Csikszentmihalyi, 1988, 1990) that has been linked to processing should help to further clarify the role of interest in cognition.

INTEREST AND DEVELOPMENT

Only a few studies have addressed the relation between interest and development. Consistent with the organization of our discussion of interest and learning, we first focus on individual interest and then on situational interest as a developmental condition and outcome.

Individual Interest as a Developmental Condition and Outcome. Two lines of empirical studies that have focused on individual interest can be identified: those that address the influence of an existing interest on the subsequent activity of an individual, and those that investigate the changing role of interest in learning at different developmental stages.

As Renninger (this volume) indicates, studies that have focused on the influence of interest on subsequent activity suggest that young children are overwhelmingly influenced by their individual interests across a diverse set of problem-solving contexts. In older children and adults, on the other hand, the effect of interest appears to be task specific. For example, interest seems, at least in certain conditions, to influence reading more than writing (Hidi & Anderson, this volume) or mathematics (Renninger, this volume). Furthermore, Renninger reports that within-subject analyses of student performance in both reading and mathematics indicate that the text difficulty/level of problem further influences the impact of interest on learning (Renninger, 1991, this volume).

From a Piagetian (1968, 1981), Wernerian (1978), and/or Vygotskian (1967) perspective, it might be presumed that the preoperational child first uses individual interest as a forum for exploring properties of objects. Such focused practice appears to facilitate the child's actions with objects, viewed as interests and noninterests. Older students, in contrast, are usually required to engage in a range of tasks to which they respond differentially. As such, they presumably need to attend to classes of objects and events that are not necessarily of interest to them (see Renninger, this volume).

Study of the relation between the development of interest and the varying task requirements of different domains (e.g., reading, math) is in its infancy, as is an understanding of the differing effects of students' individual interests, the role of task difficulty in interest, the implications of gender differences in what is identified as inherent, and the links among interest, motivation, achievement, and temperament. Based on findings to date, it appears that interest serves differing roles in development as a function of age (Todt, 1978). Moreover, findings that suggest different effects of interest on performance across domains, or subject areas, also suggest that the nature of the task and the specific role of interest as a facilitator or scaffold for access, attention, or recall may have both universal and idiosyncratic aspects that need to be teased out. In an effort to study the changing role of interest over time, Krapp and Fink's (this volume; Fink, 1991) longitudinal studies of preschool and kindergarten children indicate that at this age children's interests are relatively stable, increasingly complex, and progressively more differentiated over time. Other studies have focused on an observed decline in school content-area related interests that begins around age 11. This trend is most pronounced in mathematics and science but holds across school subject areas and school culture. It is also observed to be more pronounced for girls than for boys (Lehrke, 1988; Lehrke, Hoffmann & Gardner 1985; Todt 1985).

Of major concern in recent research on interest development have been the questions of how students gain and change interests in content areas such as math and science, and how related gender differences can be explained. Developmental changes in interest can be observed during early puberty, when peers have the most important influence (Todt, 1985). Todt also argues that theories and results related to the development of vocational interests (Barak, 1981; Gottfredson, 1981) may help to explain developmental changes in subject matter interests. Other related issues involve the integration of gender roles into self-concept, and awareness of social-status differences, both of which are apparent at much earlier ages. Clarifying the role of interest in students' learning and development, and its subsequent implications for theory, research, and practice, provides a detailed agenda for future research.

Situational Interest as a Developmental Condition or Outcome. Whereas the possibility of short-term effects may make situational interest seem to be less relevant to developmental considerations than individual interest, several important questions have emerged from research on situational interest that can be related to development.

Hidi (1990) suggested that situational interest and individual interest are not dichotomous phenomena that occur in isolation. On the contrary, these types of interest can be expected to interact and influence each other's development. More specifically, she argued that situational interest, triggered by environmental factors, may evoke or contribute to the development of long-lasting individual interests. Future research will be needed to examine the extent to which situational interest serves as a developmental condition for individual interests. Because specific curiosity and exploration are related to certain aspects of situational interest, further research into the relation of interest and these topics may provide further clarification of the role of situational interest in the origins of interest development (Krapp, in press).

There has been very little research on how situational interest changes with age. In one of the few related studies (Hidi & McLaren, 1990), it was reported that children in grades 4 and 6 had interest ratings of topics and themes only moderately correlated with adult's ratings. A subsequent qualitative analysis of the topical rating differences showed that children tended to be generally less interested in social science topics than adults, and that children were most interested when they had moderate knowledge of the topics. Whether these findings would hold up across different age groups in a variety of domains has yet to be determined.

CONCLUSIONS

Research on interest has typically been undertaken based on practical considerations involved in students' learning, such as interest as a facilitator for skill development, learning from text, or student motivation. As the chapters collected in this volume demonstrate, however, the research to date has focused primarily on interest as an independent variable. As such, the variables studied, the questions posed, and the methodologies employed have been driven by a need to establish how interest affects achievement, cognition, vocational choices, and so on, rather than questions related to the nature, determinants, and functions of interest per se. Although this has served to link research on interest to other paradigms and to practice, there has been little effort, prior to this volume, to address the larger issues of how research programs on interest might complement one another, or what a coherent set of questions on interest might address.

The present volume was compiled to facilitate discussion of how different approaches to interest might be better understood, and how subsequent investigation of interest might be designed to further our understanding of the role of interest in learning and development. Questions that are informed by these chapters but remain, as yet, unanswered include: (a) How can different conceptualizations of interest be related so that they fit together as aspects of a larger construct? Even if all the conceptualizations cannot be unified into a coherent theory of interest, consideration of the range of foci in interest research should make possible an exchange of different viewpoints within the context of a more general field of interest research. (b) What kind of research strategies and methods fit the demands of educationally/ ecologically relevant interest research? Some problems of past research may have been the result of not considering this question. (c) How might existing theories and research results be utilized in everyday practice? This goes well beyond the metatheoretical problems of theory construction. It involves the research problems that are selected, the concepts that are used, and the ways in which interest is operationalized via instructional procedures and measurements.

REFERENCES

Allehoff, W. H. (1985). *Berufswahl und berufliche interessen.* Göttingen: Hogrefe.

Allport, G. W., Vernon, P. E., & Lindzay, G. (1960). *A study of values* (3rd ed.). Boston: Houghton–Mifflin.

Anderson, J. R. (1976). *Language, memory, and thought.* Hillsdale, NJ: Lawrence Erlbaum Associates.

Anderson, R. C. (1982). Allocation of attention during reading. In A. Flammer & W. Kintsch (Eds.), *Discourse processing* (pp. 287–299). Amsterdam: North–Holland.

Anderson, R. C., Mason, J., & Shirey, L. (1984). The reading group: An experimental investigation of a labyrinth. *Reading Research Quarterly, 20*, 6–38.

Anderson, R. C., Shirey, L. L., Wilson, P. T., & Fielding, L. G. (1987). Interestingness of children's reading material. In R. E. Snow & M. J. Farr (Eds.), *Aptitude, learning, and instruction. Vol. 3: Conative and affective process analyses* (pp. 287–299). Hillsdale, NJ: Lawrence Erlbaum Associates.

Arnold, F. (1906). The psychology of interest. I/II. *Psychological Review, 13*, 221–238/291–315.

Atkinson, J. W. & Raynor, J. O. (Eds.) (1974). *Motivation and achievement.* Washington, DC: Winston.

Baldwin, J. M. (1897). *Social and ethical interpretations in mental development: A study in social psychology.* London: Cambridge University Press.

Baldwin, J. M. (1906). *Thought and things: A study of the development and meaning of thought* (Vol. I). New York: Macmillan.

Baldwin, J. M. (1907). *Thought and things: A study of the development and meaning of thought* (Vol. III). New York: Macmillan.

Barak, A. (1981). Vocational interests: A cognitive view. *Journal of Vocational Behavior, 19*, 1–14.

Berlyne, D. E. (1949). Interest as a psychological concept. *The British Journal of Psychology, 39*, 184–195.

Berlyne, D. E. (1960). *Conflict, arousal and curiosity.* New York: Grove Press.

Berlyne, D. E. (1974). Novelty, complexity, and interestingness. In D. E. Berlyne (Ed.), *Studies in new experimental aesthetics* (pp. 175–180). New York: Wiley.

Bransford, J. S. (1979). *Human cognition: Learning, understanding, and remembering.* Belmont, CA: Wadsworth.

Brown, A. L. (1982). Learning and development: The problems of compatibility, access and induction. *Human Development, 25*, 89–115.

Brown, J. S., Collins, A. & Duguid, P. (1989). Situated cognition and the culture of learning. *Educational Researcher, 18* (1), 32–42.

Claparède E. (1909). *Psychologie de l'enfant et pédagogie expérimentale* (2nd ed.). Geneve: Kundig.

Clark, M. S., & Fiske, S. T. (Hrsg.) (1982). *Affect and cognition.* Hillsdale, NJ: Lawrence Erlbaum Associates.

Csikszentmihalyi, M. (1975). Beyond boredom and anxiety. San Francisco: Jossey–Bass.

Csikszentmihalyi, M. (1988). Motivation and creativity: Towards a synthesis of structural and energistic approaches to cognition. *New Ideas in Psychology, 6*, 159–76.

Csikszentmihalyi, M., & Csikszentmihalyi, I. S. (1988). *Optimal experience: Psychological studies of flow in consciousness.* New York: Cambridge University Press.

Csikszentmihalyi, M., & Csikszentmihalyi, I. S. (1990). Flow: The psychology of optimal experience. New York: Harper & Row.

Day, H. I. (Ed.) (1981). *Advances in intrinsic motivation and aesthetics.* New York: Plenum Press.

Deci, E. L. (1975). *Intrinsic motivation.* New York: Plenum Press.

Deci, E. L., & Ryan, R. M. (1985). *Intrinsic motivation and self-determination in human behavior*. New York: Plenum Press.

Dewey, J. (1913). *Interest and effort in education*. Boston: Riverside Press.

Dweck, C. S. (1985). Intrinsic motivation, perceived control, and self-evaluation maintenance: An achievement goal analysis. In C. Ames & R. Ames (Eds.), *Research on motivation in education* (Vol. 2, pp. 289–305). New York: Academic.

Dweck, C. S., & Leggett, E. L. (1988). A social–cognitive approach to motivation and personality. *Psychological Review, 95*, 256–273.

Elliott, E. S., & Dweck, C. S. (1988). Goals: An approach to motivation and achievement. *Journal of Personality & Social Psychology, 54*, 5–12.

Entwistle, N. J., & Ramsden, P. (1983). *Understanding student learning*. London: Croom Helm.

Evans, K. M. (1971). *Attitudes and interests in education* (2nd ed.). London: Routledge & Kegan.

Eysenck , M. E. (1982). *Attention and arousal*. New York: Springer–Verlag.

Fink, B. (1991). Interest development as structural change in person–object relationships. In L. Oppenheimer & J. Valsiner (Eds.), *The origins of action: Interdisciplinary and international perspectives*. New York: Springer–Verlag.

Fransson, A. (1977). On qualitative differences in learning: IV—Effects of intrinsic motivation and extrinsic test anxiety on process and outcome. *British Journal of Educational Psychology, 47*, 244–257.

Friedman, M. I., & Willis, M. R. (1983). *Human nature and predictability*. Hampshire: Gower.

Gardner, P. L. (1975). Attitude to science: A review. *Studies in Science Education, 2*, 1–41.

Garner, R., Gillingham, M. G., & White, C. S. (1989). Effects of "seductive details" on macroprocessing and microprocessing in adults and children. *Cognition and Instruction, 6*, 41–57.

Görlitz, D., & Wohlwill, J. F. (1987). *Curiosity, imagination and play*. Hillsdale, NJ: Lawrence Erlbaum Associates.

Gottfredson, L. S. (1981). Circumscription and compromise: A developmental theory of occupational aspirations. *Journal of Counseling Psychology. Monograph. Nr. 6, 28*, 545–579.

Heckhausen, H. (1980). *Motivation und Handeln*. Berlin: Springer.

Herbart, J. F. (1806/1965). Allgemeine Pädagogik, aus dem Zweck der Erziehung abgeleitet. In J. F. Herbart (Ed.), *Pädagogische schriften* (Vol. 2). Düsseldorf: Kupper.

Hidi, S. (1989, March). *Interest and its contribution as a mental resource for learning*. Paper presented at the annual meeting of the American Educational Research Association (AERA), San Francisco.

Hidi, S. (1990). Interest and its contribution as a mental resource for learning. *Review of Educational Research, 60* (4), 549–571.

Hidi, S. & Baird, W. (1983, November). *Types of information saliency in school texts and their effect on children's recall*. Paper presented at the National Reading Conference, Austin, TX.

Hidi, S., & Baird, W. (1986). Interestingness—A neglected variable in discourse processing. *Cognitive Science, 10*, 179–194.

Hidi, S. & Baird, W. (1988). Strategies for increasing text-based interest and students' recall of expository texts. *Reading Research Quarterly, 23,* 465–483.

Hidi, S., & McLaren, J. (1990). The effect of topic and theme interestingness on the production of school expositions. In H. Mandl, E. de Corte, N. Bennett, & H. F. Friedrich (Eds.), *Learning and instruction* (Vol. 2.2, pp. 295–308). Oxford: Pergamon.

Hidi, S., Baird, W., & Hildyard, A. (1982). That's important but is it interesting? Two factors in text processing. In A. Flammer & W. Kintsch (Eds.), *Discourse processing* (pp. 63–75). Amsterdam: North–Holland.

Hofer, M. (1986). *Sozialpsychologie erzieherischen handelns.* Göttingen: Hogrefe.

Holland, J. L. (1985). *Making vocational choices: A theory of vocational personalities and work environments.* Englewood Cliffs, NJ: Prentice–Hall.

Iran–Nejad, A. (1987). Cognitive and affective causes of interest and liking. *Journal of Educational Psychology, 79,* 120–130.

Izard, C. E. (1977). *Human emotions.* New York: Plenum Press.

James, W. (1912). *The principles of psychology* (3rd ed.). New York: Holt, Rinehart & Winston.

Jenkins, J. J. (1979). Four parts to remember: A tetrahedral model of memory. In L. S. Cermak and F. I. M. Craik (Eds.), *Levels of processing in human memory* (pp. 429–446). Hillsdale, NJ: Lawrence Erlbaum Associates.

Kahnemann, D. (1973). *Attention and effort.* Englewood Cliffs, NJ: Prentice–Hall.

Kay, P. R. (1982). Interests measurement. In H. E. Mitzel (Ed.), *Encyclopedia of educational research.* New York: Free Press.

Kerschensteiner, G. (1926). *Theorie der Bildung.* Leipzig: Teubner.

Kintsch, W., & van Dijk, T. A. (1978). Toward a model of text comprehension and production. *Psychological Review, 85,* 363–394.

Krapp, A. (1979). *Prognose und Entscheidung.* Weinheim: Beltz.

Krapp, A. (Chair). (1988, April). *Differences in student performance across subject areas as a function of interest.* Symposium conducted at the Annual Meeting of the American Educational Research Association (AERA), New Orleans.

Krapp, A. (1989a). Neue ans tze einer pädagogisch orientierten interessen-forschung. *Empirische Pädagogik, 3,* H.5 .

Krapp, A. (1989b, September). *Interest, learning and academic achievement.* Paper prepared for the symposium "Task Motivation by Interest." Third European Conference of Learning and Instruction (EARLI), Madrid, Spain.

Krapp, A. (in press). Interest and curiosity: The role of interest in a theory of exploratory action. In H. Keller & K. Schneider (Eds.). *Curiosity and exploration. Theoretical perspectives, research fields, and applications.* New York: Springer.

Krapp, A., & Schiefele, U. (1986, April). *The development of interests: Research programs in the Federal Republic of Germany.* Paper presented at the annual meeting of the American Educational Research Association (AERA), San Francisco.

Kubli, F. (1987). *Interesse und verstehen in physik und chemie.* Köln: Aulis–Verlag Deubner.

Kuhn, T. (1967). *Die struktur wissenschaftlicher revolution.* Frankfurt/Main: Suhrkamp.

Larson, R. (1988). Flow and writing. In M. Csikszentmihalyi & I. Csikszent-mihalyi (Eds.), *Optimal experience: Psychological studies of flow in consciousness* (pp. 150–171). New York: Cambridge University Press.

Lavin, D. E. (1965). *The prediction of academic performance.* New York: Russel Sage Foundation.

Lehrke, M. (1988). *Interesse und Desinteresse am naturwissenschaftlich-technischen Unterricht.* Kiel: Institut für die Pädagogik der Naturwissenschaften (IPN).

Lehrke, M., Hoffmann, L., & Gardner, P. L. (Eds.) (1985). *Interests in science and technology education.* Kiel: Institut für die Pädagogik der Naturwissenschaften (IPN).

Lepper, M. R. (1988). Motivational considerations in the study of instruction. *Cognition and Instruction, 5,* 289–309.

Lunk, G. (1926). *Das Interesse. Bd.1: Historisch-kritischer Teil.* Leipzig: Klinkhardt.

Lunk, G. (1927). *Das Interesse. Bd. 2: Philosophisch-pädagogischer Teil.* Leipzig: Klinkhardt.

Mandl, H., Stein, N. L. & Trabasso, T. (Eds.) (1984). *Learning and comprehension of text.* Hillsdale, NJ: Lawrence Erlbaum Associates.

Mandler, F. (1975). *Mind and emotion.* New York: Wiley.

Nolen, S. B. (1988). Reasons for studying: Motivational orientations and study strategies. *Cognition and Instruction, 5,* 269–287.

Oppenheimer, L., & Valsiner, J. (Eds.) (1991). The origins of action: Interdisciplinary and international perspectives. New York: Springer–Verlag.

Piaget, J. (1981). Intelligence and affectivity: Their relationship during child development. In T. A. Brown & M. R. Kaegi (Eds.), *Annual Review Monographs.* Palo Alto, CA: Annual Reviews Inc.

Prenzel, M. (1988a). *Die wirkungsweise von Interesse. Ein erklärungsversuch aus pädagogischer Sicht.* Opladen: Westdeutscher Verlag.

Prenzel, M., Krapp, A., & Schiefele, H. (1986). Grundzüge einer pädagogischen Interessentheorie. *Zeitschrift für Pädagogik, 32,* 163–173.

Renninger, K. A. (1984). Object–child relations: Implications for both learning and teaching. *Children's Environments Quarterly, 1,* 3–6.

Renninger, K. A. (1987). Do individual interests make a difference? In *Essays by the Spencer Fellows (IV).* Cambridge, MA: National Academy of Education.

Renninger, K. A. (1989). Individual patterns in children's play interests. In L. T. Winegar (Ed.), *Social interaction and the development of children's understanding* (pp. 147–172). Norwood, NJ: Ablex.

Renninger, K. A. (1990). Children's play interests, representation, and activity. In R. Fivush & J. Hudson (Eds.), *Knowing and remembering in young children* (pp. 127–165). Emory Cognition Series (Vol. III). Cambridge, MA: Cambridge University Press.

Renninger, K. A. (1991, April). Influences of interest and text difficulty on students' strategies for reading and recall. In S. Wade (Chair.), *Effects of interest on strategies and learning from text.* Symposium conducted at the annual meeting of the American Educational Research Association, Chicago.

Renninger, K. A., & Leckrone, T. G. (1991). Continuity in young children's actions: A consideration of interest and temperament. In L. Oppenheimer & J. Valsiner (Eds.) *The origins of action: Interdisciplinary and international perspectives* (205–238). New York: Springer–Verlag.

Renninger, K. A., & Wozniak, R. H. (1985). Effect of interest on attentional shift, recognition, and recall in young children. *Developmental Psychology, 21*, 624–632.

Rubinstein, S. (1958). *Grundlagen der allgemeinen Psychologie*. Berlin: Volk und Wissen.

Rumelhart, D. E. (1977). *An introduction to human information processing*. New York: Wiley.

Schiefele, U. (1988). Motivationale Bedingungen des textverstehens. *Zeitschrift für Pädagogik, 34*, 687–708.

Schiefele, U. (1990). *Zeitschrift für Experimentelle und Angewandte Psychologie 37*, 304–332.

Schiefele, U., Krapp, A., & Winteler, A. (1988, April). *Conceptualization and measurement of interest*. Paper presented at the annual meeting of the American Educational Research Association (AERA), New Orleans.

Schiefele, U., Winteler, A., & Krapp, A. (1988). Studieninteresse und fachbezogene Wissensstruktur. *Psychologie in Erziehung und Unterricht, 35*, 106–118.

Schwarz, P. A. (1971). Predictional instruments for educational outcomes. In R. L. Thorndike (Ed.), *Educational measurement* (pp. 303–334). Washington, DC: American Council on Education.

Shirey, L. L., & Reynolds, R. E. (1988). Effect of interest on attention and learning. *Journal of Educational Psychology, 80*, 159–166.

Snow, R. E., & Farr, M. J. (Hrsg.) (1987). *Aptitude, learning and instruction. Volume 3: Conative and affective process analyses*. Hillsdale, NJ: Lawrence Erlbaum Associates.

Sorrentino, R. M., & Higgins, E. T. (Eds.) (1986). *Handbook of motivation and cognition. Foundations of social behavior*. Chichester: Wiley.

Super, D. E. (1960). Interests. In C. W. Harris (Ed.), *Encyclopedia of educational research (3rd ed.)* pp. 728–733.

Thorndike, E. L. (1935). *Adult interests*. New York: Macmillan.

Tobias, S. (1978). *Overcoming math anxiety*. New York: W. W. Norton.

Tobias, S. (1990). *They're not dumb, they're different: Stalking the second tier*. Tucson, AZ: Research Corporation.

Todt, E. (1978). *Das Interesse*. Bern: Huber.

Todt, E. (1985). Elements of a theory of science interests. In M. Lehrke, L. Hoffmann & P. L. Gardner (Eds.), *Interests in science and technology* (pp. 59–69). Paper presented at the 12th IPN–Symposium, Kiel.

Travers, R. M. W. (1978). *Children's interests*. Kalamazoo: Michigan University, College of Education.

van Dijk, T., & Kintsch, W. (1983). *Strategies of discourse comprehension*. Orlando: Academic Press.

Voss, H. G., & Keller, H. (1983). *Curiosity and exploration. Theories and results*. New York: Academic Press.

Vygotsky, L. S. (1967). Play and its role in the mental development of the child. *Soviet Psychology, 3*, 62–76.

Walsh, W. B., & Osipow, S. H. (Eds.) (1986). *Advances in vocational psychology: Vol. 1: The assessment of interests.* Hillsdale, NJ: Lawrence Erlbaum Associates.

Werner, H. (1978). Process and achievement: A basic problem of education and developmental psychology. In S. S. Barten and M. B. Franklin (Eds.) *Developmental processes: Heinz Werner's selected writings, Vol. 1, General theory and perceptual experience* (pp. 23–40). NY: International Universities Press.

2 Interest: A Metatheoretical Perspective

Jaan Valsiner
University of North Carolina at Chapel Hill

The main focus of my metatheoretical analysis can be summarized by the statement: *"This volume (on 'interest') cannot be interesting in itself."* Behind this seemingly negativistic statement is of course a whole complex of unsolved problems of psychology with which different scholars over the past two centuries have been wrestling. Namely, the issues of *psychological functions* and their *contextual embeddedness* episodically become foci of attention for psychologists. Flavors of these issues can be found all through the volume, as the different contributors vary from viewing the external world as "interesting" to the other extreme of seeing "interest" in the persistent pursuits of intrapersonal kinds. Efforts to "measure" interest usually lead to the operationalization of the concept on the basis of the person's encounters with specific external object domains of the world.

In general, the problem of creating a developmental theory of interest is similar to the basic problem of most psychological terms—their embeddedness in the everyday language. This embeddedness has two faces. On the one hand, it makes psychologists' talk understandable to the laypersons; on the other, however, it introduces into psychological terminology the implicit guidance of scientific reasoning, by way of the social suggestions encoded in the connotations of everyday terms.

Furthermore, the extension of psychological terminology is held hostage by the meaning systems of everyday terms. Thus, in psychology we are faced with the dangers of *horizontal linking*. The common-sense use of "interest" can be viewed as somehow linked with "motivation," which in turn is somehow linked with "effort," and "novelty," and so on. This alley of theorizing allows for the creation of novelty in psychologists' reasoning along a path pre-encoded by common language associations between word meanings. Psychology's theoretical sphere over the recent decades has mostly developed through this route—some rather local-level explanatory term becomes linked with a neighboring one by way of their partial overlap in their semantic fields, and the network of such explanatory terms develops further by incorporating "next neighbors" along the lines of association of terms at the same level of abstractness. In parallel with this horizontal extension of explanatory terminology (and the publication of a multitude of different empirical studies "proving" the adequacy of each), psychology becomes increasingly ignorant of its own knowhow through the necessity to adhere to "cognitive economy" (see Thorngate, 1990). Ignorance, of course, does not help to solve any of the fundamental problems of our understanding of fundamental issues of psychology, among which "interest" should be considered one of the most important.

"INTEREST," AND PSYCHOLOGY'S AMBIVALENT RELATIONS WITH COMMON LANGUAGE TERMS

Over its complicated history of trying to separate itself from philosophy, psychology has constructed for itself a very ambivalent relation with its own roots. This ambivalence can be seen in its "love/hate" relation with the meanings of common-language terms and with a common-sensical under-standing of psychological functions. On the one hand, no psychologist is ever free from the common-sense and everyday-language-based inter-pretations of psychological functions. On the other hand, different efforts at purifying psychological terminology from the ill-defined concepts of everyday life have led psychologists to avoid such terms, and substitute others for them (which may remain equally vague; consider psychologists' move from the notion of "will" to the use of "intention," or from "mental" to "cognitive" science, Valsiner, 1991a).

In the recent decade, the issues of common-sense and -language in psychology have been given some attention (Siegfried, 1991; Smedslund, 1978, 1982; Valsiner, 1985a). The problem of common-sense and everyday language terminology in psychological theories remains more fundamental than the present discussion warrants, because there exists a problem of fusion of levels of analysis. "Interest," for example, is itself a concept that has been invented in everyday life to refer to a certain psychological phenomenon. As such, the everyday use of the term becomes part of the phenomenon to be explained by a scientific account (e.g., John's use of "I am interested in X" and his actions and reasoning/feeling about X all become parts of the phenomenon to be explained). Furthermore, by using a sign to refer to the mental-affective-actional phenomenon the structure of the latter becomes changed (i.e., John's statement "I am interested in X" changes his previous relation with X). This mental semiotic organization of psychological phenomena by the person creates a new state of the phenomena through humans' active construction of their psychological functions (Vygotsky & Luria, 1930): by using signs we reorganize our psychological (and social) worlds.

The constructive semiotic nature of human minds constitutes a major problem for psychologists' terminology. Whereas a person uses a term in a particular personal sense, the psychologist may try to use the same term in its more general shared meaning. Hence, in the preceding example, we will never be able to specify exactly what John's sense in saying "I am interested in X" was at the moment of saying it, but we will be tempted to make a general "diagnostic statement"—"John *has interest* in X." Because such statements can be made about any person who provides us with traces of using the word "interest" in some personal sense, it is possible to fuse the levels of sense and meaning in our psychological (inductive) generalizations. Thus, if N persons state that "I am interested in X" (statements at the level of personal sense), we might be tempted to claim that "interest in X" (statement at the level of meaning) is widely present among people, hence general. Of course by doing this we have fused the levels of the individual (and unique) use of the word in everyday life, and the psychologists' generalization (level of general shared meaning or special term) that supposedly is applicable to many persons in similar ways most of the time. By this route of inductive generalization we have created a psychological term "interest" that seems to coincide with its common-language everyday counterpart. This makes it easy to operationalize the concept in empirical investigations, because one can assume that self-reports of "interest" or raters' agreements in attributing "interest" to children observed in their play contexts are direct representations of the psychological concept.

However, such operationalization remains a methodological construction that leads to data derivation from the phenomena in ways that by their nature eliminate a relevant aspect of the phenomena from the data. Contrary to the widespread belief in most of empiricistic psychology that "data are objective" (or that "the data speak for themselves"), in any empirical research effort the investigator constructs data in the process of research. "Data" are *constructed* by the coordination of the theoretical perspective of the investigator with his or her methodological inclinations and the phenomena under study (see Valsiner, 1991b). Hence the psychological "data" in any study are in some sense external to the intrinsic organization of their "phenomena-of-origin." They adequately represent only a selected facet of the real psychological phenomena, never their entirety. The investigator superimposes the meaning he or she gives the psychological concept upon the subject through the activity of operationalizing the concept and the process of carrying out the study. Furthermore,the subject's common-sense understanding of the concept under study remains divergent from that of the investigator.

In fact, the only condition under which the investigator's use of the term would coincide with that of the subject is that of full isomorphism between the collective-cultural meaning (see Valsiner, 1989, chap. 3) and the subject's personal sense. This is a very unlikely situation in actual life. Thus the confusion of levels; "interest" in our analytic schemes is unlikely to be the same as the senses in which "interest" as an everyday concept is used by persons in their life-worlds. Because the term is the same, however, it is easy to succumb to the illusion that our meaning for it equals the personal sense of it in the minds of our subjects.

Obviously, this confusion of levels (of meaning and sense) makes the use of any common-language meaning as a theoretical concept a very difficult task for theorists. Psychologists appear to be literally captivated by everyday language. If they use everyday terms, they generally overlook the variety of dynamic uses of these terms in the personal life-words of people (their personal senses). If they try to escape this problem by inventing new terminology that by itself does not have ill-defined semantic field boundaries, as the common-language terms have, then they are faced with the task of translating the meaning of their special scientific term into everyday language. As a result of such translation (if successful), they are back at the previous problem of discrepancy between meaning and personal senses of the same term.[1]

---

[1] A good example of the latter is Pascual–Leone's "M–operator," which (as a special term strictly definable according to the given theorist's intentions) becomes translated into the common language notion of "mental energy," thus acquiring surplus meaning that starts to guide the theorist's reasoning (see Pascual–Leone, 1984).

How, then, can the study of "interest" bypass the problems posed by terms of different semanticity for the researcher and the subject? Furthermore, the problem for a developmental theory of interest is complicated by the *entifying* function of language in organizing our understanding of our psychological processes.

FROM ENTIFIED TO PROCESS-ORIENTED CONCEPTS: "INTEREST" AND "BECOMING INTERESTED"

The preponderance of common sense is to reflect upon ongoing dynamic processes in terms of entified concepts (see Bloom, 1981, pp. 36–60). The real psychological life-world of any person is uninterruptably dynamic, and every use of a word in this process provides a means of organizing that dynamic flow. The use of any entified everyday term (e.g., "I am happy"), however, introduces a static moment into that irreversible flow (i.e., from my ongoing flow of feelings I create a temporarily stable state of affairs— "being happy"—by way of having said, "I am happy"). Furthermore, everyday language can create further stability in my life-world through my use of statements like "I feel profound happiness" or "I have a happy personality." Of course, it has been merely my way of reorganizing (or controlling) the ongoing flow of my life-world that has led me to use stability-implying terms in my personal sense. From the flow of unstructured feelings I can construct an entified personality characteristic (*"have* a happy personality") that I am supposed to "possess" as an entity. Furthermore, communication using entifying concepts is useful to "cut short" other people's puzzlement about oddities in my acting or thinking.

Let us consider an example. By stating to my peers that "I *have an interest in* collecting beer cans" I am able to explain away the presence of a ridiculous number of these objects (clearly subsumed under the label "garbage" by many others) in my living room—I will not be viewed as a pathological case who keeps garbage in his living room, but an independent person whose inalienable personal interests "are in" collecting these objects. Through linking the entified concept "interest" with my peculiar, and perhaps anti-social, habit, I have attained for myself the semiotically marked social "right" to keep these beer cans in my social–personal life-world. This status allotted to me by my peers under the label of my "interest" *is meant to be relatively stable,* though changeable under my personal control (e.g., when I declare "I am no longer interested in collecting beer cans, but now I am interested in X," then my peers are expected to accept this transition from one static state of "interest" to another).

On the side of my self and its social presentation, the use of the common-language term "interest" in my explanation of my personal weirdness prevents others from looking more thoroughly into my psychological processes while I indulge in this "interest" of mine. Simultaneously, it creates a certain stability in my self-reflection, as my "interest" may be linked with lengthy and persistent activities that are self-motivated. Reference to "interest" as a reason for some activity is sufficient to keep the person involved in it, and to keep others from further inquiries into its underpinnings. Consider the following effort by an investigator to penetrate the subject's world of interest:

INVESTIGATOR: You have all these beer cans in your living room. Why?

SUBJECT: Because I am interested in collecting beer cans.

INVESTIGATOR: How interesting! And why are you interested in collecting beer cans?

SUBJECT: Because I have an interest in beer cans.

It is possible to imagine this kind of conversation proceeding for a long time, with the subject always explaining his or her activities or preferences by reference to the "interest in" them. In everyday language use, the entifying nature of our concepts thus plays an important role—it creates relative moments of stability within the never-ending flow of psychological functions taking place in irreversible time (see Valsiner, 1992b, in press).

This is the core of psychologists' theoretical problem—if the use of entification through the use of words is basic to the semiotic organization of the persons' life-worlds, then obviously no psychological analysis of interests can succumb to similar entification. In other words, the psychology of interests cannot follow the lead of equating interests with entities, but needs instead to view interest as an ongoing process in the life-world of the person. This is not to say that a subject's statement about his or her "interest" is not useful for investigators. Quite the contrary; these statements help to demarcate the episodes in the flow of the life-world where the interest-processes are declared to be active. A process-oriented approach to "interest" may, in contrast, explain the actual (as opposed to nominal) mechanisms that keep persons purposefully and persistently involved in activities or imaginary internal creativity.

From Static Attributions to Developmental Analysis of Processes

Recent calls for process-oriented theorizing can be heard rather loudly in the developmental psychology of our present time (Rogoff, 1990; Valsiner, 1984, 1987; Winegar, Renninger & Valsiner, 1989). Of course, these calls reiterate similar calls made throughout the history of psychology (Lewin, 1927, Vygotsky & Luria, 1930; Werner, 1937). A move to a process-oriented theoretical view of "interest" is based on the recognition of the process of constant irreversible person <—> environment transaction. Once an emphasis is placed upon process aspects of transactions, the question of "interest" is no longer limited to an onto-logical issue ("what *is* interest?"), but acquires a developmental focus as well ("how does whatever is interest *emerge from* whatever interest is not?"). This focus leads our investigation to a rather curious state: in order to reveal the development of "interest" our empirical investigations should trace the process of the emergence of a new structure or process from a set of phenomena that in themselves have no direct resemblance to anything our investigators' minds would recognize as "interest." In order to study interest one cannot study "interest," but something else from which recognizable "interest" emerges. In this volume, this need is exemplified in those chapters that concentrate on the study of "interest" through "P–O Relationships," rather than in itself (see chapters by Krapp & Fink; Prenzel; Nenniger; Renninger; and Schiefele).

If "interest" as a common-language based class of psychological phenomena is viewed developmentally, then it becomes impossible to locate it in any place (in the mind, in the environment), and it becomes a relational process-based concept for our scientific terminology. Thus, what we identify as "interest" in a child's persevering actions with a certain object in the environment allows us to look for psychological processes that regulate the child's self's structure in its *relation* with the structure of the object in the given field. These processes are necessarily time-linked, hence the clear necessity for investigators' use of sequentially organized units of action that reflect "interest." "Interest," then, is not in the object (hence my declaration about the present volume in the beginning of this chapter), nor in the mind of the child, but it emerges as a result of processes that link the two in irreversible time. Once we have been able to "diagnose" its presence, we have already missed the opportunity to study its emergence. Of course, we will be in a position to study its further transformation into other forms (e.g., the development of "new interests" on the basis of previous ones in ontogeny). However, the methodological paradox of development remains—the transformation of a previous pattern of "interests" into a new one in ontogeny cannot be explained by the concept of "interest" as an entity. It becomes necessary to study *developmental processes* that give rise to a class of detectable phenomena that our common sense tends to label "interests." In other words, "interest" is a descriptive term that (because of its entified static nature) cannot be transformed into an explanatory term useful for the construction of psychological theories.

Internalizing Reconstructions of Social Suggestions: A Process That Gives Rise to "Interest"

In this chapter, I view "interest" as an intermediate product of the processes of social organization of mental and affective development in ontogeny. The system of these processes has been described elsewhere (see Valsiner, 1985b, 1985c, 1987, 1989, 1992a, in press). Basically, the social world of the developing person is organized by a structure of limits (zones of "free movement"—ZFM—and "promoted actions"—ZPA) that guide the person towards acting within the set of nearest possibilities for acting and thinking (ZPD or "zone of proximal development"—defined here differently from the way others use the term). Thus, the developing person encounters both limits on the variability of possibilities, and particular suggestions for focussing upon some subrange of these possibilities. The whole process of human ontogeny is both canalized by the social world and coordinated with the active participation (self-canalization) of the developing person. In this canalized process, the developing person constructs his or her own psychological functions in the process of social experiencing. This constructive process is labelled internalization. The notion of *internalization* (and its complementary process—*externalization*) is central for understanding how phenomena that we tend to label "interests" can emerge. The developing person is actively involved in the analytic/synthetic process of "taking in" information from the surrounding socially organized world (see also Krapp & Fink; and Renninger, this volume). That process constitutes an *experiencing* of the world and leads to the internal construction of new mediating devices that are preadaptations for future experiences. Internalization involves the analysis of complex information made available in the course of experiencing, and the synthesizing of psychological (internal) phenomena that can function as a means to some end in the present or future. Internalization leads to the construction of unique intrapsychological functions on the basis of experiencing the external world. These functions become involved in the process of experiencing, as they are translated into the structure of externally observable actions. Hence, observations of "interests" in our subjects are necessarily based on products of externalization.

INTRAPSYCHOLOGICAL RECONSTRUCTION OF CONSTRAINT SYSTEMS

The nature of the internalized construction of psychological functions remains that of enabling our cognitive–affective processes by way of constraining their directions of possible movement. Thus, in the intrapsychological sphere of a developing person the emergence of new personal senses (based on collective–cultural meanings) and concepts of different (hierarchically organized) levels of abstraction allows for reorganization of the dynamic flow of affective/mental processes. This reorganization can lead to a further differentiation (or, episodically, to states of fusion or de-differentiation) of these internal processes, which are mostly available to investigators through the use of some form of introspection. Hence a different (self-) canalyzing system is constructed in the course of internalization/externalization in ontogeny, which allows for relative inconsistency between what people understand and talk about, and what they do.

"Interest" as a Temporarily-Fixed Constraint Structure in Self-Canalization

When a person is described as "having an interest" (a descriptive, entified statement), we can look for the dynamic organization of that phenomenon in the temporary fixation of some set of constraints in the intrapersonal flow of affective thinking. If I set up for myself constraints (by way of personal sense—i.e., the core of the personal–cultural world—Valsiner, 1989) then these constraints (senses) lead my mental processes towards persevering activity oriented towards some object or event in the external world, or some idea of my own making. The first of these outcomes (externally oriented action) will be available to other people who identify it as "interest." The second is available only to me through my introspection and can become available to others if I myself label it "interest" and communicate that to others. In both cases, however, it is an internally constructed set of signs that has guided me towards this perseverance in my acting, thinking and feeling. My "interest" can be described as emerging from the structure of my "personal senses" in my personal culture (see Valsiner, 1989) at a given time. Likewise, any reorganization in the structure of that self-organization may lead to the disappearance of previous "interests" and the construction of new ones (see Renninger & Leckrone, 1991; Krapp & Fink, in this volume). Thus, the main nature of "interest" is that it is constantly changing in the web of the individual's personal culture, sometimes disappearing, at other times leading to new forms of interest.

A Hypothetical Illustration: From Killing Insects to Collecting Them

Let us imagine that my personal culture includes the notions that (a) "insects are dirty"; (b) "insects are bothersome"; and (c) "we must get rid of insects." This combination of notions that I have constructed in my mind leads me to kill flies when they are around, using a special insect-killing whip (who can kill these "dirty" flies by hand?), and this killing is activated whenever any of these insects has the unfortunate fate of flying around me. Because I act in this insect-killing mode only when it is triggered by one of these bothersome creatures, no observer will probably detect in me an "interest in killing flies." Nor do I myself apply the "interest" label in my mind to this everyday activity. Also, because I do not initiate the activity myself (without triggers) and go around on a "fly-hunting trip" during which I would look for flies to kill (compare this with "interest in hunting" among people who are described as "hunters"), again my genocidal activity in respect to the insect world goes by without being described as "interest."

Now let us consider a "developmental intervention"—using textbooks on nature written by authors well-trained in the "Time–Life style" (see chapters by Garner, Brown, Sanders, & Menke; and Wade, in this volume). In these, I find some "seductive details" in addition to the basic information about insects and their lives and roles in nature. For example, let us consider a case in which the textbook includes a little "personal story" of how a famous rock star loves flies to such an extent that he (or she) always wears a necklace made of these dried insects (a somewhat perverse decoration to imagine, but, alas, in the world of celebrities one may be able to find even more extreme examples). I may have been identifying myself with that rock star for a long time, and this new "seductive detail," which is perfectly irrelevant for understanding the biology of flies (and may be ignored by all other students), becomes relevant information for reorganizing my relations with the world of insects. In my personal sense system, the notion "insects are dirty" may turn into "flies are beautiful." This mental (semiotic) constraint reorganizes the intrapsychological system that guides my actions: no longer will I use the whip to smash the bothersome flies; instead I will carefully capture these little creatures with my hands, put little pins through them, and place them in my specially purchased collection box. When my friends visit me I will show them my collection with pride and pleasure. I will go out on special "hunting trips" to find new specimens for my collection. I will explain to myself and others that "I have an interest in collecting insects," and surely people who observe me will "detect" this "interest" in my actions and their persistence.

In this (admittedly invented) example there was no role given to the notion of "interest." Instead, other personal senses that regulate the person's understanding of some class of nature (insects) were used to guide my involvement in episodic ordinary actions; and by way of the intrapersonal subjective integration of the class of insects with a strongly affective identity-figure, the old system of cognitive constraints was reorganized, with a result that became detectable as "interest" for both myself and to others. In this example, the emergence of persevering self-canalization systems in the mind creates novelty rather than following any previous external models or internally stable strategies in any faithful way.

Is Self-Construction of Novelty in the Mind a New Idea?

My claim here about the linkage between "interests" and internal canalization (internalized self-directive sign-mediational mechanisms) may look somewhat novel for the psychology of 1990s. However, this perception is merely a result of a historical myopia in the contemporary empiricistic traditions of the discipline. For turn-of-the-century developmentalists the idea of the construction of novelty was the key to understanding development (Baldwin, 1894, 1902, 1906; Morgan, 1892). The present self-canalization notion carries into the intra-psychological world Baldwin's assumption of *persistent imitation* (trying, and trying again), setting it up in conjunction with the notion of bounded indeterminacy as the central feature of development (see Valsiner, 1987, chapter 8). The developing person always constructs limited autonomy for the creation of possible future actions in imaginary possible environments. This intrapsychological process of fantasy or imagination is a central mechanism for creativity, and has been viewed as the vehicle of psychological development (Vygotsky, 1931, pp. 454–456). "Interests," then, can be viewed as an intermediate by-product of the imagination processes that guide the person's mental/affective and actional systems towards some object. In reality, the developing person does not "*have* interests," but is involved in a self-canalization process of striving towards some object. Thus, to return to beer can or insect collection, in both cases the emerged "interest" constitutes a self-constraining device for the person's further development, while these "interests" came into being on the basis of other internalized constraint systems.

METHODOLOGICAL IMPLICATIONS

My metatheoretical meditation about "interest" in this volume will remain only half complete unless the methodological implications of psychologists' increasing interest in "interest" are discussed. The processes involved in creating the phenomena of "interest" are hidden deep in the intra-psychological sphere. These processes cannot be empirically studied using consensually validated methodological imperatives of Behaviorist and its continuing Cognitivist origins. Introspection as a scientifically adequate methodological direction needs to be rehabilitated within the "scientific method" in psychology. During the twentieth century, introspection has been stigmatized as "soft" or "subjective" psychology, and its early users caricatured as non-objective "soul-searchers" for whom "scientific rigor" is foreign. Nothing can be further from the actual state of affairs (see Danziger, 1980, 1985, 1990; Danziger & Shermer, 1991 in press).

Following C. Lloyd Morgan's elaboration of issues of methodology (which has been retained in contemporary psychology in the form of misinterpretations of "Morgan's Canon"—for the full story, see Morgan, 1894, Ch. 3), suggests that *coordination* of (in contrast with "choice between") exterospective and introspective processes would actually permit the study of intra-psychological processes. The focus of this volume on the domain of "interests" leads us to a need for a careful re-evaluation of our methodological habits. Let me remind us of Morgan's argument about "two inductions":

> Our conclusions concerning the mental processes of beings other than our own individual selves are... based on a two-fold induction. First the psychologist has to reach, through induction, the laws of mind as revealed to him in his own conscious experience. Here the facts to be studied are facts of consciousness, known at first-hand to him alone among mortals; the hypotheses may logically suggest themselves, in which case they are original so far as the observer himself is concerned, or they may be derived—that is to say,

suggested to the observer by other observers; the verification of the hypotheses is again purely subjective, original or derived theories being submitted to the touchstone of individual experience. This is the one inductive process. The other is more objective. The facts to be observed are external phenomena, physical occurrences in the objective world; the hypotheses again may be either original or derived; the verification is objective, original or derived theories being submitted to the touchstone of observable phenomena. Both inductions, subjective and objective, are necessary. Neither can be omitted without renouncing the scientific method. (Morgan, 1894, pp. 47–48.)

Morgan's thesis leads to the need to go beyond psychology's eclectic ways of linking theories, methods, and phenomena in the construction of knowledge (see also Valsiner, 1991a). The present volume cannot be "interesting" in itself; theoretically, this is impossible, but taken together the chapters in this volume can lead to a rechanneling of the scientific activities of readers who concentrate on the study of complex psychological phenomena and persevere in their efforts to make better sense of them.

REFERENCES

Anderson, R. C. (1982). Allocation of attention during reading. In A. Flammer & W. Kintsch (Eds.), *Discourse processing*. New York: North–Holland.

Baldwin, J. M. (1894). Imitation: A chapter in the natural history of consciousness. *Mind, 3*, (n.s.), 26–55.

Baldwin, J. M. (1902). *Social and ethical interpretations in mental development*. New York: MacMillan.

Baldwin, J. M. (1906). *Thought and things. Vol. 1. Functional logic, or genetic theory of knowledge*. London: Swan Sonnenschein.

Bloom, A. (1981). *The linguistic shaping of thought*. Hillsdale, NJ.: Lawrence Erlbaum Associates.

Danziger, K. (1980). The history of introspection reconsidered. *Journal of the History of the Behavioral Sciences, 16,* 241–262.

Danziger, K. (1985). The methodological imperative in psychology. *Philosophy of the Social Sciences, 15,* 1–13.

Danziger, K. (1990). *Constructing the subject: Historical origins of psychological research*. Cambridge: Cambridge University Press.

Danziger, K., & Shermer, P. (1991 in press). The varieties of replication: a historical introduction. In R. van der Veer, M. H. van IJzendoorn, & J. Valsiner (Eds.), *Replicability in the study of human development*. Norwood, NJ: Ablex.

Lewin, K. (1927). Gesetz und Experiment in der Psychologie. *Symposion, 1,* 375–421.

Morgan, C. L. (1892). The law of psychogenesis. *Mind, 1,* (n.s.), 72–93.

Morgan, C. L. (1894). *An introduction to comparative psychology.* London: Walter Scott.

Pascual–Leone, J. (1984). Attentional, dialectic, and mental effort: Toward an organismic theory of life stages. In M. L. Commons, F. A. Richards, & C. Armon (Eds.), *Beyond formal operations* (pp. 182–215). New York: Praeger.

Renninger, K. A., & Leckrone, T. G. (1991). Continuity in young children's actions: A consideration of interest and temperament. In L. Oppenheimer, & J. Valsiner (Eds.), *The origins of action* (pp. 205–238). New York: Springer.

Rogoff, B. (1990). *Apprenticeship in thinking.* New York: Oxford University Press.

Siegfried, J. (Ed.) (1991, in press). *The role of common sense in psychological theorizing.* Norwood, NJ: Ablex.

Smedslund, J. (1978). Bandura's theory of self-efficacy: A set of common-sense theorems. *Scandinavian Journal of Psychology, 19,* 1–14.

Smedslund, J. (1982). Revising explications of common sense through dialogue: Thirty-six psychological theorems. *Scandinavian Journal of Psychology, 23,* 299–305.

Thorngate, W. (1990). The economy of attention and the development of psychology. *Canadian Psychology, 31,* 262–271.

Valsiner, J. (1984). Conceptualizing intelligence: From an internal static attribution to the study of the process structure of organism–environment relationships. *International Journal of Psychology, 19,* 363–389.

Valsiner, J. (1985a). Common sense and psychological theories: The historical nature of logical necessity. *Scandinavian Journal of Psychology, 26,* 97–109.

Valsiner, J. (1985b). Theoretical issues of child development and the problem of accident prevention. In T. Gärling & J. Valsiner (Eds.), *Children within environments: Toward a psychology of accident prevention* (pp. 13–36). New York: Plenum.

Valsiner, J. (1985c). Parental organization of children's cognitive development within home environment. *Psychologia, 28,* 131–143.

Valsiner, J. (1987). *Culture and the development of children's action.* Chichester: Wiley.

Valsiner, J. (1989). *Human development and culture.* Lexington, MA: D. C. Heath.

Valsiner, J. (1991a). Construction of the mental: From the "cognitive revolution" to the study of development. *Theory & Psychology, 1,* 4, 477–494.

Valsiner, J. (1991b). Integration of theory and methodology in psychology: The legacy of Joachim Wohlwill. In L. Mos & P. van Geert (Eds.), *Annals of theoretical psychology. Vol. 7. Developmental Psychology* (pp. 161–175). New York: Plenum.

Valsiner, J. (1992a, in press). Social organization of cognitive development: Internalization and externalization of constraint systems. In A. Demetriou, M. Shayer, & A. Efklides (Eds.), *The modern theories of cognitive development go to school.* London: Routledge & Kegan Paul.

Valsiner, J. (1992b). Making of the future: temporality and the constructive nature of human development. In G. Turkewitz & D. Devenney (Eds.), *Timing as an initial condition of development*. Hillsdale, NJ: Lawrence Erlbaum Associates.

Vygotsky, L. S. (1931). *Pedologia podrostka*. Moscow–Leningrad: Gosudarstvennoie uchebno-pedagogicheskoie izdatel'stvo.

Vygotsky, L., & Luria, A. R. (1930). *Tool and symbol in child development*. Unpublished manuscript.

Werner, H. (1937). Process and achievement—a basic problem of education and developmental psychology. *Harvard Educational Review, 7,* 353–368.

Winegar, L. T., Renninger, K. A., & Valsiner, J. (1989). Dependent–independence in adult-child relationships. In D. A. Kramer & M. Bopp (Eds.), *Transformations in clinical and developmental psychology* (pp. 158–168). New York: Springer.

The Relation of Interest to the Motivation of Behavior: A Self-Determination Theory Perspective

3

Edward L. Deci
University of Rochester

Anyone who has observed young children knows that it is natural for them to be active and attentive during most of their waking hours. When free from biological urges, they direct their energy and attention to activities they find *interesting*. For long periods of time they pile blocks, dress dolls, push boxes, empty jars, throw balls, or make their dinosaurs walk and talk. And they do these activities without prods or pushes; indeed, they sometimes persist in spite of prods or pushes to the contrary.

For parents, this can be both gratifying and disconcerting. Because *interest is a powerful motivator*, children entertain themselves with activities that interest them, and they learn about their world by doing so. However, they sometimes continue with these activities rather than doing other things that parents judge more important for learning or social harmony. In fact, children may resist and become irritable when their parents try to direct their attention away from what interests them.

Young children are not the only ones who are motivated by interest. Even adults can become wholly absorbed in an activity that has no payoff except the enjoyment they experience while doing it. Most often, such absorption occurs in leisure pursuits; that is, people typically pursue avocations primarily because of interest in the activities. However, interest can also be an important motivator in one's vocation. In fact, because people who are interested in their work are typically committed to doing it well, many behavioral scientists have been exploring how to make jobs more interesting for people (e.g., Hackman & Oldham, 1980; Vroom & Deci, in press). Still, adults' behaviors are less often motivated purely by interest than are children's, because with adults the motivational propensity of "interest" is often mixed with other motivational forces such as evaluation apprehension, ego-involvement, social comparison, and habit.

The purpose of this chapter is to explore the motivating aspects of interest and the relation of interest to other motivational processes. To accomplish that, I present a conceptualization of interest from the perspective of self-determination theory (Deci & Ryan, 1985, 1987, 1991).

SELF-DETERMINATION THEORY IN BRIEF

Self-determination theory distinguishes between the motivational dynamics underlying activities that people do freely and those that they feel coerced or pressured to do. To be self-determining means to engage in an activity with a full sense of wanting, choosing, and personal endorsement. When self-determined, people are acting in accord with, or expressing, themselves. As a concept, then, self-determination describes the regulation of behaviors that emanate from what we call the *integrated self* (Deci & Ryan, 1991).

In explicating the motivational basis of self-determined behavior, I initially contrasted behaviors that are done simply for the personal reward of enjoying the activity itself with behaviors that are instrumental for some other reward, such as money, praise, or grades on a report card (Deci, 1975). The former are referred to as intrinsically motivated and the latter as extrinsically motivated. Intrinsically motivated behaviors are the prototype of self-determined activity; they are of interest to one's intrinsic self (Deci & Ryan, 1991) and are thus freely undertaken. Extrinsically motivated activities, in contrast, are ones that are undertaken as a means to some end—that is, as an instrument for achieving some outcome other than the spontaneous satisfaction that accompanies the activity. Extrinsic outcomes are often administered by others and used to coerce or control—for example, teachers often dispense grades and detention to make students do particular activities. Consequently, early formulations (e.g., Deci,

1975) viewed extrinsically motivated behaviors as non-self-determined and antagonistic to intrinsically motivated (self-determined) behaviors. In later work, my colleagues and I (Ryan & Connell, 1989; Ryan, Connell, & Deci, 1985) proposed that it is possible, through the developmental processes of internalization and integration, for an extrinsic regulatory process to become part of the self and thus to be the basis for self-determined, extrinsically motivated behavior. As such, extrinsically motivated behaviors can be either self-determined or non-self-determined, depending on the extent to which their regulatory processes have been integrated into the self (Deci & Ryan, 1991).

The concept "interest" has often been associated with intrinsically motivated behaviors because people seem to adopt those behaviors out of interest. In fact, several theories of human motivation have referred to people as being *intrinsically motivated* when they are freely doing what interests them (deCharms, 1968; Deci & Ryan, 1985; White, 1959). When so motivated, their behavior is characterized by concentration and engagement; it occurs spontaneously and people become wholly absorbed in it. The purest forms of intrinsic motivation may involve the person's experiencing what Csikszentmihalyi (1975) has referred to as "flow"—a state in which the person is completely immersed in an activity and experiences a flow of awareness. This state can be thought of as a prototype of being interested.

In self-determination theory, interest is also closely linked to intrinsic motivation, though more generally it is linked to all self-determined action. In self-determination theory, interest is conceptualized as the core affect of the self—the affect that relates one's self to activities that provide the type of novelty, challenge, or aesthetic appeal that one desires at that time. Thus, interest is primarily linked to intrinsically motivated activities but can become associated with extrinsically motivated activities to the extent that their regulation has been integrated with one's intrinsic self (Deci & Ryan, 1991). Let me now elaborate.

INTRINSIC MOTIVATION AND INTEREST

From the perspective of self-determination theory, the starting point for an analysis of interest is in the relation between a person and an activity. When a person experiences interest, he or she is engaged in some activity. This could be playing softball, looking at a painting, riding a bicycle, listening to a symphony, or sensing the inner activity of breathing. Typically, activities involve objects—things that are being apprehended or manipulated—and some theorists (e.g., Krapp & Fink, this volume) use the person–object interaction as the focus of their analysis. In my view, although the object is important, it is considered an aspect of the activity, so it enters the analysis accordingly.

Because interest exists in the relation between a person and an activity, the self-determination analysis is concerned with the match between a person's needs, desires, and capacities, on the one hand, and the affordances of an activity, on the other. More specifically, we are concerned with the needs and desires that are either intrinsic to the self or have become integrated with the self (Deci & Ryan, 1991) and with the match between those needs and the affordances of various activities. Our approach, therefore, maintains that a person is not necessarily *interested* in the activities he or she is motivated to do. Often, for example, the activity is simply instrumental and is not of interest to the person. Only when the needs or desires of the self mesh with the activity will the person experience interest. This point is a very important one because, as I later argue, the quality of one's motivated behavior differs as a function of the extent to which the person is interested in the activity.

Beginning with the definition of interest as an affect that occurs in the interaction between a person and an activity, one can then move to a focus either on the activity or on the person. For example, one can explore the characteristics of activities that tend, on average, to make them interesting to a group of people (e.g., to late elementary school children). This approach, which can be found in the work of various investigators (e.g., Hidi & Baird, 1986), is quite useful for purposes of intervention. By knowing what characteristics of tasks tend to be interesting to children, one can design educational materials that, on average, will be more interesting (and thus more intrinsically motivating) for the children.

Similarly, one can treat interest as a person variable (e.g., Renninger, 1990) and focus on the degree to which a person is interested in a particular activity or class of activities (e.g., mathematics, or school work more generally). This approach is concerned with the person's enduring interests in an activity over an extended period of time (see also Krapp & Fink, this volume), and it allows interest to be treated as an individual difference or dispositional variable. Thus, one could assess the degree to which people are interested in an activity (or class of activities) and use this to predict other variables such as school achievement or classroom adjustment.

Each of these approaches represents a useful arena for research and helps to explicate an aspect of the concept "interest." However, whether one's focus is primarily on the interestingness of activities or on people's tendency to be interested, one must also, at least implicitly, consider the other. To design interesting tasks, one must understand the characteristics of the people who will engage in them; and to assess people's interest, one must do so with respect to activities, however broadly these activities are defined. Furthermore, a thorough analysis of interest requires even more than a consideration of the person and the activity, because a person–activity interaction occurs within a social context, and the context can have a considerable influence on that interaction, and thus on the person's interest.

In this chapter, I focus on the interrelatedness of persons, activities, and contexts, discussing the issues as they apply to students in educational settings. I begin by elaborating the concepts of intrinsic motivation, interest, and self-determination, emphasizing the relation of activities to persons. Subsequently, I review two bodies of research: The first explores the effects of social contexts on people's intrinsic motivation, interest, and self-determination; and the second explores the relation of intrinsic motivation, interest, and self-determination to conceptual understanding, cognitive flexibility, and creativity.

Intrinsic Motivation

Intrinsic motivation has been increasingly recognized over the past two decades as a crucial concept for understanding human motivation. To a large extent, the concept emerged from a realization that the two dominant associationist theories in empirical psychology—Skinnerian operant theory (e.g., Skinner, 1953) and Hullian drive theory (e.g., Hull, 1943)—were not adequate for explaining a variety of behaviors and phenomena that were being observed in experiments with humans and other animals. These observations involved such behaviors as exploring novel spaces (Montgomery, 1954) and manipulating objects (Harlow, 1953) that seemed to have neither a direct nor an indirect relation to reinforcements. Because the concept of intrinsic motivation received initial attention largely in reaction to the two very different reinforcement theories, it was initially formulated and defined in two quite different ways.

In response to Skinner's functional theory of reinforcement, intrinsically motivated behaviors were defined as those that occur in the absence of any operationally separable reinforcement (i.e., in the absence of an extrinsic reward). This view, although it added little to our understanding of the psychological processes underlying intrinsically motivated behavior, has served well as an "operational" definition of the concept and is the basis for the so-called free-choice measure of intrinsic motivation that has been used by numerous researchers for the past two decades (Deci, 1971).

Alternatively, in response to Hull's drive theory of reinforcement, which stated that all behavior is reducible to physiological drives, intrinsically motivated behaviors have been defined as those that are based in the innate *psychological* needs of the organism (e.g., White, 1959). The two inherent psychological needs most frequently referred to as being related to intrinsic motivation are competence (or effectance) and self-determination (or autonomy), although a third need—the need for relatedness—has also proven useful for a full explication of intrinsic motivation and self-determination (Deci & Ryan, 1991). The view that intrinsic motivation is based in psychological needs was initially articulated by White (1959), although it is traceable to the earlier work of Murray (1938) and Maslow (1943). This approach is extremely important because it elucidates the psychological processes involved in intrinsic motivation, and in so doing it addresses people's basic nature. Furthermore, it provides a basis for predicting what contextual conditions will enhance versus diminish intrinsic motivation—contexts that allow the satisfaction of one's intrinsic needs for competence, self-determination, and relatedness will enhance intrinsic motivation, whereas those that thwart the satisfaction of one or more of these needs will diminish intrinsic motivation.

Although the two approaches to defining intrinsic motivation are quite different, they are complementary in that the first approach describes the organism's actions, whereas the second sheds light on the underlying processes that motivate these actions. The idea that human beings have intrinsic psychological needs suggests that "nonreinforced" activity is motivated by those basic psychological needs. In other words, people's inherent needs to be competent, self-determining, and related motivate them to actualize capacities that allow them to function in a competent and self-determined fashion while maintaining meaningful ties to significant others.

Interest

The concept of "interest" became prominent in discussions and definitions of intrinsic motivation somewhat later than did the ideas of nonreinforcement-related activity and psychological needs. Still, it was at least implicit in all discussions of intrinsic motivation, for it is hard to talk about "intrinsically motivated" activity without describing people being interested in the activity. Stated differently, the clearest evidence in support of non-reinforcement-derivative behavior is that people (and other animals) persist at activities for no clear reason except that they seem to find the activities interesting.

Because, in self-determination theory, interest is explicated in terms of the interaction between a person and an activity, operating within a social context, I now consider each of the three elements in turn.

The Person. Central to the psychology of a person is the developing self (Deci & Ryan, 1991; Ryan, 1991), which consists of innate capacities, intrinsic psychological needs, and the developmental process of organismic integration through which the person develops. Interest occurs at the moment of a match between these organismic conditions and the affordances of the situation. In other words, one experiences interest when one encounters novel, challenging, or aesthetically pleasing activities or objects in a context that allows satisfaction of the basic psychological needs and thus promotes development.

The *experiential component* of a person's interest is the uniquely recognizable awareness that the person has come to associate with particular physiological activity (James, 1890). Each of us has a personal understanding of what it means, experientially, to be interested. There is a certain quality of attention and a certain sense of delight, for example. The experiential quality of interest has a positive hedonic valence and is related to the feelings of excitement and enjoyment, although there is lack of agreement about whether interest, excitement, and enjoyment are the same or different affective experiences. Izard (1977), for example, considered interest–excitement to be one emotion and enjoyment to be another, and Reeve (1989) has distinguished interest and enjoyment empirically. Although I think interest, excitement, and enjoyment are all slightly different experiences, I often look to their convergence as a means of assessing intrinsic motivation. When a person reports interest, excitement, and enjoyment with respect to an activity, one can be reasonably sure that the person is intrinsically motivated for that activity.

Interest also has a *dispositional component.* Through experiencing interest when relating to particular activities, a person develops an interest for, or an enduring desire to interact with, those activities. Such interests can be narrowly defined (e.g., playing tennis) or more broadly defined (e.g., engaging in athletics) and once identified can be assessed and used to predict qualities or quantities of behavior and development. Thus, for example, if one were to assess a child's interest in reading, one could use that to predict the child's intrinsically motivated activity (and achievement) concerning reading. In other words, one could predict the extent to which the child would engage in reading without being prodded and without needing an extrinsic incentive. The more broadly one defines dispositional interest, the more broad can be the outcomes one predicts. In the next section, I address how these enduring, dispositional interests develop.

The Activity. The referent of a person's interest, whether one is dealing with an immediate experience or a dispositional tendency, is an activity that typically includes some object. These referents are activities that, at a particular time (or perhaps ongoingly), have an optimal relation to the condition of the organism—that is, to one's desires and inclinations, if biological urges do not interfere. When that relation is optimal, one experiences interest and begins to develop a dispositional preference for that activity or class of activities.

Considerable research has focused on the characteristics of tasks (and objects) that tend to make them interesting to people. Two closely related characteristics seem to be central: *optimal challenge* and *novelty*. Activities or ideas that people find interesting are usually optimally discrepant from what they know or can do. These activities require that people "stretch" their capacities or expand their cognitive structures. Interest is what people are likely to feel when they encounter such optimally challenging tasks, and those are the tasks people freely seek. For example, people often speak of preferring to play squash with others who are just a little better than they are—that is, who provide a challenge. (Of course, if people's primary motivation is to win rather than to enjoy the game, they may prefer a poor player, but then interest is not central to those interactions.)

Danner and Lonky (1981) did a study in which children's reasoning capacities were preassessed. The researchers then made a variety of activities available to the children, using the type of "interest center" structure often available in "open classrooms." The results indicated that when the children were free to select their own activities they tended to go to those that were slightly beyond their existing capacities. In a complementary study, Harter (1978) found that children expressed greatest pleasure (for example, by smiling) when they worked on tasks that were moderately difficult (i.e., optimally challenging) for them.

Closely related to the idea of optimal challenge are those of novelty (Berlyne, 1971) and optimal discrepancy between an input and a cognitive structure (Hunt, 1965). The concepts of novelty and discrepancy are slightly different, and each differs slightly from optimal challenge, because each comes from a different theoretical tradition. Still, they share the common idea that people tend to freely seek and be interested in those activities or inputs that are optimally challenging, in other words, that are not fully mastered but are not so discrepant as to be frustrating.

Of course, not all challenges or novel inputs interest an individual, but where there *is* interest, there is likely to be optimal challenge or novelty. The additional factor that is necessary to explain what inputs are interesting to people can be called *preferences*. In essence, these are dispositional interests. People have preferences among optimally challenging activities (or objects) because of the personal relevance or aesthetic appeal of the activities or objects. In general, these preferences develop as a function of three critical factors: innate capacities, environmental affordance, and interpersonal contexts.

First, people tend to prefer those activities for which they have some innate capabilities, and the stronger their capabilities, the more likely they are to find the activities interesting. Researchers have often found, for example, that perceived competence is correlated with interest and intrinsic motivation (Grolnick, Ryan, & Deci, in press; Ryan & Grolnick, 1986), and it is sometimes said that geniuses "have to do what they do" in the sense that their superior ability is so compelling that it dominates their interest. I am here making two related points. One is that people tend to have stronger preferences (or dispositional interests) for activities at which they are more competent or have greater potential. The other is that, regardless of people's level of proficiency, they are more interested in activities that provide optimal challenge. Beginners and accomplished performers alike are more interested in optimally challenging activities, though of course the activities that are optimally challenging for accomplished performers are much more difficult than those that are optimally challenging for beginners.

Second, preferences (or enduring interests) are also influenced by the activities available in people's environments. Although the tendency to engage in challenges and develop competencies is innate and is influenced by inherent capacities, the specific activities toward which one directs one's energies are affected by the affordances that are available. A child who lives on a small farm on the side of an Alp, surrounded by snow, mountain goats, and wild flowers, will tend to develop different preferences from those of a child who lives in the Galapagos, surrounded by ocean, turtles, and sunshine. Whereas the former might be interested in farming, the latter may develop a preference for fishing. The environmental factors are *not* determinative, and either young person could go off to the city to become a physician, but the environments do influence preferences because they constitute the challenges and gratifications that are available, and people are more likely to develop preferences for optimal challenges that are available to them than for those that are not.

Third, preferences are influenced by social contexts. Later in the chapter I will review an extensive body of research showing how social contexts influence intrinsic motivation and enduring interests. For now, let me just say that when people engage in activities within a social context that allows satisfaction of their fundamental psychological needs for competence, autonomy, and relatedness, they will be likely to maintain or develop enduring interests in those activities, whereas when they engage in activities within a social context that thwarts the satisfaction of the three psychological needs, they will lose or fail to develop enduring interests.

INTEREST AND EXTRINSIC MOTIVATION: SELF-DETERMINATION

Interest organizes some of people's attention and activity. When they feel free to do so, their attention is directed toward activities or objects that interest them. They turn to things that satisfy their intrinsic needs and to tasks for which they have developed preferences. And when people experience interest, the energy necessary for action is readily available. This unconflicted activity is what we refer to as being intrinsically motivated and is what we have been discussing so far. When people are thus motivated, the "rewards" are the spontaneous affective/cognitive experiences that accompany their behavior.

Although interest plays a central role in intrinsic motivation, interest is not central to all motivated behavior. Often, for example, people engage in activities not because the activities are themselves interesting, but rather because they are *instrumental* for some desired outcome that is quite separate from the activity itself. Such outcomes can include status, approval, money, and a host of others. In these cases, the term interest does not properly describe one's relation to the activity. One does not do the activity because one finds it interesting; one does it because it is instrumental to some other outcome. If I were to play tennis merely as a way to relate to a friend who likes tennis, I would not be playing the game because it interests me. Instead, I would be doing it because it gives me an opportunity to relate to my friend. If my friend preferred ice skating, I would probably go ice skating. Of course one could say that I am interested in relating to my friend, that I find my friend interesting. That may well be true, but it changes the referent activity. In this example the referent activity is playing tennis, and the point is that this activity is not intrinsically motivated, so the term interest is not appropriate for describing my relation to tennis.

Activities that are not themselves interesting but are done because they are instrumental for some desired outcome are said to be *extrinsically motivated*. The relation between extrinsic motivation and intrinsic motivation has received considerable attention in the past 25 years. For example, operant theorists have claimed that there is no such thing as intrinsic motivation (Reiss & Sushinsky, 1975), and instrumentality theorists have asserted that extrinsic and intrinsic motivation are additive to yield total motivation (Porter & Lawler, 1968). However, an abundance of research has now indicated that extrinsic and intrinsic motivation can be negatively interactive, with extrinsic motivation sometimes undermining intrinsic motivation because of diminishing what I have called a sense of self-determination (e.g., Deci, 1975). This research finding, which has been replicated many times, has led numerous writers and theorists to pit intrinsic and extrinsic motivation against each other, viewing them as antagonistic. This, however, is an oversimplified and inaccurate account of the relation between the two types of motivation.

Whereas many studies have shown that extrinsic rewards tend to decrease intrinsic motivation within some social contexts (Deci, 1971), other studies have found that the same rewards may enhance intrinsic motivation in other contexts (Ryan, Mims, & Koestner, 1983). Although I elaborate on this point in a later section on social contexts, I mention it here to make clear that the relation between extrinsic and intrinsic motivation is complex both because the effects of external incentives depend on the social context within which they are administered and because a person's extrinsic motivation has been found to have many forms (Ryan & Connell, 1989). Notably, research has indicated that some activities undertaken because of extrinsic prods, pressures, or inducements can leave people feeling they have no sense of freedom or self-determination, whereas other instrumental or extrinsically motivated activities, such as playing tennis to be with a friend, may allow one to feel quite free and self-determining. In recent work, my colleagues and I (Deci & Ryan, 1985; Ryan & Connell, 1989; Ryan, Connell, & Deci, 1985) have focused on the issue of how extrinsically motivated activities—ones that a person undertakes not because they are intrinsically interesting to him or her but rather because they are instrumental to a desired outcome—can vary in the extent to which they are endorsed by or emanate from one's sense of self and are thus self-determined.

Our analysis of extrinsic motivation revolves around the concept of *internalization*, which is the process through which external regulation is actively transformed into internal regulation (Schafer, 1968). Consider the case of classroom learning. Learning, as an activity, can certainly be interesting, as is so evident in young children, and we all know what it is like to be interested in learning something. The problem faced by educators and parents alike, however, is that many of the classroom activities they believe to be important for children's learning are not really interesting to children. Thus, it is up to the socializing adults to encourage children to undertake behaviors that the children would not do spontaneously (i.e., that are not intrinsically motivating). The ideal outcome of such adult–child socializing interactions is for the child to take responsibility for learning the uninteresting material, in other words, for the child to internalize the regulation for that activity. The adult may supply the initial extrinsic impetus for the action, but the goal is for the child to become self-regulating with respect to it.

By internalizing the value of an activity and the process of regulating it, a person transforms motivation by external factors into motivation by internal factors. However, there are two distinctions that are important to make at this point. First, this "now internal" motivation is still referred to as *extrinsic* motivation because there is still a goal separate from the interest and enjoyment of the activity itself. For example, if learning the multiplication tables is considered important for being able to do more advanced math and other such activities, a child may accept responsibility for learning them even though the child does not find the activity at all interesting. The child would have internalized the regulation of this activity (and thus the motivation would be internal to the child), but the activity is extrinsically motivated because it is still an instrumental one that is done now because it is instrumental to being able to do more advanced mathematics in the future. The second important point is that the concepts of interest and importance have somewhat different motivational functions. We have drawn a clear link between interest and intrinsic motivation emphasizing that an activity is intrinsically motivated if one's primary reason for doing it is the spontaneous interest and enjoyment one experiences from doing it. With extrinsic motivation, however, the concept of "importance" is more germane. One undertakes the activity primarily because it is instrumental or important for some extrinsic goal, even a goal that the person values (i.e., for which the value has been internalized) such as being able to do more advanced mathematics.

The self-determination theory formulation of internalization has differentiated the concept of extrinsic motivation even further by describing different forms of internalized extrinsic motivation (Deci & Ryan, 1985; Ryan & Connell, 1989). *Introjected* regulatory processes are processes that have been taken in or internalized by a person but never accepted as his or her own. These may take the form of controlling prescriptions, often formulated as "shoulds" or "oughts," and they typically have immediate consequences like self-administered approval or disapproval. To do something because you have learned that you should and will feel guilty if you do not is an example of introjected regulation. Gradually, however, a person may come to *identify* with the importance of the activity for him or herself in which case the regulation will have been more fully accepted by the person as his or her own—there will be less conflict and greater integration with respect to the regulation of that activity. Finally, the person may, as the developmental process continues, *integrate* that regulatory process with others so as to form greater coherence of self. Using the spatial metaphor, one would say that the regulation gradually becomes integrated into the self and thus is the basis for self-determined extrinsic motivation.

In this conceptualization, then, there are four types of extrinsically motivated activity—external, introjected, identified, and integrated—here ordered to reflect increasing degrees of self-determination. Accordingly, this view suggests that a person can gradually become self-determined with respect to the activity even though he or she may not be very interested in it. It is probable that, as the regulation becomes integrated, the person will experience greater interest in doing it, though I believe that the concept "importance" continues to be more central than interest even to self-determined extrinsic motivation.

A further proposition of self-determination theory is that the process of internalization tends to occur naturally—that is, people will be intrinsically motivated to accept values and regulatory processes—if the values are not inconsistent with their basic nature and the social context does not interfere with the process (Deci & Ryan, 1985, 1991). Out of the need for relatedness, people are motivated to find a satisfying place in the social milieu. Doing this requires sharing at least some of the values and practices of the others in that milieu. Thus, the internalization process begins because of a person's need for relatedness to others. People internalize values and behaviors that are endorsed by the social world because they want to be accepted by that world.

Internalizing a regulation merely to be accepted by others is likely to take the form of introjected regulation. The identification and integration of the regulation is not necessary for people to feel related to others, but it is necessary for them to feel self-determined. Thus, for the internalization process to be effective and to result in integrated self-regulation, it must be motivated by a combination of the psychological needs for relatedness *and* self-determination (autonomy).

Ryan and Connell (1989) recently developed a scale to assess the degree to which the regulation of school work has been internalized by middle-childhood students. They reported that the more autonomous or self-determined the students were in regulating their school-related behavior, the more likely they were to enjoy school, the less anxious they were about school, and the more proactive they were in coping with school problems.

To summarize, according to self-determination theory, internalization of the regulation for uninteresting behaviors is a natural, intrinsically motivated process. When the process functions effectively, children can become more self-determined in the regulation of extrinsically motivated behavior. As they become more self-determined, it is probable that they will be more interested in the activity, though I have emphasized that the importance of the activity rather than its interestingness is more central to extrinsic motivation (even internalized forms of it), whereas interest is more central to intrinsic motivation. As we see next, both intrinsic motivation and internalization are significantly affected by the social context within which the children are functioning.

SOCIAL CONTEXTS

Earlier I said that there are three fundamental psychological needs that are intrinsic to the self—the needs for competence, autonomy, and relatedness. Social contexts that allow the satisfaction of these three basic needs will promote intrinsic motivation, internalization, and interest, whereas those that thwart one or more of these basic needs will inhibit or undermine these intrinsic processes.

Dozens of studies in psychology laboratories, classrooms, and homes have focused on factors that enhance (versus diminish) intrinsic motivation and interest by facilitating versus forestalling the experience of competence, self-determination, and relatedness.

Numerous studies have shown that competence-promoting information enhances interest (e.g., Boggiano & Ruble, 1979; Deci, 1971; Harackie-wicz, 1979; Ryan, 1982), whereas information that signifies or ensures incompetence diminishes interest (e.g., Deci & Cascio, 1972; Vallerand & Reid, 1984). Studies using path analytic procedures (e.g., Harackiewicz, Abrahams, & Wageman, 1987) have further confirmed that competence-promoting feedback and structure are important for enhancing people's sense of competence and in turn their intrinsic motivation and interest, whereas competence-diminishing feedback and structure undermine intrinsic motivation and interest. However, studies have also shown that boosting perceived competence is not enough to maintain or enhance intrinsic motivation and interest; the person must also experience a sense of personal causation or self-determination with respect to his or her competence (Fisher, 1978; Ryan, 1982).

A tremendous amount of empirical work has focused on the distinction between contexts that support autonomy, thus facilitating intrinsic motivation and interest, and those that control behavior, thus undermining intrinsic motivation and interest by diminishing one's sense of self-determination. Early studies on this topic were laboratory experiments that explored the effects of specific external events such as the promise of a reward or the imposition of a deadline. The typical paradigm involved two groups of subjects working on the same activity under the same condition, except that one group would receive the experimental manipulation (e.g., would receive a monetary reward) and the other group would not. Subsequently, intrinsic motivation for the target task were assessed in either or both of two ways: behaviorally, by calculating the amount of time subjects spent on the task during a free-choice period when other attractive activities were available; and attitudinally, with self-reports of interest/ enjoyment for the task. Means for the groups were then compared, and results used to demonstrate that monetary rewards (Deci, 1971), good player awards (Lepper, Greene, & Nisbett, 1973), avoidance of punishment (Deci & Cascio, 1972), deadlines (Amabile, DeJong, & Lepper, 1976), imposed goals (Mossholder, 1980), and competition (Deci, Betley, Kahle, Abrams, & Porac, 1981) all tended, on average, to undermine intrinsic motivation and interest, thus suggesting that they were experienced by subjects as controlling. On the other hand, providing people with choices (Zuckerman, Porac, Lathin, Smith, & Deci, 1978) and acknowledging their perspectives or feelings (Koestner, Ryan, Bernieri,

& Holt, 1984) were found to enhance intrinsic motivation and interest, thus suggesting that they were experienced by subjects as supportive of autonomy.

Studies in public school classrooms (e.g., Deci, Schwartz, Sheinman, & Ryan, 1981) indicated that, when the general classroom contexts tended to be autonomy–supportive rather than controlling, the students displayed higher intrinsic motivation and more positive concomitants. For example, in one study of school classrooms, we (Deci, Nezlek, & Sheinman, 1981) focused on the effects of teaching styles on student motivation and self-image. In 35 fourth-, fifth-, and sixth-grade classes, we assessed whether the teachers tended to support their students' autonomy or to control their students' behavior, and we assessed the children's level of intrinsic motivation, as indicated by their curiosity and preference for challenge. We also measured their perceived competence and feelings of self-worth. Children in the classrooms of control-oriented teachers showed less intrinsic motivation, perceived themselves as less competent, and felt less good about themselves than students of autonomy-supportive teachers. This and other studies reported in this section focused only on interest, intrinsic motivation, and affective correlates such as self-esteem. In the final section of this chapter, I report studies that link interest, intrinsic motivation, and self-determination to enhanced learning.

A series of laboratory experiments by Ryan and his colleagues (e.g., Ryan, 1982; Ryan, Mims, & Koestner, 1983) explored the effects of specific events, such as limits or rewards, when they were administered within different social climates. These studies showed that, although particular events (e.g., a monetary reward) tend on average to be experienced in specifiable ways (i.e., as either autonomy-supportive or controlling) and thus have the predictable effects of enhancing or diminishing intrinsic motivation and interest, the context within which the events are administered can substantially influence their effects. For example, on average, rewards have been found to be experienced as controlling and to undermine intrinsic motivation (Deci, 1971, 1972). However, Ryan et al. (1983) showed that rewards could either enhance or undermine intrinsic motivation depending on whether the context within which they were administered was autonomy supportive or controlling. Autonomy–supportive contexts do not pressure one to act in particular ways, and they use rewards simply to convey information and/or appreciation. Controlling contexts, on the other hand, pressure people to behave, think, or feel in particular ways.

In another study from this series (Koestner, Ryan, Bernieri, & Holt, 1984), two groups of children were asked to paint pictures, and limits were set on the way they worked. However, the way the limits were communicated differed for the two groups. The children in one group were told how the task should be done, and they were told that they should be good boys (or girls) and do it the right way. The other children were told about the task and the limits, and their responses were acknowledged, but the experimenter did not use controlling words or phrases such as "should" or "be a good boy/girl." Thus, for the first group, the experimenter was being controlling by using language that tended to pressure the children, whereas for the second group the experimenter was being much more supportive of the children's initiative and autonomy by not using the controlling language and acknowledging the children's perspective. The results of the experiment showed that the children in the first group, who heard the controlling language, lost intrinsic motivation because they were performing to comply with the experimenter's demands. On the other hand, the children in the second group remained intrinsically motivated; they performed out of interest and enjoyment.

To summarize, the presence of specific events such as positive feedback or limits can influence the way a target person experiences the social context (e.g., rewards can make the context more controlling). However, interpersonal processes, as affected by factors such as the orientation of authorities in that context—authorities such as teachers or parents—are also important determinants of the quality of the context. Interpersonal aspects of the context can even change the way specific events (such as rewards) tend to be experienced. Simply stated, specific events and general interpersonal processes interact to determine the nature of the social context and thus to affect the motivation of people in that context. When the context is experienced as being controlling—as pressuring people to think, feel, or behave in some specific way—their interest will tend to be undermined and they will be motivated to maximize their extrinsic outcomes. On the other hand, when people experience the context as supporting their autonomy—as encouraging their initiation and choice— they will maintain their interest and intrinsic motivation.

The final contextual nutriment for interest is the kind of genuine interpersonal involvement that satisfies a person's need for relatedness. For children, of course, it is the relationship with parents and teachers— that is, with their significant adults—that is most important for their maintaining interest in school and developing appropriate social skills (e.g., Connell, in press; Ryan & Lynch, 1989). When they are denied the relatedness with these adults, they tend to lose interest in the activities that the adults endorse.

In one laboratory experiment with young children, for example, Anderson, Manoogian, and Reznick (1976) found that denying children desired involvement with adults led the children to lose intrinsic motivation. Most other studies exploring this issue have been done in field settings and have considered both autonomy support and interpersonal involvement by significant adults. Grolnick, Ryan, and Deci (in press) assessed third- through sixth-grade students' perceptions of their parents' involvement and autonomy support regarding homework and other school-related activities. They found that the combination of these two variables predicted what the researchers called the students' inner resources for learning; namely, their perceived control (Connell, 1985), perceived competence (Harter, 1982), and perceived autonomy (Ryan & Connell, 1989), all of which correlate with intrinsic motivation. In another study, Grolnick and Ryan (1989) used structured interviews with parents to assess their autonomy support and involvement with their children and found these variables to be related to intrinsic motivation and other important variables such as self-esteem.

Most of the studies of social-contextual influences thus far discussed used intrinsic motivation or interest as the dependent measure, and the results confirm that the convergence of autonomy support, competence-promoting feedback, and interpersonal involvement represents the optimal condition for intrinsic motivation.

Some of the aforementioned laboratory and field studies, as well as additional ones, have also explored the effects of social contexts on the internalization of regulations. For example, in the Grolnick and Ryan (1989) study, multiple-regression analysis showed that parental autonomy support was a significant predictor of internalization and that involvement supplemented that effect.

In a laboratory experiment, Deci, Eghrari, Patrick, and Leone (1991) had subjects work on a boring activity, though the activity was one that could be used to improve concentration. They found that three factors were important for promoting internalization, as assessed by subsequent self-regulation of the activity. They were: providing a rationale for doing the dull task (viz., it can improve concentration); minimizing the use of pressure and providing a sense of choice about doing the activity; and acknowledging that the subjects might find the activity uninteresting.

People's willingness to participate in uninteresting activities depends on their experiencing the activities as having personal importance or instrumental value to them. If people understand the importance of the activities, social contexts that are characterized by involvement and autonomy support will tend to foster the internalization of regulations for these uninteresting though important activities. And through internalization and integration, the activities may gradually become more interesting for the person.

PERSONS, ACTIVITIES, CONTEXTS: A SUMMARY

Thus far, I have defined interest as the core affect of self, suggesting that it occurs when there is an ideal match between a person's organismic condition and the environmental affordances. I linked interest directly to intrinsic motivation, and I also suggested that if the extrinsic regulation of an activity has been fully integrated with the intrinsic self, the person is likely to experience greater interest for the activity than if its regulation has not been fully integrated.

A particular activity will be more or less interesting to a person as a function of the degree to which it is optimally challenging for the person and the degree to which he or she has developed a preference (i.e., a dispositional interest) for the activity. The development of preferences for a particular activity is explained by the mix of innate competencies and potentials, the ongoing availability of the activity as an affordance, and the quality of the social context within which one repeatedly encounters that activity.

Social contexts play a crucial role in the immediate experience of interest (and intrinsic motivation), in the development of enduring preferences (or dispositional interests), and in the internalization and integration of extrinsic regulatory processes. Contexts that are autonomy–supportive, that provide optimal challenges and informational feedback, and within which one feels securely related to significant others will promote the experience of interest, the development of enduring interests, and the integration of regulations.

Accordingly, to facilitate a person's interest, another person—such as a parent or teacher—must take account of the person's dispositions and the available affordances, so as to create an optimal person–activity match. When there is a good match, the person will be intrinsically motivated; when there is not, the other person must provide optimal structures that can be internalized. Finally, throughout all this, the other person needs to relate genuinely to the target person and support his or her autonomy.

Having focused primarily on the characteristics and conditions that promote interest and self-determined motivation, I shall now turn to a consideration of the concomitants and consequences of interest and self-determination, particularly in the educational domain.

EDUCATIONAL OUTCOMES

The enterprise of schooling serves a variety of cultural functions (Ryan & Stiller, in press) aimed at preparing children to become productive members of society. Although people disagree about the outcomes that should represent the most important goals of the schooling endeavor, there are two that I believe to be by far the most important. One is that students gain an integrated understanding of the meaning and importance of concepts. This is often referred to as "deep learning" but can be simply stated as learning to think. The other is that students gain a strong sense of personal worth and self-understanding as well as a meaningful accommodation to the social world—an accommodation in which they not only respect the social world and are influenced by it but maintain interest, curiosity, and personal commitment.

These learning and adjustment outcomes are all too frequently confused with their more superficial counterparts. Scores on standardized tests and grades for courses are the bottom line—the currency—of education, yet there is no indication that these reflect the type of conceptual understanding or creative problem-solving that I refer to as deep learning. Indeed, it is quite possible that scores and grades are primarily reflective of a more superficial kind of learning—learning that is geared toward memorizing the kinds of facts that one might be required to reproduce on an exam. Similarly, compliance and conformity to norms are often used to signify adjustment, though there is no indication that these signify a sense of personal worth or self-understanding.

In this section, I review research that relates intrinsic motivation and interest to learning and adjustment. Some of the studies involve assessment of these motivational variables. Others predict achievement and adjustment from social context variables that have been found either to increase or to decrease intrinsic motivation and interest, thus establishing a network of relations among variables.

Several investigations by the Motivation Research Group at the University of Rochester have considered the relation among external pressures, intrinsic motivation, and educational outcomes. In one experiment, Benware and Deci (1984) asked college students to read and learn some complex text material. Half the subjects were told that they would be tested on what they learned, thus approximating the typical controlling, extrinsic conditions of many classrooms. The other subjects were told that they would have the opportunity to put their learning to use by teaching it to other students. We thought that this learning context would facilitate intrinsic motivation because the learning would have some real use—it would be a more meaningful condition for learning. The subjects all took the text home and had several days to learn it. They were asked to keep track of how long they spent reading or studying it before returning to the laboratory. When subjects returned, they were all given the same exam, which included questions to assess both rote memorization of facts and conceptual understanding of the material.

They were also given a questionnaire on which they reported how interesting they found the material and how much they enjoyed learning it. Results of the experiment indicated that, although the rote memorization of the two groups was identical, those subjects who learned in order to teach showed significantly greater conceptual understanding than those who learned in order to take an examination. When we analyzed the time that the subjects spent learning the material, there was no difference between the groups. There was, however, an important difference between the groups on another variable. Subjects who learned the material to teach it found it significantly more interesting and enjoyable than those who learned it simply to be tested. Furthermore, the degree of interest/enjoyment that subjects expressed was positively correlated with their conceptual understanding. In sum, then, this study suggests that when people are motivated by control or pressure (here manipulated by telling subjects they would be tested), intrinsic motivation and interest that students have for learning tends to be undermined. This, in turn, impairs their conceptual understanding of the material. On the other hand, when students have a meaningful reason for learning and do not feel pressured, they tend to find the material more interesting and learn it more fully.

Another experiment, by Grolnick and Ryan (1987), found complementary results with fifth-grade students. Three groups of students were given text material to read in individual sessions outside their normal classroom. Children in the first group were asked to *learn* the material because they would be tested on it and given a grade. Children in the second group were also asked to *learn* the material, but there was no mention of a test. For the children in the third group there was no mention of learning; they were simply asked to *read* the passage so they could report how interesting they found it. Thus, the first two groups were "directed" to learn, whereas the learning of the third group was nondirected or incidental. However, only the first group learned under controlling conditions, so the last two groups were both expected to be more interested in the material.

After each child read the material, he or she was examined on it, both for rote memorization and conceptual understanding. Each child was also given a questionnaire assessing his or her interest in the passages. Furthermore, 1 week later, a different experimenter went into the children's classrooms and group-administered a second exam and interest questionnaire. This had been entirely unexpected by the children, so it provided an opportunity to assess longer-term retention of material under conditions where none of the children had any specific reason to remember the material.

Results of the experiment showed that subjects in the "test" condition (which was believed to be the most controlling) reported significantly lower interest and displayed significantly less conceptual understanding than subjects in the two noncontrolling conditions. On the other hand, subjects in the test condition evidenced as much rote memorization as subjects in the directed learning condition without a test, and subjects in both directed learning conditions showed more rote memorization than those in the nondirected learning group. Finally, however, subjects in the test condition reported feeling significantly more pressured and evidenced significantly greater memory deterioration in the week following learning than did subjects in the other two conditions. It seems, then, that the standard practices of pressuring students to learn through the use of techniques like tests may result in poor affective and conceptual outcomes. Even the advantage that this method may have for fostering rote memorization appears to be very short term, as it was gone within a week.

Other studies of the antecedents of educational outcomes have used questionnaires to assess children's perceptions of the context, their intrinsic motivation for learning, and their self-perceptions (e.g., perceived competence). The relation of these to school achievement as assessed by grades and by standardized achievement was then calculated. In one such study, Grolnick, Ryan, and Deci (in press) used a questionnaire to assess children's perceptions of their home contexts—whether their parents were involved with them and supportive of their autonomy.

Also assessed were three variables that index how children feel about themselves in the school context, namely perceived control, perceived competence, and perceived autonomy in the academic domain. Using structural equation modeling, we found that the three self-perception variables (which are all correlated with intrinsic motivation) were positively predicted by the children's perceptions of their parents' autonomy support and involvement and, further, that these self-perception variables positively predicted their achievement in school.

In another study, Deci, Hodges, Pierson, and Tomassone (1990) found that perceived autonomy and perceived competence also predicted the standardized achievement scores of students with learning disabilities and emotional handicaps.

Creative and cognitive flexibility

There are two other sets of experiments that are directly relevant to our understanding of educational outcomes. Both sets use experimental methods similar to those that explored the effects of contextual factors on intrinsic motivation, though in one set the dependent variables were related to creativity and in the second to cognitive flexibility. The expectation was that intrinsic motivation would facilitate both creativity and flexibility of thought, so the studies explored the effects of contextual factors that had been repeatedly shown to undermine intrinsic motivation to see whether they would also decrease creativity or cognitive flexibility.

Amabile (1983) developed a consensual assessment method for measuring the creativity of artistic projects (e.g., collages and paintings) produced by subjects in her experiments. Using this procedure, she found that when subjects produced an artistic work in order to get a reward, to try to win a competition, or to try to be rated well by an evaluator, their works were judged to be less creative (using the consensual assessment method) than those of comparable subjects who did not expect a reward, a competition, or an evaluation. The same controlling factors that decrease intrinsic motivation also dampened creativity. Parallel results were also found in the "cognitive-flexibility" experiments. For example, subjects who were given financial rewards for solving problems had a harder time breaking mental set and solving subsequent problems than comparable subjects who had not been offered the reward (McGraw & McCullers, 1979).

It appears from all this research that children's interest, intrinsic motivation, and self-determination with respect to school-related activities lead to optimal educational outcomes. In other words, these motivationally relevant, internal states lead to enhanced conceptual understanding and more positive affective experiences. Furthermore, interest, intrinsic motivation, and self-determination have been reliably shown to be affected primarily by the autonomy support and involvement of teachers and parents. Other research (Deci, Spiegel, Ryan, Koestner, & Kauffman, 1982) has shown that a strong emphasis on performance standards leads teachers to be less autonomy-supportive. Thus, it seems incumbent upon those of us who are in the role of teacher or parent to create the social conditions that will be experienced by our children and students as encouraging them to follow their interests and to initiate their own behavior—in short, to be responsive to their own inner being.

ACKNOWLEDGMENT

Preparation of this chapter was supported by research grant HD-19914 from the National Institute of Child Health and Human Development to the author.

REFERENCES

Amabile, T. M. (1983). *The social psychology of creativity.* New York: Springer–Verlag.

Amabile, T. M., DeJong, W., & Lepper, M. R. (1976). Effects of externally imposed deadlines on subsequent intrinsic motivation. *Journal of Personality and Social Psychology, 34,* 92–98.

Anderson, R., Manoogian, S. T., & Reznick, J. S. (1976). The undermining and enhancing of intrinsic motivation in preschool children. *Journal of Personality and Social Psychology, 34,* 915–922.

Benware, C., & Deci, E. L. (1984). The quality of learning with an active versus passive motivational set. *American Educational Research Journal, 21,* 755–765.

Berlyne, D. E. (1971). What next? Concluding summary. In H. I. Day, D. E. Berlyne, & D. E. Hunt (Eds.), *Intrinsic motivation: A new direction in education.* Toronto: Holt, Rinehart, & Winston of Canada.

Boggiano, A. K., & Ruble, D. N. (1979). Competence and the overjustification effect: A developmental study. *Journal of Personality and Social Psychology, 37,* 1462–1468.

Connell, J. P. (1985). A new multidimensional measure of children's perceptions of control. *Child Development, 56,* 1018–1041.

Connell, J. P. (in press). Context, self and action: A motivational analysis of self-system processes across the life-span. In D. Cicchetti (Ed.), *The self in transition.* Chicago: University of Chicago Press.

Csikszentmihalyi, M. (1975). *Beyond boredom and anxiety.* San Francisco: Jossey–Bass.

Danner, F. W., & Lonky, E. (1981). A cognitive-developmental approach to the effects of rewards on intrinsic motivation. *Child Development, 52,* 1043–1052.

deCharms, R. (1968). *Personal causation: The internal affective determinants of behavior.* New York: Academic Press.

Deci, E. L. (1971). Effects of externally mediated rewards on intrinsic motivation. *Journal of Personality and Social Psychology, 18,* 105–115.

Deci, E. L. (1972). Intrinsic motivation, extrinsic reinforcement, and inequity. *Journal of Personality and Social Psychology, 22,* 113–120.

Deci, E. L. (1975). *Intrinsic motivation.* New York: Plenum Press.

Deci, E. L, Betley, G., Kahle, J., Abrams, L., & Porac, J. (1981). When trying to win: Competition and intrinsic motivation. *Personality and Social Psychology Bulletin, 7,* 79–83.

Deci, E. L., & Cascio, W. F. (1972, April). *Changes in intrinsic motivation as a function of negative feedback and threats.* Paper presented at the Eastern Psychological Association, Boston.

Deci, E. L., Eghrari, H., Patrick, B. C., & Leone, D. (1991). *Facilitating internalization: The self-determination theory perspective.* Unpublished manuscript, University of Rochester.

Deci, E. L., Hodges, R., Pierson, L., & Tomassone, J. (1990). *Motivationally relevant predictors of achievement and adjustment in learning disabled and emotionally handicapped students.* Unpublished manuscript, University of Rochester.

Deci, E. L., Nezlek, J., & Sheinman, L. (1981). Characteristics of the rewarder and intrinsic motivation of the rewardee. *Journal of Personality and Social Psychology, 40,* 1–10.

Deci, E. L., & Ryan, R. M. (1985). *Intrinsic motivation and self-determination in human behavior.* New York: Plenum Press.

Deci, E. L., & Ryan, R. M. (1987). The support of autonomy and the control of behavior. *Journal of Personality and Social Psychology, 53,* 1024–1037.

Deci, E. L., & Ryan, R. M. (1991). A motivational approach to self: Integration in personality. In R. Dienstbier (Ed.), *Nebraska symposium on motivation: Vol. 38. Perspectives on motivation.* Lincoln: University of Nebraska Press.

Deci, E. L., Schwartz, A. J., Sheinman, L., & Ryan, R. M. (1981). An instrument to assess adults' orientations toward control versus autonomy with children: Reflections on intrinsic motivation and perceived competence. *Journal of Educational Psychology, 73,* 642–650.

Deci, E. L., Spiegel, N., Ryan, R. M., Koestner, R., & Kauffman, M. (1982). The effects of performance standards on teaching styles: The behavior of controlling teachers. *Journal of Educational Psychology, 74,* 852–859.

Fisher, C. D. (1978). The effects of personal control, competence, and extrinsic reward systems on intrinsic motivation. *Organizational Behavior and Human Performance, 21,* 273–288.

Grolnick, W. S., & Ryan, R. M. (1987). Autonomy in children's learning: An experimental and individual difference investigation. *Journal of Personality and Social Psychology, 52,* 890–898.

Grolnick, W. S., & Ryan, R. M. (1989). Parent styles associated with children's self-regulation and competence in school. *Journal of Educational Psychology, 81,* 143–154.

Grolnick, W. S., Ryan, R. M., & Deci, E. L. (in press). Inner resources for school achievement: Motivational mediators of children's perceptions of their parents. *Journal of Educational Psychology.*

Hackman, J. R., & Oldham, G. R. (1980). Motivation through the design of work. In J. R. Hackman & G. R. Oldham, *Work redesign* (pp. 71–94). Reading, MA: Addison–Wesley.

Harackiewicz, J. (1979). The effects of reward contingency and performance feedback on intrinsic motivation. *Journal of Personality and Social Psychology, 37,* 1352–1363.

Harackiewicz, J. M., Abrahams, S., & Wageman, R. (1987). Performance evaluation and intrinsic motivation: The effects of evaluative focus, rewards, and achievement orientation. *Journal of Personality and Social Psychology, 53,* 1015–1023.

Harlow, H. F. (1953). Motivation as a factor in the acquisition of new responses. In *Current theory and research on motivation* (pp. 24–49). Lincoln: University of Nebraska Press.

Harter, S. (1978). Pleasure derived from optimal challenge and the effects of extrinsic rewards on children's difficulty level choices. *Child Development, 49,* 788–799.

Harter, S. (1982). The perceived competence scale for children. *Child Development, 53,* 87–97.

Hidi, S., & Baird, W. (1986). Interestingness—A neglected variable in discourse processing. *Cognitive Science, 10,* 179–194.

Hull, C. L. (1943). *Principles of behavior: An introduction to behavior theory.* New York: Appleton–Century–Crofts.

Hunt, J. McV. (1965). Intrinsic motivation and its role in psychological development. In D. Levine (Ed.), *Nebraska symposium on motivation* (Vol. 13). Lincoln: University of Nebraska Press.

Izard, C. (1977). *Human emotions.* New York: Plenum.

James, W. (1890). *The principles of psychology.* New York: Holt.

Koestner, R., Ryan, R. M., Bernieri, F., & Holt, K. (1984). Setting limits in children's behavior: The differential effects of controlling versus informational styles on intrinsic motivation and creativity. *Journal of Personality, 52,* 233–248.

Lepper, M. R., Greene, D., & Nisbett, R. E. (1973). Undermining children's intrinsic interest with extrinsic rewards: A test of the "overjustification" hypothesis. *Journal of Personality and Social Psychology, 28,* 129–137.

Maslow, A. H. (1943). A theory of human motivation. *Psychological Review, 50,* 370–396.

McGraw, K. O., & McCullers, J. C. (1979). Evidence of a detrimental effect of extrinsic incentives on breaking a mental set. *Journal of Experimental Social Psychology, 15,* 285–294.

Montgomery, K. C. (1954). The role of exploratory drive in learning. *Journal of Comparative and Physiological Psychology, 47,* 60–64.

Mossholder, K. W. (1980). Effects of externally mediated goal setting on intrinsic motivation: A laboratory experiment. *Journal of Applied Psychology, 65,* 202–210.

Murray, H. A. (1938). *Explorations in personality.* New York: Oxford University Press.

Porter, L. W., & Lawler, E. E. (1968). *Managerial attitudes and performance.* Homewood, IL: Irwin–Dorsey.

Reeve, J. (1989). The interest–enjoyment distinction in intrinsic motivation. *Motivation and Emotion, 13,* 83–104.

Reiss, S., & Sushinsky, L. W. (1975). Overjustification, competing responses, and the acquisition of intrinsic interest. *Journal of Personality and Social Psychology, 31,* 1116–1125.

Renninger, K. A. (1990). Children's play interests, representation, and activity. In R. Fivush & J. Hudson (Eds.), *Knowing and remembering in young children* (pp. 127–165). Cambridge, MA: Cambridge University Press.

Ryan, R. M. (1982). Control and information in the intrapersonal sphere: An extension of cognitive evaluation theory. *Journal of Personality and Social Psychology, 43,* 450–461.

Ryan, R. M. (1991). The nature of the self in autonomy and relatedness. In J. Strauss & G. R. Goethals (Eds.), *Multidisciplinary perspectives on the self.* New York: Springer–Verlag.

Ryan, R. M., & Connell, J. P. (1989). Perceived locus of causality and internalization: Examining reasons for acting in two domains. *Journal of Personality and Social Psychology, 57,* 749–761.

Ryan, R. M., Connell, J. P., & Deci, E. L. (1985). A motivational analysis of self-determination and self-regulation in education. In C. Ames & R. E. Ames (Eds.), *Research on motivation in education: The classroom milieu* (pp. 13–51). New York: Academic Press.

Ryan, R. M., & Grolnick, W. S. (1986). Origins and pawns in the classroom: Self-report and projective assessments of children's perceptions. *Journal of Personality and Social Psychology, 50,* 550–558.

Ryan, R. M., & Lynch, J. (1989). Emotional autonomy versus detachment: Revisiting the vicissitudes of adolescence and young adulthood. *Child Development, 60,* 340–356.

Ryan, R. M., Mims, V., & Koestner, R. (1983). Relation of reward contingency and interpersonal context to intrinsic motivation: A review and test using cognitive evaluation theory. *Journal of Personality and Social Psychology, 45,* 736–750.

Ryan, R. M., & Stiller, J. (in press). Culture, self, and education: A theory of motivation in internalization in schools. In P. R. Pintrich & M. L. Maehr (Eds.), *Advances in motivation and achievement: Vol. 7. Goals and self-regulatory processes.* Greenwich, CT: JAI Press.

Schafer, R. (1968). *Aspects of internalization.* New York: International Universities Press.

Skinner, B. F. (1953). *Science and human behavior.* New York: Macmillan.

Vallerand, R. J., & Reid, G. (1984). On the causal effects of perceived competence on intrinsic motivation: A test of cognitive evaluation theory. *Journal of Sport Psychology, 6,* 94–102.

Vroom, V. H., & Deci, E. L. (in press). *Management and motivation* (2nd ed.). London: Penguin.

White, R. W. (1959). Motivation reconsidered: The concept of competence. *Psychological Review, 66,* 297–333.

Zuckerman, M., Porac, J., Lathin, D., Smith, R., & Deci, E. L. (1978). On the importance of self-determination for intrinsically motivated behavior. *Personality and Social Psychology Bulletin, 4,* 443–446.

4 The Selective Persistence of Interest

Manfred Prenzel
University of Munich, FRG

Maria works as a teacher and takes courses in education in her free time. She has decided to take an introductory course in word processing and programming in BASIC. She believes that being able to use a computer will aid her in both her work and her studies. But this is not the main reason for Maria's decision. Something about computers just grabs her. She sees the computer as a mental challenge. All the students in the course, including Maria, have the opportunity to use a computer at the school. They can work on it as often and as long as they wish. At first, Maria took advantage of this opportunity in order to get some individual practice on the sample programs used in the course. Before long, she began working on a program of her own, one designed to calculate a person's ideal weight. On 12 separate occasions, Maria voluntarily went to the computer lab to develop and improve a program that gave personal feedback about changes in weight. While programming, Maria ran into a number of problems that prompted her to consult some of the literature about BASIC.

Having completed and polished up this program to her satisfaction, Maria tackled an even more complicated programming project—a program to give "tailor-made" feedback to her students about their mistakes and improvement in math drills. In the course of several more visits to the computer lab, Maria developed a first version of her program and did a test run using a math quiz. Then she modified and revised the program until it worked smoothly.

Out of a vague intention to learn something about computers, Maria has developed an ongoing interest in them. Maria has, on her own, repeatedly spent hours learning to program. Her engagement with the computer shows a remarkable amount of persistence. Among the numerous possibilities for working with a computer, Maria has chosen one particular application. The ideal weight and test feedback programs demonstrate the particular focus or the selectivity of her computer interest.

This example is representative of what might be considered a developing or emerging interest. The example exhibits all the characteristics that older as well as contemporary theories of interest have postulated: Maria is interested in a certain object, namely the computer (object relation); she wants to know more about computers and to improve her competence (cognitive or epistemic orientation); she is emotionally involved (positive affect); the computer has special importance for her (value orientation); she is engaged in activities with the computer, on her own, not caused by external contingencies (autotelic activity).

But how can we explain the selective persistence of this interest, namely: (a) the persistence, in terms of the frequency and duration of engagements with the object, and (b) the selectivity, in terms of the type and the content of the activities?

In Maria's example there are no external influences that shaped the selective persistence of her engagement with the computer. No one forced or even asked Maria to write her programs. She received no immediate profit. On the contrary, she could have chosen to spend the time amusing herself or earning money, but she voluntarily spent her time programming. Maria's work with the computer is "self-intentional." However, something must have occurred in the interaction between the person ("Maria") and the object ("computer"), something that determined the selective persistence of her engagement with it.

In the following, several contemporary explanations for the selective persistence of interests are introduced and discussed. Of special importance are the approaches that specify the conditions for the selective persistence of object-related, autotelic (self-intentional) activities. Then, a theory of the effect of interest is presented in order to explain the selective persistence of interests. Following this, qualitative data from a study of selective persistence in the domains of computers and music are described. Finally, the discussion focuses on ways in which the study of selective persistence extends our present understanding of the development of interest and its role in learning.

COMMON EXPLANATIONS FOR THE SELECTIVE PERSISTENCE OF INTEREST

This section is concerned with previous explanations for the selective persistence of interests. An explanation typical of popular, or everyday, psychology is described first. Following this, proposals from the fields of interest and intrinsic motivation research are considered.

Selective Persistence of Interest in Everyday Thinking. The word "interest" is used frequently in everyday life. It usually describes preferences for objects. For example: Maria spends most of her free time working on the computer, goes to computer stores, reads magazines about software, compares possibilities for programming in one language with programming in another. We would say: "Maria is interested in computers." Beside this descriptive use, the term *interest* also serves for explanation in everyday thinking. If we were to ask Maria (or someone else, perhaps a friend) why she does all these things, we might well receive the answer: "Maria happens to be interested in computers."

Popular psychology thus uses the concept of interest to describe and to explain the selective persistence of engagements. This kind of an explanation contains a recognition of self-intentionality—it seems that when someone is interested in a domain, he or she needs no further reason or motive to repeatedly engage in activity involving that domain. Unfortunately, such an explanation relies on circular reasoning. Aside from mentioning the idea of interest, this reason in no way clarifies interest or what might serve as a determinant of selective persistence.

Selective Persistence of Interest through Value Orientation. It is primarily in older theories of interest that one finds explanations of selective persistence that are similar to the simple, everyday explanation. Both Kerschensteiner (1928) and Lunk (1927), for example, conceived of interest as a personal disposition, or value orientation. A similar notion was proposed by Allport and Vernon (1931), who suggested that if one assumes a dispositional value system then objects and activities involving those objects can be considered to have different values. From this perspective, objects of interest are, of course, especially "valuable" and, given a choice, a person prefers to engage in activities that involve these objects.

However, because "value orientation" has been infused into the everyday explanation, these simple dispositional explanations contain no new information about the concept of interest and are especially inadequate for explaining changes in selectivity.

Selective Persistence of Interest by Development of Stable Attitudes. Strong (1943) did not define interest explicitly as a disposition, but rather as a stable attitude (a "response of liking") that could be activated by processes of measurement or application of stimuli. He formulated a simple explanatory principle about the origin of such responses: "An interest is an expression of one's reaction to his environment. The reaction of liking–disliking is a resultant of satisfactory or unsatisfactory dealing with the object" (p. 682). In other words, if an activity is satisfying to a person, it will be repeated. If an activity is not satisfying, its repetition is less likely. Strong used a hedonistic effect to explain selective persistence; however, it remains unclear what partial processes and events can be subsumed under the heading *satisfaction*. Furthermore, this does not allow for interests that change and develop. In this model, a person would always have to deal with the same domain in the same fashion.

Selective Persistence of Interest through Anticipated Satisfaction. Later theories of vocational interest were based on Strong's idea that the selection of interesting objects arose from satisfying experiences with those objects. Super and Crites (1962), as well as Barak (1981), described interest as a disposition in the sense of its being an aspect of a person's self-concept. Thus, Super and Crites (1962, p. 410) redefined Strong's notion of "satisfaction" to describe what they called "satisfaction of mastery." Barak (1981), on the other hand, differed from Strong by including additional mediating cognitions (anticipation of success and satisfaction, awareness of one's own abilities) in his model of interest development. In both of these explanations, the selective persistence of interest appears to result from satisfying experiences with specific domains of objects and activities. These satisfying experiences, in turn, led to the expectation of further satisfaction in future encounters and thereby molded the person's self-concept. Satisfying experiences, thus, were a prerequisite for further activity involving these domains.

The development of more precise models of disposition lessened the likelihood of further circular explanations of selective persistence. However, each of the models described here depended on a single "prime mover," namely the success experienced during an activity that led to satisfaction and to reinforcement of that activity. As a result, these models are considered to have inadequately accounted for the dynamic component of selective persistence as evidenced by the change and further development of interest.

Selective Persistence of Interest through Subjective Discrepancy. The idea that a person voluntarily selected objects (or stimuli) from his or her environment and engaged in activities with them was first described by Berlyne (1967, 1978) and Hunt (1965), not as a function of dispositional factors, but rather of variables located in the relation between the person and object in the environment. Berlyne based his discussions of collative variables on the relation between stimuli characteristics and the person's prior cognitive experiences. As such, he was able to explain not just specific epistemic activities, but also the diversive search for stimulation in the environment when the activation potential of the immediate surroundings was low.

Explanations that arose from discrepancy theories of intrinsic motivation typically emphasized selectivity. Such theories could be used to predict the stimulus configurations a person would select for activity involving epistemic orientation. These theories could also be used to predict the processes in the individual, associated with arousal, that could be arranged along a scale ranging from unpleasant to pleasant. However, discrepancy theories of intrinsic motivation overlooked selective persistence, which spans a sequence of related situations. In other words, these theories did not indicate which objects a person would seek out when bored, or how a person, over a period of time and in different situations, would successively analyze (and then internally construct) entire areas of knowledge by means of epistemic activities (cf. Krapp, in press; Prenzel, 1988).

Such long-term developments were described, however, in a different theory that included cognitive conflict as one of its central features. In his equilibration model, Piaget (1963, 1981) ;was able to describe and explain the selective persistence of object relations, especially during the first years of life. Although the model developed by Piaget to explain the effect of cognitive conflict was not as detailed as Berlyne's model, it did take into consideration changes in cognitive structure that in turn determined a "starting point" for new activities with objects. However, his theory did not concern itself with the development of domain-specific structures of knowledge and competency as reflected in the interests of adolescents and adults.

Selective Persistence of Interest through Experiences of Efficacy. The theory of Super and Crites took into account the significance of "satisfaction of mastery" in the development of an interest-related self-concept. Other theories of intrinsic motivation have focused more systematically on the effects of feelings of competence or efficacy.

White (1959, 1960), in particular, hypothesized that an individual's basic need for effective interaction with the environment that led to feelings of efficacy when there was a more adequate (successful) adaptation to the environment. An individual's exploration of the environment could lead him or her to orient toward specific portions of the environment for either longer periods of time and in periodic episodes. The selective persistence of object relations was thus a result of the feeling of efficacy experienced in the wake of interactions with the environment. This, in turn, led to successful adaptation. Such adaptation emerged in response to feelings of efficacy. However, it is not at all clear from this theory exactly why individuals might explore domains not found in their immediate environment.

The theories of deCharms (1968), Bandura (1982), and Deci and Ryan (1985) are further explanations of feelings of effectiveness. The early version of Deci's theory (1975), as well as research into overjustification (e.g., Lepper & Greene, 1978) propose an explanation for those situations where the persistence of interest relations can decline, namely through the undermining of intrinsic motivation by means of extrinsic stimuli.

More recent work of Deci and Ryan (1985, 1987; see also Deci, this volume) also emphasizes the significance of self-determination and competence in the development and maintenance of intrinsic motivation. They view feelings of self-determination and competence as important components of activity and describe these as necessary conditions for the selective persistence of self-intentional relations to domains. These components, however, are not sufficient conditions for selective persistence. The particular situational aspects with which a person chooses to engage in activity, and the form that this engagement assumes over time cannot be determined completely from these models.

Selective Persistence of Interest through the Search for a Feeling. An alternative consideration equates interest with emotion. According to Izard (1977), interest is a fundamental, positive emotion that is closely associated with curiosity and with processes of perception and cognition. This implies that interest is a pleasant, desirable state. In other words, pleasant feelings of interest can be brought about through object-related activity. Izard also speaks of "interest–cognition–orientations," which, on the one hand, could be described as the structural outcome of domain-related activity or, on the other hand, could aid in goal formation by helping a person "imagine the possibilities" for that activity. Thus, Izard's theory can be interpreted as suggesting that selective persistence of object relations might be attributed to emotional and cognitive goal orientations that have developed in the course of active engagement with that object.

A similar explanation of activity is found in the theory of Csikszentmihalyi (1975). Csikszentmihalyi offers both a theoretical basis and examples whereby the repeated experience of flow led to a search for flow. Engagement with subject matter at levels of difficulty corresponding to a person's ability became a means for bringing about a pleasant state (cf. "sensation seeking" in Zuckerman, 1979, or "hedonic tone" in Apter, 1982). While Izard's proposed feeling of interest and Csikszentmihalyi's flow experience may be a part of what causes selective persistence, they do not give a full explanation of this phenomenon.

In sum then, previous explanations of the selective persistence of interest indicate a number of conditions that help to resolve the inadequacy of the everyday explanation, but they do not completely explain the selective persistence of interest.

Selective Persistence in a Person–Object Theory of Interests

The present discussion of the selective persistence of interest is part of a more encompassing theory developed in Munich (Prenzel, Krapp, & Schiefele, 1986; Schiefele, 1986; and cf. the article by Krapp & Fink, this volume). This theory has described interest as a unique relation between a person and an object.[1] The general characteristics of such an interest relation are as follows:

- High cognitive complexity of the subjective object representation, and a diverse repertoire of well-developed skills related to involvement with the object.

- Emotionally positive feelings associated with the object and engagement with it.

---

[1] The reader is reminded that "object" in this sense goes well beyond common use of object to refer to a concrete, tangible thing (for further discussion of this point, see the chapter by Krapp and Fink in this volume).

- Valuing of the interest object, and "self-intentionality" of activity involving the object (i.e., activity of an autotelic, noninstrumental character).

This discussion of interests will distinguish between a momentary and a long-term relation with an interest object. The sum of a person's experiences with an interest object constitutes the "history" of that individual's interest in the object. This history includes the various activities and topics, and the frequency and duration of the episodes of engagement. This long-term relation with the interest object can be described in terms of persistence and selectivity.

Defining Selective Persistence

Persistence refers to the maintenance of a relation with an interest object that involves repeated episodes of active engagement over time. The duration and the frequency of the activities characterize persistence.

Selectivity refers to the factual form of the relation with the interest object. It involves the specific content and activities that the person prefers while engaged in the domain.

The concept of *selective persistence* combines these two aspects and describes the content-based orientation, the intensity, and even the quality of interest. Thus, the more pronounced the interest, the more pronounced will be persistence and selectivity.

The concepts of persistence and selectivity are not unique to the study of interest. They can be found in theoretical work related to interest and motivation from numerous authors (e.g., James, 1890; Lunk, 1927; Maehr, 1976; White, 1959). In recent years, however, empirical research more directly related to the relation between interest and selective persistence has become increasingly prominent in the literature (Renninger, 1989, 1990; Renninger & Leckrone, 1991; Renninger & Wozniak, 1985).

Generally, selective persistence can be found in all relations between people and various domains. Every day we interact in a certain way for various lengths of time with various objects in various domains (e.g., with our morning corn flakes, with the car, with the computer at work, etc.). Inasmuch as our relations with these objects are ongoing, selective persistence is involved. However, we are not necessarily interested in such objects; we merely use them.

The explanation of the selective persistence of interest, however, entails special and stimulating problems. For everyday object relations that have nothing to do with interest, an explanation of selective persistence seems clear. We persist in the daily shower, the bowl of corn flakes, and getting to work on time because these are necessary habits.

Selective persistence of interest relations cannot be so easily explained because of the unique nature of interests—especially the self-intentionality of interest-based activity. When a person is involved with an object of interest, no further external (i.e., foreign to the object) stimulation or instrumentalities is required. Here the criterion of self-intentionality is similar to Deci and Ryan's (1980) concept of intrinsic motivation, which is characterized by an "absence of any apparent external contingency" (p. 42).

If selective persistence of interest is to be explained in terms of certain conditions, then the only possible conditions to be considered are those found in the interaction between the person and the object of interest. The present theory of interest attempts to explain which of the processes and events that occur while a person is engaged with an object lead the person to (a) take up that object later (persistence), and (b) use certain actions to center activity around a certain aspect of the domain (selectivity).

Any explanation of selective persistence in interest must make note of the fact that people engage in activities voluntarily and repeatedly, that interests result from these activities, and that these interests are self-supporting and capable of developing on their own. Understanding why some individuals explore successively more difficult domains and develop highly specialized competencies is especially important for education.

In order to monitor the selective persistence of interest, it is important to distinguish between the general domain of objects and the individual objects contained in the domain. Generally, domains of interest are broad and abstract classes (e.g., computers, music, literature). Individual interest objects can be characterized as members of those classes with specific boundaries and elements. As time passes, an individual who is interested constructs and develops increasingly subjective representations of the interest objects. Although the characteristics of such interest objects can be uncovered by a researcher (e.g., through interviewing techniques), it is important that any patterns discovered be validated across repeated encounters with the object or domain. More accessible to researchers, however, are the concrete objects of activity ("reference objects"; cf. Prenzel, 1988). In the case of an interest in music, this could include an instrument, a phonograph record, or sheet music. Similarly, an interest in literature would involve books as reference objects, and an interest in computers could involve hardware, software, or both. These reference objects are elements of a subjectively perceived interest object. Most interest-based activities involve reference objects that readily lend themselves to empirical study. Consequently, these activities serve as convenient objective indicators of personal interest. In the following, the expression "object-based engagement" means activity involving any reference object from an entire domain.

Every activity involving a reference object of interest indicates persistence in the related domain. The persistence of a relation with an interest object is determined by the frequency and duration of activities involving reference objects from that domain. Important insights into the selectivity of the relation with an object can be found in the nature of the activities, the constellation of reference objects used, and the changes in that constellation.

Distinguishing between the interest object and the reference objects of interest provides further possibilities for the measurement of selectivity. To uncover a subjective representation of an interest object, one could ask subjects to name all the reference objects and possible activities (usually involving these objects) with which they are familiar (i.e., "the set of all known object-based engagements"). The domain "computer," for instance, could involve the hardware, operating system, software, manuals, and activities such as programming, games, hacking, etc. with which the person is familiar. Taking the analysis a step further, one could ask subjects to name the reference objects with which they have already worked and the activities they have carried out (i.e., "the set of object-based engagements already carried out").

In this way it is possible to achieve a clear picture of the subject's interest as well as a solid basis for monitoring his or her activities in order to analyze selectivity. Subjects can repeat activities that they have already carried out (repetitive engagement); they can make a first attempt at activities that they are aware of but have never carried out (imminent engagement); or they can work up a completely new activity (transcending engagement).

These distinctions then facilitate an explanation of selective persistence. The interest relation between a person and an object can be observed as a series of consecutive object-based engagements, each of which is characterized by a particular type of activity and a particular content.

To explain persistence, one must identify the conditions under which a person engages in a number of activities in a certain domain without external stimuli (e.g. monetary reward, lack of punishment). A precise explanation of persistence would allow one to predict whether a subject will take up an activity later, or how often a subject will become engaged with reference objects in a domain.

To explain selectivity, one must identify the conditions under which a person engages in particular forms of activity in a certain domain without external stimuli (e.g., monetary reward, lack of punishment). A precise explanation of selectivity would allow one to predict whether a subject will engage in a particular activity later.

Consideration of Relevant Factors

The explanations of both selectivity and persistence are understood to locate the conditions of selective persistence in the interaction between the person and the object.

The present discussion of selective persistence of interest assumes the existence of a representation system in the person. This representation system encompasses domain-specific declarative and procedural knowledge, including knowledge about the domain in question, its reference objects, the relations between the reference objects, and alternatives for activity, as well as personal talent and capabilities. A detailed description of a representation system could be based upon conceptions such as "production system" (e.g., Anderson, 1983) or "mental model" (e.g., DeKleer & Brown, 1983; Johnson–Laird, 1983). But a description of this kind, in the context of an explanation of interest, would be exceedingly elaborate. Therefore, we use the more general and older concept of "schema" (e.g., Abelson, 1981; Piaget, 1963; Rumelhart & Norman, 1978). In interest theory terminology, the representation system contains object and activity schemata, as well as the schemata of possible activities. Schemata can be both cognitive and emotional.

What happens to these schemata during an activity? Not only are they activated and applied, they are subject to alteration (cf. Flavell, 1972; Seiler, 1980). Activity and object schemata can be stabilized through repeated application; they can become more complex as their internal organization changes; they can become larger as additional elements are added. Also, the entire system of schemata can become more integrated.

On the other hand, incompatible or contradictory extensions can disturb the overall pattern (cf. Fink, 1989; Prenzel, 1988); all are cognitive effects that can result directly from an engagement. These effects, in turn, influence succeeding engagements: thus, refined activities are possible, and exploratory or epistemic activities allowing improved integration are necessary.

An engagement also involves emotional effects. Any activity that contains elements of uncertainty or involves new, complex constellations can be accompanied by arousal (Berlyne, 1967; Pribram, 1980) and feelings of rewarded exertion. While active, a person can experience emotions related to content (cf. Averill, 1980; e.g., moods of a musical composition, empathizing with characters in literature or film), or positive feelings of stimulation or fun (cf. Izard, 1977). The person can become lost in flow (Csikszentmihalyi, 1975). Successful completion of an activity may result in feelings of competence (Deci & Ryan, 1985). These emotional effects, once represented in the person, effect future engagements. The person may try to experience "pleasant" emotions by engaging in certain activities or try to avoid unpleasant states by avoiding certain engagements.

The functional pathway of these cognitive and emotional effects is embedded in a self-regulatory process. The system for self-regulation complements the representation system in that it initiates activities (on the basis of experience). Using concepts developed by Piaget (e.g., 1978, 1985) and Brown (1984), the model of effect distinguishes between two possible levels of regulation: (a) a "subconscious" self-regulation that, to a great extent, is subject to a principle of equilibration; (b) a "conscious" self-regulation, involving reflection and intent.

Subconscious self-regulation, involving the principle of equilibration, is concerned with maintaining a balance between the organism (the organism's schemata) and the environment. This balance is sustained by means of object-based engagements. According to Piaget (e.g., 1985), equilibration includes an internal need to construct and improve upon structures by means of new substructures that allow for greater detail. Equilibration also includes the need for greater integration of schemata by means of overarching structures. To a certain extent, selective persistence follows from the "logic" of the relation between the internal structure of a person and the structure of that portion of the external world with which the person is engaged. This relation is not necessarily controlled consciously.

Self-regulation at the conscious level, on the other hand, assumes a metastructure in the person. This metastructure can reflect relations among the person, the interest domain, other domains, and the processes of equilibration. Conscious regulation gives the person room to maneuver, by enabling long-term planning based upon expected consequences, freeing the person from emotional stress during difficult phases of adaptation, or aiding the person in getting through boring periods of required practice when these are seen as a necessary prelude to later, more interesting activities. In general, conscious self-regulation allows a more flexible approach to the process of engagement between person and interest object.

Hypotheses of Effect

This discussion considers persistence and selectivity, on the one hand, and the effects on their role in interest, on the other (Figure 4.1).

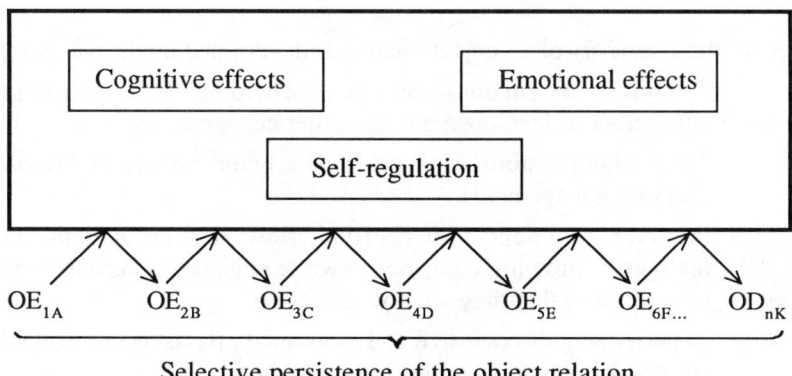

Fig. 4.1. Structure of the model of effect (OE = object engagement; 1 .... n: certain activities; A .... K: certain objects)

The cognitive and emotional effects that occur during self-regulated object engagement provide important conditions for subsequent instances of object engagement. Repeated patterns of object engagement (certain activities, certain domains) determine the selective persistence of a person's relation to the interest object. Thus, from the perspective of self-regulation, both cognitive and emotional effects present a network of conditions that affect, explain, and/or can be used to predict selective persistence.

Two assumptions are basic to the relation between self-regulation and selective persistence of interest: First, *persistence* increases when engagements with an interest object result in the following cognitive and/or emotional effects:

- Resolution of cognitive conflict, stabilization, differentiation, and integration of object-related schemata.
- Experiences of exertion, flow, enjoyment, and feelings of competence.
- Recognition of remaining potentially resolvable cognitive conflicts and development of goal schemata for future work.
- A feeling that discrepancies and emotional states can be controlled in the future as a result of object-related activities, and the development of ways to deal with them.

Second, the *selectivity* of an object relation is determined by the following:

- Conscious or subconscious goal schemata for object-based engagements developed during earlier engagements.
- Adaptation possibilities that rely on schemata developed during previous engagements.
- Previous experiences of exertion, flow, and enjoyment, and feelings of growing competence while engaged in certain forms of activity so that they are now preferred.
- Experiencing of cognitive and emotional effects as controllable entities following object-related engagements.
- Unresolved, but resolvable, discrepancies between object schemata and the interest object.

On the basis of these general, theoretical proposals, specific statements can be arrived at and empirically tested. The following describes a first attempt to formulate and test more precise hypotheses.

EXPLORATORY STUDIES

If our theoretical assumptions are correct, it should be possible to show that interest-based engagements include processes such as the experiencing of cognitive conflict, enjoyment, flow, or feelings of competence. When the object relation is primarily self-intentional (without clear extrinsic stimulation), events that accompany activity can be assumed to influence persistence. Therefore, in cases of more or less pronounced persistence, one should find correspondingly greater or lesser evidence of these processes.

In terms of selectivity, more or less frequent (persistent) activities should also yield evidence of these accompanying processes to a greater or lesser degree. An initial test of the model of effect resulted in three hypotheses:

Hypothesis 1: A person who engages in activity with an object repeatedly (high persistence) and without external prompting (self-intentional) should experience cognitive conflict, substantial enjoyment, flow, and the feeling of growing competence during engagement.

Hypothesis 2: The greater the persistence of engagement, the greater the degree of enjoyment, flow, and feelings of competence. No such relation is expected for cognitive conflict, however.

Hypothesis 3: Activities involving different aspects of the interest object and displaying different levels of persistence will entail different degrees of enjoyment, flow, feelings of competence, and cognitive conflict.

How can these hypotheses be tested empirically? The ideal design would involve a longitudinal study of considerable duration, during which each and every object-based engagement of a person is monitored and the accompanying processes measured. Methodology should allow for the description of individual episodes of object-based engagement, including the reference objects, content, and type of activity involved in those episodes. It should be possible to describe these episodes of engagement both from the observer's perspective and from the perspective of the person carrying out the activity. These descriptions should be simple, but nevertheless insightful. Ideally, the accompanying processes will be measured as the activity is being carried out; however, this is probably not practical. Even a thinking-aloud technique, or the mere presence of an observer, could disrupt more complex forms of object-based engagement (cf. Ericsson & Simon, 1984). The most reliable method of learning about the processes that accompany activity might involve allowing the person to complete an engagement and, immediately thereafter, asking him or her to recount the internal feelings or events experienced during engagement.

We are now ready to develop criteria for the conceptualization of a study of the processes involved here. These criteria pertain to the design of such a study and to the selection of an object domain, study participants, and methodology. First, the episodes of engagement must be examined in a longitudinal framework. Second, the domains should exhibit clear, comprehensible structures and include a majority of engagements that involve concrete reference objects. Third, following an activity, the subjects must be able to describe their processes. And fourth, an appropriate means of generating a protocol of comments made by subjects following engagement should be employed.

Method

In order to satisfy the preceding requirements, two domains were chosen, "computers" and "music." Engagement in both computers and music was limited to the active use of a computer or the playing of the guitar. For both of these domains, a majority of the activities involve the physical instrument itself, and most of the constituent parts of activity can be measured by means of reference objects (e.g., computer programs, musical notes). Subjects participating in the study were school-age and college students, who, on the basis of their level of cognitive development, were seen as capable of reflecting on both the engagement episodes and the accompanying processes. The participants had an interest in learning either the computer or the guitar and had no professional ambitions for either of these domains. Finally, student activities were monitored over fairly short periods of time in order to readily employ a method for recording each individual activity and describing the most important personal experiences of the subjects.

A total of 27 individuals with varying levels of interest in computers and 7 persons with a high level of interest in the guitar participated. All prospective participants were screened by means of an extensive, structured interview that verified the self-intentionality of engagement and reconstructed the preceding development of this interest. In the course of this first interview, the study participants were shown how to keep a record sheet of their engagement.

The studies were conducted over a period of from 1 to 2 months. During this time, the participants were to record each episode of engagement with the object of interest. These record sheets were then collected on a weekly basis.

The interview was used to determine both the object-related activities that the subjects had already carried out and the activities they intended to carry out in the future. This initial interview was based upon the structure of the domain as determined with the help of experts. For each domain, reference objects and content were assigned to categories of activity in a fashion similar to a two-dimensional Tyler matrix (cf. Tyler, 1949). The study participants were asked to name all the objects or topics, and all the activities relevant to the domain involved (e.g., hardware, software, components; programming, applications, exploration, games) that they could. On the basis of these responses, which were recorded using matrices on prepared forms, the participants were then asked to indicate what forms of engagement they had carried out in the past, and what forms of engagement they intended to carry out in the immediate future.

In order to verify self-intentionality, the subjects' reasons for engaging in an activity were examined. Questions were asked about support or control by parents, teachers, and peers. Included for study were only those candidates for whom the primary stimulant lay in the object itself and who did not intend to make a living this way in the future.

To acquaint subjects with the methods for keeping records, they were asked to fill out a practice sheet describing their last engagement in the domain. The concept of "interest" was not discussed with the participants, but they were told that the study had to do with a detailed reconstruction of engagements with the computer or the guitar.

Each record sheet was divided into two parts. Before beginning an engagement, participants were asked to note the date and time, their mood at the start, and the activities they intended to carry out. Immediately following an engagement, the participants were to note the individual activities (as units of activity/content, e.g., debug graphics program, play Tetris), as well as the duration of each activity. A series of rating scales (with possible values ranging from 0 to 6) for estimating the following parameters for each of the activities was included on each record sheet: the overall quality of the feeling that accompanied the activity, a subjective estimate of the level of difficulty as an indicator of cognitive conflict, the depth of involvement as an indicator of flow, and the extent of increased competence. In some of the phases of the study, subjects were also asked to quantify their feelings of rewarded exertion and various aspects of flow.

For the purposes of evaluation, the record method and rating scales establish relatively narrow boundaries for quantitative calculation. However, the estimates of accompanying processes reflected in the rating scales are idiosyncratic measures. The only comparison they permit is between engagements for the same participant, over time. Thus, whereas an average value for rating each individual's activity over time can be determined, calculations performed across the entire group of students would have yielded no meaningful results. For this reason, no tests of significance between subgroups were conducted.

Results

Detailed description of the results of this set of studies can be found elsewhere (Bogner, 1988; Forster, 1987; Prenzel, 1988). Here, only those results that are relevant to the hypotheses under immediate consideration are described. In addition, a few examples of object-based engagements are provided in order to highlight the sequences of events involved in them.

Hypotheses 1 and 2—Computer Engagements. Hypotheses 1 and 2 had to do with the persistence of interest relations. According to Hypothesis 1, persistent, self-intentional, interest-based activities should be accompanied by certain processes. The pattern of estimates in the record sheets (each record being regarded as a self-contained whole) should support this assertion. Hypothesis 2 proposes that interest relations exhibiting a higher level of persistence (as opposed to other relations exhibiting lower levels of persistence) are associated with substantially greater feelings of enjoyment, flow, and increased competence.

Over the course of approximately 1 month, the 27 participants interested in computers spent a total of 557 hours working with them ($M = 20.7$; $SD = 14.8$). During this time, 605 individual episodes of engagement were recorded in terms of activity and content. The participants persistently (albeit to varying extents) became engaged with the computer without being prompted from any external source.

For each individual participant, the estimated scale values for the process variables were averaged across all engagements. Table 4.1 shows the distribution of these idiosyncratic average values on the 6 values in the rating scale. The information in Table 4.1 has already been differentiated on the basis of persistence. The degree of persistence was used to split the total group of 27 participants into two subgroups. The subgroup with less persistence (nLP = 14) spent an average of ca. 11 hours with the computer;

the subgroup with greater persistence (nHP = 13) spent an average of ca. 31 hours with the computer.

Table 4.1

Accompanying Processes. Frequency Distributions of Individual Ratings (means) on Scale Values (LP = low persistences; HP = high persistence)

Scale Value N:	Enjoyment			Cognitive Conflict			Flow			Competence		
	All	LP	HP	All	LP	HP	All	LP	HP	All	LP	HP
	(27)	(14)	(13)	(27)	(14)	(13)	(27)	(14)	(13)	(27)	(14)	(13)
0 – 1	–	–	–	1	1	–	–	–	–	–	–	–
– 2	–	–	–	3	1	2	3	2	1	3	2	1
– 3	–	–	–	9	4	5	7	3	4	8	5	3
– 4	15	11	4	14	8	6	11	8	3	8	5	3
– 5	7	3	4	–	–	–	6	1	5	4	1	3
– 6	5	–	5	–	–	–	–	–	–	4	1	3

For Hypothesis 1, Table 4.1 shows that in computer engagements subjects experienced the following: significant feelings of enjoyment, low to moderate levels of cognitive conflict, moderate to high amounts of flow, and feelings of markedly increased competence. Comparing the distributions of average values of the two subgroups, one finds that the subgroup with greater persistence recorded higher estimates for enjoyment, flow, and increased competence.

Hypotheses 1 and 2—Guitar Engagements. A similar pattern is found among the smaller number of guitar players. The seven participants (all of whom exhibited a high level of interest) spent a total of 202 hours playing the guitar ($M = 28.86$, $SD = 15.6$), spread over 169 episodes of engagement and involving 409 individual units, or events (usually the playing of individual pieces). The estimates for the processes that accompanied engagement correspond to those of the computer study participants: the individual average values for enjoyment while engaged all lie above 3.5, the estimates of cognitive conflict are comparable to those of the computer study participants, with only one individual estimating the level of difficulty to be somewhat higher ($M = 4.7$), and the values for flow and feeling of competence lie between 3 and 4 (in the case of one participant each of these values was under 2). Thus, these results support Hypotheses 1 and 2.

Hypothesis 3—Computer Engagements. In order to test Hypothesis 3 pertaining to selectivity, engagements with the computer were classified by means of a simple taxonomy (programming, games, application, exploration, and miscellaneous). In terms of both the type of activity and the contents involved, programming and games (using game software) can be distinguished clearly from one another. Table 4.2 shows the results from a subgroup of 7 school-age participants who had a strong interest in computers. The figures in the table show the proportion of time spent programming versus time spent playing games for each participant. The table also reports the differences between the averaged estimates of processes accompanying programming versus game activities.

Table 4.2

Distribution of Time for Two Computer Activities and Differences in Activity Accompanying Processes by Students with High Interest (N = 7)

Participant	Distribution of Time (%)		Difference Values (Mean Programming — Mean Games			
	Programming	Games	Enjoy-ment	Cognitive Conflict	Flow	Compe-tence
A	80.5	15.7	.51	.73	1.83	2.45
B	57.8	20.5	.14	2.85	2.95	3.43
C	50.1	17.2	.06	− 1.01	− .49	2.07
D	10.8	62.1	− .57	− 1.61	− .74	− .21
E	44.4	34.2	− .80	2.81	.84	2.86
F	7.0	45.3	.67	.47	1.67	2.67
G	35.6	32.9	.44	.95	1.88	1.55

In the cases of participants A, B, and G, who exhibited a preference for programming, the difference values are uniformly positive. Participant D, having a clear preference for game playing, yielded uniformly negative difference values. Participants C and E yielded mixed results (partly negative, partly positive differences). Participant F spends comparatively little time programming but nevertheless indicated markedly higher values for the processes accompanying programming than for those accompanying game playing. A possible explanation for this would be that participant F is not a "hard core" game player, and that during the period of time covered by the study he was occupied primarily by activities involving hardware manipulation.

Hypothesis 3—Guitar Engagements. Corresponding analyses were carried out for the data on guitar playing. The domain "guitar" does not readily lend itself to a simple, yet sensible, subcategorization, such as computer programming versus game playing. Among others, the categories of "exercises," "practicing pieces," and "interpretation" were compared with one another. Clear differences in the accompanying processes could be discerned for all participants especially when comparing "exercises" with "interpretation" or "improvisation." Plausible explanations for these differences can be found, but it seems more sensible to attempt a detailed analysis on the basis of the pieces played rather than on the basis of the type of activity. As an example, Table 4.3 compares one participant's ratings after having played movements of a Bach suite (a total of 60 engagements) with her ratings after having played Villa–Lobos études (22 engagements).

Table 4.3

Average Estimates of Processes Accompanying the Playing of
Two Different Guitar Pieces (N = 1)

	Enjoyment	Cognitive Conflict	Flow	Competence
Bach (60 engagements)	1.63	5.50	3.96	3.59
Villa–Lobos (22 engagements)	1.22	5.82	3.91	2.96

The pieces were rather new to this participant, which explains the high level of cognitive conflict she experienced. The ratings are clearly higher in the case of the Bach piece, which is correspondingly played more often. But take careful note of an example course of engagement. During the course of the study, this participant learned to play a suite by Bach: she was already somewhat familiar with some of the movements (e.g., "Allemande"); now she began to learn the "Prelude," the "Presto," and the "Gigue." In learning the various suite movements, the same process can be observed. First, the piece is played from the sheet music and is practiced several times. Following several repetitions, the participant begins to play the piece from memory. Interpretations are attempted, until eventually the piece is mastered. However, learning of the individual movements is not characterized by successive episodes involving always the same piece. Instead, following a few attempts involving the "Gigue," the participant goes over to a more familiar piece (e.g., "Allemande"), before returning to the "Gigue" for further practice.

This "working up" of new pieces is a distinctive qualitative feature of object-related engagement. If one monitors the content of activities involving a domain such as the guitar or computers, one repeatedly finds streaks of engagement where succeeding activities are based on what went on before. These "activity chains" are centered around larger units of content which are then explored, or around attempts to solve complex problems.

Further Case-Based Considerations. Let us now take a look back at the description of computer-based activity, involving Maria, with which this chapter began. The "working up" of the two programs (ideal weight and student feedback) represents, in each case, an instance of problem-solving. Initially, we see an approximate knowledge of the possibilities of a computer program (e.g., feedback loop) and the idea for a practical application.

Similar examples can be found among other cases of computer-based interest. A teenager, for instance, repeatedly plays a labyrinth game. As he plays, he observes how the program works, then decides that he could write such a program for himself. He designs a similar labyrinth game, writes the program, improves the graphics, tests the game, and, finally, attempts to make the game capable of "learning."

A further example would be the school-age participant who notes that the material in his mathematics class is well suited to the computer's abilities to calculate functions and plot graphs. Over the course of several sessions, he writes a program designed to carry out the consecutive steps of curve analysis, thereby easing his homework worries.

The basic dynamic of developing interests can be found within such activity chains. The decisive factor at the beginning of such a chain seems to be that the person runs into a situation in everyday life that might lend itself to a computer application. To a certain extent, the person seems to interpret his or her environment in terms of possible computer applications. When, therefore, a situation arises that can be dealt with in this fashion, this constitutes a "problem." The process of solving a problem, which can extend over several engagements, is characterized by feelings of rewarded exertion, arousal, or flow. The person searches for helpful sources of information, previous knowledge is brought into play and refined, and a new level of competence is achieved. Periodically, difficulties arise, as indicated by reported feelings of frustration. These difficulties are worked at tenaciously until a solution is found. Based upon newly won competence, new areas open up—areas that contain both new problems and new possibilities for their resolution.

DISCUSSION AND PROSPECTS

Beginning with a general model of selective persistence and interest, three hypotheses were derived and tested in two different object domains.

Object-based engagements, monitored over relatively short periods of time, were accompanied by processes that offer theoretically plausible explanations for the persistence and selectivity of interest. In the absence of external provocation, feelings of enjoyment and rewarding exertion, flow, or increasing competence were found to take on the quality of "intrinsic motivation." The students' knowledge that their activities led to such feelings gave rise to particular forms of renewed engagement that reflected their feelings. This suggests that the students engaged in cognitive conflict, which could be satisfied by posing and then solving new problems. This in turn provided opportunities to again experience expectation, flow, or feelings of competence. Engagement with the interest object corresponded to a self-motivating, but also a self-developing system of circular regulation (cf. Nuttin, 1984).

Considering the small groups of subjects and measurement employing only a few scales, the empirical testing of this theoretical model is in no way complete. However, various possibilities present themselves for further studies in the context of the theory of interest effect.

Obviously, one could attempt to intensify and improve the empirical investigation by means of a design that would extend previous exploratory studies. First, engagements could be monitored over longer periods of time. This would allow a more elaborate look at the development of selective persistence and at the processes that accompany preceding activity. Second, a longitudinal study could be conducted involving individuals of differing levels of competence or interest. Whereas the use of record sheets for the making of protocols about activities and processes has been fruitful, the urge to expand the information covered by the rating scales must be balanced by the need to limit the burden placed on the subjects. To solve the problem of the idiosyncrasy of the ratings, it may be possible to anchor individual estimations by having the participants rate everyday tasks, such as homework, and then compare these estimations across participants.

The variations just mentioned serve primarily to subject the theoretical model to a more thorough empirical test. Further studies are obviously necessary. However, now that some initial empirical evidence supporting this theory of interest has been gathered, it seems sensible to orient future research more strongly toward application, in particular toward application in education. As understood in the context of this chapter, "interest" is a relatively global (one could say "holistic") concept involving cognitive, emotional, value-related, and conative components. The fact that each of these areas is already an extremely complex field of research complicates matters somewhat. For although research continues apace in each of them, we do not have at this time a basic store of concepts and verified results that would allow us to synthesize the findings coming from these different areas. In light of this inadequacy, the question arises as to the possibility of conducting meaningful basic research in the field of interest. On the other hand, "interest" is an everyday concept with which we are all very familiar. The term refers to a phenomenon that not only educators consider desirable, but that all individuals experience in their engagements with particular object domains—albeit with varying duration and intensity—and that is generally regarded as the ideal form of learning-oriented interaction with objects. Both students and teachers desire more knowledge about this phenomenon known as "interest" and the conditions surrounding it, especially the conditions that teacher and learner can recognize in the immediate environment and over which they may have some control (cf. Krapp, 1979).

The following concluding portion attempts to organize interest-oriented research into two currently relevant dimensions of educational–

psychological thought. One obvious dimension involves the discussion of learning in school and out (cf. Resnick, 1987). The interests investigated in our research began outside of school, and, for the most part, exhibited a considerable level of development. This is not meant to imply that interests can not be stimulated and developed in school, but the school environment does not allow for the persistent (in other words, long-term) pursuit of a particular topic, especially of a strongly selective (narrowly defined) topic. This can mean that persistent and selective interests have to be pursued and developed outside of school. It can also mean, however, that more room should be made inside the school for a longer and more selective development of interests (e.g., in the sense of project-oriented instruction.)

A second aspect also relates to the discussion about learning in school and out. Glaser and Bassok (1989) believe that instruction-oriented research should concentrate not only on learning in institutional settings but should also investigate the learning phenomenon in natural settings. Following research into the cognitive processes of experts (cf. Chi, Glaser, & Farr, 1988), Glaser and Bassok consider desired cognitive performance and the learner's initial state to be well described, or at least easily accessible for description. They suggest that less is known, however, in our knowledge about the difficult process of acquiring a new competency. From the perspective of a theory of interest, we can attribute to experts a highly selective and persistent interest in the object of expertise. The novice, on the other hand, seems to exhibit more of an object-related curiosity. It is unclear what motivational events occur on the long pathway from the novice to the expert stage. Can expertise in an object domain develop at all in the absence of interest? Does a person continue to engage in activity in an object domain over the longer term only when that engagement leads to processes such as those described (e.g., cognitive conflict, flow, feeling of competence) in the model of effect?

The two aspects just mentioned allow for better organization and a sharper focus for future studies of the selective persistence of interest. If we investigate longer-term involvement with objects from a theory of interest perspective, then one goal should be to analyze the development of interests outside of school. This knowledge could then be used to investigate classrooms and attempt to create the same conditions in the classroom that now lead to the development of interests outside of school. Failing that, this knowledge could be used in school to enable students to develop more interests outside of school. An additional area of concentration should be the development of object-specific interests and competencies in the case of advanced novices. In other words, the conditions contributing to the selective persistence of object-related activity at a level of moderate competence (that is, beyond initial curiosity, but well before the highly specialized interest of the expert) require more careful scrutiny.

REFERENCES

Abelson, R. P. (1981). Psychological status of the script concept. *American Psychologist, 36,* 715–729.

Allport, G. W., & Vernon, P. E. (1931). *A study of values.* Boston: Houghton–Mifflin.

Anderson, J. R. (1983). *The architecture of cognition.* Cambridge: Harvard University Press.

Apter, M. J. (1982). *The experience of motivation. The theory of psychological reversals.* London: Academic Press.

Averill, J. R. (1980). A constructivist view of emotion. In R. Plutchik & H. Kellerman (Eds.), *Emotion. theory, research and experience. Vol. 1: Theories of emotion* (pp. 305–340). New York: Academic Press.

Bandura, A. (1982). Self-efficacy mechanism in human agency. *American Psychologist, 37,* 122–147.

Barak, A. (1981). Vocational interests: A cognitive view. *Journal of Vocational Behavior, 19,* 1–14.

Berlyne, D. E. (1967). Arousal and reinforcement. In D. Levine (Ed.), *Nebraska Symposium on Motivation* (pp.1–110). Lincoln: Nebraska University Press.

Berlyne, D. E. (1978). Curiosity and learning. *Motivation and Emotion, 2,* 97–175.

Bogner, Ch. (1988). *Warum beschäeftigen sich Jugendliche mit Computern? Eine interessentheoretische Analyse.* Unpublished Master's Thesis. University of München.

Brown, A. L. (1984). Metakognition, handlungskontrolle, selbststeuerung und andere, noch geheimnisvollere Mechanismen. In F. E. Weinert & R. H. Kluwe (Eds.), *Metakognition, motivation und lernen* (pp. 60–109). Stuttgart: Kohlhammer.

Chi, M. T. H., Glaser, R., & Farr, M. J. (Eds.) (1988). *The nature of expertise.* Hillsdale, NJ: Lawrence Erlbaum Associates.

Csikszentmihalyi, M. (1975). *Beyond boredom and anxiety.* San Francisco: Jossey Bass.

deCharms, R. (1968). *Personal causation.* New York: Academic Press.

Deci, E. L. (1975). *Intrinsic motivation.* New York: Plenum Press.

Deci, E. L., & Ryan, R. M. (1980). The empirical exploration of intrinsic motivational processes. In L. Berkowitz (Ed.), *Advances in experimental social psychology* (pp. 39–80). New York: Academic Press.

Deci, E. L., & Ryan, R. M. (1985). *Intrinsic motivation and self-determination in human behavior.* New York: Plenum Press.

Deci, E. L., & Ryan, R. M. (1987). The support of autonomy and the control of behavior. *Journal of Personality and Social Psychology, 53,* 1024–1037.

DeKleer, J., & Brown, J. S. (1983). Assumptions and ambiguities in mechanistic mental modells. In D. Gentner & A. L. Stevens (Eds.), *Mental models* (pp. 155–190). Hillsdale, NJ.: Lawrence Erlbaum.Associates.

Ericsson, K. A., & Simon, H. A. (1984). *Protocol analysis: Verbal reports as data.* Cambridge: MIT Press.

Fink, B. (1989). *Das konkrete Ding als Interessengegenstand.* Frankfurt: Lang.

Flavell, J. H. (1972). An analysis of cognitive–developmental sequences. *Genetic Psychology Monographs, 86,* 279–350.

Forster, P. (1987). *Emotionale Prozesse bei interessegeleitetem Handeln.* Unpublished. Master's thesis, University of München.

Glaser, R. and Bassok, M. (1989). Learning theory and the study of instruction. *Annual Review of Psychology, 40,* 631–667.

Hunt, J. McV. (1965). Intrinsic motivation and its role in psychological development. In D. Levine (Ed.), *Nebraska Symposium on Motivation* (pp. 189–282). Lincoln: Nebraska University Press.

Izard, C. E. (1977). *Human emotions.* New York: Plenum Press.

James, W. (1890). *The principles of psychology.* New York: Holt, Rinehart, & Winston.

Johnson–Laird, P. N. (1983). *Mental models. Towards a cognitive science of language, inference, and consciousness.* Cambridge, MA: Harvard University Press.

Kerschensteiner, G. (1928). *Theorie der bildung, 2nd ed.* Leipzig: Teubner

Krapp, A. (1979). *Prognose und entscheidung.* Weinheim: Beltz.

Krapp, A. (in press). Interest and curiosity: The role of interest in a theory of exploratory action. In H. Keller & K. Schneider (Eds.). *Curiosity and exploration. Theoretical perspectives, research fields, and applications.* New York: Springer.

Lepper, M. R., & Greene, D. (Eds.) (1978). *The hidden costs of reward.* Hillsdale, NJ: Lawrence Erlbaum Associates.

Lunk, G. (1927). *Das interesse.* Leipzig: Klinkhardt.

Maehr, M. L. (1976). Continuing motivation: An analysis of a seldom considered educational outcome. *Review of Educational Research, 46,* 443–462.

Nuttin, J. (1984). *Motivation, planning, and action. A relational theory of behavior dynamics.* Hillsdale, NJ: Lawrence Erlbaum Associates.

Piaget, J. (1963). *The origin of intelligence in children.* New York: Norton.

Piaget, J. (1978). *Success and understanding.* Cambridge, MA: Harvard University Press.

Piaget, J. (1981). *Intelligence and affectivity: Their relationship during child development.* Palo Alto, CA: Annual Reviews.

Piaget, J. (1985). *The equilibration of cognitive structures.* Chicago: Chicago University Press.

Prenzel, M. (1988). *Die Wirkungsweise von Interesse.* Opladen: Westdeutscher Verlag.

Prenzel, M., Krapp. A., & Schiefele, H. (1986). Grundzüge einer pädagogischen Interessentheorie. *Zeitschrift für Pädagogik, 32,* 163–173.

Pribram, K. G. (1980). The biology of emotions and other feelings. In R. Plutchik & H. Kellerman (Eds.), *Emotion, Theory, research, and experience. Vol. 1: Theories of emotion* (pp. 245–269). New York: Academic Press.

Renninger, K. A. (1990). Children's play interests, representation, and activity. In R. Fivush & J. Hudson (Eds.), *Knowing and remembering in young children* (pp. 27–165). Emory Cognition Series, (Vol. III.) Cambridge, MA: Cambridge University Press.

Renninger, K. A. & Leckrone, T. G. (1991). Continuity in young children's actions: A consideration of interest and temperament. In L. Oppenheimer & J. Valsiner (Eds.), *The origins of action: Interdisciplinary and international perspectives.* (pp. 205–238). New York: Springer–Verlag.

Renninger, K. A. & Wozniak, R. H. (1985). Effect of interest on attentional shift, recognition, and recall in young children. *Developmental Psychology, 21,* 624–632.

Resnick, L. B. (1987). Learning in school and out. *Educational Researcher, 16,* 4, 13–20.

Rumelhart, D. E., & Norman, D. A. (1978). Accretion, tuning, and restructuring: Three modes of learning. In J. W. Cotton & R. L. Klatzky (Eds.), *Semantic factors in cognition* (pp. 37–53). Hillsdale, NJ: Lawrence Erlbaum Associates.

Schiefele, H. (1986). Interesse—Neue Antworten auf ein altes Problem. *Zeitschrift für pädagogik, 32,* 153–162.

Seiler, T. B. (1980). Entwicklungstheorien in der Sozialisationsforschung. In K. Hurrelmann & D. Ulich (Eds.), *Handbuch der Sozialisationsforschung* (pp. 101–121). Weinheim: Beltz.

Strong, E. K., Jr. (1943). *Vocational interests of men and women.* Palo Alto: Stanford University Press.

Super, D. E., & Crites, J. O. (1962). *Appraising vocational fitness.* New York: Harper & Row.

Tyler, R. W. (1949). *Basic principles of curriculum and instruction.* Chicago: Chicago University Press.

White, R. W. (1959). Motivation reconsidered: The concept of competence. *Psychological Review, 66,* 297–333.

White, R. W. (1960). Competence and the psychosexual stages of development. In M. R. Jones (Ed.), *Nebraska Symposium on Motivation* (pp. 97–141). Lincoln: University of Nebraska Press.

Zuckerman, M. (1979). *Sensation seeking: Beyond the optimal level of arousal.* Hillsdale, NJ: Lawrence Erlbaum Associates.

II INDIVIDUAL INTEREST AND LEARNING IN SCHOOL

Is Interest Educationally Interesting? An Interest-Related Model of Learning

5

James F. Voss and Leona Schauble
University of Pittsburgh

The title of this chapter poses a question, one that most people would probably answer in the affirmative. Yet, despite the presumed facilitating effect of interest, research since Dewey's (1913) treatise on the topic has been concerned largely with the difficult problem of how interest is related to other concepts such as emotion (cf. Izard, 1977; Piaget, 1981), whereas the question of how interest is related to learning has received only infrequent study (e.g., Renninger, 1989).

The position taken in this chapter is that interest indeed has the potential to be educationally interesting, but to show why this is the case, one cannot simply consider interest per se. Instead, interest must be examined in relation to its role in the learning process. Similarly, we believe that to develop an understanding of the learning process learning must be viewed in the context of the individual's overall mental functioning. Therefore, the initial section of this chapter presents a broadly based model of learning, including consideration of the role of interest. In the section that follows we consider the implications of this model for the educational context.

THE NATURE OF LEARNING

The Fragmentation of Mental Functioning in Psychology

General theories of psychology have typically had one of three foci, motivation, perception, or learning. Moreover, a theory having one of these foci typically has been thought to be weak with regard to the other two. Motivational theories have viewed an individual's behavior in relation to needs and motives that produce goal-directed action. Learning therefore is considered to be a function of motivation, but usually little is said about the mechanisms by which learning takes place. Perceptual approaches, such as Gestalt theory (e.g., Koffka, 1935), have emphasized that how one perceives, interprets, and mentally organizes the environment is critical to what one does. In this case learning tends to be viewed as the acquisition of perceptual relations; these, in turn, are stored in memory and utilized in subsequent perceptual experiences. However, as with motivational approaches, perceptual theories usually have had little to say about the mechanisms of learning.

Learning theory, derived in large part from the writings of Aristotle, the British empiricists, and the Soviet reflexology tradition of Sechenov (1863/1965) and Pavlov (1927), has generally held that learning consists of the acquisition of associations. Whereas Hullian theory (e.g., Hull, 1943) attempted to relate learning to motivation, the study of how motivation influences human learning has, until recently, consisted largely of isolated studies investigating how particular motivational variables influence learning. In recent years, however, some research (e.g., Dweck, 1986) has addressed how motivational activities such as goal setting influence student performance. With respect to perception, learning theory has had to address the idea that the organism, as an active processor of information, can select and elaborate upon the stimulus input, thus demonstrating that how input is perceived is directly related to what is learned (cf. Voss, 1979).

In recent decades, psychology has been dominated by the cognitive movement, an approach having its origins more in relation to perception than to motivation or learning, as shown, for example, by the central role played by representation in cognitive theory, that is, how the individual represents or builds models of the environment. With respect to the study of learning, although cognitive psychology has made substantial theoretical contributions, a theory of learning has not been one of them. There has been considerable research on skill acquisition (e.g., Anderson, 1982), and a number of the concepts that have been employed in this work, such as spreading activation, are associative and come from classical learning theory. Similarly, general modeling approaches such as connectionism and neural nets have associative roots. However, a cognitive theory of learning involving such topics as knowledge acquisition has not been forthcoming. Cognitive research has nevertheless demonstrated how particular factors affect the learning process, especially showing the importance of prior knowledge in the acquisition of new knowledge (e.g., Spilich, Vesonder, Chiesi, & Voss, 1979). Indeed, much of the current research on subject-matter learning conducted within the cognitive framework is concerned with how the knowledge and skills a student brings into the learning situation influence learning, or how such knowledge becomes restructured in the process of learning. This perspective implies that learning is basically a process of transfer, in the sense that to understand how learning takes place it is necessary to determine how prior knowledge and skills facilitate or perhaps retard learning (cf. Voss, 1978).

The general theoretical traditions in psychology have thus tended toward fragmentation of the perceptual, motivational, and learning components of mental functioning. We assume, however, that to under-stand the learning process we must take motivation and perceptual factors into account, for we regard them as not only germane to the learning process, but as part of that process. Humans function holistically, and the delineation of concepts such as learning, motivation, and perception is somewhat arbitrary, albeit necessary for the purpose of analysis. But in performing the conceptual dissection, it is important not to lose sight of the coordinated nature of mental functioning.

A Functionalist Framework of Learning

Staying within the general functionalist tradition (e.g., Carr, 1925; Dewey, 1896), we assume that individuals are in continual interaction with their environment, and that within this context, the primary purpose of learning, broadly conceived, is to facilitate the organism's adaptation to the environment, including not only physical and biological factors but also social–cultural components. Moreover, during the course of development, the individual is assumed to become increasingly equipped with value-related and intellectually related mental structures. Value-based "equipment" develops as the individual acquires the norms and principles of the sociocultural milieu in which he or she is raised, with the individual differentially applying such norms to his or her own situation. Beliefs are also established, and such values and beliefs are assumed to play a major role in the establishment of goals. These may include moral goals such as maintaining integrity, career goals, and social goals. Particular values and their related goals also include affect. As the person learns more about the environment, interests are developed and goals aimed at satisfying these interests. Correspondingly, interests may be established in satisfying one's goals. These interests and goals are thus based upon the respective values and beliefs, as well as affect.

The individual's goals and interests thus produce motivation, that is, a person is directed toward a particular activity that is aimed at accomplishing goals and/or exploring an interest (cf. Bolles, 1975). Motivation thus has two functions, one qualitative and the other quantitative. Qualitatively, motivation directs the individual toward selecting activities that will accomplish goals and/or satisfy interests. Quantitatively, motivation serves an energizing function, providing the effort and persistence needed to accomplish a goal or pursue an interest (Atkinson & Wickens, 1971). An interest in baseball may promote the goal of going to a game, and, if the Cubs lose, one may go to games repeatedly, until the Cubs finally win.

But if the individual had only values, beliefs, goals, and interests, and the motivation engendered by them, the likelihood of survival or success in dealing with the environment would be minimal. The individual needs intellectual "equipment." He or she builds models of the environment (Johnson–Laird, 1983), including event contingencies, and scripts (Schank & Abelson, 1977), which are sequential; and categorical relations, schema, and mental maps are also constructed. Models may be hierarchical (Spilich, Vesonder, Chiesi, & Voss, 1979), procedural (Ryle, 1949), or may consist of topic-centered information. For example, a person may have an "abortion" model containing knowledge about the political, moral, physical, interpersonal, affective, and possibly experiential components of abortion, as well as a representation of his or her own beliefs about abortion and affect related to it.

An important function of models is that they not only provide for an understanding of the environment, they also serve as a resource to consult in order to satisfy goals and interests. The use of intellectual "equipment" as a resource occurs in a number of ways. The resources enable the individual to interpret incoming information, and they help to provide the means by which goals and interests can be satisfied, constituting a major component of the problem-solving process. Furthermore, when a given goal cannot be satisfied, perhaps because of an environmental constraint, the individual may be able to adapt by using some other means derived from models. This view is essentially taken from Selz (Selz, 1922; see also deGroot, 1983), who maintained that cognitive and motivational factors exist within a given subsystem, and that the failure of one subsystem to provide the solution to a problem leads to the search for another subsystem likely to lead to the goal. The motivational and cognitive components are thus closely integrated.

Whereas mental models serve as a resource in problem solving, they also are modified and developed in the process of solving a problem. Individuals engaged in problem solving learn about ways of solving the problem, and those means are stored for future use. Indeed, the building of mental representations can become a goal or interest in its own right. Individuals may want to learn for the sake of learning, although typically learning is related to a more particular goal or interest.

A basic assumption about mental functioning within the adaptive framework is that people interpret and provide the meaning when they process input. Furthermore, the meaning is generated by what the individuals know and feel about the events; that is, interpretations are based not only upon the individual's knowledge, but upon beliefs and values, goals and interests. Because the interpretations or representations are the product of the processing, it is interpretations that are acquired, that is, an integration of environmental stimuli and the meaning provided.

How one's knowledge influences interpretation is reasonably straightforward. Having relatively little knowledge about a situation severely constrains how it can be interpreted. For example, in a recent study of novices' models of electric circuits (Schauble, Glaser, Raghavan, & Reiner, in press), undergraduates were confronted with eight small metal boxes, each containing a hidden piece of electrical equipment. Subjects knew that the boxes contained batteries, resistors, plain wire, and, in one case, nothing at all, but they did not know what was in each box. The task was to try to figure out what was in each box by plugging them, singly or in combinations, into a simple circuit containing a light bulb.

In this study, subjects approached the task in four qualitatively different kinds of ways, each characterized by a different kind of knowledge or belief about the kinds of entities involved in the task and their interrelations. For example, the simplest model specified that there were only two classes of components within the boxes, those that "worked" (that is, lit the bulb when plugged into the circuit), and those that did not "work." Students holding this model had no way to distinguish among the five boxes that did not contain batteries (and that thus did not "work" when plugged alone into the circuit). They typically made decisions about what was inside these boxes by guessing, shaking them, or hefting them in their hands. In contrast, the most knowledgeable students understood that all the resistors, the plain wire, the empty box, and even the lightbulb itself had the property of resistance. Therefore, they understood that the only way to identify them was to plug them into test circuits in combination with one or more boxes previously identified as containing batteries. Furthermore, they knew that although these components had different names, they could all be distinguished on the basis of changes in the brightness of the bulb. Clearly, for these subjects, "understanding" involved not only accessing relevant knowledge about electrical circuits and components, but also appropriately applying this knowledge to the task at hand. Although this task posed a well-formed problem with a correct solution, we do not intend to imply by offering this example that individuals with a high level of knowledge will always agree. It is important to note that knowledge does not guarantee agreement, especially in the domains of the social sciences and the humanities, or in the frontier research areas of the physical and life sciences.

Not only knowledge and beliefs, but also affect can constrain processing. As an example, assume that an American–Japanese trade agreement has just been concluded that will likely lead to the sale of more Japanese-made automobiles in the United States. An American auto worker may have little knowledge of the economics involved but may nevertheless have considerable interest because the agreement could affect his or her job status. This apprehension could generate negative affect about the agreement and about the Japanese in general, even though the individual is making essentially no effort to understand the agreement.

In addition to knowledge and affect, motivation can influence processing and learning. The powerful role of motivation in learning can be demonstrated by examples from out-of-school learning. Carraher, Carraher, and Schliemann (1985), and Schliemann and Acioly (1989) have shown that unschooled individuals can do extremely well in performing complex arithmetic operations such as selling lottery tickets. This is a testament to the ability of individuals to learn when it becomes essentially a matter of necessity, that is, when one's values, like eating and finding shelter, dictate goals. Interestingly, Carraher et al. (1985) also found that unschooled individuals tend to show less flexibility in problem solving than schooled individuals, because they apparently rely more on computational rules and thus experience difficulty when a rule does not directly apply. In related work, Hatano and Inagaki (1987) have argued that differences in level of comprehension (deeper understanding versus more superficial comprehension) may be attributed to differences in motivation, and that those with a deep comprehension are more able to adapt to circumstances, see, and even explore different facets of the issue at hand. Moreover, the motivation Hatano and Inagaki (1987) are referring to may be regarded as interest generated, for it is when someone has a strong interest in a subject that he or she is most likely to find out how something works or find out more about it.

Thus far we have described, in quite general terms, a theoretical framework for learning, summarized in Fig. 5.1. In this framework, learning involves the perception, interpretation, and storage of information about the environment under particular motivational conditions that are generated by goals and/or interests. The acquired knowledge and beliefs are then utilized to accomplish goals and to fulfill interests. In addition, knowledge and beliefs influence the perception and interpretation of new information. This new information may include feedback indicating whether goals are being achieved. In some circumstances, information from the environment may lead to the revision of goals and interests, which in turn provide the motivational conditions for additional perception, interpretation, and learning. Thus, both value-based and intellectual "equipment" affect how individuals perceive and learn from the world. In turn, when learning occurs from observation of or interaction with the environment, both forms of equipment may be modified. We now consider some mechanisms of learning.

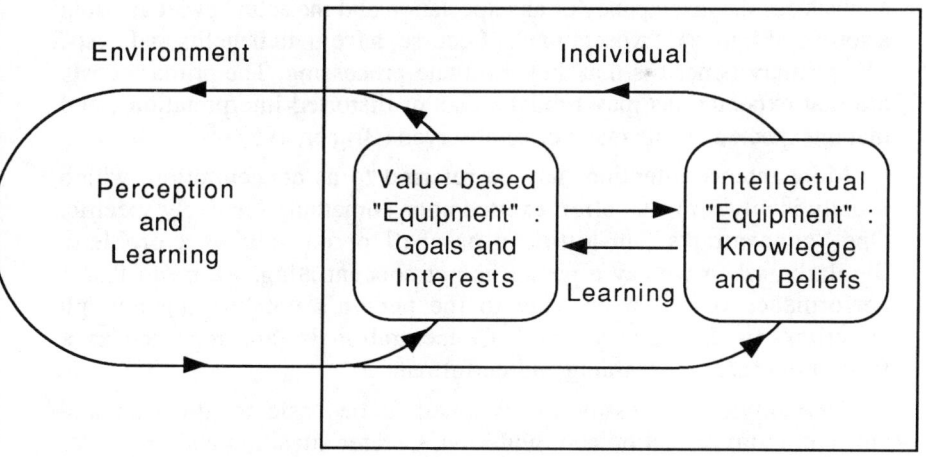

Fig. 5.1. Sketch of a general model of learning.

Some Mechanisms of Learning

Attention and Concentration. It is assumed that processing is related to attention. The environment is filled with stimulation, and the individual attends to only a small portion of it at any given time. But selection is not random; the individual attends to what is personally salient. Attention is selective, and selection is based upon goals and interests. Because of their relations to particular goals, stimuli can alert the individual so that events of potential salience receive special attention, for example, the "cocktail-party effect" (Cherry, 1953), in which the individual is sensitized to hearing his or her own name. However, much of what an individual attends to is under voluntary control, as in reading a book or watching a television program. These acts are related, of course, to one's interests and goals, because the individual selects what will be attended to, although attention may be overridden by a stimulus perceived as more salient. Absorption in a movie, for example, may give way to the smell of smoke.

Attention is also guided by expectations or predictions about what is going to happen in the environment, based upon one's models of contingent events, such as that when a stop light turns red, cars will usually stop. Expectations can also be general, such as anticipating a topic of conversation without having specific predictions regarding what will be said. Both general and specific expectations thus direct attention, while the individual works to confirm or disconfirm them. Indeed, Schank (1979) emphasizes the discrepancy of an expectation and the actual event as being a source of interest. Expectations, of course, have both benefits and costs. The primary benefit is that they facilitate processing. The primary costs are that expectations may produce bias or distorted interpretations, and that unexpected events may not be observed (Bruner, 1957).

More intense attention may be referred to as concentration, which usually involves mental effort exerted upon something relatively specific. One "concentrates" on hitting a baseball or on solving a problem. Similarly, when we say a person is not concentrating, we mean that a performance deficit exists due to the person's not "paying enough attention" to the issue at hand. Concentration is thus regarded as a facilitating factor in learning and performance.

Two related processes are assumed to be basic to attention and concentration: excitation and inhibition. Greater attending and/or greater concentrating activate representations in memory that are related to the input issue and its context. Excitation plays a major role in the direction of the activation established and in relating the new input to the existing knowledge, beliefs, affect, interests, and goals. The excitation process does not necessarily expand the number of interpretations but may result in exploring one interpretation in greater depth or in building a stronger relation.

Possibly the most important realization in recent decades about the role of associations in learning is that the links are labelled; that is, that associations are not mere connections but relations, an idea largely attributable to Selz (1922). Thus, the strength of the relation between elements is not simply a function of the frequency of their contiguous occurrence (although it may be) but of the nature of their relation. In the present context, excitation is assumed to establish these relations, with greater excitation serving to direct and to strengthen them.

It is furthermore assumed that attending or concentrating produces inhibition of information that is related to what is being processed but not relevant to the ongoing interpretation. The role of inhibition may be illustrated by the observation that when reading a novel the individual constructs a representation of the plot that is generally directly related to what has been read. However, he or she is apparently able to inhibit associations of the plot or characters and does not go off mentally in all directions. Instead, constraints are enforced. Similarly, when given the digits "2" and "3" and told to "add," a person does not say "-1" or "6." This capacity to construct the appropriate representation and inhibit others is a rather profound capability, and it certainly facilitates learning, for if the associates of given concepts were highly activated, they would quite likely produce a great deal of interference in learning. Thus, via inhibition, concentration enables one to keep mental interference to a minimum; the "noise" is kept out of the way, a process parallel to focussing attention on a particular object and interpreting it (excitation) while at the same time disregarding other environmental events. But it is also true that just as attention can be shifted when an event of high salience occurs in the environment, so concentration can be broken and shifted to a different topic.

Of considerable importance is the idea that excitation and inhibition are also related to motivation. Just as motivation influences attention in the selection of environmental information, so motivation influences concentration in the search and selection of the information in memory that provides an interpretation of that information. Furthermore, greater motivation is assumed to produce a more developed representation, deepening the interpretation and increasing the inhibition of potentially interfering information. Thus, learning is a by-product of processing because the excitation–inhibition processes provide for integration of the new information with what is already known, and the excitation–inhibition processes are a function of knowledge, beliefs, values, affect, interests, and goals. But learning is not always efficient. Indeed, it rarely is so, and in the context of the present model, ineffective learning is produced by ineffective processing. A brief discussion of some factors that may produce ineffective processing follows.

Factors Producing Ineffective Processing

Knowledge, Beliefs, and Affect. How knowledge, beliefs, and affect constrain interpretation has already been indicated. One cannot develop an appropriate interpretation when one does not have the knowledge or beliefs that relate to the input. It is possible, however, for individuals to construct an interpretation based primarily upon input information, especially if they are novices (cf. Fincher–Kiefer, Post, Greene, & Voss, 1988). The resulting interpretation is generally inferior to that of more knowledgeable individuals. Beliefs can also influence processing by yielding an interpretation based upon the individual's perspective. Such processing may not be ineffective, but it may restrict alternative interpretations. Again, affect can have a similar effect.

Motivation: Values, Interests, and Goals. It has been noted that the factors of values, interests, and goals both direct and influence the amount of processing. When they are maximally related to the task at hand so that motivation is substantial ("on task"), learning may be effective even when it is constrained by knowledge, beliefs, and affect. However, motivation that is not relevant to the task at hand can lead to ineffective processing. In the classroom, for example, poor motivation and subsequent poor processing can result from lack of interest in school work or lack of learning goals, each of which may also involve negative affect pertaining to the teacher and/or the classroom environment. The lack of a relevant interest or goal may even be due to a failure to value a school-based education.

Distraction. Motivation can produce distraction, if goals other than those required for the task at hand produce a breakdown in the inhibitory process. If an individual is attending to or concentrating on a given issue and something related to a different goal occurs, the inhibition process breaks down and the excitation process is disrupted. Although some striking environmental events, such as smelling smoke, will obviously have this effect, other more subtle events may also produce it, such as observing what another person is doing. Similarly, a person can be distracted internally by letting his or her mind "wander" to an unrelated problem or subject. Indeed, classroom attention and concentration require considerable focus, and thinking about seemingly "more important" but unrelated issues can readily disrupt the excitation–inhibition process.

Criteria for Understanding. The criteria that individuals use for establishing what is "understood" or "learned" are critical. Individuals will suspend processing when they believe learning has reached a desired or required level, and people are known to overestimate what they know (Glenberg, Wilkinson, & Epstein, 1982; Vesonder & Voss, 1985). Some individuals seem to feel that material is learned when they have obtained an "impression" of the given subject matter, whereas others will examine a subject in depth. For example, recent work concerning students' learning in a complex computer-based laboratory (Schauble, Glaser, Raghavan, & Reiner, 1991) found that successful students engaged in a search both broad and deep through the space of possible experiments, and generated explanations of their results that were consistent both internally (that is, with other knowledge) and externally (that is, with the available data). In contrast, the unsuccessful students explored very shallowly, designing only a few of the possible experiments, and their experimentation was primarily data- rather than theory-driven. They were content with post hoc explanations of unexpected results, without regard to whether those explanations were consistent with other knowledge they held about the phenomena or data they had previously generated. In school, where so much attention is given to test taking and grades, satisfaction with a very shallow degree of understanding may be extremely prevalent. For example, students studying for a test, especially those with low motivation, may study to the point of "impression" or a little beyond, especially given their tendency to overestimate their performance.

Having identified factors related to ineffective processing, this section concludes with a brief, speculative answer to the question, "What factors determine an individual's intellectual performance?" It can be argued that high quality intellectual performance is a function of at least four ingredients. As previously described, one is the individual's values, interests, and goals. A second is the person's knowledge, beliefs, and related affect. A third is experience in knowledge utilization; greater intellectual performance is associated with greater experience in using knowledge under a variety of environmental contexts and motivational states. The fourth is the effective operation of the excitation–inhibition process, leading to precise and appropriate interpretation. Thus, intellectual ability is related to the differentiation and integration of information and to the ability to relate input appropriately to what is in memory. Indeed, the last point is critical with respect to how a person generates new ideas and interprets input in ways other individuals do not. Knowledge and motivation are important, but in addition, the precision of the interpretation process is critical.

VALUES, INTEREST, AND GOALS IN SCHOOLING AND INSTRUCTION

Having sketched a model of learning in which values and interests, on the one hand, and knowledge and beliefs, on the other, play an integral role, we now turn to considering the implications of this model for schooling and instruction. There are two classes of implications. The first concerns our society's ideas about the nature and purpose of schooling, and how these ideas influence the values and interests of individuals. Second, the implications of our mcdel are worked out in a finer grained analysis within a specific subject-matter content area, science. The purpose is to illustrate how particular student errors in knowledge or strategy, often assumed to be exclusively cognitive, may in fact result from mismatches between the goals of instruction and the goals of students.

Values, Interests, and Goals in Society

Educational values are established by the culture and society in which the education takes place. They continually change in response to historical events and fluctuations in cultural notions about the nature of learning. For example, current concern about science and math education has been spurred by the poor showing of American students on cross-cultural tests (International Association for the Evaluation of Educational Achievement, 1988). This wave of consternation is only the most recent of a series of calls for curriculum and teaching reform that regularly accompany a climate of national concern about whether American students and industry will maintain a competitive position with respect to other nations (Klopfer & Champagne, 1990).

Aside from concerns about world competitiveness, over the past two decades swings in the prevailing views about education have occurred with ever-increasing frequency. The emphasis on child-centered, discovery learning periodically gives way to Back-to-Basics movements, and mainstream notions about what is important in education shift back and forth from a focus on problem solving and higher order reasoning to emphasis on drill and mastery of skills. In the United States, where education is perceived as a fundamental mechanism for achieving equal opportunity, the basic values that underlie education will probably always be subject to change and public debate. From time to time, Federal and privately funded commissions generate new recommendations for educational change and publish revised lists of national goals (for example, those published by the Carnegie Commission, and by the 1989 Education Summit with the President and State Governors in Charlottesville, Virginia). In spite of such resolve, there is probably less national unanimity on educational values than the documents imply or the public perceives.

Some value differences are obvious. In a number of American households, education is regarded as important, but the perceived importance appears to have more to do with obtaining a "good job" or going to the "right college" than intrinsic respect for the process of learning or the ability to think. Consistent with these values, pressure is high on students in some schools to obtain good grades so they can be admitted to prestigious colleges; in fact, in some circles achievement pressure begins even at preschool ages. In contrast to this near obsession with achievement and success, other families value education as an activity in its own right. Arguably, these are the familial and cultural values most likely to encourage interest in academic subject matter. And of course there are families and individuals who simply regard schooling as something that must be "put up with" until you are sixteen or until you graduate and can get a job, thus achieving a benchmark of adulthood and independence from parents.

Educational research, including most research on domains such as mathematics and science learning, typically views school learning as a process independent of the cultural context. The real question, however, is one of values. What is it that our society and students value? The columnist Mike Royko perhaps put his finger on this point when he wrote, in a column appearing in the *Pittsburgh Press* on July 1, 1990, that students know quite a bit about rock music, drugs, and sports, but cannot point to China on a map. He further asked how many parents of these same children will turn off their television set to read a book. It may therefore be unrealistic for educators to expect that children will necessarily bring to school a well-developed interest in school subject-matter or value for the activities of schooling. One primary objective of instruction within subject-matter disciplines is therefore to assist students in adopting, or at least in "trying on," the goals and interests consistent with learning for understanding.

Values, Interests, and Goals in the Classroom

An example of an experimental project with these objectives is Cheche Konnen (meaning, roughly, "Search for Knowledge" in Haitian Creole), developed to teach science and literacy in language minority classrooms (Warren, Rosebery, & Conant, in press). The objective of Cheche Konnen is to introduce students to scientific literacy by engaging them in scientific activity. Instead of working on problems and experiments presented by the teacher or the textbook, students learn to pose their *own* questions, collaboratively plan and implement research to explore these questions, analyze and interpret the data, and draw conclusions based on their research. For example, one group of students wondered why water from fountains at various locations in their school did not taste the same. The students began their exploration of this phenomenon by conducting polls of students to confirm the existence of a preference for a particular fountain, and then by conducting blind taste tests. Deciding how to carry out and interpret the results from the polls and the tests resulted in a series of discussions about issues like bias, effect size, and statistical reliability. The program of inquiry eventually led the students to conduct bacterial cultures of water samples at various sites, including not only the water fountains but also local ponds and water supplies.

In the Cheche Konnen project, students do not engage in "recipe-following" laboratory exercises in which they carry out prescribed procedures and hope to achieve the "right" answer (known by the teacher in advance). Instead, questions and issues of interest to students are used to motivate the kinds of information sought and the scientific methods employed. The purpose of the approach is not to serve as a substitute for the acquisition of basic science knowledge, but to provide a context for that acquisition. The process reflects the way that values and interests motivate learning in the practice of real science, in contrast to the more typical case where students are required to learn a set of disembodied facts and procedures. In addition, it provides experience in scientific thinking, including the often neglected issue of how a research problem is defined in the first place. This project can be characterized with respect to our framework of learning in Fig. 5.1 as beginning with students' interests, the value-based "equipment" depicted in the learning framework. These interests motivate goals, which in turn organize activity with respect to the "intellectual equipment," including information-seeking, search for understanding, and decisions about the specific strategies of scientific inquiry that should be employed.

However, it is equally possible to start with the "intellectual equipment," as does reciprocal teaching, originally developed by Brown and Palincsar (1984) to improve reading comprehension and now being applied and extended in experimental work to teach conceptual understanding in science, specifically, the molecular theory of matter (Anderson & Palincsar, 1988) and ecological cycles (Brown & Campione, 1990). In reciprocal teaching, the instructional emphasis is on developing strategies for the construction of meaning from textual material. A special role is taken by the teacher, who initially models strategies for querying phenomena and constructing explanations, but who gradually transfers control of the learning activity to the students as they become more proficient. At first, primary emphasis is placed upon strategies for monitoring one's own comprehension (e.g., questioning, clarifying, summarizing, predicting). As mastery of the comprehension-monitoring strategies increases, students are introduced to what Brown and Campione call "comprehension-extending activities," including drawing analogies, generating causal explanations, evaluating evidence, engaging in plausible reasoning, and conducting argumentation. Students take turns serving as the group discussion leader who, supported by the teacher, guides the group in interpreting, evaluating, and summarizing information. The idea is that these processes of critical thinking and learning, first modeled by the teacher and supported by the social group, will eventually be internalized by the individual and will thenceforth be available for application to novel content and even other subject matter.

The focus, then, is squarely on the acquisition of knowledge, beliefs, and strategies, the "intellectual equipment" in our learning framework. However, the focus is by no means exclusively cognitive. The cooperative nature of the procedure is an essential feature. The goal of reciprocal teaching is joint construction of meaning, and the role of the instruction in strategies is mainly to provide heuristics for getting that procedure started. New material is interpreted and evaluated by relating it to previous knowledge and beliefs, but no one person in the reciprocal teaching group, including the group leader, is responsible for knowing all the answers. Instead, the questions and knowledge resources of the group are to be drawn upon, and the entire group shares responsibility for coming to understand the material. Thus, not only are individual students' interests engaged, but in addition, the group members come to understand the goal of meaning making by practicing it, supported by the modeling of specific roles in a social learning group.

We have described two experimental projects in science instruction. In the first, learning is organized around students' values and interests. In the second, learning is organized around strategies for constructing meaning. Note that in both these projects, goal orientation plays a central role, as it does in the adaptive learning framework. In Cheche Konnen, students engage in scientific activity that is inherently goal-directed because it is organized in relation to questions that they themselves pose. In reciprocal teaching, students internalize the goal of reading to comprehend by engaging in social group practice organized around that goal.

An important feature of both of these projects is that they focus on the theoretical links between goals and performance. However, too frequently values have been disregarded in models of learning, in spite of the fact that it is values and beliefs that guide the setting of goals and the development of interests. Indeed, whereas a primary assumption of information-processing approaches to psychology is that thinking is organized in relation to a hierarchy of goals and subgoals, what the goals are and how they are established in the first place is rarely studied. More frequently, the goal is taken as the given, and research focuses exclusively on how search toward the goal proceeds. Yet, our discussion to this point suggests that there will be an interactive relation between understanding and adopting the goal of a learning activity, on the one hand, and developing the associated values and interests, on the other.

Typically, students are not expected to come to school with a mastery of the knowledge relevant to school domains; it may be useful, in addition, to take the perspective that instruction should also be directed toward helping students acquire related values, interests, and a generative understanding of the goal of complex and possibly unfamiliar learning activities such as experimentation, explanation, and reading for comprehension. Failure to learn is usually attributed to breakdown in one or another component of our functional model of learning, with little attention given to the interrelations among components. This kind of analysis is similar to psychology's multiple and fragmented pictures of mental functioning, described at the beginning of the chapter. To return to our original theme, education requires a more complex view of student learning and reasoning, one that views learning in the context of the student's overall mental functioning.

To exemplify the distinction between the traditional fragmented view and a more integrated view of learning, consider that motivation-based theories of psychology may attribute poor achievement in science to lack of interest, whereas a problem-solving theory may hypothesize that the student has weaknesses in particular cognitive strategies, for example, the widely studied scientific reasoning strategies involved in designing and interpreting experiments (e.g., Kuhn, Amsel, & O'Loughlin, 1988). However, a wider perspective on learning raises the possibility that if students show no interest in a topic or activity, this may be because they have realistic doubts about the relation between the learning activities in school and their personal long-term or immediate goals (e.g., Resnick, 1987). It is these kinds of relations that the Cheche Konnen project makes apparent. Similarly, if experimentation strategies are viewed not as basic abilities that emerge spontaneously at particular periods in development (Inhelder & Piaget, 1958), but rather as socially supported and enculturated modes of thinking, it is possible to consider how their development can be enhanced by the right kinds of cultural modelling and support. It is these kinds of links that reciprocal teaching focuses upon.

It is worth noting that this wider vision of science education, in which interests and values take an important place alongside knowledge and strategies, is in fact consistent with changes in views concerning how professional scientists reason. Inductive, positivist models of scientific reasoning have been replaced by a new attention to the social and historical character of science, in which the relevant problems for exploration, methodologies for discovery, and formal justification procedures are negotiated among the community of practitioners and the society as a whole. For the student, as opposed to the professional scientist, schooling provides the cultural milieu in which naturally evolving skills, like general induction abilities involved in reproducing favorable outcomes, can be gradually transformed into educated skills, like those required in generating and interpreting experiments. In this way, the relations between social values and schooling practices are twofold. Cultural values play a role in defining the desirable goals of schooling, such as the ability to engage in a specialized mode of thinking like scientific experimentation, and also in establishing a context where those goals can be systematically developed.

CONCLUSION

In this chapter we have been concerned with the role of interest in instruction. We have addressed this issue by considering how interest fits within larger questions about the nature of learning. We have sketched a model of learning that is broad-based and related to previous conceptions of learning as well as to motivation and perception. In doing so, we have tried to enlarge the modern cognitive conception of learning, one in which interest plays a major role. We have described interest as following and being derived from values, and, in turn, as generating the goals that motivate and direct processing. Such processing, when taken in conjunction with perceptual factors based upon what has been learned, provides at least a shadow, if not a picture, of a value-based, flexible organism quite sensitive to a wide range of physical and social stimuli and capable of learning an incredible amount about his or her environment. But what is learned, and what goals and interests a person develops, are fundamentally an issue of value.

ACKNOWLEDGMENTS

This chapter was supported by grants to the Learning Research and Development Center of the University of Pittsburgh, by the A. W. Mellon Foundation, and by the Office of Educational Research and Improvement of the Department of Education (Center for the Study of Learning). The views expressed do not necessarily constitute those of any of these organizations.

REFERENCES

Anderson, J. R. (1982). Acquisition of cognitive skill. *Psychological Review, 89,* 369–406.

Anderson, C., & Palincsar, A. S. (1988). *Teaching for conceptual understanding and self-regulation through collaborative problem solving* (Proposal submitted to the National Science Foundation). East Lansing: Michigan State University.

Atkinson, R. C., & Wickens, T. D. (1971). Human memory and the concept of reinforcement. In R. Glaser (Ed.), *The nature of reinforcement* (pp. 66–120). New York: Academic Press.

Bolles, R. C. (1975). *Theory of motivation* (2nd ed.). New York: Harper & Row.

Brown, A. L., & Campione, J. C. (1990). Communities of learning and thinking, or a context by any other name. In D. Kuhn (Ed.), Developmental perspectives on teaching and learning thinking skills. *Contributions to Human Development, 21,* 108–125.

Brown, A. L., & Palincsar, A. (1984). Reciprocal teaching of comprehension-fostering and monitoring activities. *Cognition and Instruction, 1* (2), 175–177.

Bruner, J. S. (1957). On perceptual readiness. *Psychological Review, 64,* 123–152.

Carr, H. A. (1925). *Psychology, a study of mental activity.* New York: Longmans.

Carraher, T. N., Carraher, D. W., & Schliemann, A. D. (1985). Mathematics in the streets and in the schools. *British Journal of Developmental Psychology, 3,* 21–29.

Cherry, E. C. (1953). Some experiments on the recognition of speech with one and two ears. *Journal of the Acoustical Society of America, 25,* 975–979.

deGroot, A. D. (1983). Heuristics, mental programs, and intelligence. In R. Groner, M. Groner, & W. F. Bischof (Eds.), *Methods of heuristics* (pp. 109–129). Hillsdale, NJ: Lawrence Erlbaum Associates.

Dewey, J. (1896). The reflex arc concept in psychology. *Psychological Review, 3,* 357–370.

Dewey, J. (1913). *Interest and effort in education.* Boston: Houghton–Mifflin.

Dweck, C. S. (1986). Motivational processes influencing learning. *American Psychologist, 41,* 1040–1048.

Fincher–Kiefer, R., Post, T. A., Greene, T. R., & Voss, J. F. (1988). On the role of prior knowledge and task demands in the processing of text. *Journal of Memory and Language, 27,* 416–428.

Glenberg, A. M., Wilkinson, A. C., & Epstein, W. (1982). The illusion of knowing: Failure in the self assessment of comprehension. *Memory and Cognition, 10,* 597–602.

Hatano, G., & Inagaki, K. (1987). A theory of motivation for comprehension and its application to mathematics instruction. In T. A. Romberg & D. M. Steward (Eds.), *The monitoring of school mathematics: Background papers (Vol. 2). Implications from psychology, outcomes of instruction* (Program Rep. No. 87–2, pp. 27–66). Madison: Wisconsin Center for Educational Research.

Hull, C. L. (1943). *Principles of behavior.* New York: Appleton–Century–Crofts.

Inhelder, B., & Piaget, J. (1958). *The growth of logical thinking from childhood to adolescence.* New York: Basic Books.

International Association for the Evaluation of Educational Achievement (1988). *Science achievement in seventeen countries: A preliminary report.* Oxford, England: Pergamon Press.

Izard, C. E. (1977). *Human emotions.* New York: Plenum Press.

Johnson–Laird, P. N. (1983). *Mental models.* Cambridge, MA: Harvard University Press.

Klopfer, L. E., & Champagne, A. B. (1990). Ghosts of crisis past. *Science Education, 44,* 133–154.

Koffka, K. (1935). *Principles of Gestalt psychology.* New York: Harcourt Brace.

Kuhn, D., Amsel, E. D., & O'Loughlin, M. (1988). *The development of scientific thinking skills.* San Diego: Academic.

Pavlov, I. P. (1927). *Conditioned reflexes* (G. V. Anrep, Trans. and Ed.). Oxford: Oxford University Press.

Piaget, J. (1981). *Intelligence and affectivity: Their relationship during child development*. (T. A. Brown & C. E. Kaeigi, Trans. and Ed.). Annual Reviews Monograph. Palo Alto, CA: Annual Reviews.

Renninger, K. A. (1989). Individual patterns in children's play interests. In L. T. Winegar (Ed.), *Social interaction and the development of children's understanding* (pp. 147–172). Norwood, NJ: Ablex.

Resnick, L. B. (1987). Learning in school and out. *Educational Researcher, 15* (9), 13–20.

Ryle, G. (1949). *The concept of mind*. London: Hutchinson.

Schank, R. C. (1979). Interestingness: Controlling inferences. *Artificial Intelligence, 12*, 273–297.

Schank, R. C., & Abelson, R. (1977). *Scripts, plans, goals, and understanding*. Hillsdale, NJ: Lawrence Erlbaum Associates.

Schauble, L., Glaser, R., Raghavan, K., & Reiner, M. (1991). Causal models and experimentation strategies in scientific reasoning. *Journal of the Learning Sciences, 1* (2), 201–238.

Schauble, L., Glaser, R., Raghavan, K., & Reiner, M. (in press). The integration of knowledge and experimentation strategies in understanding a physical system. *Applied Cognitive Psychology*.

Schliemann, A. D., & Acioly, N. M. (1989). Mathematical knowledge developed at work: The contribution of practice versus the contribution of schooling. *Cognition and Instruction, 6*, 185–221.

Sechenov, I. M. (1965). *Reflexes of the brain*. Cambridge, MA: The MIT Press.

Selz, O. (1922). *Zur Psychologie des produktiven Denkens*. Bonn: Cohen.

Spilich, G. J., Vesonder, G. T., Chiesi, H. L., & Voss, J. F. (1979). Text processing of domain-related information for individuals with high and low domain knowledge. *Journal of Verbal Learning and Verbal Behavior, 18*, 275–290.

Vesonder, G. T., & Voss, J. F. (1985). On the ability to predict one's own responses while learning. *Journal of Memory and Language, 24*, 363–376.

Voss, J. F. (1978). Cognition and instruction: Toward a cognitive theory of learning. In A. M. Lesgold, J. W. Pellegrino, S. D. Fokkema, & R. Glaser (Eds.), *Cognitive psychology and instruction* (pp. 13–26). New York: Plenum Press.

Voss, J. F. (1979). Organization, structure and memory: Three perspectives. In R. C. Puff (Ed.), *Memory, organization, and structure* (pp. 375–400). Hillsdale, NJ: Academic Press.

Warren, B., Rosebery, A. S., & Conant, F. R. (in press). Cheche Konnen: Science and literacy in language minority classrooms. *Cognition and Instruction*.

Task Motivation: An Interaction between the Cognitive and Content-Oriented Dimensions in Learning

6

Peter Nenniger
Universities of Kiel (Germany) and Basel (Switzerland)

The interaction of cognitive and motivational components in teaching and learning has preoccupied the educational sciences for centuries. Comenius (1627) emphasized that, in accordance with nature, effective teaching must not only facilitate learning but must also provide for its comfort and pleasure. Herbart (1806) stated that the cultivation of diversified interest is a necessary prerequisite for future learning and, therefore, a primary goal of every didactic treatment. For Herbart, this goal results from the fact that, although practical philosophy can be counted on to indicate the "necessities" ("notwendige Zwecke") of an educational concept based upon strength of moral character ("Charakterstärke der Sittlichkeit"), it gives no guidance in meeting the "possible future necessities" ("mögliche zukünftige Zwecke") of the individual during adulthood. Only an education that leads to a balanced mix of diverse interests can provide for the future.

Following Herbart's argumentation, Dewey (1913) stressed the necessity of interest for the maintenance of learning as a self-initiated, content-related activity, the mastery of which produces pleasure and satisfaction. Only a few years later, Kerschensteiner's Theory of

Education (1922) extended this same idea to aspects of value and social context.

In the second part of this century, motivational concepts related to education and instruction became more specific due to the influence of psychological research. Effective instruction came to be described in terms of the external conditions for learning (e.g., Biggs, 1979; Hameline, Nally, & Goldschmid, 1983), and the content to be learned lost much of its former importance in favor of a focus on the processes of its acquisition (cf. Wittrock, 1986a). In the last decade, however, this trend seems, at least in some fields, to have reversed itself.

In recent years, the question of how teaching can be improved to ensure effective learning has become an increasingly complex area of research. In particular, researchers have recognized that not only cognitive but also motivational components, such as interest, play an important role in student learning. Furthermore, the significant role of content in motivational processes and its concomitant effect on learning has been rediscovered.

The aim of this present chapter is to describe research that analyzes the different influences of achievement-oriented and content-oriented varia- ble structures. Different approaches to cognition and motivation are outlined in order to form a basis for a theoretical concept of academic learning, in which interest, as the crucial variable of content-oriented motivation, plays an important role. Related to these theoretical considerations, a structural model of motivationally based student learning is developed through the use of path analytic methods. With respect to the structural dependencies of this model, findings confirm that motivation plays a key role in the application of learning strategies and thereby exerts an indirect influence on information processing in learning.

The relation between motivation and the availability of learning strategies, that is, to what extent motivation is a function of the availability of learning strategies, or vice versa, remains unclear. Research into this question has yielded conflicting results (McKeachie, Pintrich, Lin, & Smith, 1986; Weinstein & Mayer, 1986), although it seems reasonable to assume a reciprocal relation between these two components of learning. In order to facilitate student learning of a task, the teacher must take into account student goal orientation and interest. These motivational antecedents lead to different learning strategies and, therefore, to different learning processes.

The first part of this chapter presents a theoretical framework for viewing content-oriented motivation or interest on the basis of general cognitive and motivational concepts and in light of studies specifically related to the role of interest in higher education. The second section describes the methodological background of a series of field experiments conducted in the United States and in Europe. In the third section the results of recent research in this field are discussed with regard to their explanatory power for understanding motivational factors, such as interest, on learning in higher education. The concluding section reconsiders the findings with regard to didactical implications for university teaching.

COGNITIVE AND MOTIVATIONAL COMPONENTS OF LEARNING

During the last few decades, most general theories of learning and instruction, as well as related suggestions for more effective teaching, have involved either a mainly cognitive or mainly motivational point of view. Concepts focusing simultaneously on both components of learning have been relatively rare.

Cognitive theories

Most contributions to the study of learning have focused on the cognitive components of learning instead of addressing the relation between cognition and motivation. For example, Ausubel, Novak, and Hanesian (1978) derive a number of related instructional guidelines from their theory of meaningful learning, in which the integration of new information into an existing cognitive structure plays an important role. Although in their complementary theory of teaching these authors argue that the motivational component of learning is less crucial in subject-matter learning than the cognitive component, they concede that motivation is necessary for the mastery of a given subject-matter discipline, and that, through a "desire for knowledge," it functions as a catalyst for meaningful learning.

Similarly, Gagne (1977, 1987) emphasizes the role of hierarchically organized conditions of learning during the acquisition of cognitive skills and ascribes to interest a mediating role in the learning process. For Gagne, motivation is a condition of learning that the instructional designer uses to channel the learner into task-related activities.

More recently, specific links between learning and various topics such as attribution, helplessness, volition, and cognition also have been described (e.g., Weinert & Kluwe 1984). On the basis of research on cognitive theory, a series of teaching methods has been proposed (cf. Kluwe, 1979; Wittrock, 1986b). Glaser (1984), for instance, proposes that training and practice in the use of procedural knowledge can improve context-specific learning abilities but admits the lack of stable findings on the effects of learning conditions.

These teaching methods are meant to enable students to learn more effectively. Dörner's research on the acquisition of knowledge structures. (cf. Dörner, 1976) describes a number of possibilities for helping students learn how to learn. However, although metacognition and, to some extent, the domain specificity of cognition are widely discussed by Dörner, the connections between these and motivation are quite general. They concern only achievement orientation and do not explicitly consider the relation between the personal meaningfulness of goal achievement and the subjective (idiosyncratic) comprehension of the contents defining the goal; that is, goals may be more or less desirable depending on the perceived characteristics of their content. Desirability of a goal, or the lack of it, then, would lead to different cognitive and metacognitive activities in working toward the achievement of the goal.

Effective learning is not only a matter of situational variables. It is the individual who actually regulates the learning process, based on his or her interpretation of the situation. Content specificity must be taken into account when considering the goals and interests of a learner. Because, however, the cognitive perspective already assumes the domain specificity of learning processes (cf. Seiler, 1973), it seems reasonable to also assume content specificity both for the reciprocal influences between cognition and motivation as well as for the metacognitive control over these two areas. This idea becomes even more plausible when one considers that, given a particular content-oriented goal, some learning steps will be more useful than others in achieving that goal. In addition, studies of the expert–novice paradigm have revealed that knowledge of the correct sequence of learning steps contributes to the effectiveness of learning. Nenniger (1986) found indications that context-specific motivation may play an important role in such learning processes.

Weinstein and Mayer (1986) extended this view of the learner as having an active role and emphasized the importance of learning strategies in the learning process. Their work suggests that there are four major components of learning: selection of information in the environment, storage of information in long-term memory, construction of new information from existing and newly perceived elements, and integration of new information into the body of the existing cognitive structure. Each of these components can be improved by activities of the learner, such as rehearsal, elaboration, and use of organizational strategies.

Levin (1986) and others argue that, in teaching students how to use learning strategies, one must take into account the properties of the task, and the learner's prior knowledge and skills. Not surprisingly, disagreement exists about which strategies have to be taught, and about how this teaching is to be done. This disagreement may be due to the general lack of empirical evidence in this field, despite a number of judicious proposals on how to teach learning strategies (cf. Chipman, Segal, & Glaser, 1985). The domain specificity of learning strategies, the teachability of metacognitive skills, and, on top of this, the role of motivation remain open questions (Chance, 1986).

In summary, then, contributions that address a cognitive perspective of learning appear to implicitly acknowledge some mediative role of motivation in learning, a role that seems related to metacognitive processes and goal formation. Furthermore, researchers increasingly ascribe more importance to domain-specific cognitive characteristics in discussing problems of learning and teaching, and largely neglect domain-specific motivation.

Motivational theories

A different line of argumentation about the relation between cognitive processes and motivation has been adopted by researchers in motivation. Instead of emphasizing the outcomes of various learning processes, these investigators have focused on the goal-related effects of activities involving the object of motivated behavior. As is made clear in the following overview of several approaches, the starting point of the line of argumentation is formed by studies of the motivating effect of the characteristics of the situational context, and the provisional endpoint is formed by studies of the motivational effect of content-related goals.

Although Berlyne's contributions on curiosity and exploratory behavior in intrinsic motivation (e.g., Berlyne, 1949, 1960, 1978) must be mentioned in any overview of work on learning motivation, the most salient example in the field remains Heckhausen's explanation of learning motivation. In the first version (Heckhausen, 1968), Atkinson's (1964) expectancy–value model was completed by additional tasks (e.g., novelty, subject matter-related incentive-value) and personality related elements (e.g., need for consent, need for self-esteem). Heckhausen and Rheinberg (1980) further differentiated the core of this model into situation–outcome, action–outcome, and outcome–consequence related expectencies. Thus, these authors distinguish between several types of learning motivation and establish a base for a more consistent explanation of the outcomes of learning-related action tendencies in light of particular task characteristics.

Heckhausen and Rheinberg's (1980) model of learning motivation based on a theory of action, for example, shows that the extent and intensity of learning depend not only on the apparent likelihood of achieving an immediate goal (e.g., passing a test on Friday) and a desired outcome (e.g., parental praise for a good grade) but also depend on additional factors, such as whether one ascribes one's success to personal effort or simple luck. This perspective recognizes, then, that motivation to learn is a function of both the learner's characteristics as well as the special conditions of the learning situation. In spite of this, motivational research still lacks a more explicit consideration of specific content-related characteristics, just as an explicit integration of the motivational concept remains missing from models of cognitive information processing.

Earlier theoretical conceptualizations of learning and teaching (e.g., Bruner, 1961, 1966; Lompscher, 1972, 1975) represented a first step in overcoming these deficiencies. The issue of content specificity found its way into these conceptualizations by virtue of their focus on school learning, the measurement of which requires a content-oriented perspective. The motivational components of learning, however, were of only secondary importance in these theories.

In his discovery–learning theory, Bruner included the structure of motives and motivational processes among the most important factors influencing the quality of learning processes but also included the degree of organization in the knowledge base, the level of intellectual skills, the mastery of heuristic methods, and the general learning attitude. Lompscher (1972), as an activity theorist, also recognized the impact of motivation on the course of a specific learning activity, which he defined by the operational skills required for the solution of a specific task.

In terms of a theory of motivation, Eccles (1983) took things one step further in this direction in that she combined different approaches to achievement and intrinsic motivation in her model of achievement motivation. Eccles showed how several expectancy and value components are related to persistence and achievement behavior. McKeachie, Pintrich, Lin, and Smith (1986) then extended this work by considering the interactions of different motivational elements (e.g., perceived self-competence, task difficulty, test anxiety) in learning-related expectancy, task value, and goal formation. In both of these approaches, however, the content relation within the task is treated only formally, focusing on the relation between motivation and learning outcome. Explicit links to the actual content to be learned remain rare.

It is only in recent years, mainly in Europe, that researchers have considered more explicitly the relation between motivation for a learning task and the content of that task. In particular, it is now acknowledged that viewing motivation exclusively from a functional point of view (i.e., with respect to initiation and maintenance of cognitive processes) is a shortcoming of current research (cf. Nuttin, 1980), and that content-specific characteristics (i.e., how the motivation associated with these cognitive processes is also linked with the semantic structure of the subject matter to be learned) also play an important role in information processing.

H. Schiefele (1974) and, more explicitly, Lind (1975) were among the first to describe content-oriented motivation. They considered Berlyne's (1960, 1978) collative stimulus properties to be the arousal potential of tasks. These stimulus properties center primarily on the formal properties of an object of motivation and not on the meaningfulness of the content to be learned. Similarly, Matushkin (1982), in his theory of "cognitive motivation," and Lehwald (1985), in his concept of "quest for knowledge" ("Erkenntnisstreben"), give more explicit consideration to content as a factor in goal-setting processes.

In the Soviet theory-of-learning tradition (e.g., Galperin 1967; Rubinstein, 1964), learning motivation is explicated against the backdrop of a theory of action. According to this tradition, motivation is the result of cognitive processes and is characterized by a series of goal-related regulating behaviors during the learning action. An individual's concrete motives can be inferred from previous regulating behaviors that began a learning activity and that lead to its further development.

Whereas Matushkin (1982) concentrates primarily on the structure of goal-oriented regulating behaviors, Lehwald (1985), on the basis of the same general concept of learning activity, focuses on curiosity. Lehwald views curiosity as an actualization of the "quest for knowledge" ("Erkenntnisstreben") that causes the learner to give preference to new information and to integrate it into his or her existing set of knowledge and skills. Thus, the quest for knowledge is explained as a regulatory scheme in which goal-oriented exploratory behavior is governed by the motivational and metacognitive components of learning activity.

As an extension of these concepts of interest, Prenzel, Krapp, and Schiefele (1986) proposed a theoretical concept in which interest is centered on content, conceptualized as the "object" of individual interest. This theoretical concept may be characterized as the "person–object theory of interest" (see the chapter by Krapp & Fink in this volume), in which interest is described as a unique relation between a person and an object domain. This relation is characterized by a specific composition of three components: cognition, emotion, and value. An important aspect of this concept of interest is its intrinsic component, called "self-intentionality." Furthermore, it is assumed that the goal of an interest-oriented action is located high up in an individual's hierarchy of values. The main effects of a sequence of interest-oriented engagements are "persistence" (the maintenance of the relation involving the object), and "selectivity" (the content-specific selection of certain characteristics of the object), which become the center of further action (see Prenzel's chapter in this volume).

By way of analogy to the expectancy by value model of achievement theory, and in light of a specific person–object relation concept of interest, Nenniger (1980, 1988b, pp. 81–95) proposed a concept of content-oriented motivation that combines the expectancy X value concept of motivation with content-oriented motives in student learning. From an expectancy X value perspective, this approach adopted the idea that both the probability of success as well as the value of goal-oriented action are involved in carrying out an action. The goals of learning-oriented activity are often determined by the content to be learned. Within this conception, two dimensions are used to specify "content" more precisely: (a) "interest in a content area," and (b) "readiness for work in a content area." Therefore, in contrast to the theory of achievement motivation, where expectations are restricted to the possible success or failure of an action and its consequences, this approach of content-oriented motivation focuses on the cognitive explorability and on the personal meaningfulness ("Sinnhaftigkeit") of a task.

Empirical study of content-oriented motivation has revealed that, in contrast to the contextually neutral achievement motivation, content motivation maintains considerable plasticity over time (Nenniger, 1987a). Findings from these studies, conducted on the basis of content-specific motivation that involved the motive dimensions "interest in a content area" and "readiness for work in a content area," have shown that the motivational structure changes during the teaching/learning process. Following approximately 1 week of learning, "active interest" (i.e., the active part of "interest") and "readiness" take on additional activating aspects. Once the teaching/learning process has been completed, these aspects again gradually recede, returning to their starting points approximately 5–7 weeks later. These findings indicate that content-specific motivation not only functions as a component in the control of the learning process but is itself a function of the learning process.

In a further analysis, Eigler, Macke, and Nenniger (1983) were able to show a high sensitivity of content-oriented motivation to different instructional conditions, again, in contrast to achievement motivation. This study, involving students majoring in mathematics, showed that content-oriented motivation developed differentially as a function of instructional method (e.g., active learning vs. receptive learning). Thus, motivation complements teaching strategy, whereby student readiness to work, student interest, and appropriate structuring of learning conditions can promote learning. This is especially true when the method of instruction reduces control over the learning process, and when learning skills are emphasized at the expense of content (cf. Nenniger, Eigler, & Macke, 1990, ch. 4). Furthermore, specific effects on causal attributions, on knowledge and skill-related information processing (cf. Nenniger, 1986, 1988b, chap. 4.4.1), and on content-related cognitive structures (cf. Nenniger et al., 1990, Study 2) have been demonstrated. These studies investigated attributions in the case of mastery learning. The results indicated that, to some extent, preferred causal attributions depend on instructional conditions and dominant motives. In an extension of Weiner's theoretical concept (cf. Weiner, 1986), it became clear that the attribution of academic achievement depends not only on a motivationally based preference for certain causal factors but also—at least when learning goals are achieved—that these preferences are embedded in a more or less stable causal structure (in the sense of a general attitude).

These findings lead to a question about the function that interests fulfill as central components of content-specific motivation in learning. For example, can interests influence the results of goal-oriented learning following the conclusion of instruction? One might conclude, on the basis of the available results, that during the process of skills and knowledge acquisition, parts of the interest dimension ("active interest") at least lead to active reinterpretation of the information to be learned. However, interest also has different effects on student learning, depending on whether the individual is learning skills or knowledge, and whether learning assessment focuses only on the outcome of learning.

Cognitive and Motivational Interaction in Learning

Several studies have begun to address the importance of an interactive view of cognition and affect in both motivation and social psychology (e.g., Isen, Daubman, & Nowicki, 1987). In particular, special attention has been given to interactions between study conditions, motivation, use of learning strategies, and academic achievement. McKeachie et al. (1986) provide an overview of this research and have developed a taxonomy of cognitive, metacognitive, and resource management strategies that forms a basis for empirical research on cognitive–motivational interactions in student learning. In their "components model of motivation," academic success is thought to result from independently chosen and consciously controlled learning activities. Academic success is a function of task-related goal orientation, self-appraisal of one's own efficiency when learning, certain anxiety factors, and individual expectations of success. From this model, one can hypothesize relational patterns between motivational and (content-related) cognitive elements of the learning task. In terms of study behavior, however, these patterns require further research.

Empirical findings available to date confirm some aspects of the model (cf. McKeachie et al., 1986, pp. 43–62). The results suggest that motivation mediates between learning conditions, learning strategies and academic performance, and the structural relations between these variables. A number of extensions of this model have been suggested in different fields of research, and, among them, the following most directly contribute to a further understanding of the role of content in the motivation of student learning.

Corno and Mandinach (1983) hypothesized that involvement in an academic task leads to more increased cognitive engagement, a supposition that was, in essence, supported by Pintrich, Cross, Kozma, and McKeachie (1986). Pintrich (1986), however, found (besides the many significant correlations between a number of motivational and learning strategy variables) only a few direct relations between cognitive, motivational, and performance variables.

In a follow-up study, Pintrich (1987) elaborated a structural model in which students' academic achievement (understood as self-regulated learning, choice persistence, and academic performance) depends on students' goal orientation, efficacy, control, and outcome beliefs, all of which are also related to perceptions of task difficulty and task-specific competence (components of the expectancy X value model of motivation, (cf. Atkinson, 1964). This analysis provides us with an approach that is based on empirical findings and that offers some insight into the general correlations between the cognitive and motivational components of academic learning.

Pokay and Blumenfeld (1990) extended Pintrich's model and used path analyses to determine the effects of prior achievement, gender, motivation, and use of learning strategies on academic achievement. Results from a study of high school students at the beginning and end of a semester confirmed the existence of differential relations between motivation and specific types of learning strategies. Specifically, Pokay and Blumenfeld found that, depending on the type of learning task, expectation of success and estimate of value had varying effects. Both factors determined the use of certain learning strategies and, therefore, had an indirect influence on learning achievement. But only expectation of success had a direct influence on learning achievement. In addition, it became clear that previous experiences with certain teachers also played a significant role. Also of importance was the content-related self-concept, which exerted a very general influence on learning achievement, on the valuing of the task, and on the use of certain learning strategies. The use of metacognitive strategies had additional effects. Whereas the use of specific learning strategies had a greater influence on immediate learning achievement, the use of metacognitive strategies had a greater influence on long-term learning achievement.

In a cross-cultural study with American (German-speaking) Swiss, and German students, Nenniger (1987b, 1988a) partially replicated and extended Pintrich's (1986) correlational study with respect to a selected number of cognitive and motivational variables. The results of the comparisons among the national samples showed significant mean differences in motivational and cognitive variables. Additionally, analyses of the respective correlational patterns revealed important contrasts in density and differentiality. Compared to American students, German-speaking students exhibited much lower correlations between the cognitive and motivational variable clusters included in the study. This resulted in the German-language students exhibiting greater variation in their learning, just as Pintrich's work would lead one to expect. Amazingly, however, the correspondence between the variable clusters in the subject groups was relatively low.

Results of a follow-up analysis of the correspondences between the observed variable patterns (Nenniger, in press) showed that the correspondences differed not only in the compared student samples, but also in the type of the patterns that were related (e.g., the correspondences of motivational with learning strategy patterns were different from those with information-processing patterns).

At this point, the question arose as to whether these differing correspondences between the variable clusters could be thought of as culturally based differences. With respect to a semantic interpretation of the related concepts, it appears that, with the exception of the concept "use of internal learning strategies," the terms motivation, learning strategies, and academic performance each have culturally different meanings.

In measuring the concept "motivation," one very clear finding was that achievement motivation played a more important role in American subjects than in German-language subjects, for whom lack of anxiety during learning seemed more important. Also, American students made greater use of study aids than German-language students.

Thus, although there is no controversy about whether content-specific learning strategies ought to be taught (e.g., Paris, Lipson, & Wixson, 1983), the necessity of generating specific learning strategies or adapting general learning strategies to new tasks and situations is of increasing importance in light of findings that indicate differential effects between achievement-related and content-related motives.

Furthermore, given findings that indicate that highly interested students have more numerous and more highly developed subject matter related associative structures than their less interested counterparts (Schiefele, Winteler, & Krapp, 1988), it appears that content-related interest influences learning and depends on content-specific knowledge and emotional feelings—variables that substantially intercorrelate and show significant effects on academic achievement.

In summary, current research on student learning in higher education suggests that motivation is a key component of both learning and instruction. However, this research also indicates that content-related influences (e.g., domain specificity, contextual interpretation, structure of the learning object) in learning must also be considered in order to specify the relation between content and motivation in learning and its implication for instruction.

EFFECTS OF ACHIEVEMENT AND CONTENT-RELATED MOTIVATION ON ACADEMIC LEARNING—EMPIRICAL STUDIES

Based on the existing research, a series of related studies was designed to evaluate the role of achievement and content-related motivation in the use of learning strategies. It was expected that differences would occur, because different students prefer different learning strategies and, therefore, employ different cognitive processes, depending on whether their motivation for learning is more content specific or achievement-oriented. In order to make this clear, the correlation between motivation, use of learning strategies, and cognitive processes were investigated within the framework of a conceptual model that included both achievement motivation and content-specific motivation.

Subjects. A total of 160 students (45 students from the University of Kiel, Germany; 50 students from the University of Basle; and 65 students from the University of Geneva, Switzerland) were evaluated during their first and second years at the university.

Instruments. All students received a modified form of Pintrich's Motivated-Learning-Strategies Questionnaire (MLSQ) (cf. Pintrich, Smith, & McKeachie, 1989) during their educational psychology class. The MLSQ is a self-report Likert–type measure, based on Weinstein's Learning And Study Strategies Inventory (LASSI) (Weinstein, Schulte, & Palmer, 1987) with scales such as "Goal Adoption," "Study Orientation," "Course Attitude," "Self-Concept," "Achievement Motivation," "Content Motivation," "Test-Anxiety," "Organization of Study Environment," "Time Scheduling," "Use of Study Aids," "Test Taking Strategy," "Note Taking Strategy," "Active Reading," "Information Processing with Respect to Memory, Comprehension, Acquisition, and Transfer," "Metacognition," and "Concentration."

Variables. Consideration of the following five latent variables, which were constructed on the basis of student responses to a selected number of the preceding scales, is critical to the present discussion: motivation, monitoring, internal learning strategies, external learning strategies and information processing. The sample items in Fig. 6.1 explain the content of these five dimensions.

These five dimensions represent a model for explaining motivated academic learning. The model contains the following components (latent variables): The first model component, Motivation, refers to emotional and motivational control mechanisms used in learning and thinking. They are represented in the following five scales: (a) Test Anxiety (8 items); (b) Self-Concept (4 items); (c) Content Motivation: Interest (4 items); (d) Content Motivation: Readiness (4 items); and (e) Achievement Motivation (5 items).

The second model component, Cognitive Monitoring, represents factors that control thinking and learning processes on the cognitive level. It consists of two scales: (a) Concentration (3 items); and (b) Meta-cognition (2 items).

The third model component, Internal Learning Strategies, represents learning strategies having to do with the internal course of learning. It consists of the four scales: (a) Note Taking (4 items); (b) Self Test of Learning Process (2 items); (c) Active Reading (3 items); and (d) Selection of Main Ideas from Text (2 items).

The fourth model component, External Learning Strategies, refers to learning strategies having to do with the shaping of external learning conditions. It consists of four scales: (a) Organization of Study Environment (4 items); (b) Use of Study Aids (3 items); (c) Organization of the Time Schedule (4 items), and (d) Test Taking (4 items).

The fifth model component, Information Processing, represents forms of behavior that describe the use of selected cognitive processes during learning. It consists of the following four scales: (a) Perception-Related Activities (3 items); (b) Acquisition-Related Activities (3 items); (c) Comprehension-Related Activities (3 items); and (d) Transfer-Related Activities (3 items).

Modeling. On the basis of these model components, a causal analysis was conducted using Wold's (1981) partial least squares procedure. This analysis used a causal model in which the component "information processing" (INF–PROC) depended on the components "internal learning strategies" (LS–INT) and "external learning strategies" (LS–EXT). "Internal learning strategies" (LS–INT) depended on "cognitive monitoring" processes (MONITOR) and "motivation" (MOTIVATION). Finally, "external learning strategies" (LS–EXT) depended on "motivation" (see Fig. 6.2).

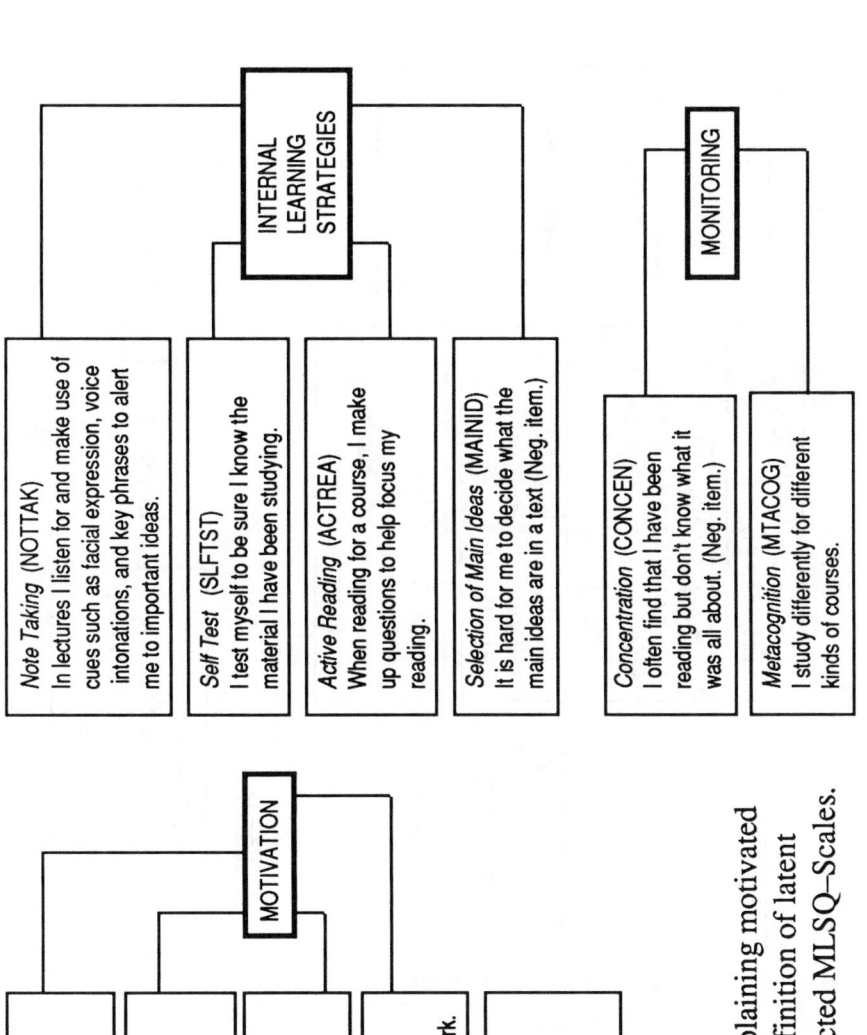

Fig. 6.1. Model for explaining motivated academic learning. Definition of latent variables based on selected MLSQ–Scales.

The figure contains the following boxes and labels:

MOTIVATION

Anxiety (ANXTY)
When I take a test, I feel I may not do as well as I could.

Self-Concept (SLFCON)
I expect to do well in college because I am smart.

Interest (CM-INT)
I have fun in elaborating new views of my subject for myself.

Readiness (CM-REA)
In my proper studies I don't need any encouragement to work.

Achievement (ACHMOT)
When work is difficult, I either give up or study only the easy parts. (Neg. item.)

INTERNAL LEARNING STRATEGIES

Note Taking (NOTTAK)
In lectures I listen for and make use of cues such as facial expression, voice intonations, and key phrases to alert me to important ideas.

Self Test (SLFTST)
I test myself to be sure I know the material I have been studying.

Active Reading (ACTREA)
When reading for a course, I make up questions to help focus my reading.

Selection of Main Ideas (MAINID)
It is hard for me to decide what the main ideas are in a text (Neg. item.)

MONITORING

Concentration (CONCEN)
I often find that I have been reading but don't know what it was all about. (Neg. item.)

Metacognition (MTACOG)
I study differently for different kinds of courses.

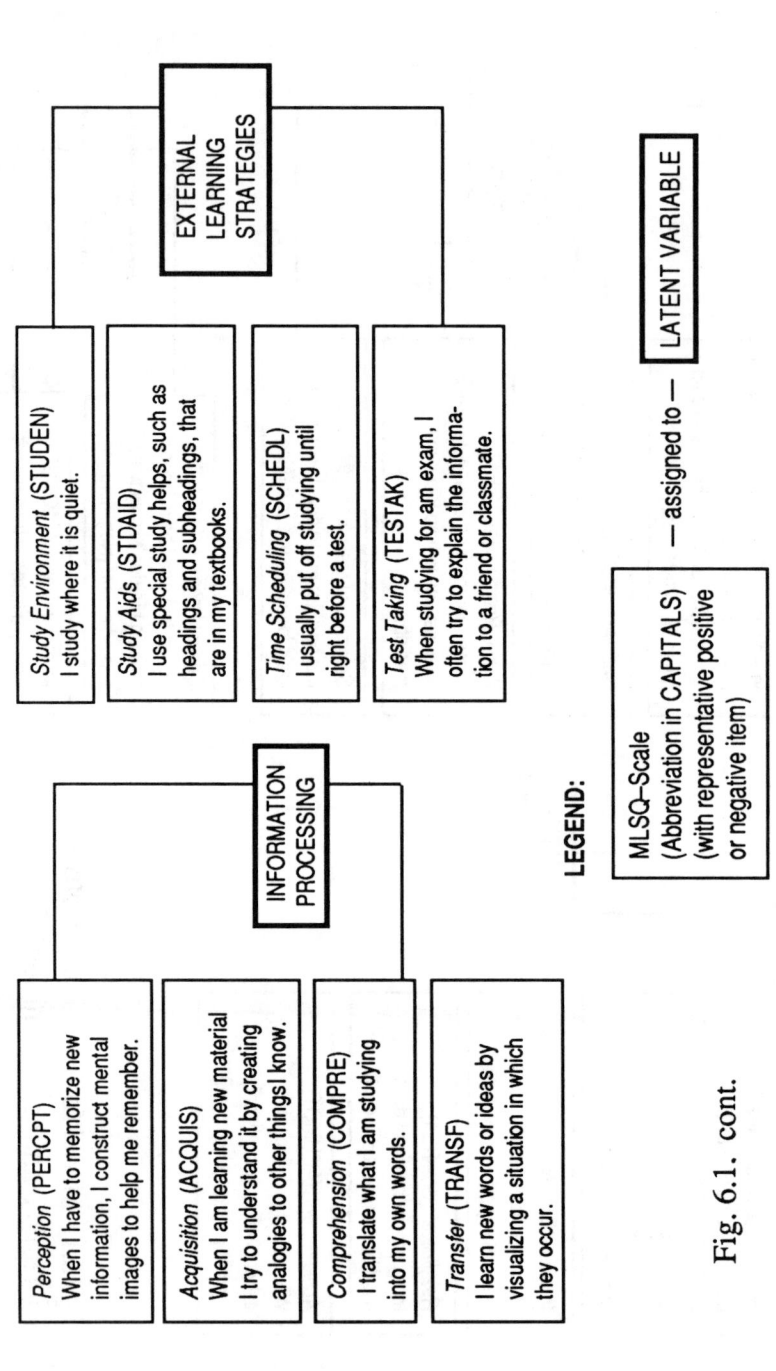

Fig. 6.1. cont.

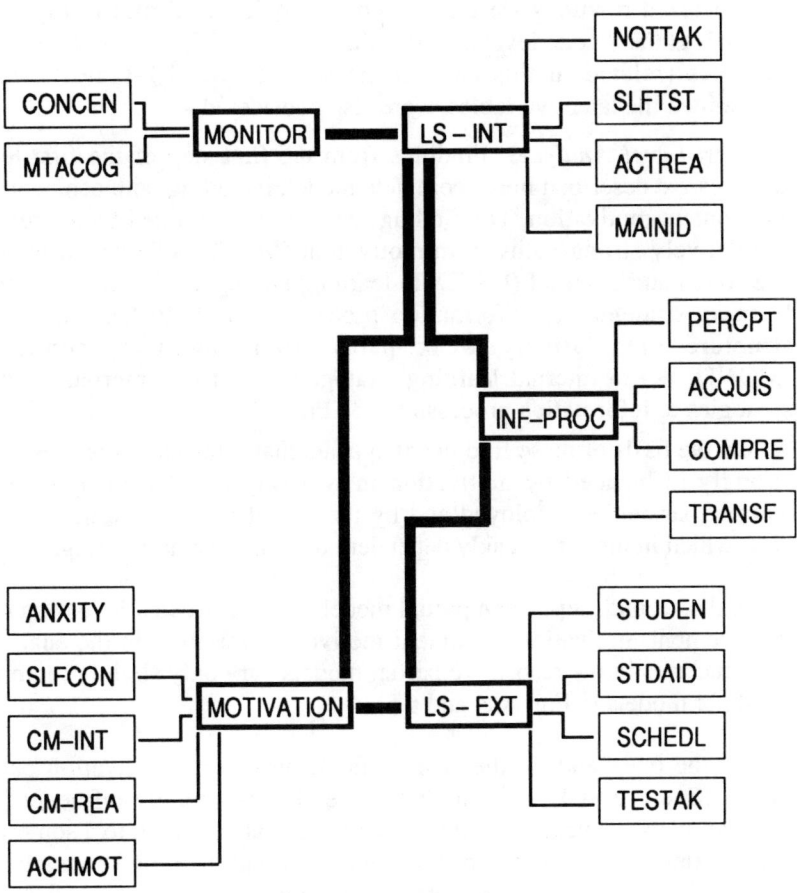

Fig. 6.2. General causal model (Internal model in bold).

The analysis of the path model was carried out in a series of steps on two levels: At the first level, only the "inner model" of the analyzed structure was considered, in that only the latent variables with their hypothesized relations were involved (see bold-faced part in Fig. 6.2). Analysis at the second level included the "outer model," in that the exterior variables (related in this case to the selected MLSQ–scales), which determined the latent variables, were also considered.

First-Level Analyses. Findings from the first step of the first-level analyses are described in the complete model, including both achievement and content motivation. The findings can be characterized by a structure of relatively strong paths from motivation (MOTIVATION) to internal (LS–INT) and external (LS–EXT) learning strategies, and from external learning strategies to information processing (INF–PROC), and by a structure of relatively weak paths from cognitive monitoring (MONITOR) to internal learning strategies, and from internal learning strategies to information processing (see Fig. 6.3).

On the basis of these findings it appears that information processing is strongly influenced by motivation in two ways, mediated by external learning strategies employed and by the use of internal learning strategies, which in turn are weakly dependent on cognitive monitoring.

In the second step, when partial models are constructed involving only achievement-motivation or content-motivation variables in the analyses, the structures in the respective partial models vary only slightly (compare the inner models in Figs. 6.4 and 6.5).

On the one hand, in the case of the achievement-motivation partial model (See Fig. 6.4), information processing is strongly influenced by motivation as a function of internal learning strategies and, to a somewhat lesser extent, as a function of the use of external learning strategies. No observable dependency on monitoring activities was found.

In the content–motivation partial model (See Fig. 6.5), on the other hand, information processing is strongly influenced by motivation as a function of internal learning strategies and, to a somewhat lesser extent, as a function of external learning strategies. The strongest path to information processing starts from monitoring activities and is mediated by internal learning strategies.

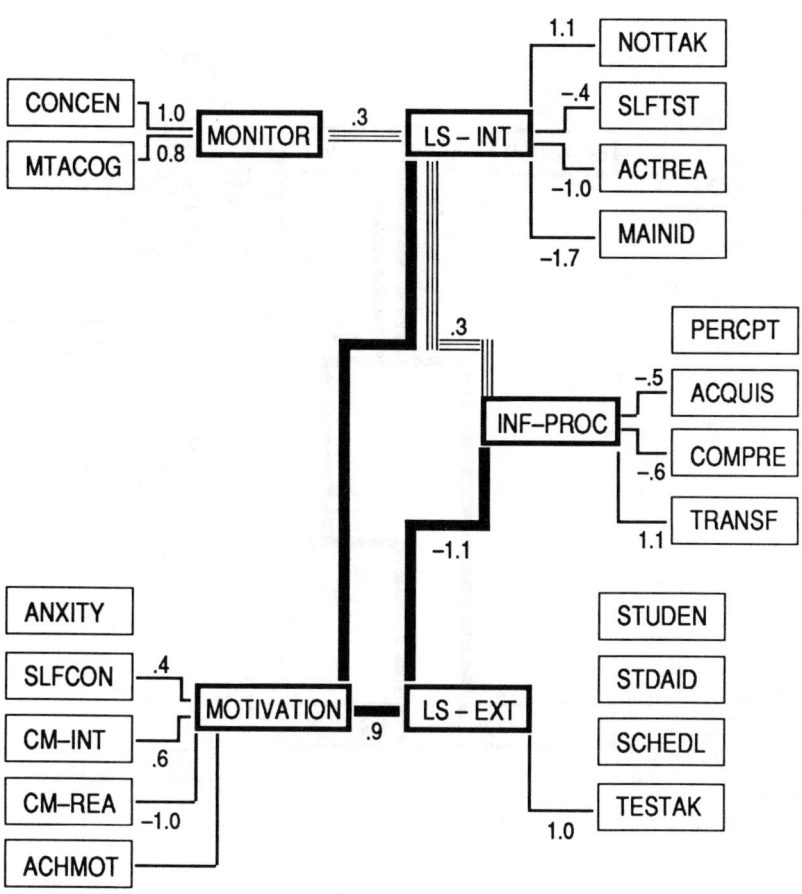

Mean Explained variance: .51
Residual variance: .72

Fig. 6.3. Complete causal model including achievement and content motivation.

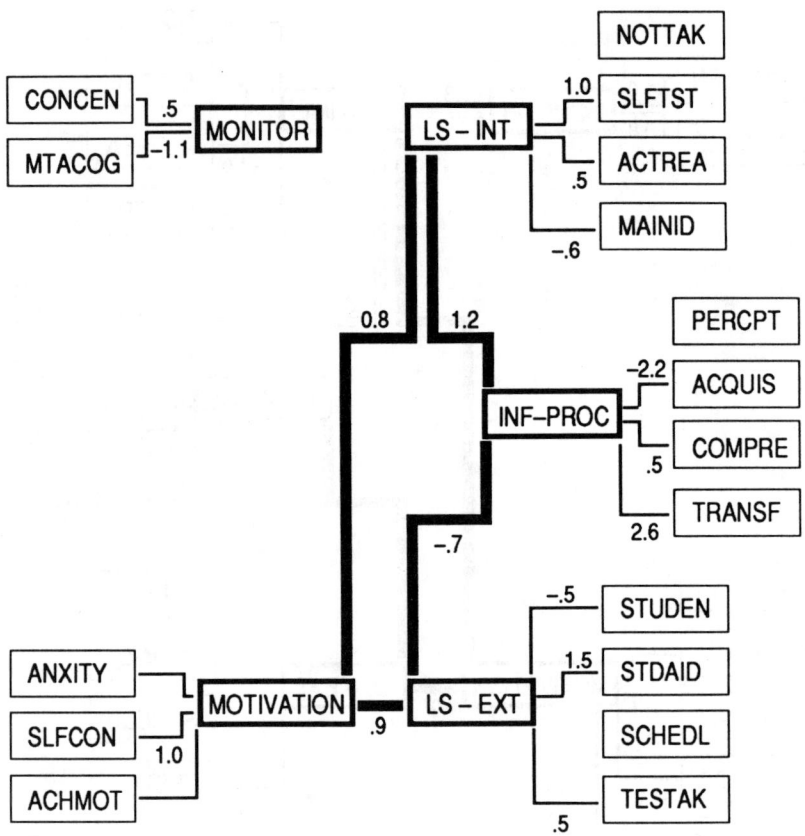

Mean Explained variance: .51
Residual variance: .67

Fig. 6.4. Achievement-orientation partial model.

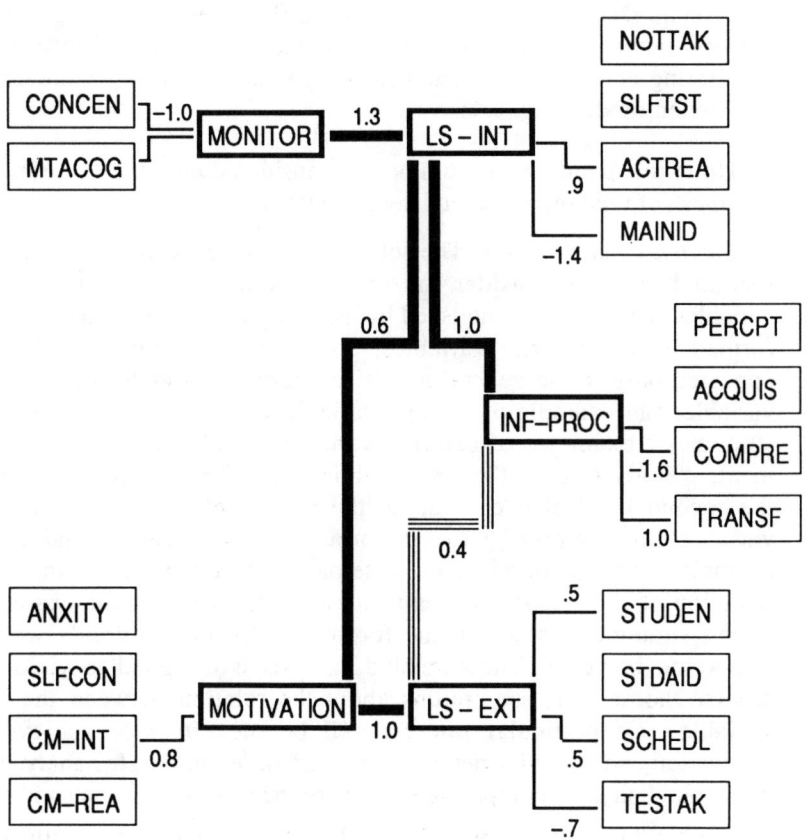

Mean Explained variance: .48
Residual variance: .72

Fig. 6.5. Content-orientation partial model.

Thus, a comparison of the partial models (See Fig. 6.6) shows a common structural nucleus with two paths of similar importance: (a) from internal learning strategies via motivation to information processing, and (b) from external learning strategies via motivation to information processing. Disregarding some marginal differences in the weights of the models' inner structures, the only difference is the lack of influence of monitoring activities in internal learning strategies in the achievement-orientation model (Fig. 6.4).

Up to this point, the discussion has considered only the "inner model" as a mesh of relations between latent variables.

Second level analyses. The following analyses were undertaken at a second level and consider the semantic background of these latent variables. This was accomplished by including the "outer model," which is formed by the exterior variables. So far, the exterior variables have appeared only in the general specification of the backdrop to the latent variables (an example of a latent variable would be "external learning strategies"; examples of external variables would be "Study Environment," "Study Aids," "Time Scheduling," and "Test taking"). Analysis at the second level also considered the weight of each of the external variables in interpreting the importance of the latent variables. For example, for the importance of "external learning strategies," the careful selection of the "study environment" and preparing for the exam, "test taking strategies," stood in the forefront. Use of study aids was also important, however. The extended analysis is designed to yield more precise theoretical assumptions about the relation between the latent variables. Of particular interest will be the effect of achievement orientation and content orientation on student learning. This analysis will be accomplished by comparing variants of the model with one another.

Within the general model (See Fig. 6.3), cognitive monitoring is mainly characterized by concentration and, to some extent, by metacognition. In the main, motivation is semantically determined by "content orientation." The most important distinctive elements of internal learning strategies are "selection of main ideas," "note taking," and "active reading," whereas "test taking" is the only unique element of external learning strategies. The main characteristics of information processing are "transfer-related activities" and, with rather marginal importance, "comprehension-related activities" and "acquisition-related activities."

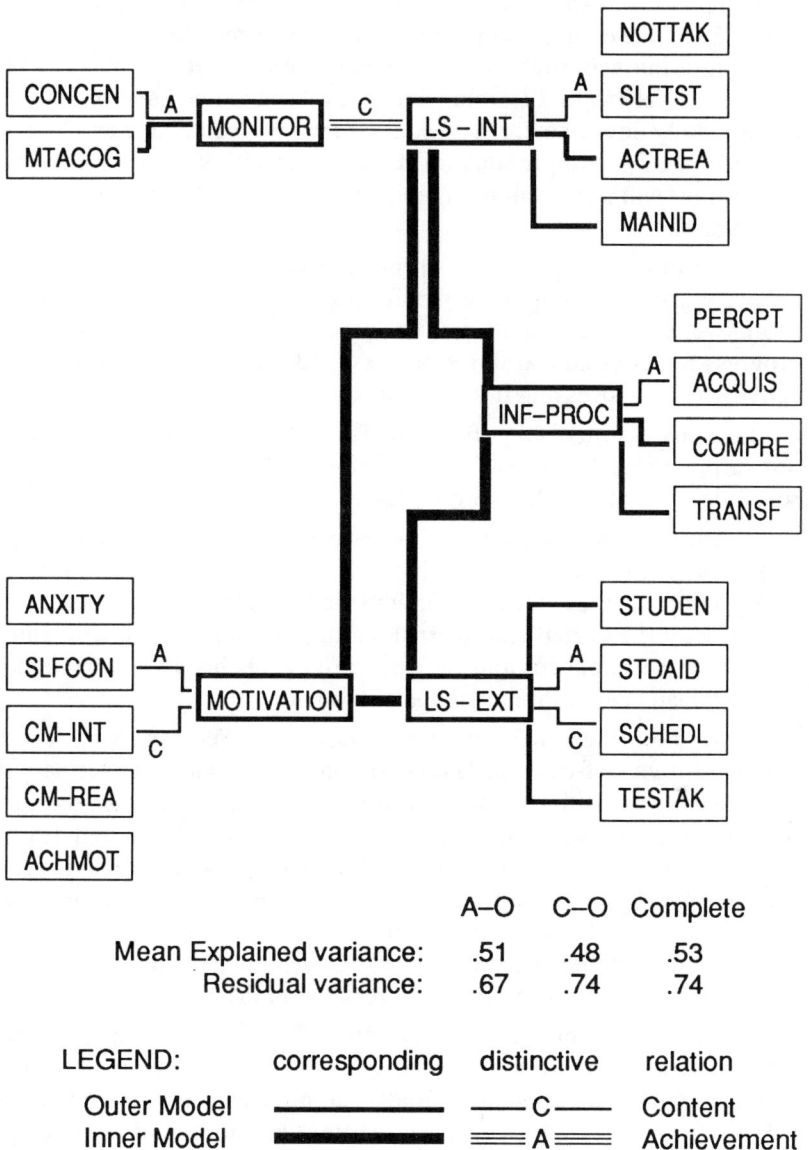

Fig. 6.6. Comparison of achievement-oriented and content-oriented causal structures.

As expected, in the partial models, the concepts take on more specific meanings. With respect to the semantic background of the concepts (See Fig. 6, 3–5), the common core of all models is formed by "metacognition" for monitoring activities, "active reading," and "selection of main ideas from texts" for internal learning strategies, "test taking" and organization of the "study environment" for external learning strategies, and "transfer related" and "comprehension-related activities" for information processing. Not surprisingly, there is no common core in the concept of "motivation."

The distinguishing features of the achievement-orientation model are "concentration" for cognitive monitoring, "self-concept" for motivation ("achievement-motivation" is of no importance!), "self-test" of learning progress for external learning strategies, and, finally, "acquisition-related activities" for processing information .

The only distinguishing features of the content motivation model are, not surprisingly, "interest" for motivation, and organization of the "time schedule" for external learning strategies.

Within this methodological framework, interpretation of the causal analyses suggests the following explanation: As a general rule, information processes are either impeded or supported by a selective preference for external and internal learning strategies that differentially depend on self-concept and on a specific, probably less achievement-oriented than content-oriented type of motivation.

From the achievement-oriented perspective (See Fig. 6.4), it seems that a positive self-concept favors comprehension and transfer activities and hinders acquisition of new information through frequent use of self-tests in learning and active reading. This pattern of internal learning strategies, however, does not include frequent selection of main ideas. On the other hand, within the same type of motivation pattern, frequent use of study aids as well as the application of test-taking strategies hinders transfer and comprehension but favors acquisition. Notably, emphasis on a well-arranged learning environment resulted in the opposite effects.

From a content-orientation perspective (Fig. 6.5), it seems that, on the one hand, interest, in conjunction with metacognition, favors transfer activities but, at the same time, hinders comprehension in learning. These effects are mediated by active reading/learning, and difficulty in identifying main ideas. On the other hand, interest also differentially effects comprehension and transfer in information processing through a decreasing use of test-taking strategies, combined, however, with an increasing organization of the learning environment and the time schedule.

Viewed in relation to the research results of both McKeachie and Pintrich (especially Pintrich, 1987, 1988; Pintrich et al., 1986; Pokay & Blumenfeld, 1990), the findings of this culturally based comparative analysis generally confirm the important correlation between motivation and the use of learning strategies. The findings, however, are still too general to prove or refute the differentiated dependency relations (made partially visible in Pintrich's study) between single motivational and learning strategy variables. Due to the highly differentiated nature of the original research question, the findings remain ambiguous. It seems reasonable to assume, however, that the narrowing down of the motivational concepts to those of achievement motivation, as attempted by Pintrich, has limited justification. Our results show that content-specific components also play an important role, at least in learning at the college level. The importance of the task-oriented self-concept found by Pokay and Blumenfeld (1990) could also be viewed as support for the importance of content-specific components.

CONCLUSIONS

This research provides further confirmation of the importance of motivational concepts in an analysis of academic learning. However, this research also reveals the need for a more careful consideration of these components of learning in terms of the content to be learned. Obviously, achievement-motivation accounts for only part of the complex mesh of factors involved in academic learning, whereas content-motivation involves another part. It seems that one must distinguish more precisely between motivation based on content and motivation based on long-term goals such as achievement. There is also a clear need to integrate the components of motivation, learning strategies, and cognition if we are to fully comprehend learning in specific environments. Any episode of structured academic learning involves a particular situation, a specific content, and clearly formulated learning goals. These aspects, however, constitute a meaningful structure and cannot be combined arbitrarily. Certain (not randomly selected) tasks are set by the teacher (not according to the whims of the students) and are performed with some (particular) goal in mind. This involves a variety of applicable learning strategies, which, however, must meet certain criteria of effectiveness based on theories of learning and teaching.

The analyses described here confirm the importance of interest as a central component of content-specific motivation. At the same time, however, it became clear that interest alone cannot adequately account for the entire motivational context of academic learning. Clearly, achievement-oriented motivation also plays an important role in students' learning. In addition, it could be seen that, although interest is a central factor in content-specific learning, students' "readiness" cannot be ignored.

One consequence of further considering content-specific components of learning could also be that, in doing so, culture-specific idiosyncrasies receive more detailed attention. Studies by Nenniger (1988a, 1989, in press), Kim (1990), and Karabenick (1990) indicate that parts of the framework for academic learning presented in the inner model (especially "motivation") are subject to cultural influences. The results of these studies indicate the desirability of increased consideration of the culture-specific conditions of learning (stimulus characteristics of the material to be presented). In addition, research results confirm the importance of personal preferences for particular *topics* during learning from texts. Content-specificity and interest in a particular object are central factors in academic learning. They determine the learning goals as well as the nature of learner engagement with the subject matter. In so doing, they also determine the quality of the learning outcome. Future research into teaching and learning should give more consideration to these factors and not interpret them only as a few among many variables in the explanation of differences in achievement. An individual's reasons for learning are not only conditional factors influencing learning in an additive fashion, but rather essential elements of that which is to be learned.

REFERENCES

Atkinson, J. W. (1964). *An introduction to motivation*. New York: Van Nostrand.

Ausubel, D. P., Novak, J. D., & Hanesian, H. (1978). *Educational psychology: A cognitive view* (2nd ed.). New York: Holt.

Berlyne, D. E. (1949). "Interest" as a psychological concept. *British Journal of Psychology, 39*, 184–195.

Berlyne, D. E. (1960). *Conflict, arousal and curiosity*. New York: McGraw–Hill.

Berlyne, D. E. (1978). Curiosity and learning. *Motivation and Emotion, 2*, 97–175.

Biggs, J. (1979). Individual differences in study processes and the quality of learning outcomes. *Higher Education, 8*, 381–394.

Bruner, J. S. (1961). The act of discovery. *Harvard Educational Review, 31,* 21–32.

Bruner, J. S. (1966). *Toward a theory of instruction.* Cambridge, MA: Belknap Press of Harvard University Press.

Chance, P. (1986). *Thinking in the classroom: A survey of programms.* New York: Teachers College Press.

Chipman, S., Segal, R., & Glaser, R. (Eds.). (1985). *Thinking and learning skills: Current research and open questions.* Hilldale, NJ: Lawrence Erlbaum Associates.

Comenius, J. A. (1627) *Magna Didactica* [Grosse Didaktik, translated and edited by A. Flitner]. Düsseldorf: Schwann.

Corno, L., & Mandinach, E. (1983). The role of cognitive engagement in classroom learning and motivation. *Educational Psychologist, 18,* 88–100.

Dewey, J. (1913). *Interest and effort in education.* Boston, MA: Riverside Press.

Dörner, D. (1976). *Problemlösen als Informationsverarbeitung.* Stuttgart, FRG: Kohlhammer.

Eccles, J. (1983). Expectancies, values and academic behaviors. In J. T. Spence (Ed.), *Achievement and achievement motives.* San Francisco, CA: Freeman.

Eigler, G., Macke, G., & Nenniger, P. (1983). Entwicklung kognitiver Strukturen—kognitive und motivationale Komponenten. In H. Mandl & L. Kätter (Eds.), *Jahrbuch Empirische Erziehungswissenschaft* (pp. 171–206). Düsseldorf, FRG: Schwann.

Gagne, R. M. (1977). *The conditions of learning* ([3rd ed.). New York: Holt.

Gagne, R. M. (Ed.). (1987). *Instructional technology: Foundations.* Hillsdale, NJ: Lawrence Erlbaum.Associates

Galperin, P. J. (1967). Zum problem der aufmerksamkeit. In J. Lompscher (Ed.), *Sowjetische beiträge zur lerntheorie: Die Schule P.J. Galperins* (pp. 15–23). Käln, FRG: Pahl–Rugenstein.

Glaser, R. (1984). Education and thinking: The role of knowledge. *American Psychologist, 39,* 93–104.

Hameline, D., Nally, J. N., & Goldschmid, M. L. (1983). Developper l'autonomie et la participation de l'étudiant dans l'enseignement universitaire. *Education et Recherche, 1,* 59–71.

Heckhausen, H. (1968). Förderung der Lernmotivierung und der intellektuellen Tüchtigkeiten. In H. Roth (Ed.), *Begabung und lernen* (pp. 193–228). Stuttgart, FRG: Klett.

Heckhausen, H., & Rheinberg, F. (1980). Lernmotivation im Unterricht, erneut betrachtet. *Unterrichtswissenschaft, 8,* 7–47.

Herbart, J. F. (1806). *Allgemeine Pädagogik, aus dem Zweck der Erziehung abgeleitet* [orig. 1806]. Düsseldorf: Küpper. (Herbart, J.F. Pädagogische Schriften Bd. 2.)

Isen, A. M., Daubman, K. A., & Nowicki, G. P. (1987). Positive affect facilitates creative problem solving. *Journal of Personality and Social Psychology, 52* (6), 1122–1131.

Karabenick, S. A. (1990). *The motivation to seek academic existence and its relation to other learning strategies: A comparison of United States and Indian college students.* Paper presented at the 22nd International Congress of Applied Psychology at Kyoto. Ypsilanti, MI: Eastern Michigan University.

Kerschensteiner, G. (1922). Der Interessenbegriff in der Pädagogik. *Pädagogische Blätter, 51*, 349–354.

Kim, Y. C. (1990). *Motivation and learning strategies of college students in Korea*. Paper presented at the 22nd International Congress of Applied Psychology at Kyoto. Daegu, Korea: Keimyung University. Kluwe, R. (1979). Wissen & Denken. Stuttgart, FRG: Kohlhammer.

Lehwald, G. (1985). Erkenntnisstreben, Lerntätigkeit und Fragestrategien. In J. Lompscher (Ed.), *Zur Psychologie der Lerntätigkeit* (Konferenzbericht, pp. 253–261). Berlin, GDR: VEB Volk & Wissen.

Levin, J. R. (1986). For cognitive principles of learning-strategy instruction. *Educational Psychologist, 21*, 3–17.

Lind, G. (1975). *Sachbezogene Motivation*. Weinheim, FRG: Beltz.

Lompscher, J. (Ed.). (1972). *Theoretische und experimentelle Untersuchungen zur Entwicklung geistiger Fähigkeiten*. Berlin, GDR: VEV Volk & Wissen.

Lompscher, J. (Ed.). (1975). *Zur Psychologie der Lerntätigkeit* [Konferenzbericht]. Berlin, GDR: VEB Volk & Wissen.

Matushkin, A. M. (1982). Psychological structure, dynamics and stimulation of learning activity [russ.]. *Woprossi Psychologii, 4*, 5–17.

McKeachie, W. J., Pintrich, P. R., Lin, Y., & Smith, D. (1986). *Teaching and learning in the college classroom: A review of the research literature*. Ann Arbor, MI: The University of Michigan. (National Center for Research to Improve Postsecondary Teaching and Learning [NCRIPTAL])

Nenniger, P. (1980). Die Bedeutung von Beiträgen der Motivationsforschung für eine Lehr–Lern–Theorie. *Unterrichtswissenschaft, 3*, 206–225.

Nenniger, P. (1986). The content-oriented task motive and its effects on the acquisition of knowledge and skills. In J. H. L. van den Bercken, E. E. J. De Bruyn, & T. C. M. Bergen (Eds.), *Achievement and task motivation* (pp. 135–145). Berwyn, PA: Swets North America.

Nenniger, P. (1987a). How stable is motivation by contents? In E. De Corte, H. Lodewijks, R. Parmentier, & P. Span (Eds.), *Learning and instruction* (pp. 159–168). Oxford, UK: Pergamon.

Nenniger, P. (1987b). *Kongnitive und motivationale Orientierung an der Universität*. Basle, CH: Universität Basel. (Psychologisches Institut / Fach Pädagogik)

Nenniger, P. (1988a). Cognitive and motivational orientations of U.S. and European students: Differences and structural correspondences. *International Journal of Educational Research, 7*, 257–266.

Nenniger, P. (1988b). *Das Pädagogische Verhältnis asl motivationales Konstrukt* (Ein Beitrag zur lehr–lern–theoretischen Analyse eines pädagogischen Paradigmas). Weinheim, FRG: Deutscher Studien Verlag.

Nenniger, P. (1989). Motivating student's use of learning strategies: Conditions and effects. In F. Halisch & S. H. L. van den Bercken (Eds.), *International perspectives on achievement and task motivation* (pp. 249–256). Berwyn, PA: Swets North America.

Nenniger, P. (in press). Motivierung studentischen Lernens im Kulturvergleich. *Zeitschrift für Psychologie*.

Nenniger, P., Eigler, G., & Macke, G. (1990). *Mehrdimensionale Zielerreichung in Lehr–Lern–Prozessen* [Studie 2]. Bern, CH: Lang. ("Collection" of the Swiss Society for Research in Education [SSRE]).

Nuttin, J. (1980). *Théorie de la motivation humaine*. Paris: Presses Universitaire de France. Paris, S. G., Lipson, M. Y., & Wixson, K. K. (1983). Becoming a strategic reader. *Contemporary Educational Psychology, 8*, 293–316.

Pintrich, P. R. (1986). Motivation, strategy use and student learning. Ann Arbor, MI: The University of Michigan (School of Education).

Pintrich, P. R. (1987). *Motivated learning strategies in the college classroom*. Paper presented at the American Educational Research Association Convention at Washington, DC. Ann Arbor, MI: The University of Michigan (School of Education).

Pintrich, P. R. (1988). A process-oriented view of student motivation and cognition. In J. S. Stark & L. Mets (Eds.), *Improving teaching and learning through research. New directions for institutional research* (pp. 55–70). San Francisco, CA: Jossey–Bass.

Pintrich, P. R., Cross, D. R., Kozma, R. B., & McKeachie, W. J. (1986). Instructional psychology. *Annual Review of Psychology, 37*, 611–651.

Pintrich, P. R., Smith, D. A. F., & McKeachie, W. J. (1989). *The Motivated Strategies for Learning Questionnaire* [MSLQ]. Ann Arbor, MI: National Center for Improving Postsecondary Teaching and Learning (The University of Michigan [NCRIPTAL]).

Pokay, P., & Blumenfeld, P. (1990). Predicting achievement early and late in the semester: The role of motivation and learning strategies. *Journal of Educational Psychology, 82*, 41–50.

Prenzel, M., Krapp, A., & Schiefele, H. (1986). Grundzäge einer pädagogischen Interessentheorie. *Zeitschrift für Pädagogik, 32*, 163–173.

Rubinstein, S. L. (1964). *Sein und Bewusstsein* (russ. orig. 1957). Berlin, GDR: Akademie–Verlag.

Schiefele, H. (1974). *Lernmotivation und Motivlernen*. München, FRG: Ehrenwirth.

Schiefele, U., Winteler, A., & Krapp, A. (1988). Studieninteresse und fachbezogene wissensstruktur. *Psychologie in Erziehung und Unterricht, 25*, 106–118.

Seiler, T. B. (Ed.). (1973). *Kognitive strukturiertheit: Theorien, analysen, befunde*. Stuttgart, FRG: Kohlhammer.

Weiner, B. (1986). *An attributional theory of motivation and emotion*. Berlin: Springer.

Weinert, F. E., & Kluwe, R. H. (Eds.). (1984). *Metakognition, motivation und lernen*. Stuttgart, FRG: Kohlhammer.

Weinstein, C. E., & Mayer, R. E. (1986). The teaching of learning strategies. In M. Wittrock (Ed.), *The handbook of research on teaching* (3rd ed., pp. 315–327). New York: Macmillan.

Weinstein, C. E., Schulte, A., & Palmer, D. (1987). *Learning and study strategies inventory* (LASSI). Clearwater, FL: H & H Publishing Co.

Wittrock, M. (Ed.). (1986a). *The handbook of research on teaching* (3rd ed.). New York: Macmillan.

Wittrock, M. (1986b). Student thought processes. In M. Wittrock (Ed.), *Handbook of research and teaching* (3rd ed., pp. 297–314). New York: Macmillan.

7 Topic Interest and Levels of Text Comprehension

Ulrich Schiefele
Universität der Bundeswehr – Munich

The relation between interest and both comprehension and learning is not a new topic, although it has long been absent from educational research (Krapp, 1989; Renninger & Wozniak, 1985; Schiefele & Winteler, 1988). Herbart (1806, 1841), one of the early pioneers of modern psychology, worked intensively in this area. He regarded the development of unspecialized, multi-faceted interest as one of the primary goals of education. In addition, Herbart assumed a very close relation between interest and learning. In his opinion, it is primarily interest that allows for correct and complete recognition of an object, leads to meaningful learning, promotes long-term storage of knowledge, and provides motivation for further learning. Herbart's work was not taken up by any immediate successor, and his theory lay dormant until the turn of the century, when leading psychologists and educators again took it up and developed it (e.g., Cattell, 1936; Dewey, 1913; Kerschensteiner, 1922; Thorndike, 1935a, 1935b).

Dewey (1913) continues to be one of the most important and influential theorizers about interest and motivation. Dewey postulated three basic characteristics of interest: (a) it is an active, "propulsive" state, (b) it is based on real objects, and (c) it has high personal meaning. In his opinion, the results of interest-based learning differ qualitatively from the results of learning that is based only on effort. Effort-based learning is mechanical and results in "trained" knowledge and habits lacking any mental purpose or worth. Interest, on the other hand, is characterized by a sense of pleasure arising out of and accompanying the activity. This sense of pleasure results from the satisfaction of psychological needs.

Dewey dismisses educational efforts toward learning that take place without regard to the material to be learned. He maintains, however, that being interested in a topic does not imply that no effort is required to learn about it. Effort is, in fact, regarded as an important part of interest-based activity. Dewey, therefore, distinguishes interest-based learning from learning that neglects a student's interests in that interest-based learning requires no coercion. According to Dewey, external attempts to "make something interesting" lead to only temporary effort and do not result in identification with the material.

Both Dewey and Herbart hypothesized that the results of interest-based learning differ qualitatively from the results achieved by mechanical or instrumentally motivated learning. Unfortunately, empirical research following their work has been limited to a few scattered studies (e.g., Bernstein, 1955; Witty & Kopel, 1936). During the last two decades, however, a series of studies focusing on the relation between interest and text comprehension has been conducted.

PRIOR RESEARCH ON THE INFLUENCE OF INTEREST ON TEXT COMPREHENSION

Although little noticed by the mainstream of text-related research, an increasing number of studies is concerned with the significance of interest for text comprehension. Initial work in this area was conducted by Asher (summarized in Asher, 1980). In recent years, more and more studies have been devoted to this topic (see the overviews by Hidi & Baird, 1986; and Schiefele, 1988).

The research has focused on two different conceptions of interest: individual or personal interest in a topic, and situational interest (Hidi, 1990). Individual interest is conceived of as a relatively enduring preference for certain topics, subject areas, or activities (e.g., Prenzel, 1988; Renninger, 1990; Schiefele, 1990a, in press b), whereas situational interest is defined as an emotional state aroused by situational stimuli (e.g., Anderson, Shirey, Wilson, & Fielding, 1987; Hidi, 1990). Research supports the general conclusion that both individual and situational interest have a positive influence on text comprehension (e.g., Anderson, Mason, & Shirey, 1984; Asher, 1980; Baldwin, Peleg–Bruckner, & McClintock, 1985; Belloni & Jongsma, 1978; Bernstein, 1955; Entin & Klare, 1985;

Hidi & Baird, 1988; Osako & Anders, 1983; Renninger, 1988; Stevens, 1979). This phenomenon is relatively independent of the age of subjects, the type of text (narrative vs. expository), the mode of text presentation (written vs. oral), and the kind of comprehension test (free and cued recall, "cloze" procedure, multiple-choice, and open-ended questions).

In spite of these positive results, the studies conducted to date are inadequate in a number of ways. The most obvious problem is the lack of an elaborated definition or theory of interest. The everyday meaning of the term *interest* is assumed to adequately delineate the concept. As a result, the measurement of interest often involves only a single rating scale where subjects are asked to indicate whether they find a topic or sentence to be extremely, quite, somewhat, hardly, or not at all interesting.

Another problem is that no attempt has been made to identify the features of interest-based text processing and to compare this mode with other modes of processing (e.g., processing based on extrinsic motivation). Only Anderson (1982) and Shirey and Reynolds (1988) have conducted studies that offer an explanation for the interest effect. They hypothesized that more attention is invested in interesting sentences. Their results, however, did not indicate that greater retention of interesting sentences is based on (consciously) increased attention.

A further crucial problem is the inadequate consideration of relevant control variables that affect interest and comprehension. Most studies have involved school-age subjects and have controlled for reading ability and text readability (e.g., Anderson et al. 1984; Baldwin et al., 1985; Cecil, 1984; Entin & Klare, 1985; Klein, 1979; Stevens, 1979). However, only a few studies have controlled for prior knowledge and intelligence. Although the influences of reading ability and readability on text comprehension have been unanimously shown to be independent of interest, these results cannot be transferred to prior knowledge or intelligence. Studies involving prior knowledge have achieved inconsistent results (e.g., Baldwin et al., 1985; Entin & Klare, 1985; Hare & Devine, 1983; Osako & Anders, 1983). Some studies have confirmed that interest affects comprehension independently of prior knowledge; others have suggested that knowledge mediates the effect of interest.

Finally, given the widespread preference for simple indicators of comprehension, studies of interest and its effect on reading comprehension do not allow any conclusions about qualitatively different levels of processing. Usually, these indicators are based on recognition tests (especially in a multiple-choice format) and, to a lesser extent, on free-recall tests and open-ended questions. Unfortunately, the use of these methods has been restricted to the measurement of purely quantitative aspects of text comprehension (e.g., number of words reproduced). In contrast, Bernstein (1955) proposed some time ago a number of qualitative comprehension indicators that could conceivably be influenced by interest, such as "word knowledge," "recognition of the main idea of a text passage," and "making conclusions about the text content."

In this chapter, I examine more thoroughly three of the problems just mentioned and offer possible solutions. Specifically, a definition of individual interest is proposed, the possible relation between interest and levels of processing or comprehension is explored, and the problem of mediating variables is discussed.

THEORETICAL CONSIDERATIONS

Conceptualization of Individual Interest

Based on older theories of interest (see overview by Schiefele & Winteler, 1988) and with reference to the interest concept of H. Schiefele and his colleagues (Prenzel, 1988; Prenzel, Krapp, & H. Schiefele, 1986; H. Schiefele, Hausser, & Schneider, 1979; H. Schiefele, Krapp, Prenzel, Heiland, & Kasten, 1983), individual interest can be interpreted as the relatively long-term orientation of an individual toward a type of object, an activity, or an area of knowledge (see also the chapter by Renninger, this volume, for a discussion of individual interest as a psychological state).

One must distinguish between two components of interest: a feeling-related and a value-related component. These components can be described more precisely using concepts from the field of motivational psychology. The taxonomy of motivational characteristics developed by Pekrun (1988) is central to such an undertaking. Using this taxonomy, it is possible to differentiate between cognitive representations of expectations, goals, and valences. Referring to this distinction, I propose to reinterpret interest as a domain-specific or topic-specific motivational characteristic of personality, which is composed of feeling-related and value-related valences. The term *feeling-related valences* is used when a topic or object is associated with feelings that precede, accompany, or follow activity involving the topic or object of interest. Typical of interest would be feelings of enjoyment or involvement. If personal significance is ascribed to a topic, one speaks of a "cognitive" or a *value-related valence*. On the basis of this distinction, it is possible to define topic interest as being composed of both feeling-related (relating a topic to particular feelings) and value-related valences (attributing personal significance to a topic).

A third important feature of interest is its intrinsic character, also termed *self-intentionality* by H. Schiefele et al. (1983). In the context of text learning, this means that the learner should be involved in a topic for its own sake and not for any external reason (e.g., passing an exam). The feeling-related and value-related valences can, therefore, be described more precisely as *intrinsic* feeling-related and value-related valences. To measure interest then, the topic valences involved must be directly related to the topic (or to reading a text on a certain topic) and not, for example, to other topics or external events. A summary of the proposed definition of individual interest is shown in Table 7.1.

Table 7.1

Definition of Individual Interest

Individual Interest (Topic Interest)	
Feeling-Related Component	*Value-Related Component*
Association of a topic or topic-related activity with positive feelings, especially enjoyment and involvement (feeling-related intrinsic valences of a topic)	Attributing of personal significance to a topic (value-related intrinsic valences of a topic)

Our discussion of the concept of "topic interest" has left aside a clarification of the term *topic*.[1] However, Hidi and McLaren (1988) have recently defined a topic as a "coherent knowledge domain of subject

---

[1] Of course, topics are not the only entities people are interested in. Krapp and Fink (1987), for example, discern three different categories of interest objects: activities, material objects, and topics.

matter" (p. 4). They cite "space travel" and "wildlife" as typical examples of topics that are of interest to school-aged children. Furthermore, Hidi and McLaren distinguish topics from "themes." Themes cut across different topics and are, therefore, more abstract generalizations of specific topic contents. For example, the themes "survival" and "future" can both be regarded as generalizations of the aforementioned topics "space travel" and "wildlife." Themes, then, can cover rather heterogeneous knowledge domains.

So far, we have only dealt with interest as a *latent* characteristic. In order to become effective, however, latent interest has to be activated by either internal or external stimuli. Therefore, it is necessary to distinguish a second form of individual interest, namely *actualized* individual interest.

Actualized interest is best described as a content-specific intrinsic motivational orientation. Basically, this means that a person in a state of being interested in a certain topic wants to learn about (or become involved with) that topic for its own sake. In other words, the interested person adopts a task- or learning-orientation (as opposed to an ego- or performance-orientation) towards a specific topic (cf. Nicholls, 1984; Nolan, 1988). It should be noted that the concepts of task- and learning-orientation are usually defined as general orientations towards learning material in school. In contrast, the interest concept is based on the idea that people develop specific relations with different subject areas.

Interest and the Concept of Motivational Orientation

The concept of different motivational orientations has recently been stressed by several authors (cf. Lepper, 1988). Motivational orientation generally describes an individual's habitual orientation toward certain goals. A good example of this is the distinction made by Nicholls (1984) between task-oriented and ego-oriented motivation (see also Nolen, 1988; Ryan, 1982). Other similar distinctions have been suggested by Dweck (1986; Dweck & Leggett, 1988) and Harter (1981). According to Lepper (1988), these efforts point to two central components of a motivational orientation conducive to learning: (a) the willingness to engage in an activity for its own sake (intrinsic component), and (b) the belief that one is the initiator of a learning activity and is solely responsible for its results. This also corresponds to Deci and Ryan's (1985) theory of intrinsic motivation, whereby intrinsically motivated behavior is based upon psychological needs for self-determination and competence.

It seems reasonable to assume a great deal of similarity between an intrinsic or task-oriented motivational orientation and the concept of interest. However, a major difference between these conceptions concerns their domain specificity. Motivational orientations are usually defined as general concepts. They are assumed to affect, for example, a student's learning behavior across different subjects. In contrast, interest is a domain-specific characteristic. It enables us to acknowledge the fact that some students are, for example, motivated to learn mathematics, whereas they really dislike learning a foreign language or chemistry.

General motivational orientations and specific interests are not, however, mutually exclusive. Presumably, a person has both more general orientations towards academic tasks *and* content-specific interests. It is believed that both general orientations and individual interests determine the strength and nature of the specific motivational orientation a student adopts in a specific situation involving a specific learning content. However, interest is expected to be more predictive of specific motivational orientations and, therefore, of outcomes of specific learning processes.

The Effect of Interest on Different Levels of Comprehension

To date, attempts to answer the question of whether interest has different effects at different levels of comprehension have yielded no clear results. Bernstein (1955), who conducted one of the first studies on the effect of interest on text comprehension, identified a number of components of comprehension, ranging from "word knowledge" to "recognition of author's intent." Bernstein's results, however, were not broken down into individual components, and it is impossible to know how many of these components were accounted for in her test of comprehension. A more informative study was carried out by Fransson (1977), who showed that students who were more interested in a topic exhibited deeper processing of a related text. Using free recall and extensive interviews, Fransson found that high-interest subjects made more connections not only between different parts of the text, but also between what was read and prior knowledge or personal experience. The subjects were also found to do more independent thinking about the text content.

In another study that centered around text comprehension, Benware and Deci (1984) demonstrated that intrinsically motivated students exhibit markedly greater conceptual comprehension of text content than extrinsically motivated students. No differences were obtained, however, in the number of details subjects were able to reproduce (rote learning).

Different types of questions were used to measure comprehension, including definitions, multiple-choice questions, and explanations. Using a different set of experimental conditions and procedures, Grolnick and Ryan (1987) came to essentially the same results as Benware and Deci.

Other studies have also attempted to investigate the effect of interest on comprehension by including various components of comprehension. Groff (1962) explored three levels of comprehension: recognition of text organization, inferences, and conclusions. Johnson and Jacobson (1968) distinguished between literal and interpretive comprehension. Similarly, Stevens (1979) differentiated between literal and inferential comprehension. Unfortunately, these studies only report overall results (which reveal significant interest effects), without separating the effects of interest on different components of comprehension. Moreover, none of these studies was based upon any particular model of text processing or representation. The criteria for judging depth of comprehension were deduced more or less intuitively.

Findings from two recent studies (Schiefele & Krapp, 1988; Schiefele, Winteler, & Krapp, 1988) revealed that university students who were highly interested in their majors did not produce any more associations with subject-related terms (e.g., "learning," "instruction," "socialization") than did less interested students. Rather, the associations of the high-interest group were more adequate in a technical sense than were those of the low-interest group. In addition, important differences in the cognitive structure of the stimulus concepts were found.

In summary, it appears that interest is of less importance when superficial knowledge, explicitly contained in a text, is required, and of greater importance when deeper comprehension of text content is required. It is presumed that an explanation of this difference can be determined only by examining mediating processes.

Mediating Processes Involved in the Effect of Interest on Text Comprehension

It would seem that the effect of interest on comprehension can only be explained by studying the *process* of interest-based learning, yet only a small number of studies concerning this issue has been conducted (Lepper, 1988; Schiefele, 1987). Such studies have usually been limited to the study of single factors, such as the role of attention while reading, and there has been a lack of more comprehensive theoretical consideration.

In this chapter, a model is presented that depicts the influence of topic interest on text comprehension as well as the processes that presumably mediate that influence (see Fig. 7.1). It is assumed that the stimulation of topic interest leads to actualized interest (i.e., a topic-specific intrinsic motivational orientation), which, in turn, exerts an influence on cognitive (e.g., elaborative processes) and emotional variables (e.g., level of activation) of the learning process. It is believed that emotional and cognitive variables interact with one another. On the one hand, emotional states presumably influence, for example, the willingness to use learning strategies, to invest effort, and to draw inferences. On the other hand, the level of cognitive involvement with the task at hand may contribute to the quality of emotional experience.

The outcome of the learning process is thought to be the result of cognitive and emotional processes. It is assumed that cognitive processes are generally more important than affective ones, at least as far as the immediate learning result is concerned. However, it is possible that this hypothesis must be modified according to the nature of the desired learning result (e.g., fact vs. conceptual understanding).

As is shown in Fig. 7.1, only indirect effects of topic interest on text comprehension are hypothesized. Thus, the effect of interest depends on its impact on the quality of the mediating emotional and cognitive processes. Because it is not possible in this chapter to focus on all of the relations between concepts shown in Fig. 7.1, only mediators of the influence of topic interest on text comprehension will be dealt with here. Specifically, previous research findings involving these mediators are discussed.

The work of Entwistle and Ramsden (1983, see also Entwistle, 1988) leads to the conclusion that intrinsic motivation to learn corresponds to a "deep approach" orientation to learning, which results in deeper comprehension. In summary, they report that intrinsically motivated students make greater attempts than other students to relate new information to prior knowledge, similar topics, concrete examples, or personal experience. The learning of extrinsically motivated students, on the other hand, is more superficial and mechanical, often involving the repeated reading of a text or outright memorization of certain passages.

In a recent study, Nolen (1988) confirmed and added to the results of Entwistle and Ramsden. She gave a scientific text to a group of school children and found that the children who exhibited a task-orientated motivation (i.e., motivation directed toward the comprehension of the

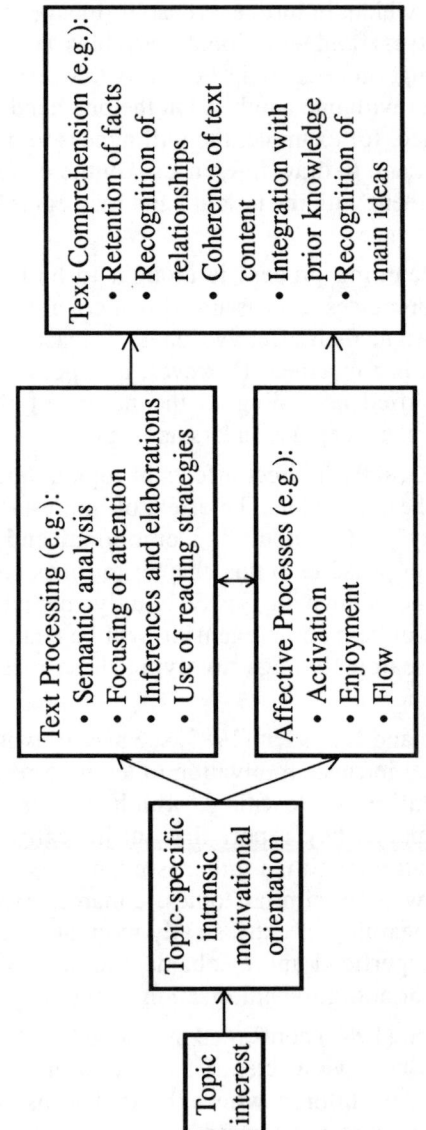

Fig. 7.1. Model of the relations between topic interest, actualized interest, text processing, affective processes, and text comprehension.

text), used learning strategies that permitted both deeper comprehension and superficial processing. Children exhibiting an ego-oriented motivation (i.e., with the primary goal of getting better grades than their peers) used only those learning strategies that allowed them to read quickly and remember the text. Self-estimation of ability to comprehend scientific texts and knowledge of learning strategies proved to be relatively unimportant in the selection of learning strategies. Unfortunately, the analysis of retention revealed little, because the texts used were obviously too difficult for the subjects and the variance in their scores was too small. Thus, no significant correlations between motivational orientation and retention were found.

Anderson (1982; see also Anderson et al., 1987) and Shirey and Reynolds (1988) investigated whether subjects invested more attention in more interesting sentences than in less interesting sentences. Two different methods for assessing attention were used: sentence reading time and reaction time to a secondary task. Slow reading and reaction times are indicative of high levels of attention. Anderson's study, which involved fourth-grade schoolchildren, showed a positive relation between interest and attention, whereas the study by Shirey and Reynolds, which involved university students, yielded a negative relation between the same factors. In both cases, interest had a significant influence on learning, but the level of attention had no corresponding effect. According to Shirey and Reynolds, these results suggest that especially adult (or skilled) readers pay less attention to interesting sentences because they know that it is easy to remember interesting material. Hidi (1990), however, has challenged that interpretation. Her work suggests that interest facilitates spontaneous, or involuntary, attention rather than intentional, or voluntary, attention. As a consequence, she maintains that interest could be associated with faster reading and reaction times, because spontaneous attention is less effortful and, thus, allows for more efficient processing of text.

One common feature of all the studies reviewed so far is that only cognitive variables (attention and learning strategies) were considered as mediating processes. As our model in Fig. 7.1 indicates, affective variables are also influential in the comprehension process. Although the assumed influence of activation on cognitive processes has been found in numerous studies (cf. Eysenck, 1982; Guttmann, 1982; Thayer & Cox, 1968), less is known about the mediating role of other affective states. Some studies suggest, however, that emotions are also of considerable significance (Bloom, 1985; Bower & Cohen, 1982; Csikszentmihalyi, 1988; Isen, Daubman, & Gorgoglione, 1987; Mandl & Huber, 1983).

Csikszentmihalyi (1975, 1988, 1990), in particular, has claimed that individuals can reach the optimum level of their cognitive capacities only when experiencing a state he has called "flow." He found that people who are strongly interested or intrinsically motivated to engage in an activity (e.g., playing chess) sometimes experience a state of optimal experience or flow. When being in flow, time seems to pass quickly, attention is sharply focused, and the individual becomes "lost" in the activity. Although the person so engaged is unconscious of self, there is, nevertheless, a feeling of control over the current activity. Csikszentmihalyi (1975; see also Csikszentmihalyi & Csikszentmihalyi, 1988) showed that the experience of flow is a powerful explanation of why people engage in certain activities without any extrinsic reinforcement.

Flow can occur to different degrees during any activity. A necessary condition is that the person sees both the level of task difficulty (or challenge) and his/her ability in the task as higher than average. It seems reasonable to conclude that readers displaying high levels of topic interest are prone to experience flow during the reading process. In fact, flow can be regarded as a state of "deep interest" (Rathunde, 1989). It remains unclear, however, whether flow is just an epiphenomenon of topic interest or whether flow actually mediates the effect of interest on comprehension processes or outcomes. To date, no conclusive empirical tests to resolve that problem have been conducted. Larson (1988) showed that essays of schoolchildren who experienced a flow-like state while writing were more exciting, better structured, and more creative than those of other students. This result, however, yields at best only indirect information about the relation between flow and text processing.

The flow model relates experiential states to both interests and cognitive or learning processes. Flow is a holistic, multi-componential state of experience that typically involves high levels of activation, enjoyment, and concentration (e.g., Csikszentmihalyi & Larson, 1987; Csikszentmihalyi & LeFevre, 1989). Thus, it would seem desirable to investigate whether flow or its components are capable of mediating the effect of interest on text comprehension.

EMPIRICAL EVIDENCE

Goals and Procedures

In the following, the results of two studies are reported that were intended to answer to the issues raised by previous studies. Specifically, our studies were designed to (a) test the impact of topic interest on various levels of comprehension, (b) examine whether interest affects comprehension independently of prior knowledge and intelligence, and (c) explore the mediating effects of selected process variables that could serve to explain the interest effect.

Both studies used the same experimental design[2] (see Table 7.2). First, subjects' prior knowledge, verbal and general intelligence, and short-term memory capacity were measured. This was followed by an assessment of subjects' topical interest in the experimental text. On the basis of the interest measure, subjects were divided into high- and low-interest groups and asked to read a text. In the final phase of the study, comprehension of the text and indicators of text processing were assessed.

Table 7.2

Design of Experimental Studies

Pre-Experimental Phase

Measurement of Control Variables: Prior Knowledge, Intelligence, Short-Term Memory

---

Experimental Phase

Measurement of topic interest

Reading phase
    Topic of text in Study I: Psychology of emotion
    Topic of text in Study II: Psychology of communication

Measurement of process variables
    Cognitive variables: Elaboration, Underlining, Note-taking
    Motivational variables: Activation, Flow

Measurement of comprehension
    Study I: Open-ended questions
    Study II: Recognition test

---

[2] A more detailed account of methodological aspects of the studies is to be found in Schiefele (1990a, 1990b, in press a).

A total of 96 male first-semester students participated in the investigations. There were 53 computer science majors in Study I and 43 social science majors in Study II. Two subjects were excluded from Study II because of outlying data. Data collection took place during regular class time; average class sizes were 25 people. A different text was used for each study.

Procedures for the two studies were the same: 2 to 4 weeks after the pretests, subjects were given written instructions asking them to evaluate sample texts from psychology textbooks. No mention was made that there would be a comprehension test later. Subjects were then told the topic and presented with a short summary of the text. Following this, they were asked to respond to the interest scale.

The next 15 minutes were allotted for reading the complete text. Subjects were allowed to make notes in the page margins and to underline portions of the text. Immediately following the reading period, the process variables of activation, flow experience, and elaborations were measured. Finally, a comprehension test was administered.

In the selection of the experimental texts, two criteria were considered. First, the subjects should have only limited prior knowledge of the text's topic. Second, interest in the topic should display large variance. Accordingly, the topic "Emotion" was chosen for Study I, and the topic "Communication" for Study II. The texts were about five pages long and consisted of three (Emotion) and four (Communication) sections.

In determining topical interest we attempted to measure intrinsic feeling-related and value-related valences. The feeling-related valences were operationalized as the expectation of experiencing certain feelings while reading the experimental text. Subjects were asked to use the following adjectives in estimating their expected feelings: ("While reading the text on '...', I expect to feel") "bored," "stimulated," "interested," "indifferent," "involved," and "engaged." When estimating value-related feelings, subjects were asked to use the terms "meaningful," "unimportant," "useful," and "worthless" to describe the value of the text's topic to them personally. Both scales relating to topic interest as well as all other scales consisted of four response categories: "not at all," "somewhat," "quite," and "completely." Individual values of topic interest were computed by adding the scores for the two components.

A more detailed description of the comprehension tests, the control variables, and the measurement of mediating variables follows.

Interest and Levels of Comprehension

Measurement of Text Comprehension in Study I. Following the work of Ballstaedt and Mandl (1987), the test of comprehension included three types of questions: 6 simple questions, 3 complex questions, and 3 deeper comprehension questions. The simple questions involved recall of concrete details (e.g., individual facts, definitions) stated explicitly in the text (e.g., "Which descriptive dimensions does Wundt consider characteristic for all emotions?"). The complex questions also related to knowledge explicitly contained in the text, but pertained to groupings of facts or relations between facts rather than to single facts (e.g., "What disadvantages are involved in the measuring of physiological changes in the study of emotions?"). The questions of deeper compre-hension required the subjects to recombine or to compare various aspects of the text and to apply the information contained in the text to a novel situation (e.g., "Two students report feeling 'very anxious' before taking an exam. What are the pros and cons of assuming that the two students are experiencing the same emotion?").

Because not all questions were assigned the same number of points, individual scores were converted into z-values. In order to arrive at only positive values, all z-values were increased by 1. Evaluation of the comprehension test was conducted by two independent trained raters, using an answer key containing model answers. In 10.3% of all evaluated answers, the raters arrived at different results.

Results of Study I. The results of the analysis of the comprehension test are presented in Table 7.3. A main effect for interest was obtained (ANOVA, $p < .005$), due in large part to the difference between the two subject groups in answering questions of deeper comprehension (planned comparison, $p < .001$). The differences in the cases of the simple (*ns*) and complex questions ($p < .05$) are distinctly smaller. The overall pattern of results confirms the hypothesis that interest exerts greater influence at deeper levels of comprehension.

In order to further examine this conclusion, the results of the compre-hension test were compared with a more objective measure, namely the length of answers given by the subjects. Analysis of the length of answers shows that, for all three question types, subjects in the high-interest group gave longer answers ($M = 21.08$ vs. $M = 18.62$ words per question). Whereas this trend lies in the theoretically postulated direction, it is not significant. Thus, the significant differences in comprehension for com-plex questions and for questions of deeper comprehension, as indicated

Table 7.3

Text Comprehension (z-Scores) as a Function of Topic Interest (Study I)

Topic Interest	SQ	CQ	DCQ	Total
Low (n = 27)	.88	.83	.74	.83
High (n = 26)	1.13	1.18	1.27	1.17

Note: SQ: Simple questions; CQ: Complex questions; DCQ: Deeper comprehension questions.

before, cannot simply be explained by the length of answers given. Instead, high- and low-interest subjects must differ in terms of the quality of their answers.

Study I shows that topic interest is a very influential motivational condition of text comprehension. The effect of interest on text comprehension is especially noticeable in the case of questions of deeper comprehension. Whether high-interest subjects actually achieve a deeper level of comprehension cannot, however, be determined with certainty from these results. An alternative explanation might be that the observed differences did not arise during processing of the text, but rather during the recall phase. One would then have to speak of a retrieval effect where low-interest subjects were also capable of answering the deeper comprehension questions, but were simply not motivated to work hard on these recall tasks.

A second problem concerns the comprehension test. As in other studies, the comprehension test in Study I is not based upon a specific theory of text processing but rather uses intuitive criteria for determining different levels of comprehension.

Van Dijk and Kintsch's Theory of Text Comprehension. The text processing theory of van Dijk; and Kintsch (1983; see also Kintsch, 1986) was used to construct a theoretically based test of comprehension, because this theory differentiates between various text representations that can also be interpreted as different levels of comprehension. Van Dijk and Kintsch distinguish between the cognitive representation of a text and the representation of the "situation" that the text describes ("situation model"). Knowledge contained in the situation model is not dependent on the text and can also be derived from other sources (e.g., learning by doing). The situation model is distinguished from two forms of text-bound representation—the verbatim and the propositional representations, which together form the "text basis." The propositional text basis consists of both a microstructure, which contains the meaning of the text, and a macrostructure, which represents the "gist" of the text. The verbatim text representation is even more closely bound to the text than the propositional and contains the representation of the text's superficial structure. An example of a purely verbatim representation would be a person who memorizes a sentence in a foreign language without knowing its meaning.

According to Kintsch (1986) and Perrig and Kintsch (1985), a propositional text representation is adequate for enabling a subject to repeat a text. *Learning*, in the sense of applying what has been read to new situations (e.g., verification of sentences in a recognition test), can only take place, however, when a situation model has been developed. In order to investigate the strength of the individual components of text representation, Perrig and Kintsch (1985) and Schmalhofer and Glavanov (1986) used recognition tests in which the subjects were asked to verify various types of sentences.

Generally, the reader of a certain text will always construct verbatim, propositional, and situational representations. The extent of each type of representation can vary immensely, however (Perrig & Kintsch, 1985; Schmalhofer & Glavanov, 1986). While reading, the three types of representation are constructed simultaneously and influence one another in a reciprocal fashion. Nevertheless, the processes involved can be distinguished from one another and are stored separately in memory (Kintsch, 1986).

Elaborations also play an important role in the model of van Dijk and Kintsch. In principle, they can be found on all three levels of text representation. Elaborations contribute to the strength and duration of the memory trace formed by the three types of representation (Kintsch, 1979). A large number of elaborations, such as mental images, associations with personal experience, and connections with prior knowledge, probably facilitate the construction of the situation model. Theoretically, one would expect to find a clear correlation between the number of elaborations and the extent of the situational text representation.

Based on this model then, it was hypothesized that high-interest subjects would build propositional and situational text representations to a greater extent than would other students. Low-interest subjects, on the other hand, were expected to acquire a mainly verbatim comprehension of the text.

Measurement of Text Comprehension in Study II. A recognition test was constructed based on techniques developed by Schmalhofer and Glavanov (1986) and Perrig and Kintsch (1985). The test contained 30 sentences, which were given to subjects in random order. Six of each of the following types of sentences were included in the test: original (O–sentences), para-phrased (P–sentences), meaning-changed (M–sentences), and correctness-changed (C–sentences). P–sentences were constructed by changing a few words. M–sentences contained correct and reasonable inferences from the text, which could be recognized as correct only on the basis of the situation model. C–sentences contradicted the corresponding original sentences and were false in terms of the situation model.

In each case, the subjects had to decide whether a sentence was presented verbatim in the original text. If the subject indicated that the sentence was not found in the text, he or she was asked to indicate whether the sentence was true or false. Based on the subject's judgment, scores for the extent of the verbatim (VERB), propositional (PROP), and situational (SIT) representations of the text were determined. The strength of individual text representations was calculated by means of d'-values[3] (cf. Egan, 1975).

The d'-value is a measure of the discriminability of two response distributions. The strength of the verbatim representation is determined by the difference between the number of "yes" answers for the O–sentences ("hit rate") and the number of "yes" answers for the P–sentences ("false alarm rate"). Similarly, the strength of the propositional representation is determined by the difference between the "yes" answers for the P–sentences and the false alarm rate for the M–sentences. Finally, the extent of the situational representation is determined by the difference between the "yes" answers for the M–sentences and the "yes" answers for the C–sentences. Determination of these differences is reasonable because the sentence pairs O–P, P–M, and M–C differ only by the contribution of one representational type (Schmalhofer & Glavanov, 1986, p. 285). All three representational forms are involved in a "yes" answer to an

---

[3] The d'-value, according to Egan (1975, p. 61), is the difference between the mean values of two distributions divided by their shared variance. Its application requires that the accumulated recognition values exhibit both a normal distribution and a homogeneous variance. Both conditions are met in the present study.

O–sentence, only propositional and situational representations are involved in the case of P–sentences, and M–sentences involve only the situational representation. In the case of the C–sentences, all three representational forms contribute to a negative response.

Results of Study II. Table 7.4 displays mean d'-values for low- and high-interest subjects. A significant main effect was obtained for type of representation (repeated measures ANOVA, $p < .05$). More importantly, the expected interaction between interest and representation appeared to be significant ($p < .01$). The pattern of results confirms the hypotheses. Low-interest subjects have a more pronounced verbatim and a less pronounced propositional and situational text representation than high-interest subjects. However, a significant difference was found only in the case of the verbatim representation (planned comparison, $p < .05$). The effect of interest on the propositional representation ($p < .10$) failed to reach an acceptable level of significance.

Table 7.4

Strength of Components of Text Representation (d'-values) as a
Function of Topic Interest (Study II)

Text Representation	Topic Interest	
	Low (n = 19)	High (n = 22)
VERB	.58	–.11
PROP	–.12	.37
SIT	.56	.72

In each recognition task, subjects were asked to decide not only whether a sentence came from the text, but also (in the case of a negative response) whether the sentence were true or false. Analysis of this verification task can yield additional insight into the type of text representation preferred by high- and low-interest subjects. Specifically, it should be indicative of the strength of the situational representation. Two ANOVAs were performed to examine the effects of interest on the verification of correct sentences (O–, P–, and M–sentences) and incorrect sentences (C–sentences). The results show that interest exerted an influence on the verification of correct sentences ($p < .05$), but not incorrect ones. Low-interest subjects were more likely than high-interest subjects to judge correct sentences to be false. A planned comparison revealed that the main effect for interest was significant only for P–sentences ($p < .01$). Low-interest subjects rejected, on the average, 21% of all P–sentences as being true, whereas high-interest subjects did so only for .08% of all P–sentences.

The results of Study II show that subjects who displayed a higher level of topic interest exhibited a less pronounced verbatim representation than low-interest subjects. Results regarding the propositional or meaning representation revealed only a nonsignificant trend in favor of highly interested students. No differences between situational representations of low- and high-interest subjects were observed. This result may indicate a lack of validity for the recognition test. The construction of meaning-changed sentences, which are crucial for calculating scores for the situational representation, is somewhat problematic. Although the whole test is based on a well-elaborated theory, there are no straightforward guidelines for constructing meaning-changed sentences. An analysis of the frequency of "yes" answers to all types of sentences shows that there were almost no differences between M– and P–sentences. This indicates that M–sentences may not have been "difficult" enough.

In support of the hypothesis that interest affects the situational representation of text, it was found that low-interest subjects rejected significantly more correct sentences in the additional verification task than did high-interest subjects.

Interest, Intelligence, and Prior Knowledge

Measurement of Control Variables. In both studies, the measurement of the various components of intelligence that could be important for text comprehension was conducted by means of several sub-tests from the IQ test by Jäger and Althoff (1983). The sub-tests used were intended to yield a score for general intelligence as well as scores for verbal intelligence and short-term memory (STM) capacity. Subjects' prior knowledge of the texts' topics was measured using 5 open-ended questions on the text content.

Results of Study I. The first step in the analysis consisted of comparing the mean values of the control variables for high- and low-interest subjects.[4] No significant differences were obtained. The mean values for the factors of general intelligence, verbal intelligence, STM capacity, and prior knowledge were nearly equal for high- and low-interest subjects. Thus, one must conclude that the differences in comprehension between the high- and low-interest groups were not attributable to these factors. This result is especially significant, as previous studies have found such factors to be of central importance in the learning of text material (e.g., Fincher–Kiefer, Post, Greene, & Voss, 1988; Perfetti, 1983; Recht & Leslie, 1988).

Contrary to expectations, prior knowledge and STM capacity did not correlate with comprehension. The indicators of verbal and general intelligence were correlated significantly only with the simple questions.[5]

In order to examine whether interest and intelligence show independent effects in the subsample analyzed here, partial correlation coefficients were computed. The results show that controlling for verbal and general intelligence did not reduce the correlations between interest and comprehension. Thus, the effects of interest and intelligence are independent of one another.

Results of Study II. Examination of the control variables in Study II revealed different results from Study I. Prior knowledge was found to be significantly correlated with interest ($r = .42$, p < .05)[6] but had no influence on the indicators of comprehension. No significant differences were found between high- and low-interest subjects in terms of intelligence. However, the level of general intelligence tended to affect text comprehension. High intelligence was associated with less pronounced propositional and more pronounced situational representations. No effect of intelligence on verbatim representation was obtained. It seems that the relation between intelligence and representation is quite different from the relation between interest and representation.

There also were no significant relations between verbal intelligence, short-term memory, and comprehension, but similar trends for general intelligence did emerge.

---

[4] It should be noted that not all subjects in both samples took part in the data collection for the control variables. This is due to the fact that participation in the seminars in which the studies were conducted fluctuated widely.

[5] A more detailed description and interpretation of these results is to be found in Schiefele (1990a).

[6] If not otherwise indicated, two-tailed tests of significance were carried out.

Next, in order to examine whether interest, prior knowledge, and general intelligence showed independent effects on text representation like those in Study I, partial correlation coefficients were analyzed. The results are summarized in Table 7.5.

Table 7.5

Zero-Order and Partial Correlations for the Relation between Interest and Components of Text Representation (Study II)

Sample	Control Variable	INT–VERB	INT–PROP	INT–SIT
TS (n=41)	–	–.50**	.34*	.08
SS1 (n=33)	–	–.46**	.33[a]	.08
SS1 (n=33)	Prior knowledge	–.57***	.36*	.12
SS2 (n=32)	–	–.49**	.38*	.08
SS2 (n=32)	Intelligence	–.51**	.51***	.02

*$p<.05$; **$p<.01$; ***$p<.001$; [a]$p=.061$.

Note: INT: Interest; TS: Total sample; SS1: Subsample 1 (all subjects who took part in the prior knowledge test); SS2: Subsample 2 (all subjects who took part in the intelligence test). SS1 and SS2 have 24 subjects in common.

The analysis of partial correlations revealed that controlling for prior knowledge and intelligence did not reduce the correlation between interest and the representational components. Note particularly that, when controlling for intelligence, the correlation between interest and PROP rises from .38 to .51. This is presumably the result of the highly negative correlation between intelligence and PROP.

The effects of prior knowledge and intelligence in both studies were relatively independent of the interest effect. The small influence of prior knowledge on comprehension was probably due to the fact that students had very little knowledge of the topics.

Interest and Mediating Processes

Measurement of Process Variables

Because the variables described here are all related to reading processes, they may serve to explain effects of interest. All of these variables were measured retrospectively, immediately following the reading of text. As depicted in Fig. 7.1, two groups of variables were distinguished: affective and cognitive processes (text processing). Activation and flow were examined as affective variables, and elaborations and learning techniques were examined as cognitive variables.

Activation. Level of activation was estimated using the "Activation–Deactivation Adjective Check List" (AD–ACL), developed by Thayer (1985, 1986). This scale allows the measurement of two independent bipolar activation dimensions: dimension A or "energetic arousal" (e.g., "energetic" vs. "sleepy"), and dimension B or "tense arousal" (e.g., "nervous" vs. "relaxed"). Only activation dimension A has been included in the present studies because it is closely related to motivational processes.

Flow. Using the concepts and methodology of Csikszentmihalyi (1975) and Massimini and Carli (1988), a questionnaire containing eight items for measuring the various components of flow was developed (e.g., "I had the impression that time went slowly while I was reading," "I was completely caught up in what I was reading"). Although the measure of flow was designed to tap a holistic state of mind covering different components, it seemed primarily to assess the experience of deep concentration. Because concentration is a central feature of flow, it becomes evident that flow is not a purely affective state.

Elaborations. A retrospective measure was employed to yield insight into elaborative processes. Subjects were asked to estimate to what extent the following four types of elaborations occurred: personal experience, content-related images, personal content-related thoughts or ideas, and paraphrasing the text in one's own words.

Underlinings and Margin Notes. Subjects were allowed to underline passages in the text and to make notes in the margins. Both methods can serve to assist remembering or comprehension of text passages (Anderson & Armbruster, 1984; Wade & Trathen, 1989).

Results of Studies I and II

In both Study I and Study II, significant correlations were found among interest and activation, flow, and elaboration (see Table 7.6 for the results from Study II). Relations between interest and underlining and note-taking turned out to be considerably weaker (see Table 7.6).

Inspection of the (5) individual flow items that were significantly related to level of interest indicated that time went by much faster for high-interest subjects, that they were much more caught up in the text, and that they experienced greater alertness and deeper concentration than low-interest subjects.

A look at the relations between individual items from the elaboration scale and interest showed that high-interest subjects more frequently reported the occurrence of mental images and personal thoughts about the text content. In addition, they tried harder to paraphrase the text.

Table 7.6

Zero-Order Correlations between Interest, Verbatim, and Propositional Text Representations, and Process Variables (Study II)

	Activation	Flow	Elaboration	Notes	Underlining
INT	.57***	.56***	.60***	.28[a]	.28[a]
VERB	−.27[a]	−.25	−.48**	−.22	−.05
PROP	.20	−.27[a]	−.27[a]	−.60***	.12

$*p<.05$; $**p<.01$; $***p<.001$; [a] $p=.061$.
Note: $n=41$; INT: Interest.

What can be said about the mediating role of the process variables studied? The results of Study I suggest a negative answer. Entering the process variables into a regression equation together with interest did not reduce the regression coefficient of interest for predicting complex questions of knowledge and questions of deeper understanding.

A different picture emerged in Study II. First, from the correlation values depicted in Table 7.6, it can be seen that cognitive process variables exhibited stronger relations to measures of text representation than did affective process variables. Not surprisingly, the amount of elaboration was negatively correlated with the strength of the verbatim representation.

An unexpectedly strong relation appears to exist between note-taking behavior and the representation of meaning.

Two separate multiple regressions were run to test mediational hypotheses. First, it was found that entering activation, flow, and elaboration into the regression equation for predicting VERB reduced the standardized regression coefficient of interest from $-.50$ to $-.29$, the latter value now being only marginally significant (F–Test, $p < .077$). Second, the inclusion of flow, elaboration, and notes in the regression equation for predicting PROP reduced the regression coefficient of interest from $.34$ to a nonsignificant value of $.17$. These results suggest that interest, in fact, exerts substantial influence on the processes that contribute to the representation of the meaning of a text.

CONCLUSION

At the outset of this chapter we took a look at the history of educational research. We found that assumptions about the relation between interest and learning were at the core of educational theories developed by scholars such as Herbart and Dewey, who both hypothesized that interest-based learning processes greatly differ qualitatively from effort-based, externally motivated learning processes. A review of more recent studies on the relation between interest and text learning revealed that most researchers have neglected to investigate the qualitative features of interest-based learning and have stressed purely quantitative outcomes.

The empirical studies reported in this chapter were designed to overcome the failure of prior research to analyze the relation between interest and comprehension more systematically. Study I confirmed that the effect of interest on comprehension is more pronounced at deeper levels of understanding. In keeping with Dewey's theory, low- and high-interest students did not differ significantly with regard to knowledge acquired by rote learning. Study II supported the results from Study I in showing that high-interest subjects displayed less verbatim and more meaning-oriented (propositional) text processing than low-interest subjects. In addition, results for control variables confirmed the independent effect of interest on text processing.

In order to gain a more detailed impression of the difference between interest-oriented and noninterest-oriented text processing styles, both studies included retrospective measures of several process variables. Analysis of these variables showed that a high level of topic interest contributes to an increased level of activation and the experience of flow. In addition, high interest subjects engaged in more pronounced elaborative processing and made more use of learning techniques. The exploration of mediating effects in Study II showed that the process variables could mediate at least part of the interest effect on comprehension. Additionally, the results suggested that cognitive process variables are more important than affective variables for mediating the effect of interest.

One problem with these results is that the measurement of process variables was almost exclusively (with the exception of notes and underlinings) based on verbal self-reports. The difficulties associated with reports of this nature are well known (Ericsson & Simon, 1980; Nisbett & Wilson, 1977). Future studies might supplement the measurement of process variables with other methods, such as think-aloud protocols (cf. Renninger, 1991) and on-line ratings.

As so often happens with research, there are more questions at the end than at the beginning. The following questions might serve as guidelines for future research.

1. Has prior knowledge been adequately measured? The tests of prior knowledge in both of the present studies were related only to knowledge explicitly contained in the texts. A possible refinement would be to include knowledge that, though not explicitly stated in the text itself, does pertain to the text's general topical domain (e.g., psychological knowledge).

2. How does the length of individual reading time influence the interest effect? At first glance, it seems reasonable that greater interest would be associated with slower reading, since greater interest would result in a more intensive processing of the text. On the other hand, it is conceivable that the interested reader simply "gobbles up" a text, finishing more quickly than an uninterested reader, who has to fight just to keep on reading (cf. Shirey & Reynolds, 1988; Hidi, 1990).

3. What influence do the instructions given before reading have on the relation between interest and comprehension? A very plausible assumption is that the interest effect is dependent on particular reading instructions. The announcement of a recall or comprehension test could, under certain conditions, hide the interest effect.

4. Are the results of the present studies also applicable to text-based, situational forms of interest? It would be interesting to apply the approach presented here to text-induced interest. This would allow

a comparison of the effects of individual and situational interest, and could thus help us to evaluate their respective merits.

5. How do the cognitive characteristics of the learner interact with interest? This is a problem of considerable significance because the results of the present studies imply that cognitive factors have effects on comprehension that are different from those of interest. A related and even more interesting question might be whether a high level of interest can compensate for deficits in cognitive functioning.

ACKNOWLEDGMENTS

Parts of the research reported in this chapter were supported by a grant from the Deutsche Forschungsgemeinschaft to Andreas Krapp and the author (Kr 716/4–1).

Preparation of the paper was facilitated by a scholarship awarded to the author by the Deutsche Forschungsgemeinschaft. Special thanks go to Steve Adams, who translated large parts of the original manuscript.

REFERENCES

Anderson, R. C. (1982). Allocation of attention during reading. In A. Flammer & W. Kintsch (Eds.), *Discourse processing* (pp. 292–313). Amsterdam: North–Holland.

Anderson, R. C., Mason, J., & Shirey, L. L. (1984). The reading group: An experimental investigation of a labyrinth. *Reading Research Quarterly, 20,* 6–38.

Anderson, R. C., Shirey, L. L., Wilson, P. T., & Fielding, L. G. (1987). Interestingness of children's reading material. In R. E. Snow & M. J. Farr (Eds.), *Aptitude, learning, and instruction. Vol. 3: Conative and affective process analyses* (pp. 287–299). Hillsdale, NJ: Lawrence Erlbaum Associates.

Anderson, T. H. & Armbruster, B. B. (1984). Studying. In P. D. Pearson (Ed.), *Handbook of reading research* (pp. 657–679). New York: Longman.

Asher, S. R. (1980). Topic interest and children's reading comprehension. In R. J. Spiro, B. C. Bruce, & W. F. Brewer (Eds.), *Theoretical issues in reading comprehension* (pp. 525–534). Hillsdale, NJ: Lawrence Erlbaum Associates.

Baldwin, R. S., Peleg–Bruckner, Z., & McClintock, A. H. (1985). Effects of topic interest and prior knowledge on reading comprehension. *Reading Research Quarterly, 20,* 497–504.

Ballstaedt, S.–P. & Mandl, H. (1987). Influencing the degree of reading comprehension. In E. van der Meer & J. Hoffmann (Eds.), *Knowledge aided information processing* (pp. 119–139). Amsterdam: Elsevier.

Belloni, L. F. & Jongsma, E. A. (1978). The effects of interest on reading comprehension of low-achieving students. *Journal of Reading, 22,* 106–109.

Benware, C. A. & Deci, E. L. (1984). Quality of learning with an active versus passive motivational set. *American Educational Research Journal, 21,* 755–765.

Bernstein, M. R. (1955). Relationship between interest and reading comprehension. *Journal of Educational Research, 49,* 283–288.

Bloom, B. S. (Ed.) (1985). *Developing talent in young people.* New York: Ballentine.

Bower, G. H. & Cohen, P. R. (1982). Emotional influences in memory and thinking: Data and theory. In M. S. Clark & S. T. Fiske (Eds.), *Affect and cognition* (pp. 291–331). Hillsdale, NJ: Lawrence Erlbaum Associates.

Cattell, R. B. (1936). The measurement of interest. *Character & Personality, 4,* 147–169.

Cecil, N. L. (1984). Impact of interest on the literal comprehension of beginning readers—a West Indian study. *The Reading Teacher, 37,* 750–753.

Csikszentmihalyi, M. (1975). *Beyond boredom and anxiety.* San Francisco: Jossey–Bass.

Csikszentmihalyi, M. (1988). Motivation and creativity: Towards a synthesis of structural and energistic approaches to cognition. *New Ideas in Psychology, 6,* 159–176.

Csikszentmihalyi, M. (1990). *Flow—The psychology of optimal experience.* New York: Harper & Row.

Csikszentmihalyi, M., & Csikszentmihalyi, I. S. (Eds.) (1988). *Optimal experience: Psychological studies of flow in consciousness.* Cambridge, MA: Cambridge University Press.

Csikszentmihalyi, M., & Larson, R. (1987). Validity and reliability of the experience–sampling method. *The Journal of Nervous and Mental Disease, 175,* 526–536.

Csikszentmihalyi, M., & LeFevre, J. (1989). Optimal experience in work and leisure. *Journal of Personality and Social Personality, 56,* 815–822.

Deci, E. L., & Ryan, R. M. (1985). *Intrinsic motivation and self-determination in human behavior.* New York: Plenum Press.

Dewey, J. (1913). *Interest and effort in education.* Boston: Riverside Press.

Dweck, C. S. (1986). Motivational processes affecting learning. *American Psychologist, 41,* 1040–1048.

Dweck, C. S., & Leggett, E. L. (1988). A social–cognitive approach to motivation and personality. *Psychological Review, 95,* 256–273.

Egan, J. P. (1975). *Signal detection theory and ROC analysis.* New York: Academic Press.

Entin, E. B. & Klare, G. R. (1985). Relationships of measures of interest, prior knowledge, and readability to comprehension of expository passages. *Advances in Reading/Language Research, 3,* 9–38.

Entwistle, N. (1988). Motivational factors in students' approaches to learning. In R. R. Schmeck (Ed.), *Learning strategies and learning styles* (pp. 21–52). New York: Plenum Press.

Entwistle, N. J., & Ramsden, P. (1983). *Understanding student learning.* London: Croom Helm.

Ericsson, K. A., & Simon, H. A. (1980). Verbal reports as data. *Psychological Review, 87,* 215–251.

Eysenck, M. W. (1982). *Attention and arousal.* Berlin: Springer.

Fincher–Kiefer, R., Post, T. A., Greene, T. R., & Voss, J. F. (1988). On the role of prior knowledge and task demands in the processing of text. *Journal of Memory and Language, 27,* 416–428.

Fransson, A. (1977). On qualitative differences in learning: IV—Effects of intrinsic motivation and extrinsic test anxiety on process and outcome. *British Journal of Educational Psychology, 47,* 244–257.

Groff, P. J. (1962). Children's attitudes toward reading and their critical reading abilities in four content-type materials. *Journal of Educational Research, 55,* 313–317.

Grolnick, W. S., & Ryan, R. M. (1987). Autonomy in children's learning: An experimental and individual difference investigation. *Journal of Personality and Social Psychology, 52,* 890–898.

Guttmann, G. (1982). *Lehrbuch der Neuropsychologie.* Bern: Huber.

Hare, V. C., & Devine, D. A. (1983). Topical knowledge and topical interest predictors of listening comprehension. *Journal of Educational Research, 76,* 157–160.

Harter, S. (1981). A new self-report scale of intrinsic versus extrinsic orientation in the classroom: Motivational and informational components. *Developmental Psychology, 17,* 300–312.

Herbart, J. F. (1806). Allgemeine Pädagogik, aus dem Zweck der Erziehung abgeleitet. In J. F. Herbart, *Pädagogische Schriften* (1965, Vol. 2, pp. 9–155). Düsseldorf: Küpper.

Herbart, J. F. (1841). Umriß pädagogischer Vorlesungen. In J. F. Herbart, *Pädagogische Schriften* (1965, Vol. 3, pp. 157–300). Düsseldorf: Küpper.

Hidi, S. (1990). Interest and its contribution as a mental resource for learning. *Review of Educational Research, 60,* 549–571.

Hidi, S. & Baird, W. (1986). Interestingness—A neglected variable in discourse processing. *Cognitive Science, 10,* 179–194.

Hidi, S. & Baird, W. (1988). Strategies for increasing text-based interest and students' recall of expository texts. *Reading Research Quarterly, 23,* 465–483.

Hidi, S. & McLaren, J. (1988, April). *The effect of topic and theme interestingness on children's school performance.* Paper presented at the annual meeting of the American Educational Research Association, New Orleans.

Isen, A. M., Daubman, K. A., & Gorgoglione, J. M. (1987). The influence of positive affect on cognitive organization: Implications for education. In R. E. Snow & M. J. Farr (Eds.), *Aptitude, learning, and instruction. Vol. 3: Conative and affective process analyses* (pp. 143–164). Hillsdale, NJ: Lawrence Erlbaum Associates.

Jäger, A. O., & Althoff, K. (1983). *Der Wilde–Intelligenz–Test (WIT).* Göttingen: Hogrefe.

Johnson, J. C., & Jacobson, M. D. (1968). Some attitudinal and comprehension factors operating in the middle grades. *Educational and Psychological Measurement, 28,* 825–832.

Kerschensteiner, G. (1922). *Theorie der Bildung.* Leipzig: Teubner.

Kintsch, W. (1979). Levels of processing language material: Discussion of the papers by Lachman and Lachman and Perfetti. In L. S. Cermak & F. I. M. Craik (Eds.), *Levels of processing in human memory* (pp. 211–222). Hillsdale, NJ: Lawrence Erlbaum Associates.

Kintsch, W. (1986). Learning from text. *Cognition and Instruction, 3,* 87–108.

Klein, H. A. (1979). What effect does non-sexist content have on the reading of boys and girls. *Reading Improvement, 16,* 134–138.

Krapp, A. (1989, September). *Interest, learning, and achievement.* Paper presented at the 3rd meeting of the European Association for Research in Learning and Instruction, Madrid.

Krapp, A. & Fink, B. (1987, April). *Development of interests as change in individual person–object relationships.* Paper presented at the biennial meeting of the Society for Research in Child Development, Baltimore.

Larson, R. (1988). Flow and writing. In M. Csikszentmihalyi & I. S. Csikszentmihalyi (Eds.), *Optimal experience: Psychological studies of flow in consciousness* (pp. 150–171). Cambridge, MA: Cambridge University Press.

Lepper, M. R. (1988). Motivational considerations in the study of instruction. *Cognition and Instruction, 5,* 289–309.

Mandl, H. & Huber, G. L. (Eds.) (1983). *Emotion und Kognition.* München: Urban & Schwarzenberg.

Massimini, F. & Carli, M. (1988). The systematic assessment of flow in daily experience. In M. Csikszentmihalyi & I. S. Csikszentmihalyi (Eds.), *Optimal experience: Psychological studies of flow in consciousness* (pp. 266–287). Cambridge, MA: Cambridge University Press.

Nicholls, J. G. (1984). Achievement motivation: Conceptions of ability, subjective experience, task choice, and performance. *Psychological Review, 91,* 328–345.

Nisbett, R. E., & Wilson, T. D. (1977). Telling more than we can know: Verbal reports on mental processes. *Psychological Review, 84,* 231–259.

Nolen, S. B. (1988). Reasons for studying: Motivational orientations and study strategies. *Cognition and Instruction, 5,* 269–287.

Osako, G. N. & Anders, P. L. (1983). The effect of reading interest on comprehension of expository materials with controls for prior knowledge. In J. A. Niles & L. A. Harris (Eds.), *Searches for meaning in reading/language arts processing instruction* (pp. 56–60). Rochester, NY: National Reading Conference.

Pekrun, R. (1988). *Emotion, Motivation und Persönlichkeit.* München/Weinheim: Psychologie Verlags Union.

Perfetti, C. A. (1983). Individual differences in verbal processes. In R. F. Dillon & R. R. Schmeck (Eds.), *Individual differences in cognition* (Vol. 1, pp. 65–104). New York: Academic Press.

Perrig, W., & Kintsch, W. (1985). Propositional and situational representations of text. *Journal of Memory and Language, 24,* 503–518.

Prenzel, M. (1988). *Die Wirkungsweise von Interesse.* Opladen: Westdeutscher Verlag.

Prenzel, M., Krapp, A., & Schiefele, H. (1986). Grundzüge einer pädagogischen Interessentheorie. *Zeitschrift für Pädagogik, 32,* 163–173.

Rathunde, K. (1989). The context of optimal experience: An exploratory model of the family. *New Ideas in Psychology, 2,* 91–97.

Recht, D. R. & Leslie, L. (1988). Effect of prior knowledge on good and poor readers' memory of text. *Journal of Educational Psychology, 80,* 16–20.

Renninger, K. A. (1988, April). *Effects of interest and noninterest on student performance with tasks of mathematical word problems and reading comprehension.* Paper presented at the annual meeting of the American Educational Research Association, New Orleans.

Renninger, K. A. (1990). Children's play interests, representation, and activity. In R. Fivush & J. Hudson (Eds.), *Knowing and remembering in young children* (pp. 127–165). Cambridge, MA: Cambridge University Press.

Renninger, K. A. (1991, April). *Influences of interest and task difficulty on students' strategies for reading and recall.* Paper presented as part of the symposium, *Effects of Interest on Strategies and Learning from Text.* American Educational Research Association, Chicago, IL.

Renninger, K. A., & Wozniak, R. H. (1985). Effect of interest on attentional shift, recognition, and recall in young children. *Developmental Psychology, 21,* 624–632.

Ryan, R. M. (1982). Control and information in the intrapersonal sphere: An extension of cognitive evaluation theory. *Journal of Personality and Social Psychology, 43,* 450–461.

Schiefele, H., Hausser, K., & Schneider, G. (1979). "Interesse" als Ziel und Weg der Erziehung. Überlegungen zu einem vernachläßigten pädagogischen Konzept. *Zeitschrift für Pädagogik, 25,* 1–20.

Schiefele, H., Krapp, A., Prenzel, M., Heiland, A., & Kasten, H. (1983, July/August). *Principles of an educational theory of interest.* Paper presented at the 7th biennial meeting of the International Society for the Study of Behavioral Development, Munich.

Schiefele, U. (1987). The importance of motivational factors for the acquisition and representation of knowledge. In P. R. J. Simons & G. Beukhof (Eds.), *Regulation of learning* (pp. 47–69). Den Haag: SVO Selecta.

Schiefele, U. (1988). Motivationale Bedingungen des Textverstehens. *Zeitschrift für Pädagogik, 34,* 687–708.

Schiefele, U. (1990a). The influence of topic interest, prior knowledge, and cognitive capabilities on text comprehension. In J. M. Pieters, K. Breuer, & P. R. J. Simons (Eds.), *Learning environments* (pp. 323–338). Heidelberg: Springer.

Schiefele, U. (1990b). Thematisches Interesse, Variablen des Leseprozesses und Textverstehen. *Zeitschrift für Experimentelle und Angewandte Psychologie, 37,* 304–332.

Schiefele, U. (in press a). Interesse und Textrepräsentation—Zur Auswirkung des thematischen Interesses auf unterschiedliche Komponenten der Textrepräsentation unter Berücksichtigung kognitiver und motivationaler Kontrollvariablen. *Zeitschrift für Pädagogische Psychologie.*

Schiefele, U. (in press b). Interest, learning, and motivation. *Educational Psychologist.*

Schiefele, U. & Krapp, A. (1988, April). *The impact of interest on qualitative and structural indicators of knowledge.* Paper presented at the annual meeting of the American Educational Research Association, New Orleans.

Schiefele, U. & Winteler, A. (1988). *Interesse—Lernen—Leistung. Eine Übersicht über theoretische Konzepte, Erfassungsmethoden und Ergebnisse der Forschung* (Gelbe Reihe, Arbeiten zur Empirischen Pädagogik und Pädagogischen Psychologie, Nr. 14). München: Universität der Bundeswehr.

Schiefele, U., Winteler, A., & Krapp, A. (1988). Studieninteresse und fachbezogene Wissensstruktur. *Psychologie in Erziehung und Unterricht, 35,* 106–118.

Schmalhofer, F., & Glavanov, D. (1986). Three components of understanding a programmer's manual: Verbatim, propositional, and situational representations. *Journal of Memory and Language, 25,* 279–294.

Shirey, L. L., & Reynolds, R. E. (1988). Effect of interest on attention and learning. *Journal of Educational Psychology, 80,* 159–166.

Stevens, K. (1979). The effect of topic interest on the reading comprehension of higher ability students. *Journal of Educational Research, 73,* 365–368.

Thayer, R. E. (1985). Activation (arousal): The shift from a single to a multdimensional perspective. *Biological Bases of Personality and Behavior, 1,* 115–127.

Thayer, R. E. (1986). Activation–deactivation adjective check list: Current overview and structural analysis. *Psychological Reports, 58,* 606–614.

Thayer, R. E., & Cox, S. J. (1968). Activation, anxiety, and verbal learning. *Journal of Experimental Psychology, 78,* 524–526.

Thorndike, E. L. (1935a). *Adult interests.* New York: MacMillan.

Thorndike, E. L. (1935b). *The psychology of wants, interests and attitudes.* New York: Appleton–Century.

van Dijk, T., & Kintsch, W. (1983). *Strategies of discourse comprehension.* Orlando: Academic Press.

Wade, S. E., & Trathen, W. (1989). Effect of self-selected study methods on learning. *Journal of Educational Psychology, 81,* 40–47.

Witty, P. A., & Kopel, D. (1936). Motivating remedial reading: The interest factor. *Educational Administration and Supervision, 22,* 1–19.

Interest as a Predictor of Academic Achievement: A Meta-Analysis of Research

8

Ulrich Schiefele, Andreas Krapp, and Adolf Winteler
Universität der Bundeswehr – Munich

The explanation and prediction of academic achievement is an important area of research in educational psychology. The prevalence of research efforts in this area reflects the fact that many decisions reached in the modern educational system are based upon predictions of school success. Such decisions include choosing the optimal time for entering school, selecting the appropriate type of school or academic track, being accepted at a certain college or university, or the choice of a particular field of study. Because these decisions can greatly influence the life of a young person, a period of careful consideration often precedes the final decision. Parents and students often seek counseling. Institutions such as schools and colleges have developed special entrance tests, and base their recommendations or decisions upon systematic diagnostic data. The estimation of a candidate's probability of future academic success is a central aspect of the decision-making process, regardless of whether the process involves personal decisions or institutional decisions (Cronbach & Gleser, 1965; Jungermann, 1976; Krapp, 1979; Lee, 1971).

Generally, every prognosis relevant to educational or academic goals is based upon two types of data: (a) data pertaining to the requirements and conditions of the desired educational path (e.g., curricular goals, level of difficulty, qualification of instructors), and (b) data pertaining to the prospective student (e.g., cognitive abilities, motivational orientation). To

183

the extent that a decision has long-term implications (i.e., when the final evaluation of a course of schooling lies far ahead in the future), the diagnosis of *enduring characteristics* of student performance prevails.

In view of the great practical importance of academic career decisions, it is not surprising that for decades scientists have invested a considerable amount of time to find highly predictive and stable determinants of academic achievement. Reviews with varying emphases and inclusiveness have been written, for example, by Bloom (1976), Fleming and Malone (1983), Lavin (1965), Sauer and Gattringer (1985), Steinkamp and Maehr (1983), and Tiedemann (1977). Occasionally, attempts have been made to summarize the various findings and to organize the great number of predictive variables into theoretically meaningful classes (e.g., Haertel, Walberg, & Weinstein, 1983; Krapp, 1984; Kühn, 1983).

Three major groups of factors that influence achievement are distinguished: student characteristics (e.g., intelligence), home environment (e.g., socioeconomic class), and school context (e.g., quality of instruction). Academic career decisions, as described before, rely primarily on student characteristics that are classified in a variety of different ways. Regardless of the theoretical foundations and the particular goals of different approaches, one usually finds three broad classes of factors that are considered to be especially relevant to a successful prognosis of academic success: (a) general cognitive factors (e.g., verbal ability), (b) general motivational factors (e.g., achievement motivation), and (c) specific preferences for particular subject areas. The latter group is commonly referred to as "interests."

Cognitive factors have been found to exhibit the greatest predictive power. In empirical studies they account for the largest part of observed achievement variance (e.g., Bloom, 1976; Kuusinen & Leskinen, 1988). There is general agreement, based on empirical evidence, that motivational or emotional factors are of less importance. A number of reviews (e.g., Kühn, 1983; Steinkamp & Maehr, 1983) and recent studies using causal modeling procedures (e.g., Parkerson, Lomax, Schiller, & Walberg, 1984; Quack, 1979; Schneider and Bös, 1985) confirm the importance of cognitive factors. As predictors, they usually explain up to 50% of the variance in achievement, calculated on the basis of correlation and regression analyses (e.g., Khan, 1969; Lavin, 1965; Nichols, 1966; Steinkamp & Maehr, 1983). However, more precise analyses of variance yield a more differentiated picture.

According to Quack (1979), considering both cognitive and noncognitive factors simultaneously, and calculating specific and confounded portions of explained variance for both groups, reveals that approximately 25% to 30% of the observable variance in academic achievement can be explained on the basis of cognitive factors alone. A further 25% portion of the observable variance is explained by noncognitive factors. According to Quack, there are two "threshold values" for the portions of variance explained by cognitive factors. The first threshold corresponds to the "pure" portion of explained variance (25% to 30%). The second threshold denotes a "ceiling value" of about 50% for the portion of explained variance that is confounded with noncognitive variables.

Schneider and Bös (1985), who used data from fourth-graders and causal modeling procedures, came to similar conclusions. Their analysis confirms that researchers have tended to underestimate the influence of noncognitive factors on academic achievement. These include motivational factors, which often influence achievement indirectly.

This chapter provides an overview of previous research results pertaining to the relation between interest and academic achievement. First, we focus on the conceptualization and operationalization of interest. Then the goals and procedures adopted by most studies on the interest–achievement relation are discussed. Results from this branch of research are reviewed in the next two sections. Whereas studies published prior to 1965 are summarized on the basis of earlier reviews, a meta-analysis is applied to studies published after 1965. The major goals of the meta-analysis were to determine the strength of the predictive value of interest and to identify variables that moderate the impact of interest on achievement. Finally, the results of the review are discussed and suggestions for future research are given.

CONCEPT AND MEASUREMENT OF INTEREST

Predictions of academic success or failure are based upon information about cognitive and noncognitive prerequisites for learning that generally correlate with academic achievement and, hence, serve to explain the variability of academic performance. With this goal in mind, the search for likely predictors of academic achievement centers around behavioral characteristics of the student that can be shown to exert a significant effect in many learning situations and in a stable manner over time. Only those factors that exhibit a general and stable influence can contribute consistently to predictions of school performance.

The goal of finding general, stable predictors of achievement has also affected studies that have included measures of interest as predictors. Many of these studies rely almost exclusively on dispositional conceptions of interest. Borrowing from theoretical models and diagnostic measures developed in vocational psychology (Allehoff, 1985; Barak, 1981; Holland, 1973, 1976; Walsh & Osipow 1986), research in this area is based on a concept of interest that has been shaped by the principles of traditional personality psychology. From this theoretical perspective, interests are conceived of as traits or dispositions. Todt (1978), for example, refers to them as "...behavioral or action tendencies that are relatively long-term and relatively generalized [and] ... that are aimed at various domains of objects, activities, or experiences" (p. 14). As a consequence, interests are usually measured with standardized tests developed in vocational psychology. Typical tests are the Strong Vocational Interest Blank, the Kuder Preference Record, or the Vocational Preference Inventory (see Walsh & Osipow, 1986). In addition, numerous questionnaires have been developed to predict achievement in particular schools, age groups, or subject areas (e.g., Carter, 1982; Harty & Beall, 1984; Hoffmann & Lehrke, 1986).

STRATEGIES AND METHODS OF RESEARCH

The analysis of the predictive power of interest has usually involved examining whether a systematic relation exists between interest and a certain achievement criterion (e.g., grade points). This has almost always taken the form of simple correlation and regression analyses. Most studies have neglected the problems of prognostic stability and causal directionality. Instead, the conclusions drawn have been largely limited to whether a portion of the observed variance in achievement could be attributed to interest with sufficient probability. Very few studies have included a test of whether and to what extent the interest measured at Time 1 actually predicted academic achievement at Time 2. Only in this case could interest truly be regarded as a causal antecedent of achievement. In addition, no study was found that tested the prognostic stability of interest by varying the time lag between measuring interest and achievement.

Almost all empirical studies have attempted to quantify the relation between interest and academic achievement by means of a more or less controlled explanation of variance. Many studies have calculated correlations without systematically controlling for alternative influence factors. By contrast, methodically more sophisticated studies have controlled for the influence of alternative predictors either by ensuring that these predictors were equally prevalent in a group of subjects or by employing statistical procedures (e.g., analysis of covariance) to eliminate the influence of these factors.

Another problem of prediction research is related to the influence of moderator variables, such as gender or age (Saunders, 1956; Zedeck, 1971). Rather different results may be obtained for the same set of predictors, depending on the number or type of included moderator variables. Often, these variables cannot independently contribute to the prediction of a criterion. They can be highly effective, however, in differentiating samples into subgroups with varying degrees of predictability (Jäger, 1978; Rosemann & Allhoff, 1982).

RESEARCH CONDUCTED PRIOR TO 1965: A SUMMARY OF REVIEWS

Although early research on noncognitive factors in academic achievement often included interest as a predictor, later research neglected this variable. Similarly, research summaries written prior to 1970 regularly include references to the effect of interests, whereas more recent review articles (e.g., Fleming & Malone, 1983; Steinkamp & Maehr, 1983; Uguroglu & Walberg, 1979; Willson, 1983) contain no mention of interest. Super (1960) summarized a series of studies published in the United States before 1957. The empirical correlations between interest scores (usually measured by vocational interest tests) and indicators of academic achievement at both the school and the college levels rarely exceeded .30. Higher correlations emerged for samples that exhibited either homogeneity in terms of ability or at least moderate variability in level of interest. Conditions characteristic of the school or college environment were also found to be of importance. For example, the prevalence of a competitive atmosphere seemed to reduce or obstruct the interest effect.

Fishman and Pasanella (1960) reviewed a total of 580 studies published between 1949 and 1959 on the relation between cognitive and noncognitive predictors and average college grades. Seven studies investigated the interest–achievement relation and yielded correlations between .05 and .26.

Lavin (1965), who relied primarily on material different from that used by Super, reached similar conclusions. In both college and high school, the correlations between interest and grades did not exceed .30. Lavin explained this by noting that, at least in the case of college students who had already selected a particular major, the level of interest in the subject matter was uniformly high. Thus, only a small degree of variance in measures of interest was found. Interest was, however, highly correlated (up to .70) with indicators of performance in specific courses. Lavin pointed out that almost none of the studies he reviewed distinguished between male and female subjects, and only some of the studies controlled for the students' ability levels. In those studies that did control for ability, however, significant correlations between interest and achievement were consistently found.

Trost (1975) described a number of other studies of the relation between interest and academic achievement that were published before 1965 (and not included in the work of either Super or Lavin). He distinguished between studies that attempted to predict overall success (final exam results or grade point average) and those that concentrated on predicting success in particular subject areas or even particular courses. Although he found somewhat higher correlations between interest and success in particular courses, he concluded that correlations between interest and achievement generally tended to be relatively small.

The findings just reported suggest that interest is moderately useful as a predictor of academic achievement. However, restrictions in the variance of interest scores, heterogeneity of ability, and the use of unspecific achievement criteria often masked the interest effect.

RESEARCH CONDUCTED SINCE 1965: A META-ANALYSIS

Goals and Selection Procedures

This chapter overviews the past 25 years of research on the interest–achievement relation and suggests guidelines for future research in this area. The main questions are the following: How large is the correlation between interest and achievement in general? Can differences be found among the various subject areas? Does the influence exerted by interest become stronger or weaker during the school years? What part does gender play in the relation between interest and achievement?

One of the greatest difficulties of summarizing interest-related research is the extremely eclectic use of the interest concept. The term *interest* is often used interchangeably with terms such as *intrinsic motivation, subject-related affect, attitude, and cognitive motivation.* As a result, some studies purportedly having to do with interest have, in fact, measured something quite different. Conversely, some studies that actually addressed interest have, for instance, labeled it attitude, liking, or curiosity. This confusion leads to problems when attempting to identify relevant studies to analyze.

The present review is limited to studies that were concerned with the relation between individual interests explicitly directed towards specific subject areas (e.g., physics) and achievement in school. Our understanding of interest follows the conceptualization of H. Schiefele and colleagues (e.g., H. Schiefele, Krapp, Prenzel, Heiland, & Kasten, 1983) who, in accordance with older theories (Dewey, 1913; Kerschensteiner, 1922), discussed interest as a domain- or content-specific motivational characteristic (see chapters by Schiefele and Krapp & Fink, this volume).

For the purposes of this review interest was operationalized as involving some kind of preference for a school subject or for activities related to that subject. Studies that did not measure interest in a specific subject area were not included in the meta-analysis. Typical examples are the studies of Khan (1969) and Lloyd and Barenblatt (1984). In investigating the predictor "academic interest," Khan (1969) determined attitudes towards school work and instructional methods in general rather than towards a particular school subject. Similarly, Lloyd & Barenblatt (1984) used the construct "intrinsic intellectual motivation," which was meant to signify a person's habitual emotional reactions to the content and process of academic learning. Content referred to any possible material covered in school. Aside from the questionable meaningfulness, in purely psychological terms, of a concept of learning motivation not related to any particular subject area, these constructs failed to fulfill the criterion of domain specificity crucial both to earlier as well as in present conceptualizations of interest.

Evaluation of achievement criteria presented less of a problem. Most of the studies relied on standardized knowledge tests, grades, or grade averages to measure achievement. Studies that involved relatively specific criteria for determining performance (e.g., solving of certain problems, memorizing of a text) were excluded from consideration. Overviews of studies addressing the relation between narrowly defined interests and specific performance criteria have been provided by Hidi (1990; see also Hidi & Baird, 1986), Schiefele (1988, this volume), and Wade (this volume).

The search for relevant studies was conducted using the databases PSYCINFO (Anglo–American literature) and PSYNDEX (German literature). In addition, periodicals were scanned; however, no unpublished dissertations were included.[1] A great variety of key words was used in the search, because relevant studies were often found hiding behind seemingly irrelevant titles. Key words included interest, academic achievement, motivation, attitude, and affect.

Sixteen publications were identified that fit the criteria they were focused on: the relation between interest and achievement. They contain 121 independent random samples (or independent single studies, respectively) from 18 different countries. The sample groups ranged in size from 49 to 15,719. The grade levels ranged from the 5th to the 12th grade. Nine different subject matter areas were covered. Finally, these studies reported a total of 189 correlations between measures of interest and measures of achievement (see Table 8.1).

More than half of all of the correlations (108 out of 189) came from studies initiated by the International Association for the Evaluation of Educational Achievement (IEA, e.g., Husén, 1967). The IEA project was carried out in 21 countries and involved a total of six school subjects. Generally, two populations were studied: 13- or 14-year-old students, usually in the 8th grade, and 18-year-old students, usually in the 12th grade. Both populations were then broken down further.

Meta-Analytic Procedures

In order to achieve a more objective summary of the studies included in this review, meta-analytical methods were adopted (Fricke & Treinies, 1985; Glass, 1976; Glass, McGaw, & Smith, 1981; Hunter & Schmidt, 1990; Hunter, Schmidt, & Jackson, 1982; Kulik & Kulik, 1989). It seemed most appropriate to use guidelines developed by Hunter et al. (1982; Hunter & Schmidt, 1990) because these authors are especially concerned with the integration of results from correlational studies.

First, all relevant study features were coded. These included: size of correlation coefficients, sample size, gender of sample, year of publication, nationality of sample, type of achievement measure, reliability of both the interest and achievement measures, source of study (IEA vs. other), subject area, and grade level. Second, correlations were

---

[1] We are currently preparing an extension of the present analysis to include doctoral dissertations.

aggregated from different subgroups of studies (e.g., all studies involving mathematics as the subject area) and compared with each other. According to Hunter et al. (1982) the best estimate of the population correlation is given by the mean value of individual correlations weighted by the sample sizes of the corresponding studies. In addition, each correlation coefficient was converted into Fisher's z before using it for any computation.

Because a major goal of the present meta-analysis was an investigation of the effects of moderator variables (i.e., sex, subject area, grade level), it was necessary to determine whether the variance between correlations was solely due to sampling error or reflected a "real" variation between population values. If a large part of the observed variance could not be attributed to sampling error, then the correlations were seen as being heterogeneous and the existence of relevant moderator variables was very likely ("model of heterogeneous effects"). If the observed variance was caused mainly by sampling error, then the "model of homogeneous effects" could not be rejected and the search for moderator variables would be unwarranted.

Three different indicators of heterogeneity have been discussed in the literature (Schwarzer, 1989). First, Hunter et al. (1982) suggested that the percentage of observed variance accounted for by sampling error should be less than 75%. Second, the same authors (see also Hunter & Schmidt, 1990) proposed a Chi^2 test in which the observed variance for a group of correlations is related to the mean value of these correlations. Third, the population (or residual) standard deviation (i.e., square root of the difference between observed variance and sampling error variance) should be larger than one-fourth of the population correlation coefficient (McDaniel, Hirsh, Schmidt, Raju, & Hunter, 1986).

In some studies the same sample was used to generate several correlation coefficients. Such coefficients are dependent on each other and, therefore, were always combined into a single mean value and then entered into the calculation of the overall mean. In these cases the original sample size of a study was used as the weight. Thus, nonindependent results were not lumped together and the sample size was not inflated.

A major disadvantage of weighting correlation coefficients with sample size is that correlations based on very large samples become too influential. In the present case this concerns most samples from the IEA project (cf. Table 8.1). In order to control for the undue impact of these studies on the meta-analytic results, analyses of both weighted and

Table 8.1

Descriptive Information on Studies Included in the Review

Author	Sample Grade	Size	Interest Measure (Item Content)	Achievement Measure[a]	Correlations
			Mathematics		
IEA Study Husén; (1967)	8	Samples from 11 countries $n > 841$ $n < 6544$ m/f	Q: Desire for further education, liking the subject, quality of grades, career goals	IEA math achievement test (Rel.=.91)	.23 .24 .26 .27 .28 .29 .32 .35 .38 .39 .42
Wendeler; (1968)	10	227 117 (m) 110 (f)	Q: Self-rating of interest in various subject-related topics (Rel.=.96)	Grades	.38
Skager et al. (1965)	10/11	524 261 (m) 263 (f)	Q: Liking of various subject-related activities	Grades	m:.35 f:.31
Todt (1978)	10/11	220 120 (m) 100 (f)	T: Preference ratings for various subject-related activities (Rel.=.85)	Grades	m:.50 f:.47
Todt (1978)	10–12	158 96 (m) 62 (f)	T: see above	Grades	m:.53 f:.40
Todt (1978)	11/12	158 (f)	T: see above	Grades	.45
IEA Study Husén; (1967)	12	Samples from 9[b] countries $n > 369$ $n < 4372$ m/f	Q: see above	see above (Rel.=.86)	.16 .29 .29 .29 .30 .32 .33 .37 .39 .40 .43 .47 .51 .52
Todt (1967)	12	208 (m)	T: see above	Grades	.37
Sjöberg; (1983)	12	174 134 (m) 40 (f)	Q: Self-rating of general interest, personal significance, importance of success in subject area	Grades	.53
Sjöberg (1984)	12	100 71 (m) 29 (f)	Q: see Sjöberg (1983)	Grades	.44

Science

Harty & Beall; (1975)	5	95 m/f	Q: Liking for science-related activities (Rel.=.78c)	Grades	.30		
IEA Study Comber & Keeves; (1973)	8	Samples from 15 countries n > 697 n < 7363 m/f	Q: Participation in science-related activities, enjoyment of science in school (Rel.=.74)	IEA science achievement test (Rel.=.83)	.09 .26 .32 .36 .39	.18 .26 .35 .37 .42	.23 .27 .35 .38 .49
IEA Study Kelly; (1978)	8	Samples from 7 countries n > 932 n < 3823 m/f	Q: General liking for science (Rel.=.76)	see Comber & Keeves (1973)	m: .22 .38 .52 f: .18 .25 .36	.31 .41 .23 .30	.37 .46 .24 .34
Napier & Riley; (1985)	11	3135 m/f	Q: 1) Liking for science classes (Rel.=.82), 2) Participation in science-related activities (Rel.= .83)	Science achievement test (Rel.= .82)	.18 .26		
IEA Study Comber & Keeves (1973)	12	Samples from 14 countries n > 491 n < 15719 m/f	Q: see above (Rel.=.76)	see above (Rel.=.82)	.21 .33 .48 .53 .64	.22 .40 .50 .58 .67	.27 .43 .51 .60

Physics

Oehlert; (1977)	5/6	100 m/f	Q: Liking of physics instruction, readiness to achieve in physics (Rel.=.83)	Achievement tests: 1) Knowledge (Rel.=.89) 2) Transfer (Rel.=.86)	.53 .50	
Todt (1978)	8/9	234 117 (m) 117 (f)	T: see above (Rel.=.98)	Grades	m: .24 f: .39	
Todt (1978)	8–10	526 263 (m) 263 (f)	T: see above	Grades	m: .22 f: .11	

Wendeler; (1968)	10	227 117 (m) 110 (f)	Q: see above (Rel.=.94)	Grades	.45
Skager et al. (1965)	10/11	524 261 (m) 263 (f)	Q: see above	Knowledge test	m:.32 f:.25
Todt (1978)	10/11	220 120 (m) 100 (f)	T: see above	Grades	m:.17 f:.33
Todt (1978)	10–12	146 89 (m) 57 (f)	T: see above	Grades	m:.43 f:.10
Todt (1978)	11/12	158 (f)	T: see above	Grades	.39
Todt (1967)	12	113 (m)	T: see Todt (1978)	Grades	.28
Sjöberg; (1983)	12	174 134 (m) 40 (f)	Q: see above	Grades	.48
Sjöberg (1984)	12	100 71 (m) 29 (f)	Q: see above	Grades	.49

Biology

Todt (1978)	8/9	234 117 (m) 117 (f)	T: see above (Rel.=.97)	Grades	m:.08 f:.07
Todt (1978)	8–10	526 263 (m) 263 (f)	T: see above	Grades	m:.13 f:.12
Wendeler; (1968)	10	227 117 (m) 110 (f)	Q: see above (Rel.=.95)	Grades	.27
Skager et al. (1965)	10/11	524 261 (m) 263 (f)	Q: see above	Knowledge test	m:.20 f:.21
Todt (1978)	10/11	220 120 (m) 100 (f)	T: see above	Grades	m:.16 f:.11
Todt (1978)	10–12	125 76 (m) 49 (f)	T: see above	Grades	m:.22 f:-.08
Todt (1978)	11/12	158 (f)	T: see above	Grades	.30

Chemistry

Wendeler, (1968)	10	227 117 (m) 110 (f)	Q: see above (Rel.=.94)	Grades	.43

Social Science

Wendeler (1968)	10	227 117 (m) 110 (f)	Q: see above (Rel.=.89)	Grades	.33
Wendeler (1968)	10	227 117 (m) 110 (f)	Q: 1) Ancient history (Rel.=.89) 2) Modern History/ Politics (Rel.=89)	Grades	.39 .35
Skager et al. (1965)	10/11	524 261 (m) 263 (f)	Q: see above	Knowledge test Grades	m:.35 f:.24 m:.35 f:.19
Todt (1978)	10/11	220 120 (m) 100 (f)	T: see above (Rel.=.96)	Grades	m:.41 f:.51
Todt (1978)	10–12	154 94 (m) 60 (f)	T: see above	Grades	m:.31 f:.20
Todt (1978)	11/12	158 (f)	T: see above	Grades	.32
Todt (1967)	12	208 (m)	T: see Todt (1978)	Grades	.26
Sjöberg (1983)	12	174 134 (m) 40 (f)	Q: see above	Grades	.41
Sjöberg; (1984)	12	100 71 (m) 29 (f)	Q: see above	Grades	.26
Hall (1975)	12 Junior Coll.	159 (m) 93 (White) 66 (Black)	Q: Interest in instruction, voluntary participation	Grades	White: .24 Black: .36

Foreign Language

IEA Study Carroll; (1975)	8	Samples from 6 countries $n > 839$ $n < 4420$ m/f	Q: desire for further education, liking the subject, quality of grades, importance of the subject (Rel.=.74)	IEA french achievement test (Reading) (Rel.= .85)	.22 .38	.24 .42	.26 .47
IEA Study Lewis & Massad; (1975)	8	Samples from 7 countries $n > 687$ $n < 2331$ m/f	Q: see Carroll (1975) (Rel.=.69)	IEA English achievement test (Rel.= .93)	.22 .38 .49	.28 .48	.28 .49
Skager et al. (1965)	10/11	524 261 (m) 263 (f)	Q: see above	Grades	m:.31 f:.16		
IEA Study Carroll; (1975)	12	Samples from 7 countries $n > 378$ $n < 3230$ m/f	Q: see above (Rel.=.70)	see above (Rel.=.83)	.26 .35 .43	.28 .39	.33 .41
IEA Study Lewis & Massad; (1975)	12	Samples from 9 countries $n > 323$ $n < 2310$ m/f	Q: see above (Rel.=.65)	see above (Rel.=.82)	.18 .27 .29	.26 .27 .31	.27 .27 .33
Sjöberg; (1983)	12	174 134 (m) 40 (f)	Q: see above	Grades (English)	.41		
Sjöberg (1984)	12	100 71 (m) 29 (f)	Q: see above	Grades (English)	.30		

Literature

IEA Study Purves; (1973)	8	Samples from 9 countries $n > 548$ $n < 7228$ m/f	Q: Frequency of reading (Rel.=.66)	IEA literature achievement test (Rel.= .79)	.10 .16 .18	.12 .17 .22	.13 .17 .22

Wendeler; (1968)	10	227 117 (m) 110 (f)	Q: see above	Grades (Rel.=.92)	.32
IEA Study Purves; (1973)	12	Samples from 9 countries $n > 464$ $n < 14204$ m/f	Q: see above (Rel.=.72)	see above (Rel.=.73)	.12 .14 .15 .16 .17 .17 .21 .24 .34

Arts/Music

Skager et al. (1965)	10/11	524 261 (m) 263 (f)	Q: see above 1) Music 2) Fine arts 3) Aesthetics	Knowledge test (music and art)	m: .26 f: .37 m: .10 f: .34 m: .26 f: .26
Skager et al. (1965)	10/11	524 261 (m) 263 (f)	Q: see above (Industrial arts)	Knowledge test	m: .24 f: .17

Note: Q = Questionnaire, T = Standardized test.

[a] Grades are either semester grades or grades for a whole school year.

[b] Despite the smaller number of countries there are 14 correlation coefficients because in some countries two different populations of the same age group were investigated.

[c] This value is the mean of .87 (internal consistency) and .69 (test–retest reliability).

unweighted correlations were conducted. However, only negligible differences between the two procedures emerged. Thus, only results based on weighted correlations are reported.

Studies Included in the Analysis

Table 8.1 overviews the studies included for review. The table is organized according to school subject and within each school subject according to grade level. For each individual study, information is provided concerning the sample and methods of measuring interest and achievement. For most of the studies, one or more overall correlations have been indicated. Some studies, however, reported separate correlations for male and female students.

Results

The Overall Interest Effect. From the studies listed previously, 121 independent correlation coefficients could be obtained. The distribution of these coefficients is depicted in Table 8.2 as a "stem and leaf" diagram (Tukey, 1977). Each digit to the left of the vertical line is part of the "stem," representing in each case the first digit of a correlation coefficient. Each of the digits to the right of the vertical line is a "leaf," representing the second digit of a correlation coefficient. For example, there are three correlation coefficients equal to or greater than .60 (namely .67, .60, .64) and 7 coefficients equal to .26.

Table 8.2

Independent Correlations between Interest and Achievement, Based on all Studies

.6	7
.6	04
.5	8
.5	011223
.4	67788999
.4	0012223334
.3	5555667777888889999
.3	000012222333334
.2	666666677777777888899999
.2	00112222233444
.1	55666777778888
.1	022334
.0	9

Note. k (number of correlations) = 121.

The values in Table 8.2 exhibit a normal distribution. All correlation coefficients are positive. The values range from .09 to .67. The mean value of the correlation coefficients equals .31, with a standard deviation of .133 (SD_r). Sampling error could account only for 2.1% of the observed variance. The population standard deviation (SD_p) amounts to .131, almost the same value as that without a correction for sampling error. Using this value for calculating the 95% confidence interval for the population correlation yields the coefficients .05 and .57.

As can be easily inferred from the results just mentioned, all three criteria of heterogeneity are met. The population standard deviation (.131) is larger than one fourth of the population correlation (.078), only 2.1% of the observed variance can be accounted for by sampling error, and the Chi^2 test is highly significant $(p < .001)$. These results suggest that the existence of relevant moderator variables is very likely.

To obtain a more precise estimate of the average population correlation, Hunter et al. (1982) recommend applying the correction for attenuation. For this purpose every correlation coefficient was weighted by both the reliabilities of the interest and achievement measures. In doing this, the correlation between interest and achievement for the whole sample of studies reached the value of .40, with a standard deviation of .158. In those cases where no reliabilities were indicated, the mean of available coefficients was used to replace missing values. The correction for attenuation was only applied in the case of the overall correlation. Because error-free measurement of variables like interest or achievement is not possible, the correction for attenuation leads to unrealistic estimations. In addition, comparability to other research results is greater when uncorrected coefficients are computed (Kulik & Kulik, 1989).

Before turning to a test of moderator variables, the influence of other, probably less important study features was investigated. First, it was confirmed that sample size was not significantly correlated with size of correlations $(r = -.14, n = 121)$. The direction of this correlation indicates that, as expected, a large sample size is associated with a smaller correlation coefficient. Further results show that studies published before 1975 yield the same values as more recent studies, and that studies conducted in the United States are not different from other studies. Also, no difference was found between IEA and other studies. Finally, we examined the influence of measuring interest and achievement simultaneously or at different times. In a meta-analysis by Uguroglu and Walberg (1979) of the relation between motivational predictors and achievement criteria, no difference between concurrent and predictive correlations could be found. Unfortunately, however, not enough studies were retained that reported an appreciable length of time between these two measurements.

Effects of the School Subject. As a first step in the analysis of moderator variables, we examined whether the strength of the interest–achievement relation varied between different subject areas. The results are reported in Table 8.3. Arts/music is not included because only one independent correlation could be derived.

Table 8.3

Interest-Achievement Correlations for Individual Subject Areas

Subject Area	r	k	SD_p
Mathematics	.32	31	.086
Science	.35	39	.140
Physics	.31	9	.117
Biology	.16	6	.027
Social Science	.34	6	.061
Foreign Language	.33	32	.099
Literature	.17	9	.040

Note: r = average weighted correlation; k = number of independent correlations; SD_p = population standard deviation.

With the exception of biology and literature, all correlation values are above the .30 mark. The correlations for biology and literature are significantly lower than for all other subjects. All correlations are significantly different from zero at the 5% level.[2] Additional analyses reveal that the correlations for biology and literature are significantly lower than are those for all other subject areas.[3]

---

[2] The significance of averaged correlations cannot be determined in the same way as that for individual correlations. The problem is the appropriate sample size. If the significance test is based on N as the total sample size, a type I error is probable. If the test is based on k as the number of correlations, a type II error is to be expected. Therefore, it is recommended that 95% confidence intervals be calculated (e.g., Schwarzer, 1989). Furthermore, as a rule of thumb, a population correlation should be at least twice as high as the population standard deviation. In the present analysis, all indications of significance are based on confidence intervals.

[3] The problem of testing the significance of the difference between two averaged correlations is similar to the problem of testing individual correlations (see footnote 2). However, in this case no rules of thumb or commonly accepted solutions are available. Schwarzer (personal communication) has suggested that in order to be significant the difference between two population correlations should exceed the corresponding average population standard deviation. Accordingly, all the following indications of significance are based on that rule.

In order to simplify the preceding results and to reveal more general trends, two groups of subject areas were formed: natural science and social science/humanities. The first group was comprised of mathematics, science, physics, and biology. The second group consisted of social science, foreign language, literature, and arts/music. The results of this analysis are depicted in Table 8.4. Although the interest–achievement correlation for natural science is higher than for social science, the difference between the two values does not exceed the average population standard deviation (SD_p = .121,) and thus cannot be regarded as significant. One should also bear in mind that the observed difference between natural science and social science/humanities is mainly due to the large number ($k = 19$) of low correlations obtained for literature. Interest–achievement correlations for social science and foreign language seem to be as high as those for math, science, and physics. From this, it can be concluded that there are basically no differences between natural and social sciences with regard to the size of interest–achievement correlations.

Effects of Grade Level. Previous research on the development of interests (e.g., Barak, 1981; Gottfredson, 1981) leads to the expectation that the relation between interest and achievement becomes increasingly stable with age. If this is true, then it might be expected that the correlation coefficients for older students would be higher than those for younger students.

Theoretically, our data allow for a comparison of the correlation values for all grade levels between 5 and 12. Unfortunately, the data are not spread evenly over the whole range of grade levels. Furthermore, some studies included students from different grade levels in one sample. Therefore, it seemed to be most reasonable to construct two larger groups, each encompassing several grade levels. The first group consisted of grade levels 5 to 10 and the second group consisted of grade levels 10 to 12.

As expected, the relation between interest and achievement was more pronounced at higher grade levels (see Table 8.4). However, the observed difference between the two grade level groups is nonsignificant. This result suggests that the relation between interest and achievement is equally strong for different age groups.

Effects of Gender. The last section of Table 8.4 shows the strength of correlations between interest and achievement for male versus female students. With the exception of the study by Kelly (1978), no other IEA study is involved here.

Table 8.4

Interest-Achievement Correlations Broken Down by Subject Area,
Grade Level, and Gender

Moderator variable	r	k	SD_p
Subject area:			
Natural Science	.34	74	.126
Social Science/			
Humanities	.25	53	.116
Grade level:			
5–10	.29	61	.108
10–12	.33	60	.155
Gender:			
Male	.35	14	.102
Female	.25	13	.063

Note: r = average weighted correlation; k = number of independent correlations; SD_p = population standard deviation.

The results show a clear and significant difference between male and female students. Interest explains 12% of observed achievement variance for males, but only 6% of the variance for females.

In summary, the results indicate that the predictive value of interest is equal for most subject areas, with the exception of biology and literature. In addition, younger students exhibit interest–achievement correlations almost as high as those of older students. A clear effect, emerges, however, for gender. Female students' academic performance is less associated with their interests than male students' academic performance.

It was not possible to examine the combined effects of all three moderator variables simultaneously, because not enough independent samples were left for such an analysis. However, the effects of pairs of factors could be tested. The results of this analysis show additive effects only in the expected directions. The highest correlation emerged for students in science at grade levels 10–12 ($r = .41$, $k = 16$, $p < .05$) and the lowest correlation ($r = .15$, $k = 9$, $p < .05$) for students in literature at grade levels 5–10.

Discussion

The Overall Interest Effect. The present meta-analysis suggests that on average and across different subject areas, types of school, and age groups, the level of interest accounts for about 10% of observed achievement variance. This estimation is in accordance with results from earlier reviews (e.g., Super, 1960). Of all the moderator variables we tested, only gender seems to have a strong impact on the interest–achievement relation. The relatively large residual standard deviations (see Tables 8.3 and 8.4) indicate that there are more relevant moderators than we were able to test here.

How strong is the predictive power of interest compared to other motivational or emotional variables? Uguroglu & Walberg (1979) reported an average correlation of .34 between measures of motivation and school achievement. A similar value has been reported by Bloom (1976), who reviewed the relation between subject-related affect and school achievement. Two other review articles contain data for the natural sciences that can be used for comparison. Steinkamp and Maehr (1983) and Willson (1983) obtained a relatively small correlation between affective predictors and school achievement ($r = .19$ and .16, respectively).

It was almost impossible to compare the predictive power of interest with that of other motivational or emotional variables because the reviews just mentioned did not differentiate between particular types of noncognitive variables. Instead, they mixed together different motivational and emotional factors in a single category. For example, Uguroglu and Walberg included such different variables as academic self-concept and achievement motivation in their category of motivation measures. Willson's (1983) study, however, included separate analyses for three different types of attitude variables (measures of attitude per se, measures of interests, and observed behavior) and indicated that interest exhibited a greater correlation with achievement (.27) than did other measures of attitude.

The Subject Area as a Moderator. Analysis of results broken down into individual school subjects revealed no striking differences. Weak interest–achievement correlations have been found only for biology and literature. This differs from Bloom's (1976) review, which indicated a stronger interest–achievement relation for mathematics than for other subjects.

It has been argued (e.g., Lehrke, 1988) that higher correlations between interest and achievement are to be expected in the natural sciences (with the exception of biology) and mathematics, because these subjects are believed to be more difficult than others and are therefore more dependent on the students' motivational level. In these cases interest seems to be an important prerequisite for persistence during early stages of the learning process. Easier school subjects, on the other hand, allow the less-interested student to also achieve good grades.

This argument might well explain the low interest–achievement correlations found for biology and literature. Also, the high mean correlation found for foreign language is to be expected, because students usually rate this subject as being disliked and very difficult (e.g., Stodolsky, 1988). Contradictory to the hypothesis, however, is the relatively high interest–achievement correlation found for social science, although it should also be noted that the mean correlation for social science is based on only six independent studies (see Table 8.3).

The present results suggest that interest exerts equal influence on achievement in all subject areas, independent of their level of difficulty. The low correlations found for literature may stem from the low reliability of performance evaluation in that area.

Grade Level as a Moderator. Our results show only a small tendency toward higher correlations in higher grade levels. Other reviews have found more pronounced differences between younger and older students. Uguroglu and Walberg (1979), for example, reported an increase in correlations of general measures of motivation from $r = .24$ (grade 1) to $r = .34$ (grade 12). Unfortunately, in the present meta-analysis the distribution of studies over all grade levels was quite unbalanced. We were not able, therefore, to perform an adequate test of the grade level hypothesis.

In the past, at least four possible explanations for an age-related increase in interest–achievement correlations have been put forward (Evans, 1971; Gottfredson, 1981; Todt, 1978, 1985). A first explanation suggests that over the school years, a selection process is at work, selecting those students who are capable of pursuing their interests. Second, during the course of schooling interest and achievement act upon one another and, thus, show an increasing convergence. A third explanation would be that interests become more and more stable as children become older. Furthermore, it has been found that during puberty the structure of interests is subject to fundamental changes that basically reflect a stronger orientation towards reality. This often results in the adoption of goals and interests more congruent with abilities and possible future vocations.

The available evidence does not support any of the aforementioned hypotheses. More research is needed to clarify the posited relations.

Gender as a Moderator. Our review strongly suggests that male students' performance accords with their interest level more than is the case for female students. In the past, gender differences have been studied especially in the domain of natural science. The findings of this line of research seem to correspond with our assertion that males have stronger interest–achievement relations than females. Many studies have found that males are more interested in the natural sciences (with the exception of biology) than are females, and that this difference becomes greater with increasing age (Comber & Keeves, 1973; Gardner, 1985; Kelly, 1978, 1985, 1987; Kelly & Smail, 1986; Schibeci, 1985).

Another consistent research finding is that male students perform better in the natural sciences than girls (e.g. Walker, 1976), whereas the latter achieve superior results in literature and English (as a foreign language). Female students also show greater interest in these subjects than do male students (Shemesh, 1990; Walker, 1976). On the basis of these results one might expect girls to show higher interest–achievement correlations than boys for literature and foreign language. This, however, was not confirmed by our analysis.

A line of research that is of relevance in the present context examined possible sex differences in basic abilities, like formal reasoning or spatial visualization. However, no unequivocal results could be obtained. Although it seems widely acknowledged that girls perform worse on most tests of mathematical ability than boys, especially after the 10th grade (see however Fennema, 1980; Fennema & Sherman, 1977), there is much controversy about the amount and relevance of the male students' superiority and its explanation (Aiken, 1987; Linn & Petersen, 1985; Shemesh, 1990; Stage, Kreinberg, Eccles, & Becker, 1985).

Some authors (e.g., Banreti–Fuchs & Meadows, 1976) have suggested that female students are more conformist than male students, and that they are more likely to invest effort in all subject areas regardless of their interests. Our analysis seems to be more in agreement with a conformity hypothesis. However, it is conceivable that there are, at least in the natural sciences, two processes at work that reduce the strength of the interest–achievement relation in females. The first factor represents sex-stereotyped low interest in science topics, and the second factor could be a strong need to conform to external performance expectations.

The Influence of Ability Factors. The present review suggests that interest contributes substantially to the prediction of school achievement. The strength of the relation between interest and achievement cannot be definitively evaluated, however, without taking into account other predictors. This is especially true for ability factors. Most studies included in our meta-analysis did not control for ability. There are, however, several studies (Barrilleaux, 1961; Frandsen & Sessions, 1953; Frandsen & Sorenson, 1969; Geffert, 1985; Hall, 1975; Skager, Bussis, & Schultz, 1965) that support the independence of interest and ability as predictors of achievement (see also Evans, 1971; Super, 1960). In addition, relatively small correlations between interest and ability have repeatedly been found (Gardner, 1985; Hungerman, 1967; Schibeci, 1985).

Steinkamp and Maehr (1983) discuss the possibility that the contributions of interest and ability to the prediction of achievement vary depending on the individual level of ability. They assume a threshold value of ability above which further differences in ability become less influential and motivational factors become more and more important. Below this threshold value differences in ability exert a dominant impact on achievement. This hypothesis, however, has not yet been tested.

Of course, a correlational analysis of the independence of interest and ability does not allow any conclusions about causal relations. Despite the evidence that interest and ability are independent predictors of achievement, it is reasonable to assume that these two factors influence each other, especially during the course of individual development. Several authors (e.g., Bloom, 1976; Evans, 1971; Frandsen & Sorenson, 1969; Johnson, 1969) have assumed a reciprocal relation according to which the perception of successful performance leads to positive affect, which in turn causes increased effort. Finally, increased effort contributes to the development of one's abilities.

Unfortunately, no empirical findings on the hypothesis of reciprocal influence between interest and achievement are available. Willson's (1983) meta-analysis suggests that the causal direction may change with age. He concludes that in lower grade levels the causal direction runs from achievement toward interest, whereas for older students it is reversed.

CONCLUSION

The results of the present meta-analysis suggest that there are several problems that deserve intensive investigation in the future. A first problem pertains to sex differences in the strength of interest–achievement correlations. Although previous research has repeatedly confirmed that female and male students differ with regard to their ability and interest in the natural and social sciences, this by no means provides a sufficient explanation for the generally low interest–achievement correlations found for girls. It seems desirable to conduct studies that are specifically designed to explore sex differences in greater detail.

Another task for future research may be the investigation of age-related trends. As we have seen, it is not possible on the basis of the studies included in our review to draw conclusion about the varying strength of the interest–achievement relation at different grade levels. More evidence on this issue would also be practically relevant. If it is true, for example, that students reorganize the structure of their school-related interests during puberty, then teachers and parents could be made aware of this fact and could work together to help channel students' interests in a productive and future-oriented direction.

The present review could only arrive at conclusions about correlational relations. There is an almost total lack of studies testing causal influences. Therefore, it remains unclear how interest and achievement on the one hand and interest and ability on the other interact with each other. From our point of view, it would be especially fruitful to address these problems with the help of causal modeling procedures (e.g., Kuusinen & Leskinen, 1988).

The results of the present analysis suggest a need for educational scientists to investigate the role of interest more intensively and systematically. Unlike other motivational factors that have received a great deal of attention (e.g., achievement motive), interest is a domain-specific concept in that students develop specific motivational orientations towards individual subject areas. Accordingly, we think that most students are not "omnivorous." They are not motivated to learn everything regardless of how meaningful it seems to be for them. In the same vein, students' appetite for knowledge is not determined by their (acquired or innate) abilities. As Csikszentmihalyi (1990) has written: "It is not that students cannot learn; it is that they do not wish to" (p. 115). Or, in Nicholls' (1990) words: "It is simply that more students might be gaining a sense of accomplishment and experiencing their work as meaningful if more researchers had been asking about the meaning of students' work rather than about their ability" (1990, p. 40).

REFERENCES

Aiken, L. (1987). Sex differences in mathematical ability: A review of the literature. *Educational Research Quarterly, 10,* 25–35.

Allehoff, W. H. (1985). *Berufswahl und berufliche Interessen.* Göttingen: Hogrefe.

Banreti–Fuchs, K. M., & Meadows, W. M. (1976). Interest, mental health, and attitudinal correlates of academic achievement among university students. *British Journal of Educational Psychology, 46,* 212–219.

Barak, A. (1981). Vocational interests: A cognitive view. *Journal of Vocational Behavior, 19,* 1–14.

Barrilleaux, L. E. (1961). High school science achievement as related to interest and IQ. *Educational and Psychological Measurement, 21,* 929–936.

Bloom, B. S. (1976). *Human characteristics and school learning.* New York: McGraw–Hill.

Carter, G. E. (1982). Assessing students' interests in chemistry. *British Journal of Educational Psychology, 52,* 378–380.

Comber, L. C., & Keeves, J. P. (1973). *Science education in nineteen countries. An empirical study.* New York: Wiley.

Cronbach, L. J., & Gleser, G. C. (1965). *Psychological tests and personnel decisions.* Urbana: University of Illinois Press.

Csikszentmihalyi, M. (1990). Literacy and intrinsic motivation. *Daedalus, 119,* 115–140.

Dewey, J. (1913). *Interest and effort in education.* Boston: Riverside Press.

Evans, K. M. (1971). *Attitudes and interests in education.* London: Routledge & Kegan Paul.

Fennema, E. (1980). Sex-related differences in mathematics achievement: Where and why? In L. H. Fox, L. Brody, & D. Tobin (Eds.), *Women and the mathematical mystique* (pp. 76–93). Baltimore/London: Johns Hopkins University Press.

Fennema, E., & Sherman, J. A. (1977). Sex-related differences in mathematics achievement, spatial visualization and affective factors. *American Educational Research Journal, 14,* 51–71.

Fishman, J. A., & Pasanella, A. K. (1960). College admission-selection studies. *Review of Educational Research, 30,* 298–310.

Fleming, M. L., & Malone, M. R. (1983). The relationship of student characteristics and student performance in science as viewed by meta-analysis research. *Journal of Research in Science Teaching, 20,* 481–495.

Frandsen, A. N., & Sessions, A. D. (1953). Interests and school achievement. *Educational and Psychological Measurement, 13,* 94–101.

Frandsen, A., & Sorenson, M. (1969). Interests as motives in academic achievement. *Journal of School Psychology, 7,* 52–57.

Fricke, R., & Treinies, G. (1985). *Einführung in die Metaanalyse.* Bern: Huber.

Gardner, P. L. (1985). Students' interest in science and technology: An international overview. In M. Lehrke, L. Hoffmann, & P. L. Gardner (Eds.), *Interests in science and technology education* (pp. 15–34). Kiel: Institut für die Pädagogik der Naturwissenschaften.

Geffert, E. (1985). Motivationale Grundlagen der mathematischen Begabung. *Zeitschrift für Psychologie, 193,* 431–441.

Glass, G. V. (1976). Primary, secondary, and meta-analysis of research. *Educational Researcher, 5,* 3–8.

Glass, G. V., McGaw, B., & Smith, M. L. (1981). *Meta-analysis in social research.* Beverly Hills, CA: Sage.

Gottfredson, L. S. (1981). Circumscription and compromise: A developmental theory of occupational aspirations. *Journal of Counseling Psychology Monograph, 28,* 545–579.

Haertel, G. D., Walberg, H. J., & Weinstein, T. (1983). Psychological performance models of educational performance: A theoretical synthesis. *Review of Educational Research, 53,* 75–91.

Hall, E. R. (1975). Motivation and achievement in black and white junior college students. *Journal of Social Psychology, 97,* 107–113.

Harty, H., & Beall, D. (1984). Toward the development of a children's science curiosity measure. *Journal of Research in Science Teaching, 21,* 425–436.

Hidi, S. (1990). Interest and its contribution as a mental resource for learning. *Review of Educational Research,* 549–571.

Hidi, S., & Baird, W. (1986). Interestingness—A neglected variable in discourse processing. *Cognitive Science, 10,* 179–194.

Hoffmann, L., & Lehrke, M. (1986). Eine Untersuchung über Schülerinteressen an Physik und Technik. *Zeitschrift für Pädagogik, 32,* 189–204.

Holland, J. L. (1973). *Making vocational choices: A theory of careers.* Englewood Cliffs, NJ: Prentice–Hall.

Holland, J. L. (1976). Vocational preferences. In M. D. Dunnette (Ed.), *Handbook of industrial and organizational psychology* (pp. 521–570). Chicago: Rand McNally.

Hungerman, A. D. (1967). Achievement and attitude of sixth-grade pupils in conventional and contemporary mathematics programs. *Arithmetic Teacher, 14,* 30–39.

Hunter, J. E. & Schmidt, F. L. (1990). *Methods of meta-analysis.* Newbury Park, CA: Sage.

Hunter, J. E., Schmidt, F. L., & Jackson, G. B. (1982). *Meta-analysis: Cumulating research findings across studies.* Beverly Hills, CA: Sage.

Husén, T. (Ed.) (1967). *International study of achievement in mathematics (Vols. 1 and 2).* Stockholm/New York: Almqvist & Wiksell/Wiley.

Jäger, R. (1978). *Differentielle Diagnostizierbarkeit in der psychologischen Diagnostik.* Göttingen: Hogrefe.

Johnson, R. W. (1969). Effectiveness of SVIB academic interest scales in predicting college achievement. *Journal of Applied Psychology, 53,* 309–316.

Jungermann, H. (1976). *Rationale Entscheidungen.* Bern: Huber.

Kelly, A. (1978). *Girls and science: An international study of sex differences in school science achievement.* Stockholm: Almqvist & Wiksell.

Kelly, A. (1985). The development of girls' and boys' attitudes to science: A longitudinal study. In M. Lehrke, L. Hoffmann, & P. L. Gardner (Eds.), *Interests in science and technology education* (pp. 269–280). Kiel: Institut für die Pädagogik der Naturwissenschaften.

Kelly, A. (1987). Die Entwicklung naturwissenschaftlicher Interessen und Einstellungen bei Mädchen und Jungen. In M. Lehrke & L. Hoffmann

(Eds.), *Schülerinteressen am naturwissenschaftlichen Unterricht*. Köln: Aulis Verlag Deubner.

Kelly, A., & Smail, B. (1986). Sex stereotypes and attitudes to science among 11-year-old children. *British Journal of Educational Psychology, 56*, 158–168.

Kerschensteiner, G. (1922). Der Interessenbegriff in der Pädagogik. *Pädagogische Blätter, 5*, 349–354.

Khan, S. B. (1969). Affective correlates of academic achievement. *Journal of Educational Psychology, 60*, 216–221.

Krapp, A. (1979). *Prognose und Entscheidung*. Weinheim: Beltz.

Krapp, A. (1984). Forschungsergebnisse zur Bedingungsstruktur der Schulleistung. In K. Heller (Ed.), *Leistungsdiagnostik in der Schule* (pp. 46–62). Bern: Huber.

Kühn, R. (1983). *Bedingungen für Schulerfolg. Zusammenhänge zwischen Schülermerkmalen, häuslicher Umwelt und Schulnoten*. Göttingen: Hogrefe.

Kulik, J. A., & Kulik, C. C. (1989). Meta-analysis in education. *International Journal of Educational Research, 13*, Issue 3.

Kuusinen, J., & Leskinen, E. (1988). Latent structure analysis of longitudinal data on relations between intellectual abilities and school achievement. *Multivariate Behavioral Research, 8*, 103–118.

Lavin, D. E. (1965). *The prediction of academic performance*. New York: Russell Sage Foundation.

Lee, M. (1971). *Decision theory and human behavior*. New York: Wiley.

Lehrke, M. (1988). *Interesse und Desinteresse am naturwissenschaftlich-technischen Unterricht*. Kiel: Institut für die Pädagogik der Naturwissenschaften (IPN).

Lewis, E. G., & Massad, C. E. (1975). *The teaching of English as a foreign language in ten countries*. Stockholm/New York: Almqvist & Wiksell/Wiley.

Linn, M. C., & Petersen, A. C. (1985). Facts and assumptions about the nature of sex differences. In S. S. Klein (Ed.), *Handbook for achieving sex equity through education* (pp. 53–78). Baltimore/London: Johns Hopkins University Press.

Lloyd, J., & Barenblatt, L. (1984). Intrinsic intellectuality: Its relations to social class, intelligence, and achievement. *Journal of Personality and Social Psychology, 46*, 655–668.

McDaniel, M. A., Hirsh, H. R., Schmidt, F. L., Raju, N. S., & Hunter, J. E. (1986). Interpreting the results of meta-analytic research: A comment on Schmitt, Gooding, Noe, and Kirsch (1984). *Personnel Psychology, 39*, 141–148.

Napier, J. D., & Riley, J. P. (1985). Relationship between affective determinants and achievement in science for seventeen-year-olds. *Journal of Research in Science Teaching, 22*, 365–383.

Nicholls, J. G. (1990). What is ability and why are we mindful of it? A developmental perspective. In R. J. Sternberg & J. Kolligian, Jr. (Eds.), *Competence considered* (pp. 11–40). New Haven/London: Yale University Press.

Nichols, R. C. (1966). Nonintellective predictors of achievement in college. *Educational and Psychological Measurement, 26*, 899–915.

Oehlert, P. (1977). *Aufstellung und erste empirische—Überprüfung eines Konstruktes zur Methode der Steuerung von kognitiven Lernprozessen durch Unterrichtsimpulse.* Unveröffentlichte Dissertation, Pädagogische Hochschule Westfalen–Lippe.

Parkerson, J. A., Lomax, R. G., Schiller, D. P., & Walberg, H. J. (1984). Exploring causal models of educational achievement. *Journal of Educational Psychology, 76,* 638–646.

Purves, A.C. (1973). *Literature education in ten countries. An empirical study.* New York: Halsted Press.

Quack, L. (1979). Zur Bedingungsanalyse der Schulleistung: Der Beitrag kognitiver und nicht-kognitiver Merkmale der Schülerpersönlichkeit. In K. J. Klauer & H. J. Kornadt (Eds.), *Jahrbuch fuer empirische Erziehungswissenschaft* (pp. 93–116). Düsseldorf: Schwann.

Rosemann, B., & Allhoff, P. (1982). *Differentielle Prognostizierbarkeit von Schulleistung.* Opladen: Westdeutscher Verlag.

Sauer, J., & Gattringer, H. (1985). Soziale, familiale, kognitive und motivationale Determinanten der Schulleistung. *Kölner Zeitschrift für Soziologie und Sozialpsychologie, 37,* 288–309.

Saunders, D. R. (1956). Moderator variables in prediction. *Educational and Psychological Measurement, 16,* 209–222.

Schibeci, R. (1985). Students' attitudes to science: What influences them, and how these influences are investigated. In M. Lehrke, L. Hoffmann, & P. L. Gardner (Eds.), *Interests in science and technology education* (pp. 35–48). Kiel: Institut für die Pädagogik der Naturwissenschaften.

Schiefele, H., Krapp, A., Prenzel, M., Heiland, A., & Kasten, H. (1983, July/August). *Principles of an educational theory of interest.* Paper presented at the 7th biennial meeting of the International Society for the Study of Behavioral Development, Munich.

Schiefele, U. (1988). Motivationale Bedingungen des Textverstehens. *Zeitschrift für Pädagogik, 34,* 687–708.

Schneider, W., & Bös, K. (1985). Exploratorische Analysen zu Komponenten des Schulerfolgs. *Zeitschrift für Entwicklungspsychologie und Pädagogische Psychologie, 17,* 325–340.

Schwarzer, R. (1989). *Meta-analysis programs (unpublished manuscript).* Berlin: Free University of Berlin, Department of Psychology.

Shemesh, M. (1990). Gender-related differences in reasoning skills and learning interests of junior high school students. *Journal of Research in Science Teaching, 27,* 27–34.

Sjöberg, L. (1983). Interest, achievement and vocational choice. *European Journal of Science Education, 5,* 299–307.

Sjöberg, L. (1984). Interests, effort, achievement and vocational preference. *British Journal of Educational Psychology, 54,* 189–205.

Skager, R. W., Bussis, A. M., & Schultz, C. B. (1965). Comparison of information scales and like–indifferent–dislike scales as measures of interest. *Psychological Reports, 16,* 251–261.

Stage, E. K., Kreinberg, N., Eccles, J., & Becker, J. R. (1985). Increasing the participation and achievement of girls and women in mathematics, science, and engineering. In S. S. Klein (Ed.), *Handbook for achieving sex equity through education* (pp. 237–268). Baltimore: Johns Hopkins University Press.

Steinkamp, M. W., & Maehr, M. L. (1983). Affect, ability, and science achievement: A quantitative synthesis of correlational research. *Review of Educational Research, 53,* 369–396.

Stodolsky, S. S. (1988). *The subject matters.* Chicago: University of Chicago Press.

Super, D. E. (1960). Interests. In C. W. Harris (Ed.), *Encyclopedia of educational research* (pp. 728–733). New York: Macmillan.

Tiedemann, J. (1977). *Leistungsversagen in der Schule.* München: Goldmann.

Todt, E. (1967). *Differentieller Interessentest (DIT).* Bern: Huber.

Todt, E. (1978). *Das Interesse.* Bern: Huber.

Todt, E. (1985). Elements of a theory of science interests. In M. Lehrke, L. Hoffmann, & P. L. Gardner (Eds.), *Interests in science and technology education* (pp. 59–69). Kiel: Institut für die Pädagogik der Naturwissenschaften.

Trost, G. (1975). *Vorhersage des Studienerfolgs.* Braunschweig: Westermann.

Tukey, J. W. (1977). *Exploratory data analysis.* Reading, MA: Addison–Wesley.

Uguroglu, M. E., & Walberg, H. J. (1979). Motivation and achievement: A quantitative synthesis. *American Educational Research Journal, 16,* 375–389.

Walker, D. C. (1976). *The IEA six subject survey: An empirical study of education in twenty-one countries.* Stockholm/New York: Almqvist & Wiksell/Wiley.

Walsh, W. B., & Osipow, S. H. (Eds.) (1986). *Advances in vocational psychology. Vol. 1: The assessment of interests.* Hillsdale, NJ: Lawrence Erlbaum Associates.

Wendeler, J. (1968). Schülerinteressen bei Gymnasiasten der 10. Klasse. *Schule und Psychologie, 15,* 114–119.

Willson, V. L. (1983). A meta-analysis of the relationship between science achievement and science attitude: Kindergarten through college. *Journal of Research in Science Teaching, 20,* 839–850.

Zedeck, S. (1971). Problems with the use of "moderator" variables. *Psychological Bulletin, 76,* 295–310.

III SITUATIONAL INTEREST (INTERESTINGNESS)

Situational Interest and Its Impact on Reading and Expository Writing

9

Suzanne Hidi and Valerie Anderson
Ontario Institute for Studies in Education

Reading and writing are crucial abilities, both in school and out. Educators who feel an obligation to bring students to the highest possible levels of competency in these basic skills have used a wide variety of teaching approaches based on theory, research, and intuition. These practical efforts have variously and somewhat haphazardly stressed what students should learn, how they learn, and even how they feel about learning, particularly with respect to their individual likes and dislikes, interests, emotions, and cultural orientations. By contrast, research over the last 20 years has had a strongly cognitive orientation, with little concern for the affective factors with which the schools have had to cope. Only recently have some cognitive researchers begun to recognize and study the affective aspects of learning.

Hidi (1990) has argued that although it is now recognized that affective factors influence the selection, processing, and retention of information, little progress has been made in actually integrating the motivational and affective aspects of learning with the cognitive ones. In Hidi's view, interest is an especially important affective factor in that it is central to intellectual functioning and, consequently, strongly influences how people select and persist in processing certain types of information in preference to others. She reviewed related research and concluded that interest has a profound effect on human functioning at both the psychological and physiological levels. Furthermore, the processing of interesting information has unique aspects not present in processing information without interest. She also proposed that current advances in neuro-cognitive research, such as the measurement of physiological concomitants of mental phenomena (Berman, 1987), may allow future researchers to integrate the physiological and psychological aspects of cognitive functioning and thus provide a more complete picture of how interest affects information processing and learning.

Among the many areas that might be developed in the field of interest, this chapter focuses specifically on the psychological aspects of children's comprehension, learning, and production of texts as a function of interest.

THE DISTINCTION BETWEEN INDIVIDUAL INTEREST AND SITUATIONAL INTEREST

As described in Chapter 1, interest research has focused either on indi-vidual (personal) interest or on interest that can be generated across individuals by certain conditions and/or stimuli in the environment. Krapp (1989) and Hidi (1990) have called this latter type of interest *situational interest*. Even though the distinction between individual and situational interest has not yet been universally acknowledged by interest researchers, they have usually dealt with one type of interest or the other. The separate conceptualizations have not only determined how interest has been viewed and researched but have reflected, to a large extent, two different ways in which the state of interest can be generated in people. Individual interest develops slowly and tends to be long-lasting. Situational interest, on the other hand, is evoked by something in the immediate environment and, consequently, may or may not have a lasting effect on personal interest and learning.[1]

Although individual interest is triggered by an individual's predisposition and situational interest by environmental factors, it must be emphasized that the two types of interest are not dichotomous phenomena that occur in isolation (Hidi, 1990). On the contrary, each can be expected to influence the other's development. Situational interest, which can only

---

[1] Recently it has come to our attention that the distinction between individual and situational interest resembles the distinction Ainley (1987) has made with respect to curiosty. She demonstrates empirically that curiosity is not a unitary concept, but one that must be divided into two factors: depth, and breadth of curiosity. Depth of curiosity describes the extent to which an individual investigates or become engaged in novel objects, events, and ideas in order to understand them. Breadth of curiosity characterizes an individual's orienation to seek more short-term change and variation.

result from an interaction between the person and the environment, may, in turn, contribute to the development of a long-lasting individual interest. This interactive process also characterizes individual interest. A person with a well-developed individual interest will have stronger reactions to certain relevant and potentially interest-evoking situations than a person without such interest.

Research on individual interest has shown that children as well as adults who are interested in a topic or an activity pay more attention, persist for longer periods of time, and acquire more knowledge than subjects without such interest (e.g., Asher, 1979, 1980; Estes & Vaughan, 1973; Fransson, 1977; Nenniger, 1987; Prenzel, 1988; Renninger, 1987, 1990). Even very young children have been found to have strong, stable, and relatively well-focused individual interests that function as powerful determinants of their attention, recognition, and memory (Renninger & Wozniak, 1985).

We wish to argue, however, that whereas research shows that individual interests have a strong impact on learning, their application in educational settings may be problematic. Most teachers would agree that individualization is important and ongoing in their classrooms. Teachers have been aware of the need to promote children's interests since Dewey's (1913) ground-breaking work on the role of interest in learning. But, as has been pointed out, until recently there has been little systematic research on interest, and educators have been left to try to take advantage of students' interests on their own. Little is known as yet about how interests develop or why some early interests lead to long-term or lifelong interests and others do not. Without this knowledge, teachers remain somewhat at a loss as to how to best nurture and use their students' individual interests. Efforts to encourage those interests have often resulted in the teacher's attempting to cater to the personal interests of each and every child in the classroom. There are clearly problems inherent in this approach. Meeting individual needs in this way is an extremely time- and effort-consuming task for teachers, particularly for the teacher who has a large group of students. It is highly questionable whether many teachers in such settings actually have enough time to provide an individual program for each student that would adequately affect learning. What is more, although it is quite likely that all children have interests of one kind or another, those interests may not be equally well expressed or appropriate in school settings.[2]

An alternative to the individualization of interests, however, might be provided by situational interest. An educational approach that focused on more generalizable situational interests would require less attention to variations across individuals and, thus, could be less taxing for the teacher. It also could help insure that all students are exposed to the basic information that is needed to promote learning. One type of situational interest that is especially relevant to education can be created by reading materials. Interest that is elicited by text through ideas, topics, and themes is a particular form of situational interest that Hidi and Baird (1988) have referred to as text-based interest. Because much of what children learn in school comes from textbooks, it seems especially opportune to determine how this potentially important source of interest might be developed and utilized. To best use text-based interest, it is essential to investigate which ideas create interest in such a way that they override individual differences. For example, in literature, certain themes and topics over the centuries have been of such universal interest as to become archetypal in their appeal (e.g., sex, death). It is reasonable to assume that this kind of universal text-based interest could also be generated by many other topics, themes, and ideas, and that texts for children could eventually be designed and chosen with this in mind.

During the last decade or so, much important research has been carried out to determine how texts can be made easier from which to learn, or "considerate," usually from an organizational or structural point of view (Armbruster, 1984). Little research has been done, however, to determine how the specific content of texts might be made more interesting or appealing and still positively affect learning. Much of this chapter is devoted to reporting the research that has examined the effects of situational text-based interest on reading and writing and the factors that contribute to this type of interest. First, however, we consider some theoretical issues that expand on the nature and importance of situational interest.

---

[2] See Renninger (this volume) for a different point of view regarding why and how individual interests should be considered in the classroom.

THEORETICAL CONSIDERATIONS OF SITUATIONAL INTEREST

Situational interest is elicited by certain aspects of a situation, such as novelty or intensity. These aspects are assumed to contribute to the "interestingness" of the situation. Although the exact qualities that elicit situational interest and determine the degree of interestingness are far from determined, research that provides insight into the creation of this type of interest has begun to increase. One important question that has not been considered is how a psychological state of interest that is due to situational factors differs from one that is due to individual predispositions. Although there is little research that directly pertains to this comparison, investigations in the area of affect may provide some evidence that certain differences exist between these two states.

The Affective Component of the State of Interest

Many of the investigators who have looked at individual interest have argued that the cognitive activities associated with such interests tend to be accompanied by positive feelings. For example, Asher (1979) looked at children's individual interest in topics and defined interest by saying that "something is interesting when you like it and would like to find out more about it" (p. 687). Prenzel (1988) hypothesized that activities involving objects of personal interest (interest engagements) would be accompanied by distinctly positive or pleasant feelings. In three longitudinal studies, Prenzel examined a small number of subjects' interactions with one of two different interest objects (computer and guitar). As predicted, the subjects' ratings of those interactions indicated that the interest engagements were accompanied by pleasant feelings. Similarly, Deci (this volume) concludes that the "experiential quality of interest has a positive hedonic valence and is related to the feelings of excitement and enjoyment." He acknowledges, however, that there is a lack of agreement as to whether interest and enjoyment are the same or different affective experiences. Earlier, Izard (1977) went well beyond arguing that interest is associated with affect to maintain that interest–excitement (distinct from enjoyment–joy) is the most frequently experienced and fundamental positive emotion, one that provides much of the motivation for learning and development of competencies and creative endeavors.

Although there seems to be considerable consistency among individual interest researchers with regard to the interest–affect association, researchers of situational interest have not been consistent on this point. Anderson (1982) reported that children reading interesting sentences showed affective responses, but he did not attempt to make any further distinctions of these responses. Iran–Nejad (1987), on the other hand, investigated the cognitive and affective causes of interestingness and liking and concluded that they arise from different causes. He asked undergraduate students to read mystery short stories with endings that varied in the degree of surprise (usually considered to be a cause of situational interest), outcome valence (the goodness or badness of the outcome), and incongruity resolution (how the reader resolves the surprise ending). The results showed that surprise had no effect on liking but did influence interest, and that outcome valence had a substantial influence on liking but no effect on interest. In addition, incongruity resolution seemed to have caused interest without directly influencing liking. Thus Iran–Nejad concluded that, although (situational) interest and liking may occur simultaneously, they are different phenomena with different underlying causes, and situational interest is not necessarily associated with positive emotions.

Berlyne (1974a, c) similarly maintained that an increase in interest is not necessarily associated with liking. In experiments on perceptual processing and verbal judgments of interestingness, he and his colleagues (Berlyne, 1974b; Crozier, 1974; Hare, 1974; Normore, 1974) found that, whereas liking (hedonic tone) tended to reach a peak at intermediate levels of uncertainty, suggesting a curvilinear relation, judged interesting-ness increased linearly with uncertainty and did not decline after a peak. The experiments also indicated that subjects tended to look longer at less pleasing but more interesting stimuli. The combined findings of Berlyne and his colleagues, like Iran–Nejad's results, further support the idea that interestingness and liking are different phenomena that may or may not occur together.

In view of the varied findings connected with situational interest, it seems reasonable to hypothesize that situational interest might not be as intensively and consistently associated with positive feelings as are activities carried out in conjunction with well-developed personal interests. Situational interest, which is most often generated by something in the immediate environment, can be spontaneous and fleeting and, as such, may be neither connected to nor the beginning of a long-standing interest. Thus, whereas situational interest may create a variety of reactions, from revulsion to amusement, it need not be necessarily connected to positive emotions or long-standing interest. Further research will be needed to more closely examine this possibility and to develop a more complete theory of how the psychological state generated by situational interest differs from that of individual interest.

Distinguishing Between Situational Interest and Curiosity

Berlyne (1960, 1974a) has also argued that a set of stimulus characteristics, called collative variables (e.g., novelty, complexity), has a powerful effect on an individual's motivational state. One state that results from these variables is curiosity. Because collative variables overlap with the stimulus characteristics that have been associated with situational interest, one may question how situational interest differs from curiosity. Even when all of Berlyne's work is considered, it is not clear how he distinguished between the two concepts. Before this point can be further discussed, however, the relevant aspects of Berlyne's theory must be summarized.

Berlyne's collative variables are structural or formal properties of stimuli that include variations along the lines of familiar–novel, simple–complex, expected–surprising, clear–ambiguous, and stable–variable (Berlyne, 1974a, p. 5). These variables affect the psychological states of individuals by eliciting conflict and uncertainty. Such changes in psychological states are related to changes in the physiological phenomena of arousal. Motivation is related to arousal in an inverted–U function; that is, the optimal motivating effect results from arousal that is neither too high nor too low. Arousal is similarly related to collative variables (characterized by an inverted–U function); thus, too much novelty may lead to high arousal and over-excitement and too little novelty may result in low arousal and boredom, but medium levels of novelty lead to moderate arousal that is optimally motivating. It is, therefore, the function of collative variables to determine how stimuli will affect arousal (arousal potential). Although a desired increase or decrease in arousal can be generally motivating (depending on the individual's existing arousal state), one of the specific functions of arousal increase is the generation of curiosity and exploratory behavior (Izard, 1977).

As mentioned earlier, it is difficult to establish with certainty how Berlyne differentiated between curiosity and interest. In his early writings, he seemed to consider interest to be more or less synonymous with curiosity (see Izard, 1977, p. 197, on this point). Berlyne's later work (1971, 1974a), however, suggests that he may have changed his mind on this point and begun to consider interestingness as a unique phenomenon. Those studies actually dealt with specific judgments of perceptual types of situational interest, although that term was not used at that time. Berlyne and his colleagues (e.g., Berlyne, 1974b; Crozier, 1974; Hare, 1974; Normore, 1974) asked subjects to judge the interestingness of visual patterns, works of art, and/or music. They concluded that collative variables increased interestingness monotonically, and more specifically found that, at least with this type of perceptual processing, interestingness is a quality that contributes to the aesthetic value of works of art.

Berlyne may have changed his view on curiosity and interest, but he did not specifically state this change, nor did he elaborate on precisely how he thought interest and curiosity differed. Although Berlyne's later research was based on perceptual situational interest, related research of the last decade has focused on semantic or text-based situational interest. In the following, we present the arguments based on this more recent research in an attempt to more clearly distinguish between interest and curiosity.

First, whereas curiosity is assumed to be a result of collative variables that create conflict and uncertainty, situational interest can be generated by stimulus characteristics that go beyond the structural and formal patterns of collative variables and are not necessarily associated with conflict and uncertainty. For example, Schank (1979) argued that some concepts like power, death, and sex are universally interesting. Kintsch (1980), who also acknowledged that interest can be created by concepts like violence and sex, called this emotional interest. With regard to text, Kintsch further proposed that another type of interest was cognitive and was determined by three interacting factors: how much the reader knows about the text's topic, the degree of uncertainty the text generates in him or her, and how well particular information can be meaningfully related to other sections of the text. Thus, although Kintsch's concept of cognitive interest specifies the aspect of uncertainty, it clearly goes beyond purely structural considerations by depending on the individual's specific content knowledge. Iran–Nejad (1987) also emphasized that the intellectual activity involved in responding to external stimuli contributed to heightened interest. He demonstrated that, in surprise-ending stories, interest is not simply the function of surprise or expectation failures in general but is specifically caused by post-surprise incongruity resolution (this volume). In addition, Anderson, Shirey, Wilson, and Fielding (1987) suggested that information that involves characters or life themes with which readers can identify and/or involves a high activity or intensity level is interesting. Hidi and Baird (1983, 1986) further reported that a character's goal-directed activities and human interest factors were highly salient, well-recalled points of school texts. Thus, many factors (e.g., life themes, sex, violence) that cannot be classified as collative variables have been associated with situational interest.

Second, the relation between curiosity and the stimulus characteristics (collative variables) that elicit it has been described by the inverted–U function discussed earlier. However, this function does not necessarily characterize the relation between situational interest and the stimulus characteristics that elicit it. For example, there is no evidence that interest generated by character identification declines after an optimal plateau. Indeed, because character identification is so closely tied to one's own character (self), it could be argued that such a decline could not exist. To carry this even further, nothing seems to be more interest-inducing than hearing one's own name being mentioned or seeing it in print. Berlyne and his colleagues' findings, which judged interestingness of perceptual patterns, showing a monotonic relation to collative variables as opposed to an inverted–U function, also support the notion that interestingness might have a different relation to stimulus characteristic than to curiosity.[3]

Third, curiosity has been traditionally associated only with quite short-term states of uncertainty that could normally be represented by a simple question. Once an answer is provided, uncertainty is reduced and so is curiosity. Situational interest may or may not be short term, and it often cannot be represented by a specific question. For example, the reader of a murder mystery is usually curious to find out who the killer is. Once the killer's identity becomes known, uncertainty is reduced and the book loses most of its appeal. Compare this experience with a person who begins reading an essay on the present state of morality and assumes that, because it is required reading for a course, it is boring. Later, the reader, rather suddenly, becomes interested in the ideas because they are original, interesting, and well-presented. At this point, she/he continues to read simply to acquire more information and more knowledge without having any question in mind that needs to be answered. The reader has become interested in the text. This situational interest, which is brought about and facilitated by the text itself (thus text-based), could but need not develop into long-term individual interest. It is, however, distinct from curiosity.

---

[3] It should be noted that whereas a curvilinear relationship may not exist between situational interest and stimulus characteristics, such a relationship may exist between interest and knowledge factors. We return to this point later in the chapter.

EMPIRICAL INVESTIGATIONS

The rest of this chapter describes the empirical investigations that Hidi and her research group have conducted over the past several years in an effort to shed light on how situational interest and, more particularly, text-based interest can be created and utilized in school settings. Although it is assumed that situational interest tends to be generated by similar stimulus characteristics across groups of individuals, some still might question whether generalizations about situational interest are possible, and might suggest that individual differences override choices and determine reactions. Recently, Sadoski, Goetz, and Kangiser (1988) empirically examined the existence of agreement among readers (central tendencies) regarding imagery and affect in stories. These authors concluded that readers demonstrated a marked consistency in their responses. Their ratings showed similar degrees of plot importance, imagery, and affect at predictable points in the stories. Their verbal reports reflected considerable agreement about what was imagined and what feelings were evoked. Many years earlier Berlyne (1974a) similarly agreed that, in spite of individual differences, people's aesthetic reactions showed an appreciable degree of consistency (p. 22). Most recently, Hayes (1991) found great consistency among readers judging college students based on application letters. Research described earlier by Schank (1979), Kintsch (1980), and Hidi and Baird (1983, 1986) also reinforces these consistencies with respect to interest.

The research that follows focuses on both the comprehension and the production of expository text. The findings clearly differentiate reading and writing, two areas that are often believed to be similar in many ways. First, the findings of the reading research are discussed, then the investigations of writing are presented and, finally, directions for future research are proposed.

Studies of the Comprehension and Recall of School Texts

Preliminary Investigations of the Relation Between Interest and Importance in School Texts and the Effect of These Factors on Learning. The first study on the comprehension and recall of text was undertaken by Hidi, Baird, and Hildyard (1982) to determine the current state of situational interest in school texts. Two major concerns were addressed. The first was the extent to which any interest generated by school texts is related to the important ideas in those texts. In other words, are the interesting text segments also the important ones? If situational interest is to have any serious impact on relevant learning, such interest should, at the very least, be focussed on important aspects of texts. The second concern was how interest and importance in texts affect students' ability to comprehend, process, and learn information.

In order to determine the relation between interest and importance in typical school texts, Hidi et al. (1982) first examined a subset of such texts from a larger sample originally collected by Kirkwood and Wolfe (1980) for a large-scale study of the readability of text materials used in the Ontario school system. The passages used in the present investigation were taken from language arts and social science textbooks used by fourth-grade students.

It was found that the texts could be classified into three distinct types: (a) typical stories with clear-cut narrative structures, (b) expository texts that dealt with facts, explanations, descriptions, and/or instructions, and (c) a group of expositions that the investigators referred to as "mixed texts" because they contained some narrative episodes or anecdotes. The narrative elements in these mixed texts frequently did not seem intended to convey essential information but rather to catch and hold students' interest. Although it has been assumed by some textbook writers that interest automatically generalizes from interesting, but trivial, information to important and/or adjacent text segments, at the point of this preliminary study these assumptions had yet to be investigated. Thus, the important question about these mixed texts was not so much whether children recalled the interesting episodes, but whether and how the episodes influenced the retention of more essential information.

First, however, the relation between important and interesting information within the three text categories was examined. Two examples of each type of text (narrative, expository, and mixed) were selected. Each text was rated sentence-by-sentence by five adult raters for importance and interestingness. The three text types were nearly equal in ideas rated as important (between 37% and 41%). Ideas rated as interesting, on the other hand, were 30.5% for mixed texts, 36.5% for narratives, and only 2.5% for expositions. Thus, the raters found the expositions almost devoid of interesting ideas, perhaps even boring.

Correlations between ratings of importance and interest for narratives and mixed texts indicated a strong relation between importance and interestingness in the narratives $(r = .70)$, but no such relation in the mixed texts $(r = .07)$. (Low interest ratings rendered similar correlations for expositions meaningless.) These results showed that only in the narrative texts were interesting ideas also important. In the mixed texts, the two characteristics did not tend to coincide. It was concluded that an inherent characteristic of stories may be that interesting ideas are also important ones, and that this quality may contribute to the ease with which narratives are understood and recalled.

Next, in order to determine the extent to which children retained the most important information from the different text types, fifth and seventh graders' immediate and delayed recall of the six texts were investigated. The test of immediate recall followed a session in which children were asked to read their passages until they felt they had learned them. The test of delayed recall was carried out 4 days later.

Immediate recall scores did not show significant grade or text differences, although students in both grades tended to recall narrations best. However, there was a significant interaction between age and text type on the delayed recall scores. Whereas the fifth graders' recall showed small differences across text types, the seventh graders' recall showed more than twice as many important idea units from narratives as from mixed texts, with recall of pure exposition half-way between the two.

If one bears in mind that both narratives and mixed texts showed similar percentages of ideas rated as interesting and important (36.5 and 30.5 percent, respectively) but had very different correlations between interestingness and importance on each of their sentences (a high correlation for narratives, a low one for mixed texts), these results are quite telling. They imply that when the interesting and important ideas in a text do not coincide and, therefore, affect processing independently, interest may actually interfere with the learning of important information. The results also raised serious doubts about the generalization of interest in texts (see also Anderson, Mason, & Shirey, 1984, on the same point) and suggested that it is quite possible that interesting episodes do not contribute to the learning of important, but marginally related ideas. The ineffectiveness of such purely interesting ideas in texts has since been supported by other studies (see Garner, this volume; Garner, Gillingham & White, 1989; Wade, this volume; Wade & Adams [in press]).

Follow-up Studies of School Texts and Learning. In order to extend the findings on how important and interesting information is currently presented in school textbooks, a more extensive set of investigations was conducted (Baird & Hidi, 1984; Hidi & Baird, 1983, 1984, 1986). These studies involved the selection and rating of a larger sample of school texts and the testing of immediate and delayed recall for some of those texts following a prescribed study period. In the first part of these investigations, 25 junior grade school chapters were selected randomly from a total of 241 science and social science chapters recommended by the Ontario Ministry of Education. Each of the 25 chapters was rated sentence by sentence, as before, by adult raters for importance and interestingness. Only about a third of the texts had a relatively high percentage of propositions rated as both important and interesting. A further 40% had few propositions rated as either important or interesting, and 20% of the texts were considered to be reasonably interesting but without important text segments. Whereas most of the 25 texts fitted into one of these three profiles, two texts could not be categorized.

Subsequently, the immediate and delayed recalls of fourth- and sixth-grade subjects were examined using four different texts at each grade level. The texts represented were selected from the 25-sample group according to the three text profiles established earlier in the investigation (interesting and important, not interesting or important, and interesting but not important). The texts were also matched for length and readability within each grade and were randomly distributed to the two groups of students. In an initial session, subjects were given 25 minutes to read and study their respective texts, after which they were instructed to write down everything they could remember, even details. One week later the tests of delayed recall were carried out with similar instructions.

Because the analysis of the ratings indicated a substantial degree of separation in patterns of perceived importance and interestingness, the crucial question was which, if any, of these two rating patterns best matched the recall patterns; that is, which provided more accurate predictions of recall, judged importance, or judged interestingness? Several stepwise regressions were performed for each of the 8 texts using immediate and delayed recall scores as dependent variables and ratings as predictors. The results showed large between-text differences and an overall weak relation between the rated importance and interesting-ness of sentences and their recall. In other words, the sentence level ratings were poor predictors of recall. Children seemed to attend equally to important and interesting information, with 40% of the highly recalled information rated as important and another 40% rated as interesting.

These results established rather conclusively that children's recall of expositions does not show a simple abstractive process in which important information is selectively recalled and unimportant information is ignored or forgotten. The interestingness of the ideas also plays a part in determining what is remembered. To further examine this effect of text-based interest on recall, Hidi and Baird (1983, 1986) performed a qualitative analysis of the recall protocols and found several patterns in the highly recalled text segments. They identified particular categories of text features that were associated with high recall, regardless of importance. For example, any text segment that contained traditional story elements with goal-directed activities and human interest factors was well recalled, even if it was not important to the main points of its text. Indeed, simple descriptions of such activities (e.g., how to build an igloo or a nest, how to make a model of a globe from an orange) proved to be highly memorable. In addition, all surprising or novel information, such as that insects feel, smell, and taste with feelers, girls build igloos, and boys learn how to cook in Sweden, was also recalled with high frequency. The high imagery value often associated with statements from the preceding categories seemed to further boost recall (e.g., "The entire population of the Far North could fit into a sports arena," "Some people think that one day cities will be built under plastic bubbles.") Finally, lists of objects, properties, countries, and quantified information figured prominently in the recall protocols. Several text features identified in this study corresponded to those Anderson et al. (1987) identified as contributing to the interestingness of text.

A Study of Strategies to Increase Text-based Interest and Subsequent Recall of School Texts. Once particular types of content-related text features had been identified as contributing to high recall, Hidi and Baird (1988) carried out a further study to establish whether texts with these features would increase interest and facilitate learning. The specific purpose of the study was to investigate the effectiveness of three text-design strategies for creating text-based interest in expository texts. The first strategy, which resulted in the base text, was to use attributes that might contribute to text-based interest as specified by Hidi and Baird (1983, 1986) and Anderson et al. (1987), such as high activity level, character identification, novelty, and life themes. The second strategy was to systematically extend the base text by adding salient descriptive elaborations to the main themes. These insertions, although interesting, were all related to important facts rather than simply being independent anecdotes. For the third strategy, the concept that interest is related to the resolution of some novel information was used (Iran–Nejad, 1987; Kintsch, 1980); the base text was manipulated so that it induced a need on the reader's part to resolve some incomplete understanding of the information given.

Participants in the study were 44 students from two fourth-grade classes and 66 students from two sixth-grade classes. The text materials were three versions of a text that dealt with three famous inventors in history. The texts included general ideas about the factors that contributed to the inventors' success and specific descriptions of some of their discoveries. The versions were produced by applying one of the three strategies just described. Texts were randomly assigned to approximately equal groups at each grade level. Subjective interest ratings of the texts were also obtained from an independent, comparable group of fourth- and sixth-grade students. The procedures involved a 25-minute session in which all students read and studied their texts. Written free recalls were obtained immediately after the study session and 1 week later.

The results showed that only the first strategy of incorporating the four attributes of text-based interest contributed to a significant increase in recall levels over those typically found for expository texts at the elementary school level. The other two strategies were found to contribute only to an increase in subjects' interest ratings. The heightened subjective interest ratings did not translate into improved recall of content. Why these subjective ratings do not translate into clear-cut quantitative differences in recall is difficult to explain. However, it has been found that quantitative analysis of recall data can give us only a limited insight into how interesting content affects the recall process. Hidi and McLaren (1988), and Schiefele and Krapp (1988) have argued that high interest does not simply increase the quantity of learning but tends to change recall patterns and results in more qualitative differences. In order to gain a clearer picture of how text interest affects recall of expository information, a qualitative content analysis was performed on the data. The results indicated that the four attributes facilitated the learning of information that was concrete, active, and personal but did not facilitate the learning of more abstract and scientific information.

Studies on the Effects of Interesting Topics and Themes on Children's Writing Performance

Although research on comprehension and learning has begun to tease out the effects of interest on performance, researchers of expository writing have yet to consider seriously the role of interest in the production of written discourse. In a literature search, Hidi and McLaren (1990) failed to find any study that systematically investigated how interesting expository topics and/or themes influence children's subsequent writing performance. Based on the rationale that interest increases learning by increasing intellectual activity, it has been assumed that, when children choose their own topics, they write better than children who are given their assignments. Although this assumption has been supported in respect to personal narrative and exciting stories, there are no scientific data to support this with respect to expositions. In the first of two studies on interest and writing, Hidi and McLaren (1990, 1991) investigated whether interest actually enhances written production of expositions on school topics. The second study focussed on how studying additional information influences writing on high- and low-interest topics.

Children's Expository Writing as a Function of Topic and Theme Interest. Hidi and McLaren (1990) predicted that the interestingness of higher-level text features, such as topics and themes, would influence children's production of expository texts. Topic was defined as a coherent knowledge domain (e.g., space travel, wildlife) that can also subdivide subject matter hierarchically (Mathematics —> Geometry —> Pythagorean Theorem) or laterally (Mathematics, History, Geography). It was expected that, because topic interest has been shown to have a facilitative effect on children's comprehension, it would have a similar effect on their writing. Themes were distinguished from topics because themes cut across knowledge domains and represent generalized forms of specific content-related knowledge. They often involve action, change, and, occasionally, causal relations. Survival, the impact of new technology, and the effect of pollution are examples of themes that apply to expository texts. Theme-related studies on the comprehension of expositions are hard to find, because themes have been considered in the literature almost exclusively in the framework of narratives (e.g., Lehr, 1987; Lukens, 1986). The researchers expected that interesting themes would also have an important facilitative effect on students' written production. More specifically, themes were expected to aid the memorial search needed for content generation by activating related, but scattered, bits of information that are not stored neatly together. Themes could also assist in organizing and constraining activated knowledge.

In the first phase of this study, teacher and student preferences for a set of social science topics and themes typically found in fourth- and sixth-grade textbooks were investigated. Both teachers and children used a 5-point scale to rate 30 topics and 20 themes. The scale ranged from 1, least preferred and uninteresting, to 5, most preferred and interesting. An analysis of the ratings showed several trends. The ratings of themes by teachers and children ranged from moderately high to high, indicating that both groups generally found themes to be interesting. The ratings of topics, however, seemed to be more affected by knowledge factors. When topics were unfamiliar or very familiar, interest ratings were low, which suggested that the optimal level for high interest in a school topic may be moderate knowledge. This has been the first experimental finding that we know of that suggests that a curvilinear relation exists between interest and knowledge factors. Whereas teachers' and students' ratings showed a moderate correlation ($r = .62$), children were less interested than their teachers in the types of topics and themes found in social science textbooks.

In a second phase of this study, the same fourth- and sixth-graders, along with a comparable group of students from a nearby school, were all asked to write a composition on either a high-interest (Space Travel) or a low-interest (Living in a City) topic. Two weeks later, the same students wrote on the opposite topic, but this time with added themes. Thus, Space Travel was paired with the theme of Survival, and Living in a City was paired with the theme of Future.

Contrary to expectations, results showed that the high-interest topic did not result in longer and/or qualitatively better expositions than the low-interest topic. Theme effects corresponded to predictions as far as quantitative results were concerned in that combining topics with interesting themes resulted in longer productions. Although this indicated that these themes had a facilitative effect on children's writing, the overall quality of the writing did not show any improvement.

In an attempt to explain the ineffectiveness of the high-interest topics, several additional analyses were conducted, including a comparison of topic relevant sentences, incorrect factual statements, and structural complexity across the two conditions. All of these data suggested that knowledge differences associated with the high- and the low-interest topics confounded our results; that is, for the low-interest topic, Living in a City, the students appeared to be drawing from a much wider knowledge base than they brought to bear on the high-interest topic, Space Travel.

Although the focus of this study was on how a generally high- and a generally low-interest topic affected children's writing performance, the same children's individual ratings of these topics were also available. Thus, it was possible to examine the impact of individual interest by examining how these ratings related to subjects' writing performance. One strong and intriguing result appeared with respect to the compositions written on Living in a City. People who were not interested in the topic performed significantly better than those who showed some interest. These differences were present in both quantitative measurements (longer productions), and in qualitative measurements (overall writing quality and quality of ideas). It was concluded that whereas high knowledge may lead to an expression of low interest, it facilitates writing. Although some children consider Living in a City to be a boring topic because they know a lot about it, the extra knowledge is still available to be called upon in a writing task. On the other hand, medium knowledge of a topic may lead to higher interest yet result in less ability to write on it.

The combined results of the investigation indicate that whereas high interest might increase cognitive effort, such as information search, inferencing, and so on, a lack of knowledge interferes with increased intellectual activity; conversely, writing on low-interest topics might be facilitated by all the relevant information stored on these boring topics. In other words, although children may be better motivated to write on high-interest topics, the lack of appropriate or sufficient knowledge to draw upon may interfere with their performance.

Tutorial Interventions Involving High and Low Interest Topics. The findings of the preceding study suggest that simply giving children high-interest topics does not guarantee improvement in their writing. In a subsequent investigation, Hidi and McLaren (1991) set out to establish whether supplementing high-interest topics with topic-relevant information could harness the motivating power of the interest created and thus improve children's writing.

Participants in the study were a different group of 60 grade-six students enrolled in the same suburban elementary school the following year. Two high-interest topics (Living in the Future and Space Travel) and two low-interest topics (Living in the City and Travelling on Land) were selected for the study. Topics were chosen on the basis of the children's ratings from study 1, which were replicated by subjects in this investigation. The students were randomly assigned a text on one of the four topics to read and study. Then they were asked to answer some questions on their texts. One week after the study sessions, children were asked to complete a writing assignment. Rather than free writing on their topics, children were given a question, written with the tutorials in mind, that could be answered by utilizing many of the ideas contained in the tutorial texts. For example, the question for Living in the Future was, "Should people look forward to living in the future?"

In the experimental group, the children's writing assignment was on the same topic as their initial tutorial texts. In the control group, however, children were asked to write about an equally interesting topic that was different from their initial tutorial text. For example, if they had read and studied the tutorial on Living in the City, they had to write about Travelling on Land. In this way, the researchers could determine the effects when no additional information on the topic was given.

The expectations were that children in the experimental condition (those who had studied topic-related information the week before) would do significantly better than those in the control condition because of their augmented knowledge. Furthermore, within the experimental condition, those writing on high-interest topics were expected to perform significantly better than those writing on low-interest topics. No significant differences were expected between high- and low-interest groups in the control condition.

Several measures of the data did not support the anticipated results. In the experimental condition, instead of the high-interest topic pair resulting in substantially longer and/or qualitatively better compositions, the reverse was true—the low-interest pair produced longer and higher quality writing. This group also reproduced more ideas from the tutorial texts in their compositions than the other children.

It was concluded that the short tutorial intervention was not effective in the utilization of high-interest topics. Children did not write quantitatively more, or qualitatively better, as a result of studying topic-relevant information in the high-interest condition. What is more, the data showed that supplementing children's knowledge of topics they already know a lot about facilitates writing performance even if the topics are judged to be boring. It may be that for tutorial intervention to be effective students must have a more extensive (prior) knowledge base than that which was available to our subjects on the high-interest topics, or a longer, more extensive, or more interpersonal tutorial experience.

The overall results suggest that a unique and unusually complex relation exists between knowledge, interest, and writing performance. Knowledge factors have an inordinate influence on writing that may dampen the motivating effect of interest on performance.

Additional Thoughts on the Effect of Interesting Topics on Children's Writing. These results seem to contradict literature that is based on the assumption that topic interest improves children's writing just as it facilitates the comprehending, learning, and enjoyment of discourse. Graves (1975, 1982, 1983), for example, has been a strong advocate of self-selected topic choices for young writers. His conclusions tend to be based on comparisons between children's writing on self-selected personal topics and writing on topics assigned by teachers. Gradwohl and Schumacher (1989) also support students' self-selection of writing topics. In their study, however, as Hidi and McLaren (1991) pointed out, self-selection versus imposed topic distinction has been confounded with personal versus school topics (e.g., hockey versus circulatory system).

Because of topical differences, the aforementioned research may not be directly comparable to that of Hidi and McLaren. Self-selected, personal topics are more likely to lead to superior writing performance because they represent children's individual interests and thus combine high knowledge and high value (Renninger 1987, 1990, this volume). Hidi and McLaren's investigations however were based on group ratings of topics. Such interest ratings reflect situational interest that is generated by the particular topic rather than subjects' individual interests. As increased situational interest is not necessarily associated with additional knowledge and value in the same way as individual interest is, self-selection of these types of topics does not guarantee improved writing.

GENERAL CONCLUSIONS

The results of the studies described here indicate that interest influences discourse processing and learning differently than it influences production. How can these findings be explained? Hidi (1990) hypothesized that the strong facilitating effect of text-based interest on knowledge acquisition is related to attentional factors. She suggested that an important aspect of information processing may be that attention is automatically rather than selectively allocated to interesting text segments. As a result, the comprehension processes that are used for interesting information may be less demanding on cognitive resources than those that are used for uninteresting information. The cognitive resources freed up by interest may then become actively involved in generating more coherent representations.

When reading is compared to the writing process, it seems that attentional factors do not play the same role in the two processes. When reading, one is dealing with discourse generated by someone else. The reader must decode the text, make sense out of it, and continuously make decisions about meaning emphasis and author intention in order to construct the appropriate representations. Attentional factors may be involved in several of these components. When writing, all the ideas must be generated by the writer. No matter how much attention is paid to the task or how efficient the allocation of attention is, insurmountable difficulties may arise in generating ideas if they are not already stored. It appears that, although having children write on interesting topics may increase motivation and cognitive effort, such an assignment neither eliminates nor enables children to overcome knowledge deficits. Children need a sufficient knowledge base for the topic on which they are writing before their production can be improved by the motivating effect of topical interest.

These results suggest that, whereas (text-based) situational interest may be a good candidate for improving children's learning from text, it may not provide the best support for enhancement of their writing proficiency. Simply giving children interesting topics without assuring that they have an appropriate knowledge base for these topics does not facilitate their writing performance. It may then be concluded that, if educators wish to use interest to improve children's writing of expository school topics, they must make sure that such knowledge is acquired by the children prior to writing. Alternatively, they may focus on individual preferences in personal topics and try to utilize these for writing. Because these types of interests usually develop together with related knowledge and values, they may prove to be good facilitators of children's written production.

REFERENCES

Ainley, M. D. (1987). The Factor Structure of Curiosity Measures: Breadth and Depth of Interest Curiosity Styles. *Australian Journal of Psychology, 39* (1), 53–59.

Anderson, R. C. (1982). Allocation of attention during reading. In A. Flammer & W. Kintsch (Eds.), *Discourse processing* (pp. 287–299). Amsterdam: North Holland.

Anderson, R. C., Mason, J., & Shirey, L. L. (1984). The reading group: An exper-imental investigation of a labyrinth. *Reading Research Quarterly, 20,* 6–360.

Anderson, R. C., Shirey, L. L., Wilson, P. T., & Fielding, L. G. (1987). Inter-estingness of children's reading material. In R. E. Snow & M. J. Farr (Eds.), *Aptitude, learning and instruction: Vol. III. Cognitive and affective process analyses.* Hillsdale, NJ: Lawrence Erlbaum Associates.

Armbruster, B. B. (1984). The problem of "inconsiderate text." In G. G. Duffy, L. R. Roehler, & J. Mason (Eds.), *Comprehension instruction: Perspectives and suggestions* (pp. 202–217). New York: Longman.

Asher, S. R. (1979). Influence of topic interest on black children's and white children's reading comprehension. *Child Development, 50,* 686–690.

Baird, W., & Hidi, S. (1984, April). *The effect of factual importance on recall from naturally occurring school texts.* Paper presented at the annual meeting of the American Educational Research Association, New Orleans.

Berlyne, D. E. (1960). *Conflict, arousal, and curiosity.* New York: McGraw-Hill.

Berlyne, D. E. (1971). *Aesthetics and psychobiology.* New York: Appleton-Century Crofts.

Berlyne, D. E. (1974a). The new experimental aesthetics. In D. E. Berlyne (Ed.), *Studies in the new experimental aesthetics* (pp.1–25). New York: Wiley.

Berlyne, D. E. (1974b). Novelty, complexity, and interestingness. In D. E. Berlyne (Ed.), *Studies in the new experimental aesthetics* (pp.175–180). New York: Wiley.

Berlyne, D. E. (1974c). Concluding observations. In D. E. Berlyne (Ed.), *Studies in the new experimental aesthetics* (pp. 305–331). New York: Wiley.

Berman, K. F. (1987). Cortical "stress tests" in schizophrenia: Regional cerebral blood flow studies. *Biological Psychiatry, 22,* 1304–1326.

Crozier, J. B. (1974). Verbal and exploratory responses to sound sequences varying in uncertainty level. In D. E. Berlyne (Ed.), *Studies in the new experimental aesthetics* (pp. 27–90). New York: Wiley.

Dewey, J. (1913). *Interest and effort in education.* New York: Houghton Mifflin.

Estes, T. H., & Vaughan, J. L., Jr. (1973). Reading interest and comprehension: Implications. *Reading Teacher, 27,* 149–153.

Fransson, A. (1977). On qualitative differences in learning: IV. Effects of motivation and test anxiety on process and outcome. *British Journal of Educational Psychology, 47,* 244–257.

Garner, R. (1991). When children and adults do not use learning strategies: Toward a theory of settings. *Review of Educational Research,* (Winter 1990), *60,* (4), 517–529.

Garner, R., Gillingham, M. G., & White, C. S. (1989). Effects of "seductive details" on macroprocessing and microprocessing in adults and children. *Cognition and Instruction, 6,* 41–57.

Gradwohl, J. M., & Schumacher, G. M. (1989). The relationship between content knowledge and topic choice in writing. *Written Communication, 6,* 181–195.

Graves, D. H. (1975). An examination of the writing processes of seven year old children. *Research in the Teaching of English, 9,* 227–241.

Graves, D. H. (1982). In R. D. Walshe (Ed.), *Donald Graves in Australia. Children want to write...* Exeter, NH: Heinemann Educational Books.

Graves, D. H. (1983). *Writing: Teachers and children at work.* Exeter, NH: Heinemann Educational Books.

Hare, F. G. (1974). Artistic training and responses to visual and auditory patterns varying in uncertainty. In D. E. Berlyne (Ed.), *Studies in the new experimental aesthetics* (pp. 159–168). New York: Wiley.

Hayes, J. R. (1991). Making personality judgements about authors. Carnegie-Mellon University. Paper presented at AERA, Chicago.

Hidi, S. (1990). Interest and its contribution as a mental resource for learning. *Review of Educational Research, 60* (4), 549–571.

Hidi, S., & Baird, W. (1983, November). *Types of information saliency in school texts and their effect on children's recall.* Paper presented at the National Reading Conference, Austin, TX.

Hidi, S., & Baird, W. (1984). *Importance and interestingness: Two factors involved in naturally-occurring school texts* (Mimeo). Toronto: Ontario Institute for Studies in Education.

Hidi, S., & Baird, W. (1986). Interestingness—A neglected variable in discourse processing. *Cognitive Science, 10,* 179–194.

Hidi, S., & Baird, W. (1988). Strategies for increasing text-based interest and students' recall of expository texts. *Reading Research Quarterly, 23,* 465–483.

Hidi, S., Baird, W., & Hildyard, A. (1982). That's important, but is it interesting? Two factors in text processing. In A. Flammer & W. Kintsch (Eds.), *Discourse processing* (pp. 63–75). Amsterdam: North Holland.

Hidi, S., & McLaren, J. (1988, April). *The effect of topic and theme interestingness on children's school performance.* Paper presented at the annual meeting of the American Educational Research Association, New Orleans.

Hidi, S., & McLaren, J. (1990). The effect of topic and theme interestingness on the production of school expositions. In H. Mandl, E. De Corte, N. Bennett, & H. F. Friedrich (Eds.), *Learning and instruction: European research in an international context* (Vol. 2.2, pp. 295–308). Oxford: Pergamon.

Hidi, S., & McLaren, J. (1991). Motivational factors and writing: The role of topic interestingness. *European Journal of Psychology of Education.*

Iran–Nejad, A. (1987). Cognitive and affective causes of interest and liking. *Journal of Educational Psychology, 79* (2), 120–130.

Izard, C. E. (1977). *Human emotions.* New York: Plenum Press.

Kintsch, W. (1980). Learning from text, levels of comprehension, or: Why anyone would read a story anyway. *Poetics, 9,* 87–98.

Kirkwood, K. J., & Wolfe, R. G. (1980). Matching students and reading materials: A cloze-procedure method for assessing the reading ability of students and the readability of textual materials. Toronto: OISE Publications.

Krapp, A. (1989, September). Interest, learning and academic achievement. Paper prepared for the symposium, *Task Motivation by Interest.* Third European Conference of Learning and Instruction (EARLI), Madrid, Spain.

Lehr, S. (1987). *The preschool child's developing sense of theme.* Paper presented at the meeting of the American Educational Research Association, Washington, DC.

Lukens, R. J. (1986). *A critical handbook of children's literature* (3rd ed.). Glensview, IL: Scott, Foresman.

Nenniger, P. (1987). How stable is motivation by contents? In E. de Corte, H. Lodjwiks, R. Parmentier & P. Span (Eds.), *Learning and instruction: European research in an international context* (Vol. 1, pp. 159–168). Oxford/ Leuven: Pergamon Press/Leuven University Press.

Normore, L. F. (1974). Verbal Responses to Visual Sequences Varying in Uncertainty Level. In D. E. Berlyne (Ed.), *Studies in the new experimental aesthetics* (pp. 109–119). New York: Wiley.

Prenzel, M. (1988, April). Task persistence and interest. In U. Schiefele (Chair.), *Content and Interest as Motivational Factors in Learning.* Symposium conducted at the annual meeting of the American Educational Research Association, New Orleans.

Renninger, K. A. (1987). Do individual interests make a difference? *Essays by the Spencer Fellows IV.* Cambridge, MA: National Academy of Education.

Renninger, K. A. (1990). Children's play interests, representation, and activity. In R. Fivush & J. Hudson (Eds.), *Knowing and remembering in young children* (pp. 127–165). Emory Cognition Series (Vol. III). Cambridge: Cambridge University Press.

Renninger, K. A., & Wozniak, R. H. (1985). Effect of interest on attentional shift, recognition, and recall in young children. *Developmental Psychology, 21*, 624–632.

Sadoski, M., Goetz, E. T., & Kangiser, S. (1988). Imagination in story response: Relationships between imagery, affect, and structural importance. *Reading Research Quarterly, 23*, 320–336.

Schank, R. C. (1979). Interestingness: Controlling inferences. *Artificial Intelligence, 12*, 273–297.

Schiefele, U., & Krapp, A. (1988, April). The impact of interest on qualitative and structural indicators of knowledge. In U. Schiefele (Chair.), *Content and interest as motivational factors in learning*. Symposium conducted at the annual meeting of the American Educational Research Association, New Orleans.

Wade, S. E., & Adams, B. (in press). Effects of importance and interest on recall of biographical text. *JRB: A Journal of Literacy*.

10 "Seductive Details" and Learning from Text

Ruth Garner
Washington State University
Rachel Brown, Sylvia Sanders, and Deborah J. Menke
University of Maryland

Textbooks, along with teacher talk, serve as the primary vehicles for knowledge acquisition in classrooms. Schallert and Kleiman (1979), in comparing textbooks with teachers, pointed out four disadvantages of textbooks. Textbooks have: (a) less likelihood of "tailoring" content to individual learners with different knowledge, interests, and skills; (b) less likelihood of activating old information and linking new information to old; (c) less likelihood of focusing attention of students on particular pieces of information; and (d) less likelihood of monitoring comprehension and recall of content. Schallert and Kleiman suggested that to learn from text students must learn to understand material that is not as well adapted to them as teachers' presentations may be.

Given current descriptions of expositions in the research literatures of psychology and education, it seems that textbooks suffer not only in comparison to teachers; they also suffer in comparison to models of ideal texts. Textbooks often present a mix of important and unimportant ideas, typically followed by a series of questions eliciting mostly detailed information (Armbruster, 1984). Topically irrelevant information is frequently included in the texts. Long digressions are common (Beck, McKeown, & Gromoll, 1989). "Big" ideas (i.e., ideas authors and teachers expect that students will understand and remember) are not signaled. To use Armbruster's label, textbooks are *inconsiderate*.

Weak signals of importance are particularly common. At the lexical level, few expressions such as "very importantly" or "of somewhat less importance" appear. At the graphic level, few variations in print size and intensity appear. At the semantic level, there are few explicit generalizations of the kind Kieras (1978, 1980, 1982) discussed (i.e., generalizations presented in the first sentence of a paragraph followed by several examples). For instance, when Baumann and Serra (1984) examined semantic signals of importance, they found that only 25% of 294 paragraphs appearing in social studies books for grades 4, 6, and 8 presented an explicit generalization at the start of the paragraph.

To understand why learning from inconsiderate textbooks is often very difficult, we must also remember that students, particularly younger students, have a limited knowledge of expository text structure. Because of a steady diet of stories at home and in the early school years, they have had little experience with exposition and, thus, have very little sense of how to identify or extract important information from text.

When Danner (1976) generated topically organized and topically disorganized expository passages that he presented orally to students in grades 2, 4, and 6, he found that passage organization affected the amount, structure, and perceived difficulty of recall in children from all three grades. Awareness of these effects increased with age.

In another study of structure, Williams, Taylor, and Ganger (1981) presented short expository texts in both topic-sentence and no-topic-sentence conditions to students in grades 4 and 6. Students were asked to select the best title for each passage from a set that included the specific topic of the text, the general topic of the text, a detail in the text, and an unrelated topic. In addition, they were asked to produce a main idea statement for each passage. Williams et al. found that the sixth graders made more appropriate specific-topic responses than did the fourth graders. There were more appropriate responses on the title-selection task than on the sentence-production task. There was no difference in performance on paragraphs with and without topic sentences.

In still another study of text structure, Taylor and Samuels (1983) asked students in grades 5 and 6 to read and recall short and long expository texts in both normally ordered and scrambled conditions. Students were labeled "aware of text structure" if, in two out of three of their recalls for normally ordered texts, they followed the author's organization. Taylor and Samuels found that these "aware" students recalled more from the normal passage than from the scrambled passage.

Students identified as "unaware" (72% of the sample) recalled no more on the normal passage than on the scrambled one. Aware readers recalled more than unaware readers on the normally ordered texts, but not on the scrambled texts.

Taken together, these studies indicate that older children demonstrate greater knowledge of the structural properties of expository text than younger children. Text manipulations designed to highlight text structure are not uniformly effective in eliciting strong main idea selection or main idea production. Children who demonstrate knowledge of expository text structure also show strong recall performance for well-organized text.

Expository text schema deficiencies first became apparent to us in a series of studies where we asked students to build paragraphs, either by manipulating sentence strips or by ordering sentences on a microcomputer screen (Garner, Alexander, Slater, Hare, Smith, & Reis, 1986; Garner & Gillingham, 1987). Students were given seven randomly ordered sentences such as the following:

4) In the past, it was common for families and friends to hold "quilting bees" to make quilts together.

2) A quilt usually has a top piece and a bottom piece.

1) Quilts are special kinds of blankets made of scraps of cloth.

7) Worms eat plants in the soil.

5) However, today, these gatherings of families and friends are less common.

3) It also has some stuffing in between.

6) Blankets are often made of synthetic materials that are machine washable.

The first sentence was an explicit generalization of the type discussed by Kieras. Sentences 2 and 3 were cohesively tied by pronoun reference. Sentences 4 and 5 were tied by conjunction. The sixth sentence presented information related to the general topic of the paragraph (blankets), but not to the specific topic (quilts). The seventh sentence presented information totally unrelated to the topic of the paragraph, information from an alternate text.

Whereas graduate students in psychology all performed the building task virtually flawlessly by eliminating topically unrelated sentences, keeping cohesively tied sentences adjacent, and placing the generalization in the conventional first-sentence position, many of the younger students did not. The youngest students often treated unimportant details or irrelevant information as first-sentence material. This result is consistent with the Williams et al. (1981) finding discussed before: younger children are less successful than older children in discriminating among abstractions, details, and irrelevant pieces of information as candidates for a passage title.

This phenomenon of students mistaking details for structurally important information is the focus of the remainder of this chapter. We discuss research that suggests that some interesting details are highly memorable, in fact so much so that they disrupt learning or even the identification of important ideas. These "seductive" details tend to be novel, active, concrete, and personally involving (Garner, Gillingham, & White, 1989). Important information, on the other hand, tends to be more abstract and general.

THE "SEDUCTIVE DETAIL" EFFECT IN RECENT RESEARCH

Some time ago, Dewey (1913) warned us about "fictitious inducements to attention" (p. 7). He suggested that when things have to be *made* interesting for people, those things are, in fact, no more interesting than before. In other words, interest is not a quality waiting around to be excited from without. Dewey's admonition finds support in the "seductive detail" literature of the past few years. In that literature, texts were "punched up" to be captivating to readers who might otherwise have little interest in the text topics. Texts were accompanied by a variety of comprehension/recall tasks.

Nonsupporting Details Embedded in Boring Texts

Powerful demonstration of the interfering effects of highly interesting details first emerged from three studies where some text details were nonsupporting, embedded, and part of generally uninteresting material (Garner et al., 1989; Hidi, Baird, & Hildyard, 1982; Wade & Adams, 1989).

By "nonsupporting," we mean simply that the vivid details were related only slightly, if at all, to the structurally important information in the texts. An example is Wade and Adams' text, wherein "big" ideas about major historical events and Horatio Nelson's role in them were interspersed with personal details about Nelson's mangled right arm and his love affair with Lady Emma Hamilton.

By "embedded," we mean that the vivid details were not separated graphically from the important ideas of the text. For instance, in the Garner et al. (1989) study, a text about insect differences presented intriguing details in the middle of the first paragraph, at the end of the second paragraph, and at the beginning of the third paragraph. None of the studies presented texts where vivid details were footnoted as intriguing asides.

The meaning of "generally uninteresting texts" is obvious. Garner et al. (1989) reported that adult raters found "big" ideas about insect differences to be very important, but not even moderately interesting. On the other hand, they found novel, active, concrete details about clicking beetles and buzzing flies to be very interesting, but not even moderately important. In all three studies, rated importance and rated interestingness diverged.

Hidi and her colleagues (Hidi et al., 1982) located texts that they were able to categorize reliably as narratives (stories found in language arts materials), expositions (material presenting facts, explanation, or instructions), or mixed texts (expositions with some narrative episodes or elements). Adults rated important and interesting information in each text. In the narratives, the most interesting ideas were also the most important. In the expositions, very few ideas were rated as interesting. In the mixed texts, no relation was found between importance and interestingness. An example of the divergence between importance and interestingness in a mixed text is the following: the big idea that ancient divers had to rely on their own lung power rather than using some form of breathing gear (very important, not particularly interesting) was interrupted by an anecdote about Alexander the Great's adventures in the sea (very interesting, not at all important here).

Fifth- and seventh-graders read and recalled information from this set of texts, both immediately and 4 days later. In delayed recall, at both grade levels, students recalled more adult-rated important information for narratives and for expositions, but not for mixed texts. In the mixed texts, fifth-graders recalled equal amounts of important and interesting information, and seventh-graders recalled more interesting information.

We designed an experiment along similar lines (Garner et al., 1989). We asked adults and seventh-graders to read a three-paragraph expository text on the topic of differences among insects. Again, information in the text was rated for importance and interestingness. Half of the readers at each age level read the text with "seductive details" (one per paragraph), half without. "Seductive details" were propositions presenting interesting but unimportant information (as rated by adults). Immediately after reading, readers completed a series of recall tasks.

Performance in recalling just the important information in the text differed dramatically by condition for both adults and seventh-graders. For instance, whereas adult readers who read the short text without the "seductive details" recalled an average of 93% of the ideas rated as most important, adult readers given "seductive details" recalled an average of only 43%. "Seductive detail" readers recalled a combination of important and interesting information. In no case did they recall all ideas that had been rated as structurally most important.

In a related study, Wade and Adams (1989) asked college students at two levels of reading ability to read and recall information from a text about Horatio Nelson. Again, information had been rated for importance and interestingness. All students, regardless of ability, remembered more unimportant than important information. All students remembered more interesting than uninteresting information.

It is clear from these three studies that when importance and interestingness diverged, interestingness was the better predictor of which information would be recalled. Important ideas about diving gear, insect differences, and territorial expansion were not particularly memorable. On the other hand, interesting details about Alexander the Great's adventures, click beetles' flipping, and Horatio Nelson's love life were highly memorable.

Supporting Details Embedded in Text

One might argue that, in the "seductive detail" effect, it is not the interestingness of the details that makes them memorable; rather, it is the irrelevance, the "standing out" against a set of propositions that are topically unified. The question might be asked: What if highly interesting information that supported structurally important information were presented in text? Would both interesting and important information then be recalled?

Hidi and Baird (1988) designed a study in which fourth- and sixth-graders read and reread a text about famous inventors in one of three conditions: (a) Base text, intended to be coherent and generally interesting; (b) Salient text, a modification of the Base text, with salient descriptive elaborations on the main themes (all supporting the structurally important ideas); or (c) Resolution text, a modification of the Salient text with a need for resolution (an element of surprise) introduced. Written free recalls were elicited immediately after reading and again 1 week later.

For the Base text, the experimenters' interest-producing strategies succeeded in producing good recall only of sentences that dealt with the active, personally involving experiences of the inventors. More abstract sentences, such as those describing general characteristics of inventors and scientific aspects of inventions, were poorly recalled. An example of a well-recalled piece of information versus a poorly-recalled piece is the following: the idea that Spenser, who invented the thermostat, worked in a lumber camp and had to open a furnace door to see if the fire needed more wood was recalled by all of the sixth graders in immediate recall and by 71% of them a week later, whereas the "big" idea that the function of the thermostat is to measure temperature in houses was recalled by only 24% of the sixth graders in both immediate and delayed settings.

Salient text elaborations tended to be well recalled. Unfortunately, little increase in recall of general, abstract "big" ideas was provided by these elaborations. The Resolution text did not improve recall of structurally important information.

These findings are not so different from findings for effects of nonsupporting details: When interesting details and structurally important ideas both appear in a text, it is the interesting details that are recalled by readers. The appropriate metaphor for attention to information in text, then, may be a light switch, which is turned on and off repeatedly (see Anderson, Mason, & Shirey, 1984, for a similar argument).

Unembedded Details in Generally Interesting Texts

What if the details were marked as details? What if they were not embedded in text? Perhaps students' abilities to differentiate unimportant from important information would increase when only the latter is elicited. In other words, perhaps what accounts for the "seductive detail" effect is not so much the topical irrelevance of the details, but their embeddedness. Perhaps general interestingness of the text is also relevant. It may be that interesting details are interesting by virtue of their being in a text dominated by very uninteresting ideas.

Recently, Garner, Alexander, Gillingham, Kulikowich, and Brown (1991) completed a study in which embeddedness of details and general interestingness of text were manipulated. It was expected that highly interesting details treated as asides would be less likely than paragraph-embedded details to be confused with structurally important information.

This expectation was based on the "subsuming" hypothesis proposed by Kieras (1982). Kieras has suggested that information that is not readily subsumed into provisionally accepted paragraph main ideas prompts revisions in main idea formulations (possibly inappropriate revisions, which are then stored and retrieved). It was also expected that highly interesting details would be less likely to be given heightened attention in generally interesting texts than in generally uninteresting ones, because in uninteresting texts, little competing information "stands out."

Forty-eight undergraduate students participated in the study. They were randomly assigned to one of four forms of text: (a) highly interesting details presented in separate paragraphs in generally interesting text (form A); (b) highly interesting details presented in separate paragraphs in generally uninteresting text (form B); (c) highly interesting details embedded in paragraphs in generally interesting text (form C); and (d) highly interesting details embedded in paragraphs in generally uninteresting text (form D).

The topic of all text forms was Stephen Hawking, the noted physicist. All forms were modified versions of an article, about 400 words in length that had appeared in *Newsweek* (Adler, Lubenow, & Malone, 1988). Forms A and C began with a paragraph that was intended to provide personally involving information about Hawking. That paragraph was the following:

> Stephen Hawking is a theoretical physicist who holds Newton's chair at Cambridge University. Though it is difficult to assess the career of a still young and still active scientist, Hawking is widely regarded as the most brilliant theoretical physicist since Einstein. Stephen Hawking is dying. Unable to speak, he is paralyzed by a progressive, incurable disease, amyotrophic lateral sclerosis, better known as Lou Gehrig's Disease. It is not clear whether or not, within the time left to him, Hawking will be able to unlock the essential secrets of the universe. He works from morning to night on Grand Unification Theory.

This paragraph was potentially interesting to readers, just as Hidi and Baird's (1988) material about Spenser's lumber camp work was, because it presented personal detail. In addition, the Hawking paragraph also touched upon one of the topics that Schank (1979) claims is nearly universally interesting: death at an early age.

Forms A and C were intended to be "generally interesting" text, in that information about Hawking's scientific work was preceded by this information (i.e., that he is racing death to complete the work). Forms B and D of the text did not contain the personally involving information. Forms B and D began with the paragraph that was the second paragraph in forms A and C. Forms B and D were labeled "generally uninteresting" text.

Paragraph topics, across forms, for the rest of the text were the following:

1. Hawking's Grand Unification Theory, an attempt to link theories of relativity and quantum mechanics, with a goal of understanding the origins of the universe;
2. The role black holes might have played in the origins of the universe;
3. "Seductive detail" information about a wager Hawking has with Kip Thorne at Caltech about black holes, involving the possibility of winning a subscription to *Private Eye*, a British satirical magazine; and
4. Hawking's 1974 paper presented at Oxford on the subject of Grand Unification.

The only other distinction among forms was in the placement of the highly interesting ("seductive detail") information. Though it appeared in all four forms, it was presented as a separate paragraph in forms A and B and embedded in the paragraph about black holes in forms C and D.

Doctoral students rated the information in the text for importance (high, moderate, or low) and interestingness (also high, moderate, or low). All doctoral students rated the following ideas as being of "high" importance: (a) Grand Unification Theory links theories of relativity and quantum mechanics; (b) Stephen Hawking is working on Grand Unification Theory; and (c) the goal of Grand Unification Theory is to explain the origins of the universe. All students rated the information about the wager with Thorne as being of "low" importance.

As expected, the patterns of interestingness ratings were reversed. The wager was rated as "high" interest by all students, whereas the Grand Unification information was rated as "low" interest by all. This meant that the Hawking text mirrored a number of other texts used in previous research in that rated importance and rated interestingness diverged.

Rated as being of moderate importance *and* of moderate interest was the information about black holes. This material might be characterized as novel, active, and concrete detail, though *not* as "seductive" (i.e., it supported structurally important ideas in text). Although the information in the paragraph about Hawking's illness was not rated formally (it only appeared in forms A and C), all eight students discussed this information using some combination of the following words: "fascinating," "intriguing," and "sad."

Undergraduate students were directed to read one of the text forms, and to try to remember the important information in the text. When they had finished reading, they exchanged their text copies for a packet of recall sheets. The students completed each sheet without being able to reinspect either the text or earlier recall sheets. In order, they responded to requests for unstructured recall of important text information (a measure comparable to those used in most previous studies), for provision of a title that "might give a reader of a science textbook a good idea of what the text is about," and for short-answer responses to five questions (three eliciting information that the doctoral students had previously rated as most important, one asking about black holes, and one asking about the wager with Thorne).

We were not certain whether the set of measures would yield redundant data. We felt that more powerful conclusions about what is memorable in text could be drawn if the same information were to be recalled in unstructured recall, structured recall (question responses), and constrained recall (a short title). We were particularly mindful of the argument that rudimentary schemas for exposition handicap students (particularly younger students) as they try to retrieve text information to complete unstructured-recall tasks. We felt strongly that unstructured recall should be supplemented with other dependent measures.

The findings from the study will not be particularly astonishing to the reader of this chapter by now: on a variety of measures, highly interesting details were very memorable, and abstract "big" ideas were not particularly memorable. For instance, in unstructured-recall responses, 35% of the undergraduate students included the information about the wager with Thorne and 96% included the information about black holes. On the average, fewer than half the ideas rated most important by the doctoral students were included in the protocols. Furthermore, in titles for the text, 8 students focused exclusively on the wager with titles such as "The Big Wager" or "A Wager about Black Holes." An additional 8 students titled the text "Black Holes." Finally, all 48 students answered the questions about black holes and about the wager correctly. In contrast, on the average only about half the questions about ideas rated most important were answered correctly.

There was also some indication that the personally involving information about Stephen Hawking (presented as the first paragraph in forms A and C) was highly memorable. Of the 24 students who read this paragraph, 22 (92%) included information about Hawking's illness in their unstructured-recall protocols. In addition, 8 of the 24 students (33%) focused exclusively on Hawking in their titles, either titling the text simply "Stephen Hawking" or combining the name with a reference to Hawking's illness (e.g., "Hawking's Battle with Lou Gehrig's Disease").

Whether highly interesting details were embedded or not made no difference whatsoever. On the other hand, there was some evidence that general interestingness of text mattered. As we had predicted, students who read "generally interesting" text (forms A and C) recalled more structurally important information in unstructured recall than students who read "generally uninteresting" text (forms B and D).

Competing Revisions of Instructional Text

In a recent study, Duffy and his colleagues (1989) used texts that once again presented some important information and some highly interesting information. In an unsuccessful attempt to replicate Graves et al. (1988), Duffy et al. presented one of three revisions or the original of a 400-word history text to 11th-grade students. (See Graves, Prenn, Earle, Thompson, Johnson, and Slater, 1991, for an update of this research.) A revision prepared by composition teachers clarified the structure of the text (i.e., signaled superordinate ideas) and provided cohesion. On the other hand, a revision prepared by an editor and writer from *Time–Life Books* lengthened the text by adding "vivid anecdotes" that emphasized relatively unimportant information. A revision prepared by text linguists addressed some structural and cohesion concerns. The *Time–Life* revision fits Hidi et al.'s (1982) "mixed text" category. The vivid anecdotes in that revision would fit our definition of "seductive details."

Students read and studied the text. After a brief interval, they were given either a free-recall or a short-answer test. Then, they rated the interestingness of the text. Significantly more propositions (and more superordinate propositions) were recalled from the composition teachers' revision than from any other version of the text. Short-answer recall was also superior for the composition teachers' revision. The composition teachers' revision was even accorded the highest student ratings for interestingness. It seems that, once again, we have evidence that "seductive detail" versions of text diminish recall of structurally important ideas.

CONCLUSIONS

The "seductive detail" effect in learning from text is very strong. Novel, active, concrete, and personally involving details are highly memorable to readers. General, abstract, and structurally important ideas are remembered less well.

The effect holds for children (Garner et al., 1989; Hidi et al., 1982) and for adults (Garner et al., 1989; Wade & Adams, 1989). It holds for academically proficient college students (Garner et al., 1989) and for low-ability college students (Wade & Adams, 1989). It holds when details are truly "seductive," that is, when they do not support the structurally important ideas of the text at all (Duffy et al., 1989; Garner et al., 1989; Hidi et al., 1982; Wade & Adams, 1989) and when they are somewhat supporting (Garner et al., 1991; Hidi & Baird, 1988). It holds when salient details are inserted unsystematically in text (Hidi et al., 1982; Wade & Adams, 1989) and when they are separated from paragraphs presenting structurally important information (Garner et al., 1991). It holds for generally uninteresting texts (Garner et al., 1989; Wade & Adams, 1989) and for generally interesting texts (Garner et al., 1991, for two recall measures; Hidi & Baird, 1988).

In the absence of an alternative to textbooks or substantially improved textbooks, the question arises: How can students cope with this highly informing medium? We suggest that the metacognitive literature, a fertile area of inquiry for psychologists and educators for about a decade, may offer some insights for both theory and practice.

Metacognition, Selective Attention, and "Seductive Details"

We suggested earlier, in discussing the light switch metaphor for attention to information in text, that an image of students "switching attention on" to a "seductive detail" and then off to abstract principles and then on again to the next "seductive detail" (and so on) captures the findings of the research reviewed in this chapter.

Think for a moment about the consciousness of the switching operation. Are students performing deliberately and planfully when they switch attention on and off in this manner? One of the contributions of metacognitive views of the world is the notion that when students engage in a task (such as learning from text) strategically, they can monitor their performance and deliberately invoke activities that enhance their performance (Garner, 1987). They can regulate their own cognitions.

It is our sense from observing both children and adults attempting to learn from text that much of their attentional activity is *not* strategic, conscious, or selective. Miller's work (1990) suggests developmental constraints on use of selective attention. Miller traces the following pattern of development of selective strategies: (a) some systematic (often spatial) movement through an information array, an absence of selection (though Miller's stimuli were doors to be opened to reveal categories of objects, text can be thought of in much the same way—a straightforward top-to-bottom pass through each sentence in a paragraph, with no extra attention given to any particular sentence); (b) partial production of the selection strategy (with text, one can imagine students at this level according some important ideas *and* some vivid details extra attention, an imperfect application of the selection strategy); (c) production of the selection strategy, but without full benefits (with text, students at this third level would accord extra attention to structurally important ideas but would not remember all of them later); and (d) production of the selection strategy with full benefits (in the case of text, students at this top level would accord extra attention to structurally important information and would recall this information when it was elicited later).

Miller's work also suggests that there are certain conditions under which students are more likely to employ sophisticated selection strategies. One important condition is a meaningful context. Boring tasks involving boring textbooks (and perhaps little awareness of the purpose of the task or the text) almost certainly produce low motivation to perform, minimal invoking of effortful strategies, and, most likely, poor performance.

Another condition mentioned by Miller is provision of developmentally appropriate instruction. Students can be taught to be more selective (i.e., to use the selection strategy with text). Teachers can "think aloud" about important ideas and interesting ideas in text, perhaps rereading the former ("Oh, the author thinks this is important. She underscored the entire sentence. I'm going to reread that and make certain I understand it. I'll want to remember that idea") and smiling or wincing at the latter ("Neat, a fly moves its wings 200 times a second. Interesting. Probably not real important to remember, though"). Modeling how importance and interestingness diverge and how one can allocate extra attention to important ideas allows students to "see" a selection strategy in action. This could *not* be accomplished if "seductive details" were eliminated from text, an unhealthy suggestion sometimes made to writers. It could be accomplished more readily if abstract principles were signaled for readers, a healthy suggestion made too infrequently to writers.

Interestingness and Interests

One of our concerns in reporting the "seductive detail" effect to educators has been that they might infer that, because details in textbooks can distract students from main ideas, they should be wary of assessing and responding to students' topical preferences. We have worried that teachers might decide not to present texts to students on the basis of expressed interest in the topics. In other words, we have been concerned that consumers of this research literature might confuse *interestingness* research with *interest* prescriptions.

In fact, we strongly approve of finding out what topics interest students and then providing text and nontext material to them on high-interest topics. In our collective experience, there are too many examples of teachers who assume that children of a certain age, gender, or ethnicity like to read and hear about certain topics in the absence of any confirming information from the best possible informants, the students.

There are also examples of teachers who ignore the issue of interest, selecting topics and texts solely on the basis of prescribed content. In fact, learning of content is diminished in instances of very low personal interest in a topic (Asher, 1980; Renninger, 1989; see also chapter by Renninger, this volume).

These points bring us back to Dewey (1913). His admonition to avoid trying to *make* something interesting does not extend to trying to find out what is of interest to persons who are learning from text. He points out that persons are always interested in one direction rather than another; conditions of total lack of interest or of impartially distributed interest are mythical.

What teachers do need to do to assist students with "seductive details" is to help students become active, planful regulators of their own cognitions (including their own attention), and, just as importantly, they need to employ meaningful activities, where students are most likely to care about understanding and remembering structurally important information in text.

REFERENCES

Anderson, R. C. (1982). Allocation of attention during reading. In A. Flammer & W. Kintsch (Eds.), *Discourse processing.* New York: North–Holland.

Adler, J., Lubenow, G. C., & Malone, M. (1988, June). Reading God's mind. *Newsweek,* pp. 56–59.

Anderson, R. C., Mason, J., & Shirey, L. (1984). The reading group: An experimental investigation of a labyrinth. *Reading Research Quarterly, 20,* 6–38.

Armbruster, B. B. (1984). The problem of "inconsiderate text." In G. G. Duffy, L. R. Roehler, & J. Mason (Eds.), *Comprehension instruction* (pp. 202–217). New York: Longman.

Asher, S. R. (1980). Topic interest and children's reading comprehension. In R. J. Spiro, B. C. Bruce, & W. F. Brewer (Eds.), *Theoretical issues in reading comprehension* (pp. 525–534). Hillsdale, NJ: Lawrence Erlbaum Associates.

Baumann, J. F., & Serra, J. K. (1984). The frequency and placement of main ideas in children's social studies textbooks: A modified replication of Braddock's research on topic sentences. *Journal of Reading Behavior, 16,* 27–40.

Beck, I. L., McKeown, M. G., & Gromoll, E. W. (1989). Learning from social studies texts. *Cognition and Instruction, 6,* 99–158.

Danner, F. W. (1976). Children's understanding of intersentence organization in the recall of short descriptive passages. *Journal of Educational Psychology, 68,* 174–183.

Dewey, J. (1913). *Interest and effort in education.* Boston: Houghton Mifflin.

Duffy, T. M., Higgins, L., Mehlenbacher, B., Cochran, C., Wallace, D., Hill, C., Haugen, D., McCaffrey, M., Burnett, R., Sloane, S., & Smith, S. (1989). Models for the design of instructional text. *Reading Research Quarterly, 24,* 434–457.

Garner, R. (1987). *Metacognition and reading comprehension.* Norwood, NJ: Ablex.

Garner, R., Alexander, P. A., Gillingham, M. G., Kulikowich, J. M., & Brown, R. (1991). Interest and learning from text. *American Educational Research Journal, 28,* 643–659.

Garner, R., Alexander, P., Slater, W., Hare, V. C., Smith, T., & Reis, R. (1986). Children's knowledge of structural properties of expository text. *Journal of Educational Psychology, 78,* 411–416.

Garner, R., & Gillingham, M. G. (1987). Students' knowledge of text structure. *Journal of Reading Behavior, 19,* 247–259.

Garner, R., Gillingham, M. G., & White, C. S. (1989). Effects of "seductive details" on macroprocessing and microprocessing in adults and children. *Cognition and Instruction, 6,* 41–57.

Graves, M. F., Slater, W. H., Roen, D. D., Redd–Boyd, T., Duin, A. H., Furniss, D. W., & Hazeltine, P. (1988). Some characteristics of memorable expository writing: Effects of revisions by writers with different backgrounds. *Research in the Teaching of English, 22,* 242–265.

Graves, M. F., Prenn, M. C., Earle, J., Thompson, M, Johnson, V., Slater, W. H. (1991). Improving instructional text: Some lessons learned. *Reading Research Quarterly, 26* (2), 110–122.

Hidi, S., & Baird, W. (1988). Strategies for increasing text-based interest and students' recall of expository texts. *Reading Research Quarterly, 23,* 465–483.

Hidi, S., Baird, W., & Hildyard, A. (1982). That's important but is it interesting? Two factors in text processing. In A. Flammer & W. Kintsch (Eds.), *Discourse processing* (pp. 63–75). Amsterdam: North–Holland.

Kieras, D. E. (1978). Good and bad structure in simple paragraphs: Effects on apparent theme, reading time, and recall. *Journal of Verbal Learning and Verbal Behavior, 17,* 13–28.

Kieras, D. E. (1980). Initial mention as a signal to thematic content in technical passages. *Memory and Cognition, 8,* 345–353.

Kieras, D. E. (1982). A model of reader strategy for abstracting main ideas from simple technical prose. *Text, 2,* 47–81.

Miller, P. H. (1990). The development of strategies of selective attention. In D.F. Bjorklund (Ed.), *Children's strategies: Contemporary views of cognitive development* (pp. 157–184). Hillsdale, NJ: Lawrence Erlbaum Associates.

Renninger, K. A. (1989, March). *Interests and noninterests as context in reading comprehension and mathematical word problem solving.* Paper presented at the meeting of the American Educational Research Association, San Francisco.

Schallert, D. L., & Kleiman, G. M. (1979). *Some reasons why teachers are easier to understand than textbooks* (Reading Ed. Rep. No. 9). Urbana: University of Illinois, Center for the Study of Reading.

Schank, R. C. (1979). Interestingness: Controlling inferences. *Artificial Intelligence, 12,* 273–297.

Taylor, M. B., & Samuels, S. J. (1983). Children's use of text structure in the recall of expository material. *American Educational Research Journal, 20,* 517–528.

Wade, S. E., & Adams, B. (1989, March). *The effect of interest on sensitivity to importance and learning.* Paper presented at the meeting of the American Educational Research Association, San Francisco.

Williams, J. P., Taylor, M. B., & Ganger, S. (1981). Text variations at the level of the individual sentence and the comprehension of simple expository paragraphs. *Journal of Educational Psychology, 73,* 851–865.

11 How Interest Affects Learning from Text

Suzanne E. Wade
University of Utah

A great deal of concern has been voiced recently about students' lack of basic knowledge, or "cultural literacy" (cf. Bloom, 1987; Hirsch, 1987; Ravitch & Finn, 1987). At the same time, textbooks—a major conveyor of knowledge in schools—have been widely criticized as being poorly written, superficial, watered down, and uninteresting (Anderson, Hiebert, Scott, & Wilkinson, 1985; Armbruster, 1984; Beck, McKeown, & Gromoll, 1989; Bowen, 1984; Fiske, 1984; Larkin, Hawkins, & Gilmore, 1987; Solozano, 1986; Tyson & Woodward, 1989). Therefore, it is not surprising that researchers, educators, and now the news media have been asking how texts can be written in ways that both inspire students and facilitate learning.

Much of the research on learning from text has focused on those characteristics that facilitate learning, particularly text structure. Text structure refers to the logical connections among ideas as well as the subordination of some ideas to others (Meyer & Rice, 1984). As a result of this research, we know that older and better readers are more able than younger and poorer readers to identify and use an author's structure, to discriminate important from unimportant information, to remember key ideas, and to recall information in an organized manner (cf. Brown & Smiley, 1977, 1978; Meyer, Brandt, & Bluth, 1980; Smiley, Oakley, Worthen, Campione, & Brown, 1977).

In addition to increasing our basic understanding of the reading process, research on structural importance has produced some practical results that have improved both text design and instruction. For example, Armbruster (1984) has described characteristics of texts that make their

255

structure easier to follow, such as giving the reader information about the structure by means of *signals* (e.g., introductions, headings, and typographic cues); making clear how words, clauses, sentences, and ideas are related to one another; and providing just enough examples, details, and other kinds of elaborations to make the content meaningful to the reader. The research has also shown that teaching students how texts are conventionally organized in different domains and how to identify a text's structure can facilitate recall (cf. Bartlett, 1978; Taylor & Beach, 1984). In addition, teaching students how to represent the hierarchical organization of information in a text through schematizing, outlining, and other techniques has been found to enhance comprehension and learning (cf. Cook & Mayer, 1983; Holly & Dansereau, 1984).

Only in the last few years have researchers begun to address another central issue in text comprehension—the role of interest. Earlier work in this area tended to examine the effect of personal preference, or topic interest, generally finding that having a high interest in a text's content facilitates reading comprehension (cf. Asher, Hymel, & Wigfield, 1978; Baldwin, Peleg–Bruckner, & McClintock, 1985; Belloni & Jongsma, 1978; Stevens, 1980). More recently, researchers have begun to investigate how comprehension and learning are affected by *text-based interest*—elements within texts that create interest for the majority of readers (Hidi & Baird, 1986, 1988).

This new research emphasis is timely because publishers are being exhorted to produce texts that are more lively, personal, vivid, and dramatic—in other words, more interesting. For example, Tyson and Woodward (1989) call for authors of textbooks to be those who can write "in the style used by skillful popularizers" (p. 17). Another textbook critic (Sewall, 1988) argues that "all good writing has a human voice and makes use of strong verbs, vivid anecdotes, lively quotations, and other literary devices" (p. 557). However, as this chapter shows, some popular strategies for creating interest may not facilitate, indeed may even interfere with, the learning of important information.

The purpose of this chapter is to review the theoretical and empirical work on text-based interest in order to understand what it is and how it affects learning. Toward these ends, three questions are addressed. First, what kinds of information in a text are interesting, particularly to the students who are the consumers of these texts? Perhaps some writers and textbook publishers have too narrowly defined interest, thus limiting themselves to interest-evoking strategies that may interfere with learning. Second, how does text-based interest affect what students learn from text?

That is, if the information in a passage varies in both interest and importance, what kinds of information are most and least likely to be remembered? The answer to this question will contribute to our understanding of how interest interacts with importance to affect learning outcomes. Third, how does text-based interest affect where students focus their attention in a text? Previous research indicates that skilled readers selectively allocate cognitive resources such as attention to important information that is difficult to remember (Brown, Smiley, & Lawton, 1978; Masur, McIntyre, & Flavell, 1973). Do skilled readers also devote extra attention to interesting information? Does interesting information require extra attention to be learned? The answer to this last set of questions will further our understanding of how interest affects the strategic use of cognitive resources. The chapter concludes with a discussion of the implications of this body of research for writing expository curriculum materials, for educational practice, and for future research. Ultimately, it is hoped that work in this area will help writers and teachers present subject-matter knowledge in ways that not only make it more interesting but also make important information more memorable.

WHAT IS INTERESTING IN A TEXT

One way that writers have attempted to create text-based interest is by embedding personalized anecdotes and highly interesting but nonessential details in expository materials (Hidi, Baird, & Hildyard, 1982; Pearson, Gallagher, Goudvis, & Johnston, 1981). This was true of two Time–Life editors who participated in a study that compared their revisions of textbook history passages with those of text linguists and college composition teachers (Graves, Slater, Roen, Redd-Boyd, Duin, Furniss, & Hazeltine, 1988). One of the Time–Life editors described his rationale for adding interesting but nonessential information this way: "To enrich the content, I inserted 'nuggets' gleaned from library sources. Nuggets are vivid anecdotes and details that remind us that PEOPLE, not events, make history. A Time–Life story is not so much a sequence of events as a string of nuggets" (p. 248). The following are examples of nuggets from the Time–Life revision of a passage about the Vietnam War: "They [the Vietcong] darted out of tunnels to head off patrols, buried exploding booby traps beneath the mud floors of huts, and hid razor-sharp bamboo sticks in holes" (p. 265). These are good examples of what Garner, Gillingham, and White (1989) have aptly termed *seductive details*—highly interesting but unimportant details (see also Garner, Brown, Sanders, &

Menke, this volume). In this case, they evoke vivid images as well as feelings of fear and perhaps anger.

The Time–Life editors seem to have achieved their goal of making the passages more interesting—at least for adults. For example, journalists, educators, and textbook writers generally found the Time–Life versions more interesting than the original textbook passages (Graves & Slater, 1989). Even, the researchers in the Graves et al. (1988) study seem to have considered the Time–Life versions more interesting than those written by the text linguists and composition teachers, who had emphasized clarity and structural cohesion in their revisions. To quote the researchers, the revisions of the Time–Life editors "went beyond such matters [as organization and coherence] and were intended to make the texts interesting, exciting, vivid, rich in human drama, and filled with colorful language" (p. 249).

However, as Duffy, Higgins, Mehlenbacher, Cochran, Wallace, Hill, Haugen, McCaffrey, Burnett, Sloane, and Smith (1989) have pointed out, what adult writers consider interesting may not be what students find interesting. Because students are the consumers of texts, it is worth investigating this issue from their point of view. Therefore, Duffy et al. had 11th-grade students rate the texts revised by the Time–Life editors, text linguists, and composition teachers on two criteria: how easy it was to learn the information in the texts and how enjoyable the texts were. The versions written by the composition teachers—not the Time–Life editors—received the highest ratings.

Although there appears to be little consensus between the adults and students in these studies regarding which of the passages were most interesting or enjoyable, there is some consistency among theorists as to what makes information in a text interesting. For example, Schank (1979) argues that certain kinds of topics are inherently interesting. These include death, danger, chaos, destruction, disease, injury, power, money (in large quantities), sex, and romance—the usual content of nuggets and seductive details mentioned earlier in this chapter.

Schank further argues that these topics can be made more or less interesting by two conditions. One is the unexpectedness of events—something is interesting in direct proportion to its unusualness or abnormality. Therefore, *John entered the room by climbing through the window* would be more interesting than *John entered the room by coming through the door*. The other condition is personal relatedness. The death of a friend or acquaintance is likely to be more interesting than the death of a stranger. According to Schank, "if someone you knew died from having sex for a lot of money, that would be interesting by my rules" (p. 281). This event meets all the criteria that create interest: three inherently interesting topics (death, sex, and a lot of money), unexpectedness (dying from having sex, having sex for a lot of money), and personal relatedness (someone you knew). However, unlike topics that are inherently interesting, both unexpectedness and personal relatedness are relative to the experiences and knowledge of the individual. What is unusual for some people may be usual for others. Likewise, whether people experience personal relatedness is dependent on the people they know and the kinds of characters and events they identify with.

Anderson, Shirey, Wilson, and Fielding (1984) have also identified a number of attributes that contribute to text-based interest. One is character identification, which is similar to Schank's notion of personal relatedness. Simply put, people are likely to be interested in characters with whom they can identify. Anderson et al. argue that character identification is probably greatest when the character matches the reader in sex, age, lifestyle, and values. Another attribute is novelty, which is similar to Schank's notion of unexpectedness. Ordinary happenings are presumably boring, whereas unusual events can be exciting. A third attribute, which Schank does not mention directly, is activity level. This represents the idea that intense feelings or actions will be more interesting than descriptions of passive states or situations that lack action.

Kintsch's (1980) distinction between *emotional interest* and *cognitive interest* adds another dimension to text-based interest. Emotional interest is aroused when events have a direct emotional impact—as sex and violence will usually have—and when stories invite a vicarious experience in the reader. Thus, emotional interest is similar to the notions of inherent interest and personal relatedness, or character identification. Cognitive interest, on the other hand, is quite different. One way to create cognitive interest is to have events unfold in an unusual or surprising way. However, Kintsch argues that unexpectedness or novelty, must be optimal: if a situation is entirely familiar and predictable, it will not generate much interest. Conversely, an event that is too unfamiliar or unexpected is also unlikely to be considered interesting. Interest is greatest at some point between total predictability and the inability to predict anything. However, there is a caveat to this generalization: an unpredictable event or statement may be interesting if, with hindsight, the reader is able to see how it fits into the text's overall structure. Because this can only be judged after reading, Kintsch (1980) has called this *postdictability*. Thus, to be interesting, "the text as a whole must hang together and make sense to the reader, so that he is able to construct a coherent macrostructure in which each text unit has its place and is meaningfully related to other sections of the text" (p. 89).

Cognitive interest is also determined by the reader's background knowledge. Interest tends to be low with little or no relevant background knowledge, increases as more is known, and diminishes again as the reader reaches the point where nothing new can be learned from the passage. Finally, cognitive interest is also affected by writing style. Something may be interesting not because of *what* is said but because of *how* it is said. For example, writers can increase cognitive interest by violating semantic rules, as poets often do, or by choosing unusual or vivid words.

In summary, theories of interest describe a number of factors that interact to determine whether a text will be considered interesting or not. But what does the empirical work in this area tell us about the kinds of information readers find interesting in school texts? When researchers have investigated the relation between what students rate as interesting and as important, they have usually found a divergence between the two (Garner et al., this volume). For example, Hidi et al. (1982) found no relation between interest and importance in expository texts, which emphasized facts, explanations, and/or instructions; in fact, their subjects rated few ideas as at all interesting. In mixed texts (expository material containing narrative anecdotes), only the anecdotes were considered interesting—but again they were rated as unimportant. Only in narrative texts were interest and importance found to be highly related. Similarly, Garner et al. (1989) found that adults rated seductive details in expository texts as very interesting but not at all important; in contrast, main ideas were rated as very important but not at all interesting.

Drawing on these findings, we (Wade & Adams, 1990) designed an experiment to examine the relation between interest and importance in biography because this genre is expository in nature but narrative in structure. Like many narratives, a biography deals with living beings and often describes the events of a person's life in chronological order. In fact, Webster (1988) defined biography as "a life story" (p. 140). However, like an exposition, the biographical passage used in this study deals with factual information—in this case, descriptions of historical events and explanations of their causes and consequences.

In the study, 52 college students were asked to rate sentences for interest and importance in a lengthy biographical sketch of Horatio

Nelson. Subjects were randomly assigned to one of two counterbalanced conditions—rating for interest first or rating for importance first. Subjects were given the text in manuscript form and asked to read it for a general understanding. Then they were given the text divided into segments of one sentence, each followed by a 4–point scale, with 1 as not at all interesting, or not at all important, and 4 as very interesting, or very important. Using this rating scale, subjects first identified one-quarter of the total number of sentences they considered the least interesting (or important). They then repeated this procedure, with the rating progressing from least to most interesting (or important), until they had rated all of the sentences. This procedure, similar to the one developed by Johnson (1970) and used in previous research (e.g., Brown & Smiley, 1977, 1978), produces ratings of relative interest and importance, taking into account the context in which information is embedded.

When the interest and importance ratings were combined, four categories resulted. The categories with the most sentences were high interest/high importance (43) and low interest/low importance (41); only 13 sentences were classified as high interest/low importance, and 15 were rated as low interest/high importance. Thus, interest and importance were found to be highly related in this biographical passage, as Hidi et al. (1982) found for narratives. A content analysis was then conducted to examine what characteristics distinguished the sentences in each category.

The category of high interest/high importance contained the main ideas of the passage—that is, the key, subsuming, and abstract concepts. Specifically, these were descriptions of the major historical events, along with explanations of their causes, outcomes, and historical significance, and descriptions of the personal attributes that were responsible for Nelson's success. Perhaps because the text was a biography, elements of narration, suspense, unexpectedness, and personal relatedness were associated with many of these main ideas. In this chapter, the sentences in this category are referred to as *main ideas*. Two examples are presented here:

1. It was his knowledge of navigation and his talent for getting along with his men that helped him to rise so rapidly in the service.
2. The Battle of Trafalgar was the greatest naval victory in British history, and it won the war for Great Britain.

The category of high interest/low importance covered topics that have many of the properties of absolute interest, embellished with vividness, concreteness, novelty, and personal relatedness. Specifically, they were details of Nelson's injuries, his love life, and his death—concepts that are inherently interesting but were not related to the key ideas of the passage. Thus, they are referred to in this chapter as *seductive details*. The following are examples:

1. During the battle, Nelson's right arm was badly mangled up to the elbow.
2. She [Lady Emma Hamilton] fell in love with the battered, one-eyed, one-armed naval hero and became his mistress.

The category of low interest/high importance consisted of factual details related to the main ideas; thus, they are referred to as *important factual details*. These were mainly the details of major historical events and of Nelson's role in them. They are important because they represent the what, when, where, and how of events that embellish our understanding of them. In the passage, they may lack interest because they do not refer to topics that have direct emotional appeal; furthermore, they do not include the conditions of unexpectedness (or novelty) and personal relatedness (or character identification) posited by the models of text-based interest. This is apparent in the following examples:

1. Nelson first distinguished himself by blockading Toulon, a port city on the coast of France, and capturing Corsica.
2. Nelson led a small landing party in an attack on the strongly fortified port of Santa Cruz de Tenerife in the Canary Islands.

Finally, information that was rated as low interest/low importance consisted primarily of common, everyday facts or events found in any biography, which have nothing to do with the main ideas and do not meet the criteria of inherent interest or unexpectedness. For the sake of economy, these are referred to as *boring trivia*. Two examples are:

1. His father was rector of the local church, and his mother was a member of the Walpole family.
2. During a brief cease-fire in the war, Nelson lived in England in a country house he had bought in 1801.

In summary, research has found that readers generally identify vivid, personalized, dramatic details and anecdotes as interesting. This finding is consistent with theories of interest because these kinds of information involve topics of inherent interest, personal relatedness, and unexpectedness. Unfortunately, as seductive details, they are usually unimportant and unrelated to the main ideas of a text. They also have the potential to bias readers' perceptions of characters and events. However, there is also evidence that interest is not confined exclusively to seductive details. For example, Duffy et al. (1989) found that text versions written by composition teachers, which emphasized clarity and structural cohesion, were rated by students as more enjoyable than the Time–Life versions, which relied heavily on seductive details and personalized anecdotes. Furthermore, main ideas may also be as interesting as seductive details to many readers in some types of texts. So far, this appears to be true of narrative texts (Hidi et al., 1982) and of biography (Wade & Adams, 1990). In the biographical passage used in the Wade and Adams study, descriptions of major historical events and explanations of causes and outcomes were rated as interesting. The fact that structurally cohesive texts and main ideas are considered enjoyable or interesting in some circumstances may reflect Kintsch's notion of cognitive interest.

EFFECTS OF INTEREST ON WHAT IS LEARNED

Popular wisdom holds that if we can find ways to make texts more interesting, students will learn more. This belief is expressed in the following quote by a journalist (Graves & Slater, 1989): "The Time–Life editors spice the descriptions with details, such as 'swarms of buzzing insects' and traps filled with 'razor-sharp bamboo sticks'. In contrast to the detached style of the original passage, this technique helps the reader see what happened. This, in turn, creates a more memorable passage because the reader has images to fall back on" (pp.13–14). However, some educators have questioned whether the Time–Life editors' techniques for making expository texts more interesting will, in fact, make their content more memorable. As one educator put it, "Would students learn more—over the long haul—from a text if it were written in 'Timese'? I doubt it" (Graves & Slater, 1989, p. 18).

Research findings support this educator's skepticism. Although Graves et al. (1988) initially found that the Time–Life versions were recalled better by students than the versions written by either the text linguists or the composition teachers, other researchers who have attempted to replicate Graves et al.'s findings using the same materials have found quite the opposite to be true. Using more rigorous research designs, Britton, Van Dusen, Gulgoz, and Glynn (1989) and Duffy et al. (1989) found that significantly more information was recalled from the composition teachers' versions than from any of the others. Later, in another replication, even Graves (1990) produced results favoring the composition teachers' versions.

These findings are consistent with the research on text-based interest, which has found that the practice of adding anecdotes and seductive details does not facilitate and may even interfere with the learning of important information. For example, Hidi and Baird (1988) found that adding interesting details and elaborations to highlight certain abstract or scientific concepts had no effect on the recall of those concepts, although the details themselves were well recalled. Similarly, Garner et al. (1989) found that inserting seductive details in a text significantly reduced the number of main ideas (although not the number of related details) that adults recalled. Seductive details had an even more detrimental effect on the recall of seventh graders, who not only recalled fewer main ideas but also fewer relevant details than a comparison group, who read the passage without seductive details. Findings are also consistent with research investigating the effect of related and unrelated details on recall. Mohr, Glover, and Ronning (1984) found that the number of unrelated details in a passage was negatively correlated with the recall of major ideas. Similarly, Bradshaw and Anderson (1982) found that major ideas are recalled better when they are presented alone than when they are studied along with unrelated facts. In both studies, major ideas were recalled best when they were embellished with supporting details, added only to elaborate the main idea.

In our own research in this area (Wade & Adams, 1990), we examined how interest and importance interact to affect what is learned because previous research has found both to be powerful predictors of learning. Results were expected to indicate which of the four categories of information (seductive details, main ideas, important factual details, or boring trivia) established in the rating study would be most and least memorable. We also hypothesized that one reason poorer readers are less sensitive to structural importance than good readers (Meyer et al., 1980; Smiley et al., 1977) may be that they are more affected by the interestingness of information in a text. As a consequence, we expected that good readers would recall more important than interesting information, whereas poorer readers would recall more interesting than important information.

In this experiment, 48 college students read the same text on Horatio Nelson, which had been rated for interest and importance. They also completed a written free-recall test, either immediately following the reading (immediate recall) or 1 week later (delayed recall). We found that interest was a better predictor of recall than structural importance for *both* ability groups. Although good readers remembered significantly more than poor readers, there was no difference in their patterns of recall. The two kinds of information that had been rated as interesting in the rating study described earlier—seductive details and main ideas—were recalled significantly better by both groups than was uninteresting information. In fact, details supporting the main ideas, which had been rated as important but uninteresting, were least memorable. These were the results for both immediate and delayed *overall* recall, in which at least 25% of the idea units in a sentence were recalled. (See Table 11.1 for overall recall results of both the immediate and the delayed conditions.) We also analyzed results using more stringent criteria (referred to as *complete* recall), in which 66% or more of the idea units in a sentence had to be recalled to receive credit. Results were similar except that in the complete recall condition no significant difference was found between the number of main ideas and seductive details that were recalled.

In summary, interest has a powerful effect on recall for even skilled readers. Across studies, seductive details are most memorable. Unfortunately, the practice of adding them to texts to increase the memorability of important information does not seem to work and in some cases may be detrimental to that objective. However, when important information is interesting—as is frequently the case for main ideas in narratives and biography—there is a greater likelihood that it will be remembered. The problem seems to be with purely expository information, which is usually considered by readers to be uninteresting, as in the case of main ideas and supporting details in expository texts (e.g., Garner et al., 1989; Hidi & Baird, 1988) and of historically important factual details in biography (Wade & Adams, 1990). Clearly, strategies are needed to make these kinds of information more memorable and, if possible, more interesting.

EFFECTS OF INTEREST ON SELECTIVE ATTENTION

The findings just discussed raise the question of *why* some kinds of information are recalled better than other kinds. The theory of selective attention (Anderson, 1982) may offer one explanation. This theory holds that the more attention a reader focuses on a text element, the better it will be recalled. In studies that have examined the effect of importance on selective attention strategies, this has certainly been found to be true. For example, in studies where certain kinds of information are made important by means of objectives (Rothkopf & Billington, 1979), adjunct questions embedded in the text (Reynolds & Anderson, 1982; Reynolds,

Table 11.1

Means and Standard Deviations for Overall Recall
(Wade & Adams, 1990)

Sentence Type	Immediate	Delayed
High Int/High Imp*		
(Main ideas)		
M	4.60	3.24
SD	1.27	1.26
High Int/Low Imp		
(Seductive details)		
M	6.50	4.88
SD	1.74	1.52
Low Int/High Imp		
(Important factual details)		
M	2.90	1.05
SD	1.59	1.03
Low Int/Low Imp		
(Boring trivia)		
M	3.49	2.16
SD	1.24	1.10

*Int = Interest; Imp = Importance

Note: Total possible recall equals 10. Of the 112 sentences in the text, 80 were analyzed. Selection was based on the mean scores for both importance and interest that were closest to either 1 (lowest in importance and interest) or 4 (highest in importance and interest). Thus, the sentences that were not used in the analysis were those with the least agreement among subjects in the rating study or that were rated as being in the middle of the rating scale—that is, close to the 2.5 median. To reflect the proportional differences that exist in each category, 30 high importance/high interest, 10 high importance/low interest, 10 low importance/high interest, and 30 low importance/low interest sentences were selected for analysis. The data in categories containing 30 sentences were divided by 3 in order to make all recall conditions numerically equivalent. Post hoc analyses revealed that the means in each sentence category for overall recall were significantly different (Newman–Keuls, $p < .05$).

Standiford, & Anderson, 1979), or text structure (Cirilo & Foss, 1980), expert readers have been found to allocate extra attention to important information and, because of this, to learn more than younger and poorer readers.

But what happens to this seemingly linear, positive relation among importance, selective attention, and learning when the variable of text-based interest is added? Because interesting information is often vivid, dramatic, suspenseful, and/or personalized, it may not require much effort to learn; at the same time, interest may attract a good deal of the reader's attention. If this is the case, then attention would appear to be a related phenomenon, but not the reason that interesting information is memorable. Therefore, if interesting information does not require extra attention to be learned, yet even skilled readers devote a good deal of attention to it, then they are not reading *strategically*; that is, they are not selectively allocating cognitive resources to information necessary for them to meet their learning goals. The problem is even greater if they devote extra attention to interesting information that is unimportant. Findings from the research described next, which investigated the influence of interest on selective attention, support this hypothesis.

The influence of interest on where attention is directed and on subsequent action and memory begins at an early age. Renninger and Wozniak (1985), for example, report that 3- and 4-year-old children are much more likely to shift their attention to identified interest objects in their peripheral visual field than to identified objects of noninterest. Furthermore, they are more likely to recognize and recall objects that are identified interests. In fact, 3-year-olds can recall an item of interest placed in the medial position in a 9-item series better than objects in any of the other positions, despite the fact that the medial position is ordinarily the most difficult to recall. Only as children get older are they able to recall objects in other positions as well. For example, the 4-year-olds in the Renninger and Wozniak study recalled the noninterest item in the last serial position as often as the interest item in the medial position, whereas the 3-year-olds recalled the interest item more often than the item in the last serial position. This finding may be evidence of the beginning of a rehearsal strategy (Renninger, 1990). It appears that the pervasive influence of interest on information processing and recall may change with age, as children develop strategies for learning (see chapter by Renninger, this volume).

Yet, the strong influence of interest never disappears. Anderson et al. (1984) found that third- and fourth-graders allocated more attention to interesting sentences and recalled them better than uninteresting ones. In this study, children read a series of unrelated sentences that had been previously rated for interest by an equivalent group of subjects. In addition to sentence recall, two measures of attention were collected. The first was reading time, a measure of attention duration, which assumes that the longer subjects spend reading a text element, the more attention they are allocating to it. Reading times were obtained by recording how long subjects spent reading sentences presented individually on a computer screen before they pressed a space bar on the keyboard to call up the next sentence. The second measure of attention was reaction time to outside stimuli, which reflects attention intensity. Reaction times were obtained by recording the amount of time it takes for subjects to respond to a tone periodically sounded in the earphones they were wearing. The assumption here is that the longer it takes subjects to respond the more they are absorbed in reading the sentences. Results of a causal analysis indicated that attention was not a mediating variable between interest and learning. In other words, subjects could have learned the interesting sentences without allocating extra attention to them. Thus, paying as much or more attention to interesting sentences as to uninteresting ones does not seem to be an effective or efficient strategy.

In a follow-up study, Shirey and Reynolds (1988) investigated whether adults are more strategic than children in the way in which they direct their attention to a text. They had college students read the same sentences which had been previously rated for interest by their peers. Unlike the children in the Anderson et al. (1984) study, adults allocated less attention to interesting sentences yet still recalled them better. Shirey and Reynolds concluded that mature readers are more strategic in how they allocate cognitive resources, giving more attention to information that cannot be easily remembered.

However, this finding may not hold for connected prose, in which sentences vary in both interest and importance. To find out, we (Wade & Schraw, 1990) examined the selective attention strategies of college students reading a revised version of the Horatio Nelson passage. Given the results of previous research on selective attention, we hypothesized that mature readers would allocate extra attention to important but uninteresting parts of a text and the least attention to unimportant parts— namely, seductive details and boring trivia.

In this study, we investigated the relation between attention allocation and recall for the four categories of information developed in the Wade and Adams study: main ideas, seductive details, important factual details, and boring trivia. The text was revised to include more sentences that might be rated as high interest/low importance and low interest/ high importance. This revision, in fact, did produce a more equal distribution of sentences in each of the four categories when it was later rated for interest and importance by a group of college students. The text was then presented to another group of subjects on a computer screen, which automatically recorded the amount of time each subject spent reading individual sentences before calling up the next sentence. After reading the entire text in this way, subjects completed a written free-recall test.

Recall patterns were identical to the immediate overall recall results obtained in the Wade and Adams study: seductive details were best recalled, followed by main ideas, with important factual details being least well recalled. However, reading times reveal an intriguing pattern (see Table 11.2). Readers spent twice as much time on the important factual details as they did on main ideas or boring trivia, yet the important factual details remained least memorable. From these results, we hypothesized that readers may realize the need to devote extra time to important factual details because they are so difficult to process and remember. This would suggest that when it comes to this kind of information, mature readers are acting strategically in allocating their cognitive resources.

Mature readers also appear to be strategic in allocating time to main ideas and boring trivia; that is, they spend relatively little time on these two types of information, possibly for different reasons. In the case of main ideas, where interest and importance converge, they may believe that this kind of information is quite memorable, which indeed is the case. Thus, they may assume that main ideas require a minimal amount of attention. On the other hand, readers may give little attention to information that is unimportant and uninteresting, perhaps because they assume it does not need to be learned. If these conjectures are true, then we can begin to develop a model of the mature reader as one who first discriminates between important and unimportant information, then allocates extra attention only to the important information that requires it. This model suggests that mature readers are highly efficient and strategic.

However, when it comes to seductive details, readers appear to be anything but efficient and strategic. Although seductive details had been rated as unimportant and have been found to be the most memorable kind of information across studies, readers in this experiment spent over 50% more time reading them than they did reading main ideas. Thus, vivid anecdotes and irrelevant details on topics of absolute interest inserted into a text are truly seductive because readers devote a good deal of time to information that is neither important nor difficult to remember.

Table 11.2

Means and Standard Deviations for Overall Recall and Reading Times
(Wade & Schraw, 1990)

Sentence Type	Recall	Reading Times
High Int/High Imp*		
(Main ideas)		
M	9.79	5.41
SD	3.58	1.56
High Int/Low Imp		
(Seductive details)		
M	14.68	8.52
SD	3.61	1.74
Low Int/High Imp		
(Important factual details)		
M	5.88	10.23
SD	4.04	2.42
Low Int/Low Imp		
(Boring trivia)		
M	6.77	5.79
SD	3.69	1.51

*Int = Interest; Imp = Importance

Note: Total possible recall equals 26; reading times are recorded in seconds. Of the 150 sentences in the text, 99 were used in the analysis. Selection criteria were as follows: to be considered high or low, a sentence's mean rating for interest and importance had to be at least 1/3 of a standard deviation above or below the grand mean of 2.5. In addition, for the categories of high interest/high importance and low interest/low importance, the means for both interest and importance could be no more than one standard deviation apart. For the categories of high interest/low importance and low interest/high importance, the two means for each sentence had to be at least one standard deviation apart. The result was 26 sentences in each category except for high interest/low importance, which contained 21 sentences. The data in this category were multiplied by 1.23 in order to equate all cells. Reading times have been corrected for words/syllables. Post hoc analyses revealed that the means for both recall and reading times were significantly different (Newman–Keuls, $p < .05$), except for the difference in recall between low interest/high importance and low interest/low importance.

However, when it comes to seductive details, readers appear to be anything but efficient and strategic. Although seductive details have been rated as unimportant and have been found to be the most memorable kind of information across studies, readers in this experiment spent over 50% more time reading them than they did reading main ideas. Thus, vivid anecdotes and irrelevant details on topics of absolute interest inserted into a text are truly seductive because in attending to them readers devote a good deal of time to information that is neither important nor difficult to remember.

In summary, the research on interest and selective attention reveals that strategies for learning develop with age, transcending but never fully overcoming the pervasive influence that interest has on young children. Mature readers are more strategic than younger readers, focusing a good deal of attention on important factual information that is uninteresting and not easily remembered. Even though main ideas are important to remember, strategic readers devote less reading time to them, perhaps because they know that main ideas are quite memorable. They also spend relatively little time on boring trivia, presumably because this kind of information is not worth remembering. However, this model of efficiency and strategic decision-making breaks down when it comes to highly interesting but unimportant information. Even strategic readers appear to be seduced by this kind of information, devoting relatively large amounts of time to it, despite the fact that it is highly memorable and not important.

Why do readers spend so much time reading seductive details, and is it the same kind of attention that they devote to uninteresting factual details? Although this question needs to be investigated using different research methods, we hypothesize that readers use a qualitatively different kind of attention for seductive details than they do for factual information that they believe is important to learn. For important factual details, readers may exert concentrated effort, or *will*, which requires strong activation of attentional resources and a conscious knowledge that it will achieve some particular end such as improved recall (Norman & Shallice, 1980). In contrast, readers may spend time rereading, visualizing, thinking about, and perhaps savoring the surprise and emotional response that seductive details elicit.

Attempts to explain these findings are only conjectures at this point. More research is needed to test these hypotheses and understand why the relation between selective attention and recall is so different for the four categories of information and how the quality of attention may vary. To do so, different research methods—both quantitative and qualitative—are needed to expand our knowledge and produce converging lines of evidence. Research methods might include verbal report data obtained by means of think alouds and interviews and other measures of attention such as reaction times to a secondary task and/or eye movement data.

SUMMARY AND CONCLUSIONS

This chapter began an expression of the hope that the literature on text-based interest can ultimately suggest ways to make texts more interesting and, at the same time, make important text information more memorable. Research findings certainly suggest what not to do, but they also offer some promising new directions.

As a result of research in this area, we know that vivid, personalized anecdotes and seductive details will usually be considered interesting. However, this is not a viable strategy for creating interest for several reasons. First, the research has consistently found that adding seductive details, or any kind of detail unrelated to the main ideas, does not facilitate and often has a detrimental effect on the learning of important information (Bradshaw & Anderson, 1982; Garner et al., 1989; Hidi & Baird, 1988; Mohr, Glover, & Ronning, 1984; Wade & Adams, 1990). Second, seductive details attract a good deal of a reader's attention, which could otherwise be devoted to essential information. Even skilled adult readers with sophisticated learning strategies direct much of their attention to seductive details, despite the fact that these details do not need extra attention to be remembered and are not important to begin with (Wade & Schraw, 1990). Third, adding interesting but unimportant information increases passage length, as in the case of the Time–Life versions that were over 80% longer than other versions (Duffy et al., 1989). Finally, strategies for evoking emotional interest may bias readers' interpretations of events by using words and images that evoke fear and perhaps hostility.

Fortunately, interest also has the potential to enhance the learning of essential information. For example, the structurally cohesive texts written by the composition teachers were not only considered more enjoyable by readers but also were recalled better than the Time–Life editor's versions (Duffy et al., 1989). In addition, we found that main ideas in biographical text were rated as interesting and recalled relatively well (Wade & Adams, 1990). These findings may be related to Kintsch's (1980) idea of cognitive interest, which occurs when learners are able to make sense of what they read and when they believe that they are learning something new.

Research is now needed to understand fully why structurally cohesive texts and certain kinds of main ideas may be interesting, and how such findings can be applied to the writing of expository materials in different domains. One possibility is that a coherent text makes comprehension easier, and therefore more enjoyable, because it makes relations among ideas more explicit. This was a conclusion Beck, McKeown, Omanson, and

Pople (1984) reached to explain why basal stories that were revised to improve their coherence were recalled better than the original versions, despite the higher readability levels of the revised stories. It was also a conclusion that Britton, Van Dusen, Glynn, and Hemphill (in press) reached when they found that the Time–Life passages in the Graves et al. (1988) study required the readers to make far more inferences of various kinds than did the composition teachers' versions. Having to make inferences requires time and cognitive effort, thus rendering comprehension a process that is more controlled than automatic.

Of particular concern is how writers and teachers can increase the interestingness and memorability of important factual information. Apparently, extra reading time and even concentrated effort are not enough. In addition to being uninteresting, factual information may be unfamiliar and unconnected for many readers (Bransford, Stein, Shelton, & Owings, 1981). Thus, we need to continue research already under way that investigates ways that writers and teachers can (a) focus students' attention on both the main ideas and on important supporting details, which will require the most effort to learn, and (b) help students link factual content to related and superordinate concepts and to their own prior knowledge. One way to accomplish these goals is to make students aware of the *signals* in texts such as previews, summaries, and adjunct questions that cue readers to important information (Armbruster, 1984; Meyer, 1979). Another way is to introduce strategies for organizing information that show the relations among concepts (cf. Holly & Dansereau, 1984). Especially for younger readers, examples need to be identified as such, explicitly related to generalizations, and contrasted with other examples (Brophy, 1990). Such interconnectedness of information can help readers understand how ideas are related and the significance or relevance of facts. The more connected knowledge is in memory, the easier it is to access in new situations (Spiro, Vispoel, Schmitz, Samarapungavan, & Boerger, 1987). Thus, connected knowledge is usable knowledge.

Finally, research on text-based interest needs to be conducted with different populations of readers. We need to know how readers' strategies for dealing with information that varies in interest and importance develop with age and reading ability. We also need to know how gender, amount of relevant background knowledge, and differences in cultural background affect what is considered interesting in a text, what kinds of information are memorable, and how interest affects selective attention strategies for learning important information.

In summary, rather than focusing on topics, words, and writing techniques that arouse emotional interest, strategies are needed that increase cognitive interest. Otherwise, nuggets and seductive details may characterize a whole new generation of textbooks. The result may be texts that are longer and contain more irrelevant detail. Thus, contrary to the writers' best intentions, students could be reading more but learning less.

REFERENCES

Anderson, R. C. (1982). Allocation of attention during reading. In A. Flammer & W. Kintsch (Eds.), *Discourse processing*. New York: North–Holland.

Anderson, R. C., Hiebert, E. H., Scott, J. A., & Wilkinson, I. A. (1985). *Becoming a nation of readers*. Washington, DC: National Institute of Education.

Anderson, R. C., Shirey, L. L., Wilson, P. T., & Fielding, L. G. (1984). *Interestingness of children's reading material* (Tech. Rep. No. 323). Urbana–Champaign: University of Illinois, Center for the Study of Reading.

Armbruster, B. B. (1984). The problem of "inconsiderate text." In G. G. Duffy, L. R. Roehler, & J. Mason (Eds.), *Comprehension instruction: Perspectives and suggestions* (pp. 202–217). New York: Longman.

Asher, S. R., Hymel, S., & Wigfield, A. (1978). Influence of topic interest on children's reading comprehension. *Journal of Reading Behavior, 10,* 35–47.

Baldwin, R. S., Peleg–Bruckner, Z., & McClintock, A. H. (1985). Effects of topic interest and prior knowledge on reading comprehension. *Reading Research Quarterly, 20,* 497–504.

Bartlett, B. J. (1978). *Top-level structure as an organizational strategy for recall of classroom text*. Unpublished doctoral dissertation, Arizona State University, Tempe.

Beck, I. L., McKeown, M. G., & Gromoll, E. W. (1989). Learning from social studies texts. *Cognition and Instruction, 6,* 99–158.

Beck, I. L., McKeown, M. G., Omanson, R. C., & Pople, M. T. (1984). Improving the comprehensibility of stories: The effects of revisions that improve coherence. *Reading Research Quarterly, 19,* 263–277.

Belloni, L. F., & Jongsma, E. A. (1978). The effects of interest on reading comprehension of low-achieving students. *Journal of Reading, 22,* 106–109.

Bloom, A. D. (1987). *Closing of the American mind*. New York: Simon & Schuster.

Bowen, E. (1984, December 3). A debate over dumping down. *Time,* p. 68.

Bradshaw, G. L., & Anderson, J. R. (1982). Elaborative encoding as an explanation of levels of processing. *Journal of Verbal Learning and Verbal Behavior, 21,* 165–174.

Bransford, J. D., Stein, B. S., Shelton, T. S., & Owings, R. A. (1981). Cognition and adaptation: The importance of learning to learn. In J. A. Harvey (Ed.), Cognition, social behavior, and the environment (pp. 93–110). Hillsdale, NJ: Lawrence Erlbaum Associates.

Britton, B. K., Van Dusen, L., Glynn, S., & Hemphill, D. (in press). The impact of inferences on instructional text. In G. H. Bower & A. C. Graesser

(Eds.), *Psychology of learning and motivation* (Vol. 25). New York: Academic Press.

Britton, B. K., Van Dusen, L., Gulgoz, S., & Glynn, S. M. (1989). Instructional texts rewritten by five expert teams: Revisions and retention improvements. *Journal of Educational Psychology, 81*, 226–239.

Brophy, J. (1990). The de facto national curriculum in elementary social studies: Critique of a representative sample. *Elementary subjects center series no. 17.* MSU: The Center for the Learning and Teaching of Elementary Subjects.

Brown, A. L., & Smiley, S. S. (1977). Rating the importance of structural units of prose passages: A problem of metacognitive development. *Child Development, 49*, 1–8.

Brown, A. L., & Smiley, S. S. (1978). The development of strategies for studying texts. *Child Development, 49*, 1076–1088.

Brown, A. L., Smiley, S. S., & Lawton, S. C. (1978). The effects of experience on the selection of suitable retrieval cues for studying. *Child Development, 49*, 829–835.

Cirilo, R. K., & Foss, D. J. (1980). Text structure and reading time for sentences. *Journal of Verbal Learning and Verbal Behavior, 19*, 96–109.

Cook, L. K., & Mayer, R. E. (1983). Reading strategies training for meaningful learning from prose. In M. Pressley & J. R. Levin (Eds.), *Cognitive strategy research: Educational applications* (pp. 81–126). New York: Springer–Verlag.

Duffy, T. M., Higgins, L., Mehlenbacher, B., Cochran, C., Wallace, D., Hill, C., Haugen, D., McCaffrey, M., Burnett, R., Sloane, S., & Smith, S. (1989). Models for the design of text. *Reading Research Quarterly, 24*, 434–457.

Fiske, E. B. (1984, July 29). Next education debate: Quality of textbooks. *The New York Times* (Section I, pp. 1, 35).

Garner, R., Gillingham, M. G., & White, C. S. (1989). Effects of "seductive details" on macroprocessing and microprocessing in adults and children. *Cognition and Instruction, 6*, 41–57.

Graves, M. (1990, April). *Effective instructional texts: Some lessons learned, some not learned, and some questions.* Paper presented at the annual meeting of the American Educational Research Association, Boston.

Graves, M. F., & Slater, W. H. (1989, April). *Some qualitative assessments of two versions of a passage from a high school history textbook.* Paper presented at the annual meeting of the American Educational Research Association, San Francisco.

Graves, M. F., Slater, W. H., Roen, D., Redd–Boyd, T., Duin, A. H., Furniss, D. W., & Hazeltine, P. (1988). Some characteristics of memorable expository writing: Effects of revisions by writers with different backgrounds. *Research in the Teaching of English, 22*, 242–265.

Hidi, S., & Baird, W. (1986). Interestingness—A neglected variable in discourse processing. *Cognitive Science, 10*, 179–194.

Hidi, S., & Baird, W. (1988). Strategies for increasing text-based interest and students' recall of expository texts. *Reading Research Quarterly, 23*, 465–483.

Hidi, S., Baird, W., & Hildyard, A. (1982). That's important but is it interesting? Two factors in text processing. In A. Flammer & W. Kintsch (Eds.), *Discourse processing* (pp. 63–75). New York: North–Holland.

Hirsch, E. D. (1987). *Cultural literacy: What every American needs to know.* Boston: Houghton Mifflin.

Holly, C. D., & Dansereau, D. F. (Eds.) (1984). *Spatial learning strategies: Techniques, applications, and related issues.* Orlando: Academic Press.

Johnson, R. E. (1970). Recall of prose as a function of the structural importance of the linguistic units. *Journal of Verbal Learning and Verbal Behavior, 9,* 12–20.

Kintsch, W. (1980). Learning from text, levels of comprehension, or: Why anyone would read a story anyway. *Poetics, 9,* 87–89.

Larkin, A. G., Hawkins, M. L., & Gilmore, A. (1987). Trivial and noninformative content of elementary social studies: A review of primary texts in four series. *Theory and Research in Social Education, 15,* 299–311.

Masur, E. F., McIntyre, C. W., & Flavell, J. H. (1973). Developmental changes in apportionment of study time among items in a multitrial free recall task. *Journal of Experimental Child Psychology, 15,* 237–246.

Meyer, B. J. (1979). Organizational patterns in prose and their use in reading. In M. L. Kamil & A. J. Moe (Eds.), *Reading research: Studies and applications.* Twenty-eighth Yearbook of the National Reading Conference.

Meyer, B. J., Brandt, D. M., & Bluth, G. J. (1980). Use of top-level structure: Key for reading comprehension of ninth grade students. *Reading Research Quarterly, 16,* 72–101.

Meyer, B. J., & Rice, G. E. (1984). The structure of text. In P. D. Pearson (Ed.), *Handbook of reading research.* New York: Longman.

Mohr, P., Glover, J., & Ronning, R. R. (1984). The effect of related and unrelated details on the recall of major ideas in prose. *Journal of Reading Behavior, 16,* 97–109.

Norman, D. A., & Shallice, T. (1980). *Attention to action: Willed and automatic control of behavior.* (Tech. Rep. No. 806). San Diego: University of California, Center for Human Information Processing.

Pearson, P. D., Gallagher, M., Goudvis, A., & Johnston, P. (1981). *What kinds of expository materials occur in elementary school children's textbooks?* Paper presented at the National Reading Conference, Dallas.

Ravitch, D., & Finn, C. E. (1987). *What do our 17-year-olds know? A report on the first national assessment of history and literature.* New York: Harper & Row.

Renninger, K. A. (1990). Children's play interests, representation, and activity. In R. Fivush & J. Hudson (Eds.), *Knowing and remembering in young children* (pp. 127–165). Emory Cognition Series (Vol. III). Cambridge: Cambridge University Press.

Renninger, K. A., & Wozniak, R. H. (1985). Effect of interest on attentional shift, recognition, and recall in young children. *Developmental Psychology, 21,* 624–632.

Reynolds, R. E., & Anderson, R. C. (1982). Influence of questions on the allocation of attention during reading. *Journal of Educational Psychology, 74,* 623–632.

Reynolds, R. E., Standiford, S. N., & Anderson, R. C. (1979). Distribution of reading time when questions are asked about a restricted category of text information. *Journal of Educational Psychology, 7*, 183–190.

Rothkopf, E. Z., & Billington, M. J. (1979). Goal-guided learning from text: Inferring a descriptive processing model from inspection times and eye movements. *Journal of Educational Psychology, 71*, 310–327.

Schank, R. C. (1979). Interestingness: Controlling inferences. *Artificial Intelligence, 12*, 273–297.

Sewall, G. T. (1988). American history textbooks: Where do we go from here? *Phi Delta Kappan, 69*, 552–558.

Shirey, L. L., & Reynolds, R. E. (1988). Effect of Interest on attention and learning. *Journal of Educational Psychology, 80*, 159–166.

Smiley, S. S., Oakley, D. D., Worthen, D., Campione, J. C., & Brown, A. L. (1977). Recall of thematically relevant material by adolescent good and poor readers as a function of written versus oral presentation. *Journal of Educational Psychology, 69*, 381–387.

Solozano, L. (1986, April 14). Textbooks: Crisis of competence. *U.S. News & World Report,* 68.

Spiro, R. J., Vispoel, W. P., Schmitz, J. G., Samarapungavan, A., & Boerger, A. E. (1987). Knowledge acquisition for application: Cognitive flexibility and transfer in complex content domains. In B. C. Britton (Ed.), *Executive control processes* (pp. 177–199). Hillsdale, NJ: Lawrence Erlbaum Associates.

Stevens, K. (1980). The effect of topic interest on the reading comprehension of higher ability students. *Journal of Educational Research, 73*, 365–668.

Taylor, B. M., & Beach, R. W. (1984). The effects of text structure instruction on middle-grade students' comprehension and production of expository prose. *Reading Research Quarterly, 19*, 134–146.

Tyson, H., & Woodward, A. (1989). Why students aren't learning very much from textbooks. *Educational Leadership, 47*, 14–17.

Wade, S. E., & Adams, B. (1990). Effects of importance and interest on recall of biographical text. *JRB: A Journal of Literacy, 22*, 331–353.

Wade, S. E., & Schraw, G. (1990, December). *Effects of importance and interest on strategic reading.* Paper presented at the Annual Meeting of the National Reading Conference, Miami.

Webster's New World Dictionary of American English (1988). Third College Edition, V. Newfeldt & D. B. Guralink (Eds.). New York: Simon & Schuster.

IV V SPECIAL APPROACHES TO EXPLAIN INTEREST EFFECTS

12

Importance, Interest, and Selective Attention

Larry L. Shirey
Santa Clara County Office of Education — San Jose, California

Although researchers have been aware of the effects of interest on memory since perhaps the middle of the last century (Renninger, 1990), little research has isolated the components of interest and studied their impact on reading. A number of years ago, when a small group of researchers at the Center for the Study of Reading at the University of Illinois attempted to conceptualize why interest influenced memory for what was read, these questions arose from a more general discussion of the effects of important text elements on reading comprehension.

Investigators long have noted that important text elements tend to be learned and recalled better than those elements that are less important (Newman, 1939; Johnson, 1970). Furthermore, text elements can become important in different ways. They can attain importance because they relate to instructions or objectives stated prior to reading (Ausubel, 1960; Rothkopf & Kaplan, 1972), because of their relevance to a reader's perspective or point of view (Anderson & Pichert, 1978; Pichert & Anderson, 1977), because of cues inserted into the text by the author (Rothkopf, 1966; Reynolds, Standiford, & Anderson, 1979), because of the structure of the text in which they occur (Kintsch & van Dijk, 1978; van Dijk; & Kintsch, 1983), because they represent conceptual or relational links between text elements and text ideas (Frase, 1969), or because they are interesting to the reader (Asher, 1980).

However, researchers at the Center for the Study of Reading concluded that importance was perhaps a confusing term to apply to all of the aforementioned characteristics of text. It was thought that importance might imply having some content value, and text characteristics such as interest might not fit within that connotation. Therefore, the group at the Center for the Study of Reading chose the term *salient* to describe the characteristics of text that appear to improve comprehension. The term salient was used to describe any feature (text- or task-related) that made an element of text more prominent. The underlying assumption behind this was that any text element that could be made salient would enable the reader to better recall and understand it; and, in turn, this increased recall would be attributed to the extra attention allocated to that text element.

In this chapter, the importance of a text segment refers to the relation of that segment to the structure of the text or to the parameters of the reading task assigned to the text. The interestingness of a text segment refers to the relation of a text segment to the reader of the text. The specific relations among importance, interest, and attention are first overviewed, with specific focus on that research that emerged from Anderson's (1982, 1983) studies of selective attention.

Anderson, Reynolds, and their colleagues (Anderson, 1982; Reynolds & Anderson, 1982; Reynolds, Standiford, & Anderson, 1979) developed a selective attention model to describe the effect that adjunct questions in text had on the level of attention allocated to text elements and subsequent learning (as measured by recall) of those elements. In order, the three steps, or stages, of this model of attention include:

(1) Text elements are processed at some minimal level and graded for importance.

(2) Extra attention is devoted to elements in proportion to their importance.

(3) Because of the extra attention, or a process supported by the extra attention, important text elements are learned better than other elements.

An implication of the selective attention model is that there is a causal, not just a correlational, relation among interest, attention, and learning. The fact that text elements that have been rated as important are subsequently better recalled or learned is well established in educational and psychological research (e.g., Brown & Smiley, 1977). Similarly, a good deal of research has determined that more attention is allocated to information that has been rated as important—attention being measured in a number of ways, including reading times (Cirilo & Foss, 1980) and eye movement patterns (Just & Carpenter, 1980). Taken together, these two findings may suggest that a positive linear relation exists between importance, attention, and learning. However, what is proven by these two separate findings is solely that correlational relations exist between importance and learning, and between importance and attention.

The causal model implies a linear, and in this case positive, relation among the variables, such as the following graphic representation (where "— (+) —> means positively related to"):

importance — (+) —> attention — (+) —> learning

The relation between attention and learning, in this case, is spurious because both variables are affected by importance, as the following figure portrays.

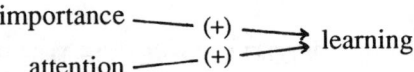

Instead, Anderson's selective attention model suggests that important (and/or interesting) text elements are better learned because extra attention is allocated to them. Notable implications for the learning process can be derived from such a model. Regardless of whether attention is causally related to learning or simply supports the learning process, the selective attention model predicts positive relations among importance, attention, and learning.

Briefly, a causal model includes four entailments that, if supported, allow researchers to make causal claims for their results. These entailments include:

1. (x) is related to (y) at a traditional level of significance.
2. (x) is related to (m)* at a traditional level of significance.
3. (m) is related to (y) at a traditional level of significance.
4. When the relations of (x) to (m) and (m) to (y) are partialled out in a hierarchical regression analysis, the relation between (x) and (y) is significantly reduced.

   * Where (m) is the mediating variable between (x) and (y) in the following relation: (x) — (+) —> (m) — (+) —> (y)

Causality can be claimed only if each of these four entailments is met. In most of the research dealing with attention as a mediating variable, only the first two entailments are evaluated; hence conclusions of a causal nature, even if only implicitly made, are presumably premature.

Considerable research using different approaches and methodologies provides results that can be interpreted in terms of a selective attention model. The work of Goetz, Schallert, Reynolds, and Radin (1983) suggests that reading time (or attention) is a likely explanation for the well-documented effects on learning of being given a perspective from which to read. In this study, students who were given a perspective from which to read spent longer on text segments that contained information relevant to that perspective and subsequently recalled the perspective-relevant information more completely. Rothkopf and Billington (1979), who used eye movements in addition to reading time as measures of attention, reported similar findings, as did Cirilo and Foss (1980), whose findings suggest that text elements that play an important role in a passage have more attention allocated to them and are better learned.

DEVELOPMENTAL LEVEL OF THE READER

In order for extra attention to be allocated to important information, that information must first be identified as important by the reader. The work of Brown and her colleagues (e.g., Brown, 1980) suggests that young children's ability to identify important information in texts is very limited and develops rather slowly. Young children are only able to make such distinctions with very simple written materials or with intense instruction and significant interaction with materials (Danner, 1976). However, if asked about which elements of text are important, children appear to be very likely to respond as adults would (Brown & Smiley, 1977). In other words, when probed, children can and will respond similarly to adults; however, when left to generate their own answer about what is important, these answers are more idiosyncratic.

Briefly, in the Brown and Smiley study, students aged 8, 10, 12, and 18 read and rated the elements of stories in terms of how important they were for understanding the story. These ratings were compared with the importance ratings of a group of college students who had performed the same task. The results demonstrated that the 8- and 10-year-old students were unable to distinguish important elements (as determined by adults) but that the 18-year-olds and, to some extent, the 12-year-olds were able to mirror the adult rating patterns. Third-, fifth-, and seventh-grade students were then tested for their recall of the stories. The more mature readers recalled more than the less mature readers, but overall, students at all grade levels recalled proportionally more story elements that were rated as important (by adults) than elements rated as unimportant. Even without being able to identify important information, young children still learned that information better. Based on these findings, Brown (1980) claimed that young children's recall patterns appear to approximate the recall patterns of adults but their importance ratings are idiosyncratic.

Pichert (1979), however, has disputed the notion that young children's importance ratings are idiosyncratic. His work demonstrates that, when given explicit instruction in the task parameters, even third-grade students exhibit a relatively high level of correspondence with adults. In this research, third-, fifth,- and seventh-grade students were given a specific perspective from which to rate the importance of the elements of a story. Each element was read aloud to the student. He or she was then reminded of the perspective and requested to determine how important the story element was to that perspective. This frequent reminder was employed so that each student kept the perspective in mind throughout the rating task. Results established that even third-graders can to a degree identify information important to a perspective in a similar manner to adults if they are provided with a perspective or focus for their reading. Control students (students not assigned a perspective from which to rate importance) exhibited a different pattern of results. Specifically, the third-grade control students were unable to identify important information (as determined by control adults); the performance of fifth-grade control students began to reflect adult ratings; and the performance of seventh-grade control students mirrored that of adult readers.

Based on these findings, Pichert posits that young children, in the absence of explicit external parameters, adopt default perspectives that may be idiosyncratic. As outlined in Pichert and Anderson (1977), it appears that adults (when not assigned a specific perspective) adopt a default perspective that matches more closely the perspective of the author. In other words, adults adopt a perspective based upon external cues provided by the author. The idiosyncratic nature of children's default perspective suggests that this perspective is based upon internal criteria, such as their interest in the text.

The notion that children's default perspectives are based primarily upon an internal criterion such as interest may also explain the finding that children are able to recall information rated as important by adults without being able to identify such information in the text. In Pichert's research, the third-, fifth-, and seventh-grade students read and recalled the stories 8 weeks after they had rated them for importance. The results of the recall tests provide additional support for the idea that young children learn information that is relevant to internal criteria such as interest. Whereas children's importance ratings at all grade levels were similar to those of adults when perspectives were given, the correlation between third-grade importance ratings and recall was very low. The best predictor of third-grade recall was importance ratings by the control group—the group assigned no perspective. To understand this result, however, one must be aware that, while reading the story, the children were not continually reminded of their perspective, as they had been in the "importance rating" portion of the study. The inference, then, is that, young children not explicitly reminded of the external task criteria fell back on a default strategy during the reading of the story. In other words, the third-grade students identified interesting information as important and also learned that information better.

In summary, these findings suggest that young children are not very effective at identifying the importance of text information embedded in the text (external criteria). It is only when they are continually and explicitly reminded of their task that children's importance ratings begin to resemble those of adults. Instead, young children are more likely to identify information on the basis of interest (internal criterion).

Interest in a topic is assumed to be an internal criterion because, like knowledge or schematic understanding of a topic, it has developed over time and resides within the reader. As such, interest is posited to be in the reader's understanding of the text, rather than in the text itself.

INTEREST IN LEARNING AND RECALL

In a number of studies, Asher and his colleagues (Asher, 1979; Asher & Geraci, 1980; Asher, Hymel, & Wigfield, 1978, Asher & Markell, 1974) investigated the effect of interest on the learning and recall of text material. Here interest referred to an interaction between the reader and the material. A similar methodology was used in each of the studies. First, subjects rated their interest in some topics and their lack of interest in others. They then read some stories judged to be interesting topics and some judged to be uninteresting topics. Variables such as vocabulary, text difficulty, story length, sex, and race were investigated along with the effect of interest. General results across studies showed that fifth- and sixth-grade students demonstrated better learning and recall of interesting information than of uninteresting information, that boys are more sensitive to the interest rating of stories than are girls, and that there is a significant interaction between the differential interest rating of the stories and the sex of the student (in other words, boys remember more from stories that are interesting to boys, and girls remember more from stories that are interesting to girls).

Two studies by Anderson, Mason, and Shirey (1984) also documented the powerful effects that interest has on the learning of text elements read by children, although interest was not the major focus of these studies. In the first of these two studies, reading in a classroom reading group was simulated. Third-grade students were grouped and took turns reading out loud the experimental materials—materials that had been previously rated for interest value by an independent group of third-graders. Following this reading group simulation, the students individually were given a cued recall test on the materials that were read in the simulated reading group. In the second study, third-grade students read by themselves.

Results of these studies mirrored the findings of the research by Asher and his colleagues. Like the fifth- and sixth-grade students, the third-grade students recalled significantly more information from sentences that were rated as interesting than from sentences that were not. Boys recalled more from sentences that were interesting to boys, and girls recalled more from sentences that were interesting to girls. Moreover, a nearly significant interaction between the sex of the student and rated interest of the material read suggests that boys are more sensitive to the rated interest level of reading material than are girls.

As a follow-up, Anderson and his colleagues attempted to determine why it is that interest has such tremendous effects on the recall of elementary school children and what the specific relation between interest and attention was. In two studies (Anderson, 1982) fourth-grade students read on a computer screen sentences that had previously been rated for interest by an independent group of students. These students were told to read each sentence and then rate it as to how interesting it was to them.

The computer kept track of how long it took the subjects to read each sentence (thus obtaining a measure of duration of attention). Additionally, the students wore headphones and were instructed to press a key on the computer keyset as soon as they heard a computer generated tone. The computer measured the time between the onset of the tone and when the student pressed the key (thus obtaining a measure of depth of attention). Results of these studies replicated the findings related to interest of the previous two studies with third-grade students: interesting information was learned better.

In addition, these studies were designed to test the four entailments of Anderson's causal model of selective attention: (a) Is the interest level of the material positively related to recall of the material? (b) Is interest positively related to attention? (c) Is allocation of attention related to recall? and (d) Is attention a mediating variable between interest and recall?

Both studies supported the first entailment that the interest level of the material is positively related to recall of the material. Both studies also supported the second entailment of the causal model, that interest is positively related to attention. In these studies, this entailment held for both duration and depth of attention. As the rated interest value of the sentence increased, so did the length of time that the fourth-grade students spent reading that sentence. Similarly, as the rated interest value of the sentence increased, the amount of time that elapsed between the sound of the tone in the headphones and the student pressing the computer key also increased.

The third entailment posited that attention allocated during the reading of a text element is positively related to recall of that text element. In these studies, as both duration and depth of attention allocated to a given sentence increased, recall of that sentence increased. It should be noted that, in the first of the experiments, the relation between reading time and recall, though positive (recall still went up 4.2% for each 100 millisecond increase in reading time), did not reach the level of significance selected for the study ($p > .01$).

The fourth, and final, entailment posited that if interest is positively associated with recall because, and only because, attention serves as a mediating variable, then the relation between interest and learning should disappear when the relation between recall and attention is statistically removed. Data from these studies failed to support this final entailment. Factoring out measures of attention in the two studies had practically no effect on the association between interest and recall.

This finding led Anderson and his colleagues (Anderson, 1982; Anderson, Shirey, Wilson, & Fielding, 1986) to infer that attention does not play a significant role in the effects of interest on recall. Rather, attention was conceptualized as an epiphenomenon that occurs in the vicinity of interesting text elements, but does not causally effect what is recalled.

RESEARCH ON INTEREST AND ADJUNCT QUESTIONS

In studies manipulating the interest level of text elements it does not appear that attention lies on the causal path between importance (as defined by interest) and learning. Children allocate more attention to interesting sentences, and children recall interesting sentences significantly better— but the extra attention allocated to interesting information is an epi-phenomenon of the process of learning, not the result of attention to the information. However, findings from studies of the use of adjunct questions to manipulate the importance level of text elements indicate that readers allocate more attention to information made important by adjunct questions and subsequently recall that information significantly better (Reynolds & Anderson, 1982; Reynolds, Standiford, & Anderson, 1979; Rothkopf & Bisbicos, 1967). The general methodology of adjunct question research has been to present questions of an identifiable type to subjects as they read a text. It has been well established that asking such questions has a strong effect on the learning of text information.

Selective attention has been the leading explanation posited to account for the outcome that readers selectively pay more attention to information that is related to the adjunct question. Furthermore, research has demonstrated that children do have more difficulty selectively attending to important information (Lane & Pearson, 1982), yet adults apparently do not have this deficiency (Reynolds & Anderson, 1982).

Comparison of the interest study with the adjunct question research is problematic for at least two reasons. First, importance or salience was defined differently in the two studies. In one it referred to the relation to the adjunct question, in the other it referred to the rated interest of the text element. Second, the age of the subjects used in these experiments differed. The adjunct question research focussed on adult, mature readers as subjects while the interest research used elementary school children who, presumably, did not have the same level of reading ability or maturity as the college students.

In an effort to address the two previously stated problems (definition of salience and age of research subject), the Anderson et al. (1984) studies were replicated using adult, mature readers as subjects (Shirey & Reynolds, 1988). In this research, college-age subjects read sentences from a computer terminal. The sentences had previously been rated for interest by an independent group of college students. Like the third-graders, the college students wore headphones as they read. A computer-generated tone occasionally sounded through the headphones, and the computer measured the time interval between this tone and when the subject pressed a key on the computer keyset. The computer also recorded the subjects' reading time for each sentence. Following the reading task, the subjects were asked to recall the sentences. Finally, each subject was presented with a list of all sentences and asked to rate how interesting they found each sentence.

Results from the study were subjected to the four entailments test of Anderson's causal model for selective attention in order to establish the role (if any) that attention plays between interest and learning. Although two measures of interest were available for each sentence (an interest rating by an independent group and an interest rating by each subject), the independent group rating was employed as the measure of interest in the analyses. Separate analyses using each measure of interest were employed with no significant differences obtained between the two sets of analyses (individual interest was a somewhat stronger predictor in the test of the first entailment). However, there was concern that the previous reading and recall of a sentence would have some unknown effect on rating the interest of that sentence. Therefore, the analyses using the individual measure of interest were discarded.

Findings from these analyses indicate that the first entailment was supported—the interest rating of the sentence was a highly significant positive predictor of recall for that sentence. In addition, findings from the analysis of the second entailment indicated that interest is positively related to measures of attention. Analysis of the data from this study indicated that, for adult readers, the rated interest value of the sentence is *negatively* related to both duration and depth of attention. The more interesting sentences were read faster by the college students. Moreover, faster reaction times to the tones were associated with the more interesting sentences. These results were interpreted as indicating that mature adult readers allocate *fewer* cognitive resources to information that is interesting to them.

Given that the second entailment of the causal analysis was not supported by the data, investigation of the third and fourth entailments of the causal model was inappropriate. Findings from this study suggest that although important and interesting text elements are better learned, why this information is better learned—at least as far as support for a causal model is concerned—is less clear.

It appears that there are two effective forms of learning characteristic of the mature reader: attention-intensive learning of important information and learning of interesting information that requires no extra allocation of attention (Reynolds & Shirey, 1988). Young children (defined as immature readers), on the other hand, appear to demonstrate an attention-intensive form of learning when reading interesting material. Further research is necessary in order to fully understand these differences between mature and immature readers—including tests of the causal model with young children in which information is made important through processes like the use of adjunct questions.

IMPORTANCE, INTEREST, AND SELECTIVE ATTENTION

Asher (Asher, 1979, 1980; Wigfield & Asher, 1984) proposed two hypotheses for understanding why readers tend to remember interesting material better than uninteresting material. First, Asher (1980) suggested that "children may have more elaborate and differentiated cognitive structures with respect to high interest topics" (p. 527). In other words, children might tend to be interested in topics with which they are already familiar. The basis for this hypothesis is Ausubel's (1963, 1968) notion that the operative schema understanding that a reader has for a text contains slots, or placeholders, for that information. The learning of this "slotted" information occurs because the information to be learned fits the slots that already exist in the reader's schematic understanding of that information. Because the learning of information does not require extra attention, or cognitive effort, on the part of the reader (Anderson, Reynolds, Schallert, & Goetz, 1977), this hypothesis is not attention intensive.

As a second hypothesis, Asher (1980) states that children "might work harder on interesting material" (p. 527). This is similar to Anderson's selective attention hypothesis that, in brief, states that extra attention is allocated to interesting information, which, in turn, results in enhanced learning of interesting information. In contrast to the "slot" hypothesis, this hypothesis is, by definition, attention intensive.

Most research in the area of allocation of attention to important information supports Anderson's selective attention hypothesis (Anderson, 1982). However, this research has focused primarily on modifying the importance of text elements by manipulating specific *task parameters* or *text characteristics*. Subjects have been given objectives to consider while reading; they have read text from an assigned perspective or point of view; they have been given questions to answer while reading;

and they have read passages where the importance of the text elements varies because of the structure of the text.

Unlike task parameters such as instructions, objectives, or text characteristics, and, unlike other determinants, interest as a determinant of salience changes with an individual reader. Interest is not a text or task characteristic. It is a factor that the reader brings to the reading situation (a reader-specific, or internal, characteristic). In the Anderson et al. (1986) study, fourth-grade students allocated more attention to and recalled more sentences that were rated as interesting. However, there was no evidence that attention played a significant causal role in the effects of interest on learning. These young readers did appear to attend selectively to interesting information, but this time was spent ineffectively because it did not directly result in any increases in information learned. It was primarily the results of this study that lead Anderson (Anderson, 1982; Anderson et al., 1986) to discount the selective attention hypothesis as a general explanation of the effects of importance on learning.

Results from the Shirey and Reynolds (1988) study demonstrated that interest also had significant effects on recall of sentences for college-age students. Very interesting sentences were recalled significantly better. However, there was no significant positive relation between interest and the amount of attention allocated. Subjects spent no more time on interesting sentences than they did on sentences that were rated uninteresting. These results suggest that information that is interesting to the more mature reader is readily learned with no costs in terms of additional expenditure of cognitive resources. These results are not particularly surprising because other research (Steffensen, Joag–dev, & Anderson, 1979) has demonstrated that adults spend less time reading and better remember information that is culturally relevant.

At first glance, these two studies appear to paint a rather confusing picture concerning the effects of interest on allocation of attention and learning during reading. They indicate that older and younger (or more mature and less mature) readers exhibit different patterns of selective attention. Fourth-grade students allocate more attention to and learn more interesting information, whereas college-age students learn interesting information better without exhibiting extra allocation of cognitive resources. When these results are combined with results of previous research demonstrating that attention is a causal mediator between importance and learning, mature readers appear to be more effective and efficient than less mature readers in their allocation of attention to interesting material. They are more effective presumably because they can successfully allocate cognitive resources to information that is relevant to task-related or external criteria, such as objectives and adjunct questions, and they are more efficient because they do not allocate extra attention to information made important by criteria internal to the reader—in this case, interest.

SUMMARY

The findings reviewed in this chapter suggest that any understanding of the effects of interest on attention and learning can be accomplished only within the context of a model of attention allocation during reading that incorporates, at a minimum, external factors (task demands, text characteristics, etc.), internal factors (interest, as well as cultural relevance and background knowledge), and the developmental level of the reader. Furthermore, it appears that external and internal criteria have different effects on the reader's allocation of attention. It is necessary to examine the reader's ability to determine the parameters of the reading task, to decide which information is interesting or important, and to evaluate the effectiveness of these strategies. It is the increasing effectiveness and efficiency of these processes that characterizes the development of reading skills.

It seems reasonable to conclude that two forms of learning characterize the mature adult reader: (a) externally (related to text and task) driven learning that is explained by a selective attention model of learning, and (b) internally (related to the reader) driven learning that occurs without extra effort, or input from interest, on the part of the reader—learning that is perhaps supported by a more elaborate schematic understanding. These findings are important for organizing instruction for young children. First, they suggest that the processes by which young readers learn information from text is different from those of mature, adult readers. Theories developed from research with older subjects may not be relevant to young readers. Second, even among similarly aged young students, various underlying reading processes may exist. These processes probably advance through numerous stages of development before appearing as mature strategies. Third, adults appear to have a significant role in young children's understanding about importance.

Further research to evaluate the developing nature of reading strategies is clearly needed to address such questions as: How do the effects of internal and external parameters on learning change as the reader's strategies mature? Will other internal characteristics (e.g., cultural relevance) exhibit the same effects on attention and learning as does interest?

It is clear that the evidence presented in this chapter is by no means conclusive regarding external and internal parameters of adult readers' learning and their development. Indeed, it is perhaps cavalier to suggest that learning can be divided into two discrete categories. However, with respect to issues related to the understanding of interest, importance, and attention, these processes appear to have varying roles in the learning of readers at different levels of ability or maturity.

REFERENCES

Anderson, R. C. (1982). Allocation of attention during reading. In A. Flammer & W. Kintsch (Eds.), *Discourse processing* (pp. 292–305). New York: North–Holland.

Anderson, R. C. (1983). *An approach to causal analysis*. Paper presented at the annual National Reading Conference, Austin, TX.

Anderson, R. C., Mason, J., & Shirey, L. L. (1984). The reading group: An experimental investigation of a labyrinth. *Reading Research Quarterly, 20*, 6–38.

Anderson, R. C., & Pichert, J. W. (1978). Recall of previously unrecallable information following a shift in perspective. *Journal of Verbal Learning and Verbal Behavior, 17*, 1–12.

Anderson, R. C., Reynolds, R. E., Schallert, D. L., & Goetz, E. T. (1977). Frameworks for comprehending discourse. *American Educational Research Journal, 14*, 367–381.

Anderson, R. C., Shirey, L. L., Wilson, P. T., & Fielding, L. G. (1986). Interestingness of children's reading material. In R. E. Snow & M. J. Farr (Eds.), *Aptitude, learning, and instruction: Conative and affective process analysis*. Hillsdale, NJ: Lawrence Erlbaum, Associates.

Asher, S. R. (1979). Influence of topic interest on Black children's and White children's reading comprehension. *Child Development, 50*, 686–690.

Asher, S. R. (1980). Topic interest and children's reading comprehension. In R. Spiro, B. Bruce, & W. Brewer (Eds.), *Theoretical issues in reading comprehension*. Hillsdale, NJ: Lawrence Erlbaum, Associates.

Asher. S. R., & Geraci, R. L. (1980). *Topic interest, external incentive and reading comprehension*. Unpublished manuscript, University of Illinois, College of Education.

Asher, S. R., Hymel, S., & Wigfield, A. (1978). Influence of topic interest on children's reading comprehension. *Journal of Reading Behavior, 10*, 35–47.

Asher, S. R., & Markell, R. A. (1974). Sex differences in comprehension of high- and low-interest reading material. *Journal of Educational Psychology, 66*, 680–687.

Ausubel, D. P. (1960). The use of advance organizers in the learning and retention of meaningful verbal processing. *Journal of Educational Psychology, 51*, 267–272.

Ausubel, D. P. (1963). *The psychology of meaningful behavior*. New York: Grune & Stratton.

Ausubel, D. P. (1968). *Educational psychology: A cognitive view*. New York: Holt, Rinehart, & Winston.

Brown, A. L. (1980). Metacognitive development and reading. In R. Spiro, B. Bruce, & W. Brewer (Eds.), *Theoretical issues in reading comprehension* (pp. 453–481). Hillsdale, NJ: Lawrence Erlbaum, Associates.

Brown, A. L., & Smiley, S. S. (1977). Rating the importance of structural units of prose passages: A problem of metacognitive development. *Child Development, 48*, 1–8.

Cirilo, R. K., & Foss, D. J. (1980). Text structure and reading time for sentences. *Journal of Verbal Learning and Verbal Behavior, 19*, 96–109.

Danner, F. W. (1976). Children's understanding of intersentence organization in the recall of short descriptive passages. *Journal of Educational Psychology, 68*, 174–183.

Frase, L. T. (1969). Paragraph organization of written material: The influence of conceptual clustering upon the level and organization of recall. *Journal of Educational Psychology, 60*, 394–401.

Goetz, E. T., Schallert, D. L., Reynolds, R. E., & Radin, D. I. (1983). Reading in perspective: What real cops and pretend burglars look for in a story. *Journal of Educational Psychology, 75*, 500–510.

Johnson, R. E. (1970). Recall of prose as a function of the structural importance of the linguistic units. *Journal of Verbal Learning and Verbal Behavior, 9*, 12–20.

Just, M. A., & Carpenter, P. A. (1980). A theory of reading: From eye fixations to comprehension. *Psychological Review, 87*, 329–354.

Kintsch, W., & van Dijk, T. A. (1978). Toward a model of text comprehension and production. *Psychological Review, 85*, 363–394.

Lane, D. M., & Pearson, D. A. (1982). The development of selective attention. *Merrill–Palmer Quarterly, 28*, 317–337.

Newman, E. B. (1939). Forgetting of meaningful material during sleep and working. *American Journal of Psychology, 70*, 680–690.

Pichert, J. W. (1979). Sensitivity to what is important in prose. (Tech. Rep. No. 149). Urbana–Champaign, IL: Center for the Study of Reading.

Pichert, J. W., & Anderson, R. C. (1977). Taking different perspectives on a story. *Journal of Educational Psychology, 69*, 309–315.

Renninger, K. A. (1990). Children's play interests, representations, and activity. To appear in R. Fivush & J. Hudson (Eds.), *Knowing and remembering in young children* (pp. 127–165). Emory Cognition Series (Vol. III). Cambridge, MA: Cambridge University Press.

Reynolds, R. E., & Anderson, R. C. (1982). Influence of questions on the allocation of attention during reading. *Journal of Educational Psychology, 74*, 623–632.

Reynolds, R. E., & Shirey, L. L. (1988). The role of attention in studying and learning. In E. T. Goetz, C. E. Weinstein, & P. Alexander, (Eds.), *Learning and study strategies: Issues in assessment, instruction, and evaluation* (pp. 77–100). Washington, DC: Academic Press.

Reynolds, R. E., Standiford, S. N., & Anderson, R. C. (1979). Distribution of reading time when questions are asked about a restricted category of text information. *Journal of Educational Psychology, 7*, 183–190.

Rothkopf, E. Z. (1966). Learning from written instructive materials: An exploration of the control of inspection behavior by test-like events. *American Educational Research Journal, 3*, 241–249.

Rothkopf, E. Z., & Billington, M. J. (1979). Goal guided learning from text: Inferring a descriptive processing model from inspection times and eye movements. *Journal of Educational Psychology, 71*, 310–327.

Rothkopf, E. Z. & Bisbicos, E. E. (1967). Selective facilitative effects of interspersed questions on learning from written material. *Journal of Educational Psychology, 58*, 56–61.

Rothkopf, E. Z., & Kaplan, R. (1972). Exploration of the effects of density and specificity of instructional objectives on learning from texts. *Journal of Educational Psychology, 63*, 295–302.

Shirey, L. L., & Reynolds, R. E. (1988). Effect of interest on attention and learning. *Journal of Educational Psychology, 80*, 159–166.

Steffensen, M. S., Joag–dev, C., & Anderson, R. C. (1979). A cross-cultural perspective on reading comprehension. *Reading Research Quarterly, 15*, 10–29.

van Dijk, T. A., & Kintsch, W. (1983). *Strategies of discourse processing.* New York: Academic Press.

Wigfield, A. & Asher, S. R. (1984). Social and motivational influences on reading. In P. D. Pearson, (Ed.), *Handbook of reading research.* New York: Longman.

13 Interest and Learning: A Biofunctional Perspective

Asghar Iran–Nejad and Carl Cecil
University of Alabama

Webster's New World Dictionary defines *interest* as a "feeling of wanting to know, learn, see, or take part in something." That interest motivates learning is hardly a question. It is not as obvious that the intellectual activity involved in learning causes interest (Iran–Nejad, Clore, & Vondruska, 1981; Kintsch, 1980). In this chapter, we argue that interest is both a cause and a consequence of learning. We define learning as the constructive, dynamic, and creative reconceptualization of internal knowledge (Iran–Nejad, 1990); a definition in sharp contrast to the common assumption that learning is internalization of external knowledge. An adequate account of interest, however, must go beyond dictionary and conceptual definitions to discuss the psychological states and processes involved. We propose a biofunctional theory to explain (a) how learning causes interest, (b) how interest causes learning, and (c) how learning processes produce learning.

The chapter consists of three major parts. The first part elaborates on the conceptual definition of interest and uses the surprise-ending story to illustrate its different aspects. The second part discusses interest as a challenge to the structural tradition in cognitive psychology. And the third part proposes a biofunctional theory of interest and learning.

INTEREST AS A CAUSE AND CONSEQUENCE OF LEARNING

Constructive Versus Unconstructive Intellectual Activity

To cause interest, intellectual activity must be constructive (see Iran–Nejad, Clore, & Vondruska, 1981). Specifically, two antithetical modes of ongoing intellectual functioning are distinguishable, which can be contrasted by pointing to the salient aspects of the psychological states characteristic of them. The first mode, the obverse side of ongoing intellectual activity, is constructive: it tends toward schema formation and it generates curiosity, suspense, certainty, and coherence. The second mode, the converse side, is unconstructive: it pulls the ongoing schema to pieces and generates fear, stress, uncertainty, and incoherence (Csikszentmihalyi, 1988; Iran–Nejad; & Ortony, 1984).

What are the cause and the consequence of unconstructive intellectual activity? Anxiety (interest going awry) is the concept that comes to mind (Csikszentmihalyi & Csikszentmihalyi, 1988; Epstein, 1986; McReynolds, 1986; Voss, 1984). If anxiety and interest are counterparts, differing only in the mode of intellectual functioning (constructive versus unconstructive), then anxiety must be viewed, like interest, as a cause and consequence of creative (but unconstructive) reconceptualization of internal knowledge. This rather counterintuitive implication seems less far-fetched if one bears in mind that anxious people are capable of destructive intellectualization that increases their anxiety instead of reducing it (Epstein, 1986).

Dynamic Versus Active Self-Regulation of Intellectual Activity

A central tenet of modern cognitive psychology is that human beings have *active* control over their internal constructive processes. This idea places the locus of control inside the organism and is often contrasted with the behaviorist dictum that learning is *passive* and controlled by external stimulation. The active construction hypothesis assumes that there is only one internal source of self-regulation: the central executive process (see, for example, Andre & Phye, 1986; Bransford, 1979).

Active internal control is often discussed in terms of the computer metaphor (Neisser, 1967). According to Andre and Phye (1986), the controlling mechanism—the central executive—"keeps track of what information is being processed and controls the flow of processing to determine which activities occur and which processing components receive system resources" (p. 9). Two kinds of activity occur in the system: controlled construction under the conscious attention of the active learner, and automatic activation of previously overlearned structures outside the learner's span of conscious control (Anderson, 1987; Schneider & Shiffrin, 1977). Learning (as opposed to automatic replay of overlearned connections) occurs under the active control of the central executive. Nonexecutive components cannot contribute to learning because they are inherently static and passive. The active learning hypothesis explains intentional learning but not incidental learning (McLaughlin, 1965), learning without knowing (see Johnson & Hasher, 1987), and insight, all of which seem to occur spontaneously outside the narrow zone of the learner's focal attention.

One way to account for spontaneous learning is to postulate more than one internal source of control (Iran–Nejad, 1990). Learners have *active internal control* over their internal processes (e.g., attention). However, active internal control alone cannot be the entire story of internal self-regulation. We believe, the system must have a second and fundamentally different way of regulating internal learning processes: *dynamic internal control* (Iran–Nejad, 1989a). Whereas the source of the first kind of internal control is the system as a unitary whole (the individual), the source of the second kind of control over the activity of the system components resides within the components. Dynamic internal control, then, is the capacity of the nervous system components to regulate their own activity. It is the prerequisite for active internal control, is sensitive to varying internal contexts, and uses local resources (cf. Navon & Gopher, 1979).

Dynamic self-regulation can be illustrated as follows: imagine a man who has lived all his life in his home town. He flies to a strange town for a job interview, arrives at the hotel late, and goes to sleep immediately. Even before he awakens, the stage is dynamically set for him to function in the new town rather than in overlearned home town ways. He senses that he is breathing the air in the new place before he opens his eyes. It appears as if spontaneous reorganization, unrestrained by any inflexible automatization of habits, has followed the mental experience of the trip every step of the way to the present moment. Furthermore, this occurs so naturally that he becomes aware mainly of the interest- or anxiety-creating aspects of the process. Something other than active intentional control must have been regulating this kind of functioning of the system. Presumably, it is this kind of dynamic intellectual activity that makes reconceptualization of internal knowledge possible and is the cause and consequence of interest or anxiety.

Creative Versus Habitual Intellectual Activity

Research in cognitive science has consistently shown that prior knowledge influences learning (Anderson, Spiro, & Montague, 1977; Bower, Black, & Turner, 1979; Schallert, 1976; Thorndyke, 1977). The nature of this influence, however, has been a matter of debate (Alba & Hasher, 1983; Iran–Nejad, 1980; Jenkins, 1974; Thorndyke & Yekovich, 1980). Any account of the role of prior knowledge should explain why our job candidate did not automatically lapse into previously overlearned routines, and which aspects of the trip resulted in interest or anxiety.

The influence of prior knowledge on subsequent learning is often described as a prediction-based process (Iran–Nejad, 1987; Kintsch, 1988), consisting of a spreading–activation network (Collins & Loftus, 1975) and an active control component. The network is the storehouse of past knowledge structures that the active control component uses to formulate hypotheses, make predictions, evaluate input, and store the product in long-term memory (Rumelhart, 1977). Learning is internalization of external knowledge: external events fill the slots of pre-existing nodes. Prediction-based learning tends to undermine the role of interest perhaps because intellectual activity does not generate interest in the habitual–automatic mode, with or without an active control component.

Our job candidate does not lapse into prior overlearned routines perhaps because intellectual functioning operates, as a rule, not in a habitual spreading–activation mode, but in a creative reconceptualization-of-internal-knowledge mode, which generates either interest or anxiety. Learning as reconceptualization of prior knowledge requires that we take into account postdiction processes, where previously learned knowledge can be spontaneously reinterpreted with the benefit of hindsight. Postdiction generates interest because it permits creative knowledge construction where prior connections do not exist or are unavailable to foresight (Iran–Nejad, 1987; Kintsch, 1980).

At present, not much empirical evidence exists for the idea that postdiction-based functioning is the brain's natural style. For more than three decades, the prediction-based approach has been the dominant view (Minsky, 1975; Rumelhart, 1975; Schank, 1979). The notion that prior knowledge affects learning in the habitual-automatic mode has created much research that has emphasized the relearning and recalling of frequently enacted scripts such as eating or shopping. This research is based on questions addressing the organizational principles of static schemata.

Whereas importance and typicality—variables sensitive to organizational structures of habitual schemata and to active utilization of them in the habitual–automatic mode—have been widely investigated, interest and motivation have not been part of the structural research tradition. For example, whereas entertainment is often the principal function of stories, the stories used in the research in the structural tradition have been "dismally lacking in surprise and interest" (De Beaugrande, 1982, p. 413). Perhaps the reenactment of overlearned knowledge structures is not interesting or interest and motivation were not considered important to understanding the role of background knowledge in learning.

An Example: Comprehension of the Surprise-Ending Story

Learning as reconceptualization of internal knowledge is a hypothesis about the process of the contribution of prior knowledge to the acquisition of new knowledge. Our definition of interest suggests that this process has inherent informational and motivational causes and consequences. It also appears to complicate our understanding of the nature of learning and interest. How one comes to reconceptualize one's existing knowledge has long been a challenge in philosophy (Petrie, 1981), psychology (Nisbett & Ross, 1980), and education (Bereiter, 1985) and recent treatments of the problem (Rumelhart, 1980; Vosniadou & Brewer, 1987) have rarely been satisfactory (Lehnert, 1981; Murphy & Medin, 1985).

In this section, we use the surprise-ending story to illustrate what reconceptualization is and how it causes interest. There are two main reasons for this choice. First, reconceptualization of internal knowledge and interest occur dramatically in situations involving surprise (Berlyne, 1974). Outside the structural tradition, Donchin (1981) stated: "the concept of surprise has virtually replaced the concept of reinforcement. Things appear to be learned if, and only if, they are surprising" (p. 508). Secondly, the surprise-ending story is a compelling case for understanding reconceptualization because it requires the reader to develop and maintain two incompatible schemata, one after another (Iran–Nejad, 1989b).

The challenge is to specify how events already encoded into the first schema can be used to construct the second. What seems to be required is two antithetical characteristics of ongoing mental structures: they must be capable of manifesting inordinate stability and unrestrained flexibility (Iran–Nejad, 1986). Intellectual functioning is inordinately stable indeed (Kuhn, 1962; Mahoney, 1977; Nisbett & Ross, 1980). Bacon (1920) said: The "human understanding when it has once adopted an opinion draws all things else to support and agree with it" (p. 50). Less is known about when and how mental structures manifest unrestrained flexibility, but reconceptualization seems impossible without it. Each of the two schemata involved in the comprehension of the surprise-ending story is very stable. Moreover, each imposes incompatible interpretations on story events, generate incompatible inferences, and support incompatible judgments about characters. The change from one incompatible schema to another represents an extreme example of interschema reconceptualization. The nature of the role flexibility plays in this process is, therefore, of paramount importance for understanding how learning occurs. Consider the following story from Thurmond (1978), used in our research. A nurse, Marilyn, leaves the hospital where she works after a late night shift. As she is driving home on the large city freeway she notices she is running out of gas. She goes to her usual station. The attendant, Gabriel, fills the tank, cleans the windows, and returns the change. As she is about to leave, he asks her to go in the station office to see his birthday gift. She consents and follows him. Once inside, he locks the door and gets a gun from a drawer. The paragraph prior to the surprising ending describes her going into shock as he pushes her to the floor.

In one experiment (Iran–Nejad, 1989b), subjects read the story (without the surprising ending) and rated thematic inferences derived a priori from a Gabriel–Bad schema (e.g., *Gabriel threatened Marilyn with a gun*) or from a Gabriel–Good schema (e.g., *Gabriel protected Marilyn with a gun*). The results (Fig. 13.1, bottom) showed that subjects rated Gabriel–Bad thematic inferences as specifically stated in, directly implied by, or consistent with the story. By contrast, Gabriel–Good thematic inferences were rated inconsistent with the story. Having read the no-surprise story, subjects held the stable view that Gabriel was a wolf in sheep's clothing and not a good Samaritan.

A second group of subjects read the same story with the surprising ending in which Gabriel told Marilyn, "Sorry I had to scare you like that; I was scared myself when I saw that dude on the floor in the back of your car." These subjects rated the thematic inferences in a manner directly opposite to the first subjects (Fig. 13.1, top). They rated the Gabriel–Good thematic inferences as specifically stated in, directly implied by, or consistent with the story; Gabriel–Bad inferences were rated inconsistent with the story.

These results imply that the story created opposite schemata in subjects. Subjects in the surprise condition read the story and, like the no-surprise subjects, constructed a stable Gabriel–Bad schema first. Then,

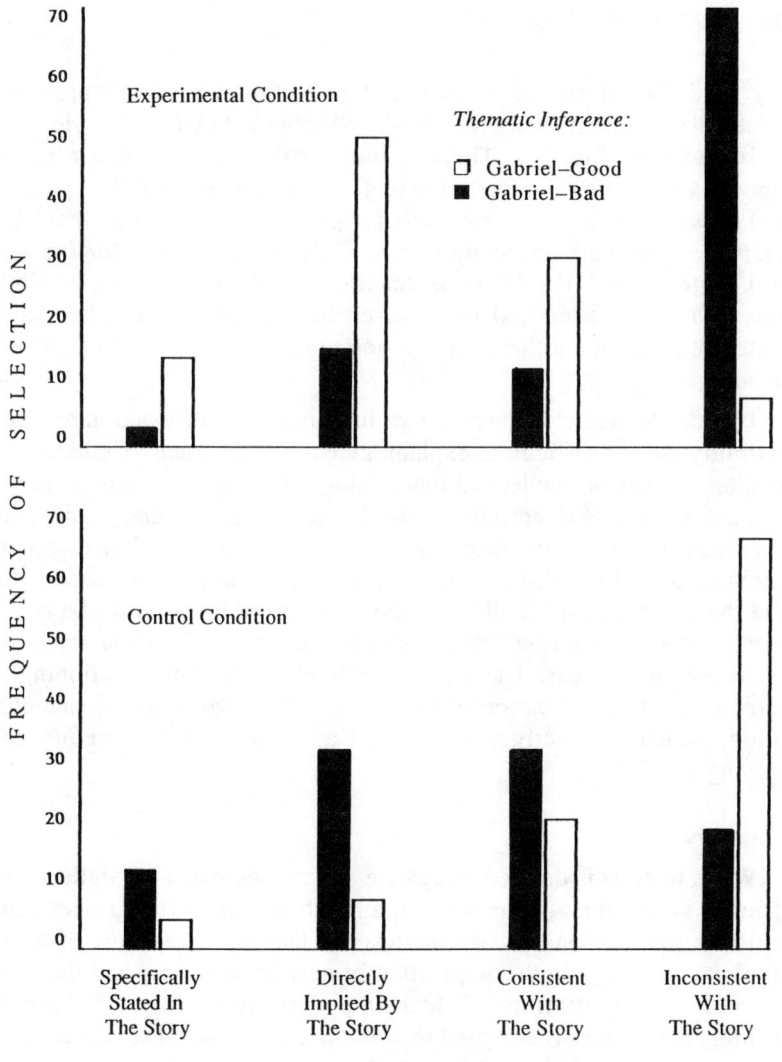

Fig. 13.1. Percentage of times each of the four categories of the congruity scale used in the Special Recognition test was selected by subjects in the Experimental (top panel) and Control (bottom panel) in response to Gabriel–Good (light bars) and Gabriel–Bad (dark bars) thematic inferences. From "A nonconnectionist schema theory of understanding surprise-ending stories" by A. Iran–Nejad, 1989, *Discourse Processes, 12,* p. 140. Reprinted by permission.

they read the surprising ending and reconceptualized the previously learned events into a stable Gabriel–Good schema in which Gabriel risked his life to save Marilyn. There is inordinate stability when a schema imposes a consistent interpretation (e.g., *Gabriel protected Marilyn with a gun*) on an event (e.g., *Gabriel pulled a gun out of the drawer*) that has an otherwise opposite interpretation (e.g., *Gabriel threatened Marilyn with a gun*). Unrestrained flexibility is manifested when an event, which has already been encoded and internalized in one schema, is available for reinterpretation in another, without any constraints imposed by previous encoding.

The antithetical characteristics of inordinate stability and unrestrained flexibility are not difficult to explain, given the constructive, creative, and dynamic aspects of intellectual functioning. The constructive aspect allows ongoing intellectual activity to build internally coherent and stable schemata. The creative aspect allows schema construction to proceed uninhibited by difficult-to-change, static, long-term memory connections. And the dynamic aspect allows previously encoded events to be reinterpreted without requiring immediate attention from the capacity-limited active control process. The same aspects of intellectual functioning that were central to the creation of interest are also central to reconceptualization, which is exactly what interest as a cause and consequence of learning implies.

Summary

When interest is defined as a cause and consequence of intellectual (as opposed to emotional) functioning, a number of important issues can be explored: the relation between interest and learning, the nature of the role of prior knowledge in the acquisition of new information, and the role of internal self-regulation of learning processes. Interest is not a phenomenon to be investigated in isolation, as the interest created by the surprise-ending story illustrates.

INTEREST AS A CHALLENGE TO THE STRUCTURAL TRADITION

Not until the early 1980s, when attention began to turn to nonstructural aspects of cognition, did the need for a better understanding of the dynamic aspects of mental functioning become clear (Brown, Bransford, Ferrara, & Campione, 1983; Hidi, Baird, & Hildyard, 1982; Iran–Nejad, 1980; Renninger & Wozniak, 1985; Schallert, 1982). However, before a comprehensive approach to learning and interest could be examined, many of the central assumptions of the structural tradition had to be questioned. The computer-inspired notion that knowledge schemata were program-like, long-term memory structures was seen as the immediate barrier because it precluded the flexibility required for the interest-creating process of reconceptualization (Hidi & Baird, 1986; Iran–Nejad, Clore, & Vondruska, 1981).

A few researchers, however, tried to incorporate motivation and learning directly into structuralism. Although much of this research was controversial and has been abandoned by its authors (Black & Wilensky, 1979; Bower & Mayor, 1985; Rumelhart, 1984), structural theories continue to be used (Lang, 1984; Yussen, Huang, Mathews, & Evans, 1988), perhaps because the reasons why dynamic aspects present an insurmountable challenge for the structural tradition are difficult to expose. A closer look at progress in the extended structural tradition is necessary to determine the future viability of the approach.

The Structural–Affect Theory

This theory was proposed by Brewer and Lichtenstein (1981) to fill the gap that existed in story research because structural theories had ignored the fact that the main function of stories is entertainment (Kintsch, 1980). The structural–affect theory argued that story affect is a function of the interaction of two sequential structures: an underlying sequence of events arranged in the form of an abstract script in long-term memory, and a surface order of events as they appear in the actual story text.

According to Brewer and Lichtenstein (1981), the order of story events causes surprise if it omits a significant event from one's underlying script for those events. For instance, in a butler-did-it-murder plot, the underlying script includes (a) *The butler put poison in the wine* (the significant outcome-relevant event), (b) *The butler carried the wine to Lord Higginbotham,* (c) *Lord Higginbotham drank the wine,* and (d) *Lord Higginbotham fell over dead.* To cause surprise, a story must omit (a) and present (b), (c), and (d). The view that withholding outcome-relevant information causes surprise, although intuitively attractive, is problematic (Iran–Nejad, 1986).

Two Schemata, Not Just One. One difficulty is that the reader is likely to be surprised when reading (b), (c), and (d) only if s/he does *not* bring to bear a butler-did-it underlying structure before reading (d), because this could spoil the surprise. In other words, according to the structural–affect theory, the butler-did-it underlying script provides the plan for the interpretation of events (b), (c), and (d) while event (a) is withheld. On the contrary, what must be withheld is the entire poisoning-Lord-Higginbotham schema (underlying structure and all), not just one significant event from it. Moreover, the reader must construct a different (serving-Lord-Higginbotham) schema before reading (d). Under these two conditions, the reader is likely to be surprised upon encountering (d). Only then, when the reader has already been surprised, does the poisoning-the-master script come into play to resolve, rather than cause, the surprise. Furthermore, resolution of the surprise requires reinterpretation of events previously encoded, not with the the poisoning-the-master script, but with the serving-the-master schema. Thus, according to the two-schemata hypothesis, the script that is expected to breathe significance into (a) is not even part of the surprise-production package. After all, there can be unresolved surprises when the previously encoded events are unavailable for reinterpretation.

Understanding the butler-did-it surprise-ending story, therefore, requires two incompatible schemata, not just one. Whereas one schema is enough to create the surprise, it cannot be the schema that instills significance into outcome relevant events. Another way to state this is that postdiction-based processes of reinterpretation, not prediction-based processes of interpretation, must construct a poisoning-the-master schema.

Could the structural–affect theory be saved by assuming that a single abstract structure, sufficiently abstract to be applicable to both presurprise and postsurprise processes, is used to construct the two incompatible schemata? Because structuralism dictates that different meanings *must* emerge out of separate underlying structures (Chomsky, 1965, Rumelhart, 1975), linking two incompatible schemata to a single less abstract one would be tantamount to abandoning the structural approach. Even if the structural-affect theory were to include more than one underlying structure for the surprise-ending story, static long-term memory structures of the kind postulated in the structural tradition could do little more than get in the way. All one needs to assume is that the surprise-ending story should create and uphold two mutually incompatible schemata in the reader: a serving-the-master schema to guide prediction-based processes prior to (d) and a poisoning-the-master schema that results from the operation of postdiction-based processes afterwards (Iran–Nejad, 1980, 1986).

The Role of Information Withholding. A second problem is that people usually omit significant underlying events from all types of stories. Scripts are used to generate expectations for omitted discourse events (Rumelhart, 1980), and to explain how people use their knowledge to fill in what is left out of a communication (Minsky, 1975). Whereas a story about eating at a restaurant might not mention that meals were ordered, it will not surprise the reader that the diners paid the bill.

If withholding the significant event is not a sufficient condition for generating surprise, is it necessary? Iran–Nejad (1984, 1986) addressed this question empirically using two versions of the Marilyn story. One version was the surprise-ending story; the second version was identical but presented explicit outcome-relevant information early in the story. (Right before Marilyn left the freeway for Gabriel's gas station, "she felt she could hear somebody breathing behind her in the car" and "she even felt breath on the back of her neck.") If, as structural–affect theory maintains, withholding ending-relevant information were the critical factor, then providing this information early in the story should remove the surprise from the ending. The results showed that the version that revealed ending-relevant information early was no less surprising than the one that withheld this information.

In summary, the structural–affect theory extended structuralism to include affect. The issues discussed here suggest that the result was hardly a viable approach to the study of motivational factors like surprise.

The Network Theory of Emotion

Another test of the viability of structuralism was the network theory of emotion. Bower (1981) argued that distinct emotions can be represented as nodes and connections in a semantic network in accordance with associative principles (Anderson & Bower, 1973). He used the electrical network as an analogy in which "terminals correspond to concepts or event nodes (units), connecting wires correspond to associative relations with more or less resistance, and electrical energy corresponds to activation that is injected into one or more nodes (units) in the network" (p. 134).

Evidence for the network theory of emotion comes mainly from experiments investigating the influence of mood states on learning and remembering (Bower, 1981; Bower & Cohen, 1982). Bower, Monteiro, and Gilligan (1978), for example, induced a happy mood in subjects to be taught one word list and a sad mood in subjects to be taught another. Subjects also recalled both lists in a sad or a happy mood. Recall was better when word-list mood matched recall mood. The researchers argued that associative connections between the ongoing mood (represented as a distinct emotion node) and the word list facilitate recall if the mood state is the same and inhibit recall if the mood state is different.

Can the network theory of emotion explain the reconceptualization of internal knowledge involved in the comprehension of the surprise-ending story? It is difficult to see how, once established, mood-dependent associations can change. Such associations gain in excitatory strength if the same mood is injected into them and in inhibitory strength if the opposite mood is injected. Events with excitatory connections with one emotion cannot have excitatory connections with its opposite emotion. The events in a surprise-ending story must be encoded in one mood and subsequently reinterpreted in the opposite mood. The network model suggests that two sets of automated paths should get in the way of reinterpretation. First, the excitatory connections between the encoding emotion and the encoded story events should make these events less available to the opposite emotion later, rendering reinterpretation unlikely. Second, the long-term inhibitory paths between the encoding emotion (which is receiving excitation from story events) and the opposite emotion (which is to guide the process of reinterpretation) should make the latter emotion unavailable to top-down, and less available to bottom-up, processing.

Reinterpretations of prior events are not limited to surprise-ending stories. Bower and Cohen (1982) acknowledged that subsequent changes in evidence, value, importance, uncertainty, and mood are potential causes of reinterpretation. To enable their network model to deal with these (post-encoding) changes, the authors defined reinterpretation as reappraisal and added a control system to the spreading–activation theory to deal with reappraisals of earlier emotional representations.

However, the appraisal system operates under the slow, capacity-limited control of the central processor and involves a complex, time-consuming sequence of steps. For each of the previously encoded events to be reappraised, the central processor must apply cognitive interpretation rules, apply emotional interpretation rules to products of the previous step, assess the importance of the results, make intensity adjustments according to the degree of importance, coordinate interaction with other emotions, modulate reactions to external situations, and store the results in long-term memory (see Bower & Cohen, 1982). Such an elaborate sequence of steps might deal with conscious reinterpretations. It sheds no light on spontaneous reinterpretations of previously encoded events.

According to network theory (Bower & Cohen, 1982), the mood-dependent "filter admits material congruent with the perceiver's mood but casts aside incongruent material" (p. 291). Our examples show that surprising events actually pull previously encoded information out of an opposite schema for use in a subsequent schema. In the butler-did-it murder plot, the serving-the-master schema is such a stable combination that no one ever suspects the butler! Nevertheless, the surprising event *Lord Higginbotham fell over dead* is not ignored. This event is incongruous with the serving-the-master schema as well as with its previously instantiated nodes: *normal wine, enjoyment, loyal butler, living master*, and so on. This incongruity makes the surprising event inaccessible to prediction processes (the more stable the presurprise expectation-generating schema, the less accessible the surprising event). It should also make the information in the previously instantiated nodes of the serving-the-master schema inaccessible to postdiction processes. The examples show, however, that postdiction processes can reach deep into the incompatible, previously encoded events, pull out whatever is compatible, reinterpret it into concepts (*tainted wine, suffering, traitorous butler*, and *dead master*) congruous with the surprising event, and produce the spontaneous conclusion the butler was trying all the time to murder, not serve, the master.

Thus, neither the inflexible spreading–activation network nor the prediction-driven appraisal system could regulate the (spontaneous) process of creative reconceptualization. Theoretically, it is difficult to see how the network theory can handle the processes involved in interest (Iran–Nejad, 1980). A similar, empirically based conclusion was reached in a review of research on the network theory of emotion (Bower & Mayor, 1985).

The Link between Interest and Attention

Cognitive Appraisal as a Prerequisite of Interest. Theories of emotion view cognitive appraisal as a prerequisite (Lazarus, 1984; Mandler, 1975), or intellectual activity as entirely unnecessary (Zajonc, 1984), for emotions. The same could be true of interest, which is often viewed as a basic emotion. Alternatively, interest may not be an emotion at all (Iran–Nejad, 1983, 1987; Ortony, Clore, & Collins, 1988). Moreover, spontaneous intellectual activity, and not cognitive appraisal, might be the real source of interest (Iran–Nejad, Clore, & Vondruska, 1981).

Because Bower & Cohen (1982) equated appraisal with attention, they described their appraisal theory as a selective attention model (Schneider & Shiffrin, 1977; Shiffrin & Schneider, 1977). External cues preattentively activate several competing hypotheses about an external event by means of passive spreading–activation. Then the central processor actively focuses attention on one hypothesis at a time, appraises its relative importance (unexpectedness, arousal level, affective value, and so on), determines its interest level, and stores the product. Therefore, the network model of emotion suggests that appraisal is a prerequisite for interest.

Bower and Cohen (1982) also equated appraisal with interpretation, and reappraisal with reinterpretation. To be sure, it is often necessary to reinterpret past events in the light of a more recent interpretation by consciously reallocating attention (processing time, resources, and strategies) to them (Bower & Cohen, 1982). However, reallocation of attention—reappraisal—is not always necessary for reinterpretation. Spontaneous reinterpretations are also possible and often necessary. In addition, there is no evidence that reinterpretations that require reappraisal cause interest; and there are indications that the effort involved in such reinterpretations may inhibit interest (Hidi, 1990). In sum, whereas the structural tradition must assume cognitive appraisal, there are strong indications that interest does not require it.

A closer look at the parallel between the network model of emotion and the network model of attention shows why neither can permit reinterpretation without reappraisal. Both approaches contrast conscious, active, flexible, and capacity-limited attention allocation with unconscious, passive, unalterable, and capacity-free automaticity (Langer, Blank, & Chanowitz, 1979). Schneider and Shiffrin (1977) suggested that because automaticity "operates through a relatively permanent set of associative connections in long-term store" (p. 2) and because "once learned, an automatic process is difficult to suppress, to modify, or to ignore" (p. 2), no reinterpretation can occur in the automatic spreading–activation mode. It can occur in the limited-capacity attention mode but requires refocusing of attention on the previously learned events. Therefore, according to network models, cognitive appraisal is a prerequisite to reinterpretation.

Importance, Interest, and Attention. The assumption that events are important by virtue of their connections with a long-term memory schema has made structural importance a widely investigated variable. It is generally assumed that (a) stimulus events are first minimally processed and appraised for relative importance, (b) more important events are then given extra attention, and (c) the more attention, the better the event is learned. One might extend this theory by further assuming that events are interesting because they are important (e.g., Shirey & Reynolds, 1988) and find a place next to importance for interest in the above (a)-to-(c) formula.

Hidi, Baird, and Hildyard (1982) questioned the correlation between interest and structural importance. They argued that interesting but unimportant events are also learned (see Hidi & Baird, 1986). Subsequent research showed that the relation between interest, attention, and learning is more complex than schema theory suggests. Using reading time, response time to a secondary probe, and sentences rated for interest value, Anderson and his colleagues (Anderson, 1982; Anderson, Shirey, Wilson, & Fielding, 1986; Reynolds & Anderson, 1982) examined the relation between interest, attention, and learning. Interesting sentences (a) were learned better, (b) took longer to process, and (c) elicited longer response time to a secondary probe. However, when measures of attention were partialled out, the relation between interest and learning did not change, suggesting that attention (extra reading/probe time) was not what caused learning. As Anderson (1982) put it, "the pause to savor an interesting sentence is not the pause that supports the process that gives birth to learning" (p. 301). In fact, there is evidence that the relation between reading/probe time and learning can be negative (Graesser & Riha, 1984; Shirey & Reynolds, 1988).

If attention is equated with appraisal—active allocation of extra resources for grading stimulus importance—the conclusion that no attention is involved in the learning of interesting events is reasonable. In fact, such an inference is required by our claim that interest needs no appraisal. There may be more to attention, however, than active allocation of extra resources. Attention may be involved in spontaneous intellectual activity that is, as noted earlier, the cause of interest. For instance, unlike important stimuli, interesting events might attract attention spontaneously (Hidi, 1990). The spontaneous attention hypothesis suggests that the conventional definition of attention is problematic (Iran–Nejad, 1990).

If we ignore the traditional dichotomy (or contrast) between control (or attention) and automaticity (or no attention), spontaneous attention could be equated with automatic attention that requires fewer central resources. In structural schema theory, for example, attention is automatic to those external events that are internally important—they fill the slots of long-term memory schemata automatically. Active attention to a relevant schema, then, provides automatic (or spontaneous) attention to its slots (events). This theory implies that both active and spontaneous attention are regulated by a single internal source of control—the central executive. The same constant amount of attentional resources is shared by all the slots of the schema, with the bulk of resources going to the focal attention slot and the rest to spontaneous attention slots.

At least two problems make the single-source theory untenable. First, it implies, paradoxically, that the more knowledge one has of a domain— the more slots there are in the schema for a domain—the more rigid one's spontaneous attention to events relevant to that domain, because of increasingly thinning attentional resources. Second, this theory makes spontaneous attention entirely dependent on past connections and prediction-based processes. As a result, spontaneous attention applies to spontaneous interpretations, but not to spontaneous reinterpretations that require, according to structural theories, conscious allocation of attention.

A solution to the dilemma has been reached by postulating (a) transient schemata (Iran–Nejad, 1980) and (b) two independent sources of internal self-regulation (Iran–Nejad, 1989a). As already discussed, spontaneous attention is regulated by dynamic internal control using local resources and active attention can be regulated by executive control using central resources.

The two-source theory has none of the problems of the single-source view. It allows both spontaneous interpretations and reinterpretations. Furthermore, the more (dynamic) spontaneous components there are in a schema, the more effort-free local resources are available to the whole schema, making ongoing processing increasingly less dependent on effortful allocation of central resources. On the other hand, the more dynamic components there are in a schema, the more the likelihood of spontaneous interest-creating reinterpretations when the internal context changes—or, in other words, the more one already knows about a domain, the more the interest associated with subsequent learning. All these considerations suggest that dynamic (spontaneous) attention may provide the link that relates interest and attention.

Attention and Control. Structural theories have equated attention with control. Controlled (or "attention-full") processing is said to be sequential and to consume capacity resources, whereas automatic (attention-free) processing is said to run in parallel and to use no capacity resources. This account appears to confound the influence of learning processes and sources of control. A clearer understanding of processing time, interest, and learning must separate the contributions of these different factors.

Attention may be viewed as a learning process that is either focal or global. Sources of control (sources that regulate attention or other learning processes) can be external, active, or dynamic. As a learning process, attention can occur under direct external control, as in surprise (passive focal attention) or seeing a forest when one's eyes fall on a landscape (passive global attention). Active attention occurs under the control of the central executive and requires allocation of central resources, as in paying attention to a difficult sentence (active focal attention) or trying to remember someone's name by thinking about the party at which the person was introduced (active global attention). And, finally, dynamic attention occurs under the control of the components of the system, as in having an insight (dynamic focal attention) or having the entire theme of a book in mind for the duration of the time one is reading it (dynamic global attention).

Processing time, therefore, is a complex function of the interaction of sources of control and learning processes. Active (focal or global) attention to an event might take time because it must be regulated sequentially and requires allocation of central resources. Dynamic attention—of the kind involved in the processing of interesting information—might take less time because it is simultaneous and uses local processing resources in parallel. On the other hand, learning of interesting information might take extra time if reconceptualization of internal knowledge involves a global shift from one schema (or topic) to another (Blanchard & Iran–Nejad, 1987).

Failing to consider the interaction of sources of control and learning processes in interpreting processing-time data can result in confusion about the role of such learning processes as attention. The single-source theory of internal control (or attention), for example, implies that active allocation of extra resources requires extra time. Extra allocation of resources is necessary for the cognitive appraisal process that determines interest. This theory predicts a positive correlation between processing time and interest, which has not received consistent support and has led to the conclusion that attention may be unnecessary for the learning of interesting events.

Berlyne (1960) postulated two kinds of attentional responses to surprising/novel stimuli: a passive (involuntary) orienting response and an active (voluntary) perceptual exploration process. The orienting response is immediate and the time it takes is usually negligible. Perceptual exploration, like cognitive appraisal, can take time. Berlyne's theory and structuralism postulate different active attentional processes, but they both predict a positive correlation between extra processing time and interest/learning.

The active perceptual exploration hypothesis may be more realistic than the active cognitive appraisal hypothesis. Blanchard and Iran–Nejad (1987) showed that the sentence *I saw a man on the floor in the back of your car* takes 1810 milliseconds to comprehend when it is not surprising but 3,095 milliseconds when it is surprising. The active appraisal hypothesis implies that only minimal processing of the physical sentence is necessary. It is the cognitive appraisal process itself that takes the extra time to determine the importance (unexpectedness, arousal level, and so on) of the meaning of the sentence. Thus, no extra time is needed to visually explore the sentence itself, especially because it is straightforward and easily held in short-term memory. The active perceptual exploration hypothesis predicts the opposite. The extra time is spent in visually exploring the sentence (which seems to suggest an opposite interpretation of the story) to make sure that it is actually saying what it appears to be saying. Eye movement patterns supported the perceptual exploration hypothesis, in that subjects spent most of the extra time rereading the sentence.

The visual exploration hypothesis is counterintuitive. It suggests that to comprehend the sentence subjects moved their active attention, not further up in the processing (or structural) hierarchy, but further down toward the physical stimulus. Then, immediately after this one-second "downward" excursion, they pressed a key to indicate they had comprehended the sentence. It is not clear how active attention can regulate all the processes required for understanding surprising events, especially if these involve reconceptualization of knowledge. Reconceptualization seems to require preshift encoding of the surprising physical sentence, a shift in topic from one schema to another, and a postshift reexamination of the physical sentence. The entire process took an extra 1,285 milliseconds as compared to the same physical sentence when it was not surprising, barely enough time to read the sentence one additional time. It can be concluded, therefore, that the process of reconceptualization is for the most part regulated dynamically, while focal attention is given to the encoding or reexamination of the physical stimulus. The core of this dynamic process is reinterpretation of prior knowledge. We believe this dynamic reinterpretation makes surprising story endings interesting (Iran–Nejad, 1987).

Moreover, although extensive reinterpretation is involved, it takes no extra time because no cognitive reappraisal is required for reinterpretation. There is no need to redetermine the importance of every previously encoded event for the new schema perhaps because appraising importance is not a part of the comprehension process.

In short, the intellectual activity involved in reconceptualization is dynamic for at least two reasons. First, reinterpretation cannot be a passive replay of the connections established at the time of the original encoding of events. These connections were established in the context of an opposite schema. Second, it is not possible to actively retrieve previously encoded events (from the memory of the original encoding schema) and reinterpret them in the context of the reconceptualization schema. For the Marilyn story, this would take several minutes instead of a mere 1,285 milliseconds. Thus, the interest-producing process of reinterpretation may be characterized as being regulated dynamically by knowledge components that serve in the incompatible schemata.

Summary

The structural tradition does not adequately account for the relation among interest, attention, and learning. We have argued that surprising events produce interest because they involve dynamic reinterpretation of previously learned information. Moreover, to explain the processing time associated with attention, the role of different kinds of attention and different sources of self-regulation must be considered.

A BIOFUNCTIONAL EXPLANATION OF THE CONCEPT OF INTEREST

Structural theories are *cognitive theories of knowledge*, whereas the biofunctional model is a *cognitive theory of how the nervous system works*. The goal is to describe how the brain, as an integrated system, makes knowledge, interest, attention, learning, and remembering possible. Biofunctional theory is neither about the software of the mind nor the hardware of the brain. It is a theory that explains how the biofunctional properties of the brain and its psychologically relevant components translate into mentalistic concepts (Iran–Nejad, 1980, 1987; Iran–Nejad & Ortony, 1984). Many of the alternative explanations discussed earlier were derived from research on biofunctional theory (Iran–Nejad, 1987, 1989b; Blanchard & Iran–Nejad, 1987; Diener & Iran–Nejad, 1986;

Iran–Nejad & Ortony, 1985) and experience with this perspective (Iran–Nejad, 1986, 1989a, 1990).

Some Basic Assumptions

The major aspects of the biofunctional theory of the nervous system (see Fig. 13.2, from left to right) are sources of control, characteristics of the brain hardware, the functional manifestation of the operation of the nervous system, experiential manifestations and judgments, and transient structural manifestations.

What is strikingly absent in this model is a long-term memory store. We believe a biologically realistic account of psychological phenomena is possible only if mental content and schemata are seen as transient dynamic patterns instead of as long-term static knowledge representations (Iran–Nejad & Ortony, 1984). Live, ongoing awareness is the only kind of knowledge in the system; there is no static knowledge, innate or acquired. This approach tries to understand not how knowledge could be stored or organized in the brain, but how the brain creates, changes, and recreates ongoing knowledge structures.

Sources of Control

Of primary importance in the creation, change, and recreation of knowledge are sources of control (Figure 13.2, double ovals) that initiate and regulate intellectual activity in the nervous system. They are mediated by interest/anxiety (dynamic control factors), intention/effort (active control factors), and external stimulation (external control factors).

Dynamic control originates in the biofunctional properties of the nervous system (hardware characteristics). Starting from this origin, Fig. 13.2 (left-to-right arrows) shows the ongoing intellectual functioning that causes interest (constructive mode) or anxiety (unconstructive mode). Curiosity, suspense, certainty, and coherence are consequences of intellectual activity in the interest mode, whereas fear, stress, uncertainty, and incoherence are consequences in the anxiety mode (box with two-way arrow connected to interest/anxiety). Note that cognitive appraisal is not a prerequisite for interest or its associated concepts.

In general, the left-to-right arrows show the direction of causality from the brain to the mind and the right-to-left arrow represents the direction of causality from the mind to the brain (see Sperry, 1968). However, the boxes represent simultaneous aspects, not sequential stages or hierarchical levels. The experience of interest is a direct consequence of

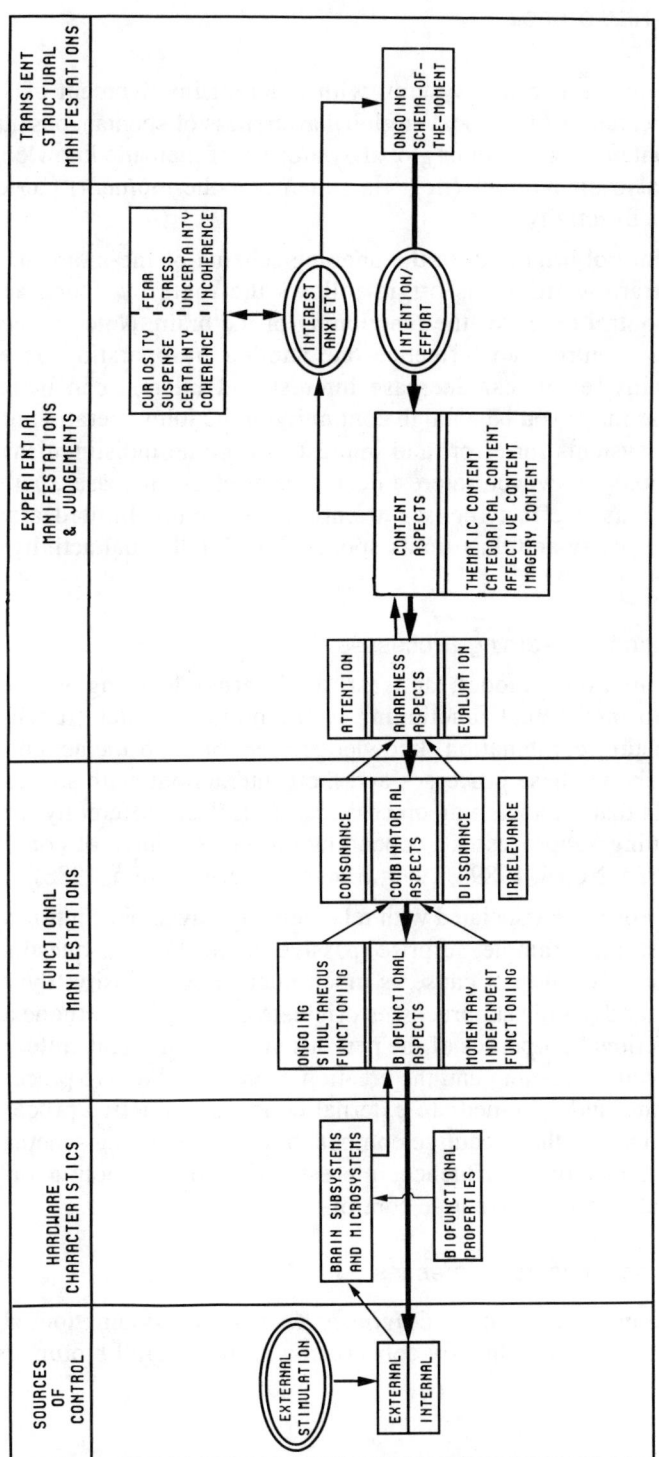

Fig. 13.2. Principal aspects of biofunctional cognition.

the activity in the nervous system, with inherent involvement of such aspects as awareness (e.g., focal or global awareness of spontaneous attention) and content (e.g., focal or global awareness of thematic knowledge). Interest is also an indirect (i.e., via schema-of-the-moment) cause of nervous system activity.

Active control originates in the ongoing schema-of-the-moment. The right-to-left arrow from this origin follows the route by which active (effortful) control regulates the functioning of the brain. Note that active and dynamic control can influence one another by operating on each other's origins (effort can increase interest and interest can increase effort). There may even be enough continuity in the joint operation of the two control systems for effort and interest to become indistinguishable. More commonly, however, interest decreases as effort increases, perhaps because increased effort focuses attention on a more limited area of intellectual activity and thus limits spontaneous intellectual activity and interest.

Self-Regulation of Learning Processes

In the biofunctional model, at least six internal learning processes contribute to intellectual functioning in the nervous system: attention, inquiry, closure, combination, knowledge creation, and metacognition. Table 13.1 shows these processes and their interactions with sources of control. Note that each learning process manifests itself differently (hence, related learning subprocesses), depending on which source of control is dominant (Iran–Nejad, 1989a, 1990; Iran–Nejad & Chissom, 1988).

The subprocesses associated with relatively high dynamic control cause more interest. For example, surprise (passive inquiry) or self-questioning (active inquiry) would not cause as much interest as curiosity (dynamic inquiry). Only dynamic subprocesses originate directly in the (nonexecutive) biofunctional properties of the nervous system and are, therefore, directly involved in learning and the creation of interest. Passive processes, which operate under immediate external control, and active processes, which originate in (the executive component of) the ongoing schema-of-the-moment, can only influence interest indirectly by acting on the biofunctional origins of dynamic control.

Knowledge as Ongoing Awareness

Biofunctional Properties as Origins of Knowledge. Assumptions about knowledge creation are directly concerned with the overall biofunctional organization of the nervous system. The brain is not seen as a patchwork of areas, centers, or regions. For example, vision requires more than a visual cortex. Instead, highly dynamic subsystems capable of interacting with inordinate stability and unrestrained flexibility are essential. The nervous system is thought of as an indefinite (but not inordinately large) number of such specialized subsystems (Iran–Nejad & Ortony, 1984).

It is often assumed that brain regions store experiences in a hierarchical fashion, with simple experiences toward the periphery and more complex materials toward the center. In the biofunctional model, brain subsystems create (but do not store) equally complex mental experiences. Individual subsystems create simple meaningless experiences. Meaningful experiences are complex, and are constructed by many subsystems working together. An experience created when focal attention centers within a brain subsystem (e.g., looking at a word) is made meaningful by

Table 13.1

Sources of Self-Regulation and Learning Processes

Learning Processes	Learning Subprocess	Sources of Self-Regulation		
		External	Active	Dynamic
Attention	1. Reactive	High		
	2. Deliberate		High	
	3. Alertful			High
Inquiry	1. Surprise	High		
	2. Self-Questioning		High	
	3. Curiosity			High
Closure	1. Orientation	High		
	2. Prediction		High	
	3. Postdiction			High
Combination	1. Independent	High		
	2. Sequential		High	
	3. Simultaneous			High
Knowledge Creation	1. Categorical	High		
	2. Propositional		High	
	3. Thematic			High
Metacognition	1. Piecemeal	High		
	2. Procedural		High	
	3. Reflective			High

Note: Adopted from "Associative and nonassociative schema theories of learning," by A. Iran–Nejad, (1989), *Bulletin of the Psychonomic Society, 27*, p. 3. Copyright 1988 by Psychonomic Society, Inc. Reprinted by permission.

the combination of experiences created simultaneously in spontaneous global attention involving many other subsystems (Iran–Nejad, 1980, 1987; Iran–Nejad & Ortony, 1984).

Each brain subsystem creates a qualitatively different subjective or phenomenal experience. This is simply an extension of the commonly held view that there is, for instance, a visual system that creates visual imagery that is a different experience from auditory or affective imagery. Each subsystem comprises a large number of homogeneously specialized microsystems. All the microsystems in the visual subsystem, for instance, are homogeneously specialized to create visual imagery. In contrast to the traditional view of microphysiological units of analysis as nerve fragments, synapses, or even chemical particles, the biofunctional model depicts brain microunits as organic microsystems capable of functioning both independently and simultaneously. Nerve fragments can store static knowledge, but a nerve fragment can no more create ongoing awareness than an isolated filament can create ongoing light.

Thus, the nervous system is composed of many specialized microsystems organized into many specialized subsystems. A brain microsystem is *specialized* in that it can generate a characteristic feeling of awareness (subjective experience) in the same way that a *color-coded* light bulb can generate ambient light of a characteristic color (Iran–Nejad, 1980, 1987). Knowledge is live awareness created and upheld from one moment to another by varying constellations of microsystems distributed across diverse subsystems (Iran–Nejad & Homaifar, 1991).

Types of Knowledge Creation. Biofunctionally, the brain engages in two different kinds of knowledge creation activity: (a) simultaneous functioning, an *ongoing* activity in which brain subsystems work together, and (b) component independent functioning, a *momentary* change in the activity of a constellation of brain microsystems (see functional manifestations in Fig. 13.2, combination subprocesses in Table 13.1). Using the light bulb analogy, think about a burning constellation of color-coded light bulbs that can either stay on continuously or generate momentary blinks (like the lights in a highway traffic arrow). Constellations of brain microsystems function analogously by engaging in ongoing activity or firing momentary blinks.

If the brain engages in two different ways of knowledge creation, two different kinds of knowledge should result. In the biofunctional model, whole-level (or mass-level) *thematic* knowledge is created and upheld by the ongoing functioning of brain microsystems and subsystems working together as a unitary mass. On the other hand, momentary independent functioning generates component-level (or unit-level) *categorical* knowledge such as images, concepts, or ideas (see the knowledge creation processes in Table 13.1). After its momentary firing, a unit-level category might become an ongoing component of the theme of the schema-of-the-moment.

Interest and Surprise-Ending Stories

The surprise-ending story illustrates how sources of control, learning processes, and kinds of knowledge interact to create two ongoing schemata and how both schemata generate interest in much the same way.

Interest and Pre-Surprise Schema Construction. Iran–Nejad (1989a) identified five major phases of schema construction in the comprehension of the surprise-ending story.[1]

Phase 1, category generation: early in the story, comprehension is merely the creation of categorical or unit-level knowledge. External and active sources of control interact with learning processes (Table 13.1) to regulate word and sentence perception. Here, momentary independent functioning is the principal learning process.

Phase 2, theme announcement: as a microsystem constellation fires its categorical knowledge, it also announces (or broadcasts) a theme. The theme circulates instantaneously in the nervous system and serves as a momentary internal context for activation of theme-relevant microsystems and reinterpretation of previously fired categories that are now ongoing components of the schema-of-the-moment. At first, theme announcement goes no farther than immediate focal attention to the meanings of words and sentences (i.e., category generation). so there is no dynamic reinterpretation of previously encoded events. Phase 2 begins when dynamic spontaneous attention to previous story events can occur during active attention to a current event, resulting in momentary creation of new themes. (Recall that it was simultaneous functioning that generated thematic knowledge.) Not every new theme that is announced, however, finds complete support in prior internal knowledge. Comprehension, therefore, must go beyond theme announcement.

Phase 3, theme completion: this begins when an announced theme reaches completion. A complete theme (Phase 3) differs from an

---

[1] Iran-Nejad (1989a) used the term *landmarks*. Our choice of the term *Phases* was influenced by Shuell (1990).

incomplete theme (Phase 2) in that only a complete theme can stay continuously in spontaneous global attention. In previous phases, active control dominated and dynamic control was dependent on it. With Phase 3, dynamic control becomes the dominant source of internal self-regulation. Only dynamic control can regulate the ongoing simultaneous functioning that upholds the current theme in spontaneous global attention.

With theme completion, the stage is set for learning as the constructive, dynamic, and creative reconceptualization of internal knowledge. Specifically, a thematically complete schema is not necessarily complete in categorical content. The ongoing theme in spontaneous global attention must now serve as the internal context for the reinterpretation of subsequent knowledge—for seeing newly fired categories in light of the new theme.

Phase 4, theme integration: the ongoing theme accomplishes two vital functions: (a) it becomes a spontaneous internal context for reinterpreting events that receive focal attention, and (b) it sets up a momentary state of *unclosure* that has dynamic momentum toward closure. It is this thematically complete but categorically incomplete state of unclosure that constitutes the interest-creating discovery module (ICDM) that is the heart of the human internal motivational system (IMS). While in ICDM, the individual tends to experience curiosity, suspense, certainty, or coherence in the constructive mode, and fear, stress, uncertainty, or incoherence in the unconstructive mode.

Phase 5, categorical completion: theme integration moves comprehension toward the last phase in schema construction, wherein a thematically complete schema reaches closure when it acquires full categorical completion.

Interest and Post-Surprise Schema Construction. The five phases described for presurprise schema construction also construct the post-surprise schema, except that theme integration and categorical completion might follow theme completion without delay. In postsurprise schema construction, there is no delay if the same categorical knowledge used for theme integration and categorical completion of the presurprise schema can be used again, after reinterpretation, for theme integration and categorical completion of the postsurprise schema (Iran–Nejad, 1989a). In other words, as soon as the theme of the surprising information is announced, it instantaneously circulates throughout the nervous system and momentarily replaces the presurprise theme. The new theme then serves as the reinterpretation context for previously encoded knowledge, which in turn participates dynamically in the categorical completion of the new theme.

Thus, the same ICDM (interest-creating discovery module) of the IMS (internal motivation system) that created interest during the construction of the presurprise schema creates the interest that results from comprehension of surprising information. This analysis is compatible with the definition of interest as a cause and consequence of learning (i.e., reconceptualization of internal knowledge). Moreover, nothing in the process indicates that interest is an emotion.

Postdiction as a Dynamic Reinterpretation Process

Redefining Postdiction: Themesight Versus Hindsight. Biofunctional theory predicts that interest will result from dynamic reconceptualization of internal knowledge. The five phases of schema construction differ most directly in the degree and manner of the involvement of dynamic reinterpretation of internal information in the context of a new ongoing theme. We identified the basic process as postdiction, which can now be defined more precisely as understanding with the benefit of *theme*sight, as opposed to *hind*sight. The core of this definition is that, given the ongoing theme, reinterpretation occurs spontaneously under dynamic self-regulation. Prediction, by contrast, occurs deliberately under active self-regulation.

The source of themesight might be the theme that is already in spontaneous global attention, as in theme integration and categorical completion during presurprise schema construction. Themesight may also arise in a theme announced by active focal attention to a currently encoding event, as in theme integration and categorical completion during postsurprise schema construction. In both cases, however, themesight can use only internal knowledge. If this is available, postdiction will be instantaneous. Otherwise, understanding will be gradual (due to delays in theme integration and categorical completion) or will fail altogether.

Failure of Postdiction Processes. Prediction-based theories assume that active attention during comprehension must be focused on the ongoing schema so that predictions can be made to facilitate selective attention. Interest results from incongruity defined as failure (Schank, 1979), or disruption (Mandler, 1982), of these active expectations. Iran–Nejad (1987) defined incongruity as failure of postdiction, as opposed to prediction, processes, and tested the null hypothesis that it causes interest.

In one study, subjects read stories that varied in the degree to which their endings (a) were surprising and (b) resolved postsurprise incongruity. Subjects who read stories that did *not* resolve incongruity rated low- and high-surprise endings as being significantly different in surprise but not in interest. By contrast, the low- and high-surprise endings that did resolve incongruity were rated as significantly different in both surprise and interest. There was also a high correlation between ratings of surprise and interest for incongruity resolved conditions ($r = .43$, $p < .001$), but the correlation was only marginal (due to partial resolvedness of the endings) for unresolved conditions ($r = .17$, $p < .05$). A second study replicated these results.

It appears that whether surprise causes interest depends on what happens after the surprise, at least in stories of this kind. Contrary to the hypothesis that postsurprise incongruity causes interest (Mandler, 1982), there was an increase in interest only when story endings resolved postsurprise incongruity: only successful postdictions caused interest. The biofunctional model implies that success in postdiction occurs to the extent that ICDM follows its course through all the necessary phases of schema construction. The story endings in this study were designed to contain a theme (theme announcement). In all endings, resolved or unresolved, the main character died or his or her life was saved. The unresolved endings, however, did not permit theme completion because no information was given as to who did the killing (or saving), why, and how. Without theme completion, the previously encoded story events could not be dynamically reinterpreted to permit theme integration and categorical completion. As a result, ICDM failed to follow its course and no interest was created.

Interest and Affect. As noted earlier, interest has seldom been distinguished from emotion (Bower & Cohen, 1982) or positive affect (Langsdorf, Izard, Rayias, & Hembree, 1983). In his early research, Berlyne (1960) viewed interest to be, like hedonic tone, a function of a quantitative arousal (potential) dimension. Berlyne's (1974) later findings showed that interest and hedonic tone behaved differently as a function of arousal potential. More recently, Schank (1979) postulated that interest is a combined function of an absolute qualitative dimension (represented as a marker stored with affective concepts such as death or sex in long-term memory) and a relative intensity dimension (such as degree of surprise).

Mandler (1982) was probably the first to distinguish interest and affect theoretically. Like Schank (1979), he assumed that interest is caused by incongruity per se. He further maintained that positive or negative affect is caused by successful accommodation of incongruous information.

In the biofunctional model, the underlying causes of interest are different from those of emotion or affect (Iran–Nejad, Clore, & Vondruska, 1981; Mandler, 1982). The model implies that affect is caused by the valence potential (i.e., goodness/badness or pleasure/displeasure) of the *content* of mental activity (Iran–Nejad & Ortony, 1985), not by schema construction phases. Some contents are positive, some negative, but both can be interesting or uninteresting. In the Iran–Nejad (1987) study, valence potential was operationalized by the goodness or badness of story outcome. The results showed that interest and affect behaved in opposite ways with regard to the independent variables manipulated. Overall, surprise had no effect on liking but influenced interest; outcome valence had a substantial influence on liking but had no effect on interest; and incongruity resolution did not influence liking but did cause interest.

Summary

The biofunctional model provides a theoretical analysis of interest, its origin in the nervous system, the processes by which it is created, its role as a cause and consequence of internal self-regulation of learning processes, and its predominantly intellectual nature. This section illustrated how these ideas might be tested empirically and reported the results of some of the experiments designed to test the prediction that dynamic reinterpretation of internal knowledge causes interest.

CONCLUSIONS AND IMPLICATIONS

The research reviewed here supports the theoretical conclusion that before interest can be a cause of learning, it must be its consequence. The empirical conclusions, however, must be modest and tentative, because only the first step toward providing a research foundation for this position.

One area of future research might test predictions associated with phases of schema construction during story comprehension. These phases represent the interaction of sources of control (external, active, dynamic), attention (focal, global), and kinds of knowledge creation (categorical, propositional, thematic). Stories are a natural domain to explore how these and similar factors (Table 13.1) influence interest and learning. Once we have a clearer idea of the biofunctional phases of schema construction in stories, further research can determine the role of these phases in the creation of interest in other types of text, such as exposition.

The biofunctional theory might also explain sentential interest. For instance, Schank (1979) argued that sentences such as *He drank a bottle of Mr. Clean* are interesting because they are unusual. However, it may not be their unusualness per se that makes them interesting, but their potential for causing reconceptualization. Sentences such as *Adult wolves carry food home in their stomachs and bring it up again or regurgitate it for the young cubs to eat* (Hidi, 1990) may also be interesting to the extent that they cause reconceptualization of one's knowledge of how animals feed their young.

In the implications of the biofunctional model for the nature of the role prior knowledge plays in the creation of interest lies another area of promising research. The model implies that the more extensive one's domain knowledge, the more one's interest in that domain. More prior knowledge provides more opportunity for reinterpretation when reconceptualization occurs. Further research might explore how far this hypothesis can go in explaining individual interests.

The idea that interest is caused by ongoing intellectual functioning is not new. It is implicit in the traditional notion of intrinsic motivation (Deci & Ryan, 1985), but it is difficult to determine exactly what intrinsic motivation means. Many authors speak of intrinsic needs that individuals must satisfy, which implies that some kind of goal appraisal is a necessary condition for interest. The core of the biofunctional internal motivational system is an ICDM that does not require prerequisite appraisal. In this sense, the model is closer to the theory proposed by Csikszentmihalyi and Csikszentmihalyi (1988), who postulate a flow process that requires no appraisal mediation. As they put it, "the mountaineer does not climb in order to reach the top of the mountain, but tries to reach the summit in order to climb" (p. 33). More generally, the model is compatible with Bartlett's (1932) constructive theory of remembering, Dewey's (1896) functional perspective, and foundational research on distributed learning and remembering (Iran–Nejad, 1980, 1988; Iran–Nejad & Homaifar, 1991).

ACKNOWLEDGMENTS

We wish to gratefully acknowledge the valuable assistance of Valerie Anderson on an earlier draft of this chapter. We also thank Suzanne Hidi, Ann Renninger, and Emily Smith for their insightful comments. This research was supported in part by a National Academy of Education Spencer Fellowship and by the Bureau of Educational Research and

Service, University of Alabama. We are greatly indebted to Jim McLean for his support. Correspondence and requests for reprints should be sent to Asghar Iran–Nejad, Behavioral Studies, The University of Alabama, Box 870231, Tuscaloosa, AL 35487.

REFERENCES

Alba, J. W., & Hasher, L. (1983). Is memory schematic? *Psychological Bulletin, 93*, 203–231.

Anderson, J. R. (1987). Skill acquisition: Compilation of weak-method problem solutions. *Psychological Review, 94*, 192–210.

Anderson, J. R., & Bower, G. H. (1973). *Human associative memory.* Washington, DC: Winston.

Anderson, R. C. (1982). Allocation of attention during reading. In A. Flammer & W. Kintsch (Eds.), *Discourse processing* (pp. 292–305). Amsterdam: North–Holland.

Anderson, R. C., Spiro, R. J., & Montague, W. E. (Eds.). (1977). *Schooling and the acquisition of knowledge.* Hillsdale, NJ: Lawrence Erlbaum Associates.

Anderson, R. C., Shirey, L. L., Wilson, P. T., & Fielding, L. G. (1986). Interestingness of children's reading material. In R. Snow & M. Farr (Eds.), *Aptitude, learning, and instruction: Cognitive and affective process analyses* (pp. 287–299). Hillsdale, NJ: Lawrence Erlbaum Associates.

Andre, T., & Phye, G. D. (1986). Cognition, learning, and education. In G. D. Phye & T. Andre (Eds.), *Cognitive classroom learning: Understanding, thinking, and problem solving* (pp. 1–20). Orlando: Academic Press.

Bacon, F. (1920). *The new organon and related writings.* New York: Liberal Arts Press.

Bartlett, S. F. (1932). *Remembering: A study in experimental and social psychology.* Cambridge, England: Cambridge University Press.

Bereiter, C. (1985). Toward a solution of the learning paradox. *Review of Educational Research, 55*, 201–226.

Berlyne, D. E. (1960). *Conflict, arousal, and curiosity.* New York: McGraw–Hill.

Berlyne, D. E. (1974). *Studies in the new experimental aesthetics.* New York: Wiley.

Black, J. B., & Wilensky, R. (1979). An evaluation of story grammars. *Cognitive Science, 3*, 213–230.

Blanchard, H. E., & Iran–Nejad, A. (1987). Comprehension processes and eye movement patterns in reading of surprise-ending stories. *Discourse Processes, 10*, 127–138.

Bower, G. H. (1981). Mood and memory. *American Psychologist, 36*, 129–148.

Bower, G. H., Black, J. B., & Turner, T. J. (1979). Scripts in comprehension and memory. *Cognitive Psychology, 11*, 177–220.

Bower, G. H., & Cohen, P. R. (1982). Emotional influences in memory and thinking: Data and theory. In M. S. Clark & S. T. Fiske (Eds.), *Affect and*

Cognition: The Seventeenth Annual Carnegie Symposium on Cognition (pp. 291–331). Hillsdale, NJ: Lawrence Erlbaum Associates.

Bower, G. H., & Mayor, J. D. (1985). Failure to replicate mood-dependent retrieval. *Bulletin of the Psychonomic Society, 23*, 39–42.

Bower, G. H., Monteiro, K. P., & Gilligan, S. G. (1978). Emotional mood as a context for learning and recall. *Journal of Verbal Learning and Verbal Behavior, 17*, 573–585.

Bransford, J. D. (1979). *Human cognition.* Belmont, CA: Wadsworth.

Brewer, W. F., & Lichtenstein, E. H. (1981). Event schemas, story schemas, and story grammars. In J. D. Long & A. D. Baddeley (Eds.), *Attention and performance IX* (pp. 363–379). Hillsdale, NJ: Lawrence Erlbaum Associates.

Brown, A. L., Bransford, J. D., Ferrara, R. A., & Campione, J. C. (1983). Learning, remembering, and understanding. In J. H. Flavell & E. M. Markman (Eds.), P. H. Mussen (Series Ed.), *Handbook of child psychology. Vol. 3: Cognitive development* (pp. 263–340). New York: Wiley.

Chomsky, N. (1965). *Aspects of a theory of syntax.* Cambridge: MIT Press.

Collins, A. M., & Loftus, E. F. (1975). A spreading activation theory of semantic processing. *Psychological Review, 82*, 407–428.

Csikszentmihalyi, M. (1988). The flow experience and its significance for human psychology. In M. Csikszentmihalyi & I. S. Csikszentmihalyi (Eds.), *Optimal experience: Psychological studies of flow in consciousness* (pp. 15–35). New York: Cambridge University Press.

Csikszentmihalyi, M., & Csikszentmihalyi, I. S. (1988). Introduction to Part IV. In M.Csikszentmihalyi & I. S. Csikszentmihalyi (Eds.), *Optimal experience: Psychological studies of flow in consciousness* (pp. 251–265). New York: Cambridge University Press.

De Beaugrande, R. (1982). The story of grammars and the grammar of stories. *Journal of Pragmatics, 6*, 383–422.

Deci, E. L., & Ryan, R. M. (1985). *Intrinsic motivation and self-determination in human behavior.* New York: Plenum Press.

Dewey, J. (1896). The reflex arc concept in psychology. *Psychological Review, 3* (4), 357–370.

Diener, E., & Iran–Nejad, A. (1986). The relationship in experience between various types of affect. *Journal of Personality and Social Psychology, 50*, 1031–1038.

Donchin, E. (1981). Surprise... surprise? *Psychophysiology, 18*, 493–513.

Epstein, S. (1986). Anxiety, arousal, and self-concept. In C. D. Spielberger & I. G. Sarason (Eds.), *Stress and anxiety: Volume 10 a sourcebook of theory and research* (pp. 265–305). New York: Hemisphere.

Graesser, A. C., & Riha, J. R. (1984). An application of multiple regression techniques to sentence reading times. In D. E. Kieras & M. A. Just (Eds.), *New methods in reading comprehension research* (pp. 183–218). Hillsdale, NJ: Lawrence Erlbaum Associates.

Hidi, S. (1990). Interest and its contribution as a mental resource for learning. *Review of Educational Research, 60*, 549–571.

Hidi, S., & Baird, W. (1986). Interestingness—a neglected variable in discourse processing. *Cognitive Science, 10*, 179–194.

Hidi, S., Baird, W., & Hildyard, A. (1982). That's important, but is it interesting? Two factors in text processing. In A. Flammer & W. Kintsch (Eds.), *Discourse processing* (pp. 63–75). Amsterdam: North–Holland.

Iran–Nejad, A. (1980, February). *The schema: A structural or a functional pattern* (Tech. Rep. No. 159). Urbana: University of Illinois, Center for the Study of Reading.

Iran–Nejad, A. (1983). Qualitative and quantitative causes of the experience of affect. *Dissertation Abstracts International, 43,* 3847A.

Iran–Nejad, A. (1984, May). *Qualitative and quantitative aspects of the comprehension of surprising information.* Paper presented at the annual meeting of the Midwestern Psychological Association, Chicago.

Iran–Nejad, A. (1986). Understanding surprise-ending stories. *Journal of Mind and Behavior, 7,* 37–62.

Iran–Nejad, A. (1987). Cognitive and affective causes of interest and liking. *Journal of Educational Psychology, 79* (2), 120–130.

Iran–Nejad, A. (1988). *Toward a Bartlettian constructive theory of learning.* Unpublished manuscript.

Iran–Nejad, A. (1989a). Associative and nonassociative schema theories of learning. *Bulletin of the Psychonomic Society, 27,* 1–4.

Iran–Nejad, A. (1989b). A nonconnectionist schema theory of understanding surprise-ending stories. *Discourse Processes, 12,* 127–148.

Iran–Nejad, A. (1990). Active and dynamic self-regulation of learning processes. *Review of Educational Research, 60,* 573–602.

Iran–Nejad, A., & Chissom, B. (1988, August). *Active and dynamic sources of self-regulation in learning.* Paper presented at the annual meeting of the American Psychological Association.

Iran–Nejad, A., Clore, G. L., & Vondruska, R. J. (1981, October). *Affect: A functional perspective* (Tech. Rep. No. 222). Urbana: University of Illinois, Center for the Study of Reading.

Iran–Nejad, A., & Homaifar, A. (1991). Assoziative und nicht-assoziative Theorien des verteilten Lernen und Erinnerns. In S. J. Schmidt (Ed.), *Gedachtnis* (pp. 206–249). Frankfurt/Main, Germany: Suhrkamp Verlag.

Iran–Nejad, A., & Ortony, A. (1984). A biofunctional model of distributed mental content, mental structures, awareness, and attention. *The Journal of Mind and Behavior, 5,* 171–210.

Iran–Nejad, A., & Ortony, A. (1985). Qualitative and quantitative sources of affect: How valence and unexpectedness relate to pleasantness and preference. *Basic and Applied Social Psychology, 6,* 257–278.

Jenkins, J. J. (1974). Remember that old theory of memory? Well, forget it! *American Psychologist, 29,* 785–795.

Johnson, M. K., & Hasher, L. (1987). Human learning and memory. *Annual Review of Psychology, 38,* 631–668.

Kintsch, W. (1980). Learning from text, levels of comprehension, or: Why anyone would read a story anyway. *Poetics, 9,* 87–98.

Kintsch, W. (1988). The use of knowledge in discourse processing: A construction integration model. *Psychological Review, 95* (2f), 163–182.

Kuhn, T. S. (1962). *The structure of scientific revolutions.* Chicago: University of Chicago Press.

Lang, P. J. (1984). Cognition in emotion: Concept and action. In C. E. Izard, J. Kagan, & R. B. Zajonc (Eds.), *Emotions, cognition, and behavior* (pp. 192–226). New York: Cambridge University Press.

Langer, E., Blank, A., & Chanowitz, B. (1979). The mindlessness of ostensibly thoughtful action: The role of placebic information in interpersonal interaction. *Journal of Personality and Social Psychology, 36,* 635–642.

Langsdorf, P., Izard, C. E., Rayias, M., & Hembree, E. A. (1983). Interest expression, visual fixation, and heart rate changes in 2- to 8-month-old infants. *Developmental Psychology, 19,* 375–386.

Lazarus, R. S. (1984). On the primacy of cognition. *American Psychologist, 39* (2), 124–129.

Lehnert, W. G. (1981). Plot units and narrative summarization. *Cognitive Science, 4,* 293–331.

Mahoney, M. J. (1977). Publication prejudices: An experimental study of confirmation bias in the peer review system. *Cognitive Theory and Research, 1,* 161–175.

Mandler, G. (1975). The search for emotion. In L. Levi (Ed.), *Emotions: Their parameters and measurement* (pp. 1–15). New York: Raven Press.

Mandler, G. (1982). The structure of value: Accounting for taste. In M. S. Clark & S. T. Fiske (Eds.), *Affect and cognition* (pp. 3–36). Hillsdale, NJ: Lawrence Erlbaum Associates.

McLaughlin, B. (1965). "Intentional" and "incidental" learning in human subjects. *Psychological Bulletin, 63,* 359–376.

McReynolds, P. (1986). Changing conceptions of anxiety: A historical review and a proposed integration. In C. D. Spielberger & I. G. Sarason (Eds.), *Stress and anxiety: Volume 10, A sourcebook of theory and research* (pp. 131–157). New York: Hemisphere.

Minsky, M. (1975). A framework for representing knowledge. In P. H. Winston (Ed.), *The psychology of computer vision* (pp. 211–277). New York: McGraw–Hill.

Murphy, G. L., & Medin, D. L. (1985). The role of theories in conceptual coherence. *The Psychological Review, 92,* 289–316.

Navon, D., & Gopher, D. (1979). On the economy of the human processing system. *Psychology Review, 86,* 214–255.

Neisser, U. (1967). *Cognitive psychology.* New York: Appleton–Century–Crofts.

Nisbett, R., & Ross, L. (1980). *Human inference: Strategies and shortcomings of social judgment.* Englewood Cliffs, NJ: Prentice–Hall.

Ortony, A., Clore, G. L., & Collins, A. (1988). *The cognitive structure of emotions.* Cambridge, MA: Cambridge University Press.

Petrie, H. G. (1981). *The dilemma of enquiry and learning.* Chicago: University of Chicago Press.

Renninger, K. A., & Wozniak, R. H. (1985). Effect of interest on attentional shift, recognition, and recall in young children. *Developmental Psychology, 21,* 624–632.

Reynolds, R. E., & Anderson, R. C. (1982). Influence of questions on allocation of attention during reading. *Journal of Educational Psychology, 74,* 623–632.

Rumelhart, D. E. (1975). Notes on a schema for stories. In D. B. Bobrow & A. M. Collins (Eds.), *Representation and understanding: Studies in cognitive science* (pp. 211–236). New York: Academic Press.

Rumelhart, D. E. (1977). Toward an interactive model of reading. In S. Dornic (Ed.), *Attention and performance* (Vol. 4), (pp. 573–603). London: Academic Press.

Rumelhart, D. E. (1980). Schemata: The building blocks of cognition. In R. J. Spiro, B. C. Bruce, & W. F. Brewer (Eds.), *Theoretical issues in reading comprehension: Perspectives from cognitive psychology, linguistics, artificial intelligence, and education* (pp. 33–58). Hillsdale, NJ: Lawrence Erlbaum Associates.

Rumelhart, D. E. (1984). The emergence of cognition from sub-symbolic processes. *Proceedings of the Sixth Annual Conference of the Cognitive Science Society,* (pp. 59–62). Boulder, CO: Institute of Cognitive Science and the University of Colorado.

Schallert, D. L. (1976). Improving memory for prose: The relationship between depth of processing and context. *Journal of Verbal Learning and Verbal Behavior, 15,* 621–632.

Schallert, D. L. (1982). The significance of knowledge: A synthesis of research related to schema theory. In W. Otto & S. White (Eds.), *Reading expository material* (pp. 13–48). New York: Academic Press.

Schank, R. C. (1979). Interestingness: Controlling inferences. *Artificial Intelligence, 12,* 273–297.

Schneider, W., & Shiffrin, R. M. (1977). Controlled and automatic human information processing: I. Detection, search, and attention. *Psychological Review, 84,* 1–66.

Shiffrin, R. M., & Schneider, W. (1977). Controlled and automatic human information processing: II. Perceptual learning, automatic attending, and a general theory. *Psychological Review, 84,* 127–190.

Shirey, L. L., & Reynolds, R. E. (1988). Effect of interest on attention and learning. *Journal of Educational Psychology, 80,* 159–166.

Shuell, T. J. (1990). Phases of meaningful learning. *Review of Educational Research, 60.*

Sperry, R. W. (1968). Mental unity following surgical disconnection of the cerebral hemispheres. *Harvey Lectures, 62,* 293–323.

Thorndyke, P. W. WWW(1977). Cognitive structures in comprehension and memory of narrative discourse. *Cognitive Psychology, 9,* 77–110.

Thorndyke, P. W., & Yekovich, F. R. (1980). A critique of schema-based theories of human story memory. *Poetics, 9,* 23–49.

Thurmond, P. J. (1978). If cornered, scream. *Ellery-Queen's Mystery Magazine, 71,* 66–68.

Yussen, S., Huang, S., Mathews, S. & Evans, R. (1988). The robustness and temporal course of story schema's influence on recall. *Journal of Experimental Psychology, 14,* 173–179.

Vosniadou, S., & Brewer, W. F. (1987). Theories of knowledge restructuring in development. *Review of Educational Research, 57,* 51–67.

Voss, J. F. (1984). Learning and learning from text. In H. Mandl, N. Stein, & T. Trabasso (Eds.), *Learning and comprehension of text* (pp. 193–212). Hillsdale, NJ: Lawrence Erlbaum Associates.

Zajonc, R. B. (1984). On primacy of affect. *American Psychologist, 39* (2), 117–123.

14

Good Strategy Instruction is Motivating and Interesting

Michael Pressley, Pamela Beard El-Dinary, Marilyn B. Marks,
Rachel Brown, and Shelly Stein
University of Maryland

Competent academic performance is complex, the product of many inter-actions among students' knowledge of strategies; metacognitive under-standings about when, where, and how to use strategies students know; prior knowledge based on experiences in the real world and in symbolic worlds (e.g., text, television); and motivational beliefs (e.g., "I can learn what is taught in school by expending effort," is a belief supporting motivation; "I cannot learn what is taught because I have low ability," undermines motivation; Borkowski, Carr, Rellinger, & Pressley, 1990; Pressley, Borkowski, & Schneider, 1989). The evidence is growing that diverse academic tasks such as writing, reading comprehension, and mathematical problem solving can be understood in terms of these components (see Pressley & Associates, 1990).

Much of the research of the 1980s in cognition and instruction involved efforts to teach strategies (see Pressley, Goodchild, Fleet, Zajchowski, & Evans, 1989), enhance metacognition about those strategies (e.g., O'Sullivan & Pressley, 1984; Pressley, Levin, & Ghatala, 1984), assess coordinations between strategies and prior knowledge (e.g., Bjorklund, 1989), and determine motivational manipulations that can increase articulated interaction of strategies with general and domain-specific knowledge (e.g., Borkowski et al., 1990). Moreover, much of this work was quite successful, demonstrating that strategies can be taught and can improve students' academic performances dramatically, at least when students remain under strong instructional control. Unfortunately, however, there was little evidence in this body of work that academic performances were improved in a general, cross-situational fashion. For example, as long as students were cued to use strategies in conjunction with their knowledge base, all went well. Once left to their own devices to accomplish academic tasks, students rarely seemed to continue using the strategies they had been taught. In short, there is no quick fix leading to autonomous academic competence.

The absence of a quick fix for effective educational practice makes sense, however, given one model of mature cognition. Learning how to coordinate a repertoire of complex strategies with ever-expanding meta-cognition, world knowledge, and motivational understandings requires years. It is the culmination of cognitive development.

This perspective has led to long-term, school-based interventions aimed at stimulating student knowledge of strategies, metacognition about strategies, world knowledge, and motivation (see Pressley,. El-Dinary, Gaskins, Schuder, Bergman, Almasi, & Brown, in press). We have studied two such programs in some detail in recent years, one being the Benchmark School in Media, Pennsylvania, which serves bright underachievers, the other the SAIL (Students Achieving Independent Learning) program, operating in some Chapter 1 schools in the Montgomery County, Maryland public schools. In addition we are currently studying cognitively oriented instruction in some other settings, including research on the various ways reciprocal teaching (Palincsar & Brown, 1984) is carried out in schools (Marks & Pressley, in preparation). Particularly relevant here is that all of the programs we have studied involve multiple efforts to increase students' interest in academic work and to motivate them to use strategies.

The purpose of this chapter is to provide information about how academic interest and motivation are cultivated in the strategies instruction programs we have been studying. Just as Krapp, Hidi, and Renninger; (this volume) have argued that cognitive theories of learning have often ignored motivation and interest, we contend that the motivational and interest components in effective cognitive instructional programs have been largely downplayed and understudied. Consideration of how schooling environments can foster academic motivation and interest seems particularly critical in light of analyses such as that of Schiefele, Krapp, and Winteler (this volume), which identifies clear associations between academic interest and academic achievement.

One immediately obvious motivational feature of these settings is that task involvement and task orientation are encouraged much more than ego involvement and ego orientation (Nicholls, 1989). This contrasts with traditional models of American schooling in which there is an emphasis on establishing who's smart and who's not through student competition for grades and positive evaluations of their abilities relative to classmates (see Henry, 1963; Holt, 1964). That is, traditional schooling has a heavy ego emphasis.

In good strategies instruction classrooms, teachers are concerned with each student's improvement. The goal is to teach every student how to carry out tasks more competently and with less effort. Whether one student in the class reads, writes, or solves problems better than another is irrelevant. This emphasis on task competency and improvement rather than on ability differences is pedagogically sound, with substantial evidence of greater interest in, effort at, and commitment to learning when task involvement/ orientation is emphasized rather than ego enhancement (Nicholls, 1989). There are many different ways by which the improvement of each student is motivated in these classrooms, encouraging interest and commitment to learning. Several of the distinctions offered in this volume are helpful in classifying the various classroom practices we have been observing.

Krapp et al. (this volume; see also Hidi, 1990) argue that much of the study of interest as a psychological state can be conceptualized either as work on individual differences in interest or as work on situational characteristics affecting interest across persons. This is an appealing breakdown for us because we have observed explicit efforts by teachers to exploit the particular interests of individual children, as well as those of groups of children, in order to motivate their learning of strategies. In addition, we have observed efforts to design learning environments that promote academic interest and motivation in all students. The short-term goal of these interventions is to create actualized states of interest in terms of Krapp et al.'s framework—attention to and pleasure in doing particular academic tasks. The implicit theory is that years of interest and pleasure in carrying out specific tasks are critical if students are ever to develop a general disposition to be interested in and motivated by academic matters (see Deci, this volume, for a formal elucidation of how interesting interactions with particular activities can lead to enduring motivation to pursue such activities).

Throughout the instruction we have been watching, there have also been attempts to increase what Deci (this volume) refers to as competence, autonomy, and relatedness—fundamental psychological needs intrinsic to the self. Efforts are made to increase students' *competence* (i.e., proficiency in executing strategies being taught) and *autonomy* (i.e., ability to generalize strategies to new situations in the absence of teacher prompting to do so). Moreover, the instruction is undertaken in order to foster *relatedness* among students and between students and teacher (i.e., classrooms are organized so that students view them as members of communities supportive of their efforts to improve rather than as competitive arenas where class members compete for the approval of an ever-judgmental teacher).

To provide the reader with a vision of the type of instruction we have been studying, we first present an overview of the components of effective strategy instruction. Then, examples of instructional practices we have observed that promote student interest and motivation are reviewed. These are classified with respect to whether they (a) promote motivation by accommodating to individual differences in students or by changing the environment so that it is generally more motivating, and (b) are intended to affect competence, autonomy, or interpersonal relatedness.

In the concluding section, we analyze how interest can promote student motivation. There are also some brief considerations of an emerging hypothesis about motivational components in good strategy instruction, and instructional recommendations that are warranted based on what is known already.

THE NATURE OF EFFECTIVE STRATEGY INSTRUCTION

In good strategies instruction classrooms, it is possible every day to observe salient and explicit instruction aimed at fostering the development of multiple strategies, understandings about when strategies being taught are appropriate, and, in turn, acquisition of nonstrategic world knowledge through application of the strategies being learned, knowledge that is then available to mediate future learning. Common components of the programs we are studying include the following (adapted from El-Dinary & Pressley, in preparation):

- Teaching is decidedly long-term. These teachers explicitly believe (and act on their belief) that effective strategies use develops through years of instruction.
- Strategies instruction is not a stand-alone entry in the curriculum. Rather, it is integrated with ongoing instruction. For instance,

reading strategies are taught and practiced as part of readings that would normally occur during reading group instruction.

- Teaching of single strategies is not emphasized. Rather teachers view acquisition of repertoires of effective and complementary strategies as the ideal.

- Explicit explanation of one or more academic strategies occurs in every class. Sometimes these are new strategies and sometimes these are strategies covered previously. In these explanations, teachers elucidate the component processes comprising the strategies. Teachers frequently explain how the various strategies covered in the curriculum can be used in conjunction with one another.

- Most lessons include teacher modeling of one or more strategies. Typically, teachers model by thinking aloud as they perform a task, in the sense of mental modeling as described by Duffy and Roehler (e.g., 1989). Teacher modeling is intended to elucidate how flexible coordination and adaptation of strategies occurs.

- Teachers discuss, endorse, and model flexible strategy use. They also explicitly acknowledge that individual students will differ in their use of strategies.

- Students are often prompted to model and explain the strategies they are learning, so that they and other students can focus on the thought processes being used.

- Teacher guidance is the most prominent mode of instruction throughout the school year. The guidance includes hints and cues about how strategies might be applied to newly encountered content as well as hints, cues, and elaborations about student adaptations of strategies and the responses produced as a function of strategy execution and adaptation, consistent with Duffy and Roehler's (e.g., 1987, 1989; Duffy, Roehler, & Rackliffe, 1986) concept of responsive elaboration.

- Teachers consistently send the message that student thought processes are what count, rather than getting a specific, "correct" answer.

In summary, the classroom instruction we have been watching features explanation and modeling of strategies. This instruction occurs every day for several years and involves authentic academic content. As teacher-guided practice of strategy use proceeds, students model and explain strategies to one another. The coordinated use of multiple strategies to accomplish academic tasks is experienced in a number of different ways—through observation of teachers and peers and through the personal experience of applying and adapting the strategies to academic tasks. Because all this occurs in the ongoing curriculum, the message communicated to students is that everyday academic cognition is strategic processing.

MOTIVATING PRACTICES DURING GOOD STRATEGIES INSTRUCTION

The strategies instruction teachers we have been studying make many efforts to motivate students' use of the strategies being explained, modeled, and practiced. These teachers do not have one coherent model of motivation that is guiding their instructional practice. Rather, they engage in a number of particular policies and practices—policies and practices of which they are consciously aware (e.g., Pressley, Gaskins, Cunicelli, Burdick, Schaub–Matt, Lee, & Powell, 1991; Pressley, Schuder, Montgomery County SAIL Faculty, Bergman, & El-Dinary, in preparation). These policies and practices combine to produce a motivating classroom environment and school day, and classrooms in which children become ever more strategic, ever more knowledgeable in general, ever more capable at coordinating all that they have learned to accomplish new academic tasks, and ever more motivated to take on such tasks because of their positive experiences in school.

Each of the practices reviewed is analyzed with respect to whether it motivates by linking with the individual interests of particular students, or reflects a change in the overall learning environment and situational interests that might be expected to affect most students. In addition, each practice is classified with respect to whether it is aimed at increasing competence, autonomy, and/or relatedness. To be sure, such classifications cannot always be clear-cut, but we believe attempting them provides clarification about the relation between the various dimensions of strategies instruction classrooms. Ultimately, an understanding of such relations may enable us to troubleshoot in classrooms that are not as effective in helping students to develop strategies. To provide some additional order to the presentation, instructional components aimed at competence are discussed first, before proceeding on to discussion of components that affect autonomous learning and interpersonal relatedness. In general, this coincides with an ordering from components that affect the overall environment to those that are aimed at meshing with particular student interests and competencies.

Ensuring Success When Strategies are Taught

Teachers show students that they can succeed in academic tasks by applying the strategies they are learning. This is accomplished by teacher scaffolding of student use of strategies with demanding tasks (Wood, Bruner, & Ross, 1976), providing just enough support so that students can succeed. For example, teachers make sure students get a chance to be successful by waiting for them to respond (Tobin, 1987). If they do not respond, the teacher reframes the question or provides hints as to how to proceed until the student makes some progress. The teacher poses questions that permit him or her to assess and then advance student processing (Gaskins, Anderson, Pressley, Cunicelli, & Satlow, in press, provide important data on this point).

The success component is notable because many of the students we were observing in these settings had experienced difficulties in other educational settings or would be "at risk" for experiencing academic difficulties. For example, Benchmark School students typically had failed in school for 1 to 2 years before they came to Benchmark. Many of the Montgomery County SAIL classrooms serve students who are disadvantaged relative to the rest of the country (e.g., in the school with the largest SAIL program, 60% of the students are eligible for and receive free breakfasts and lunches). It is no small matter that these children do well when they learn and use strategies.

This is an across-the-board environmental manipulation. Such scaffolded practice is designed to encourage the development of competence in executing the strategic procedures that are being learned. Success with strategies should also encourage increased use of them, with increased competence in strategy execution (i.e., relatively low-effort execution) depending in part on how much students are willing to apply the strategies they are learning consistently. Of course, consistent use is more likely when there was previous success in their use.

Reinforcing Thinking That Reflects Strategic Engagement

Feedback and reinforcement (often in the form of teacher attention and praise) are provided not for the "correctness" of responses, but for thought processes reflecting use of effective strategies. Consider the following fieldnote excerpts illustrating how a SAIL teacher's feedback focussed on student thought processes:

(Guided practice of "Magic Number" following independent practice of the activity.)

Teacher: Tell us what you did... You know how to do this. You're all terrific problem solvers. I'm not interested in the answer... I want to see how you did it... Make sure you understand the information.

Student 1: I had 199.

T: Tell me what you did. (T guides S1 to figure out how he got 199, an incorrect answer.)

Student 2: I had a different way of doing it.

T: Show me.

(S2 writes $7 + 3 = 10$ and $129 + 10 = 139$. T has S2 explain the process; S3 knows another way to solve the problem.)

T: Show me...These are all different ways to solve the problem. There's more than one way....

(Much later)

T: Remember what we are focusing on when we check these?

S: The strategy we used. (T emphasizes the point, elaborating on how people can have different ways of solving the same problem. T has another student give his answer and explain the reasoning behind it.)

T: Someone else either who has the same answer with different reasoning or a different answer?

And so it goes. There are many discussions during effective strategies instruction, with teachers giving attention and praise to students when they demonstrate effective use and adaptation of strategies.This is a general learning environments intervention. It is aimed at having students recognize that they are competent and to increase their competence by encouraging use and practice of the strategic processes being taught.

Emphatically Encouraging the Attribution That Performance Improvements Are Due to Use of Strategies

Teachers do much to point out that student performance improvements *follow* use of the strategies being learned. Teachers encourage students to understand that using effective strategies is what *caused* their success. They make the case to students that learning strategies is important. The following example illustrates a teacher attributing success to strategy use:

Teacher: If you look at these [first problems in the set], they're easy. You don't need to use a strategy. But the strategy helps you when the material is difficult. Mary (fictional name) used visualization.

Another teacher offered the following remarks to her students during problem-solving instruction:

Teacher: Do you think many kids could solve this in their heads? Probably not, but manipulation helped us. Sometimes, when reading a story, it's hard to understand and keep track of everything. (Teacher gives example—all the characters in yesterday's mice story.) But we can act it out to help us.

These examples show how students were encouraged to attribute their academic successes to *strategy effort* (see Borkowski et al., 1990; Clifford, 1984).

This approach contrasts with a frequent recommendation in the motivational literature that students be encouraged to attribute their success to effort alone (e.g., Weiner, 1979). Such recommendations are problematic, because effort alone often does not produce acceptable performance. Rather, what is required is effort that is expended to carry out strategies that are within one's capabilities (e.g., imagery only works for children with sufficient functional working memory capacity; Cariglia–Bull; & Pressley, 1990; Pressley, Cariglia–Bull, Deane, & Schneider, 1987) and that are well matched to the task (e.g., understanding & remembering), the materials (e.g., social studies or science text), and the context (e.g., school); that is, the effects of effort are determined by the same forces that determine the effects of any cognitive input (see the tetrahedral models of Brown, Bransford, Ferrara, & Campione, 1983, or Jenkins, 1979).

Thus, teachers teach strategies that are within their students' capacities and that are appropriate given the task, materials, and context. They also emphasize that effort expended through appropriate strategies is producing the benefits that are experienced. Effective strategy teachers make it unambiguous that comprehension is improved when students expend effort applying comprehension strategies, that writing is better when students use writing strategies, and that problem solving proceeds gainfully when students apply strategies aimed at enhancing solution finding; that is, the teacher often points out linkages between the use of particular strategies and particular academic outcomes. Teachers do not, however, teach a separate lesson on how strategy X might be helpful in a given situation. Rather they convey the linkages between strategies and success during "teachable moments" as these arise during explanations, modeling, and practice of strategies (cf. Bruner, 1977). Thus, when a student encounters an unfamiliar vocabulary word in a text, the teacher might encourage the student to select from one of several problem-solving strategies for dealing with the word (e.g., rereading previous text, skipping the word and being alert to subsequent context clues, using picture clues). As the child zeroes in on the meaning of the item, the teacher might point out to the student the power of the problem-solving strategies that were used to mediate the discovery of the meaning.

This is an across-the-board environmental manipulation, although it is deployed on an individualized basis, immediately after students experience strategy-mediated success. It is aimed at increasing the likelihood that students will use the strategies they are learning. Presumably, the greater their use of strategies, the more competent their use. Increasing knowledge of strategy utility increases willingness to use strategies autonomously (i.e., when students are reading, writing, and problem-solving on their own; e.g., Brown et al., 1983) as do the aspects of instruction taken up next.

IMPROVING METACOGNITIVE KNOWLEDGE ABOUT STRATEGIES

Another way of increasing long-term use of strategies is to ensure that students know when and where it is appropriate to use the strategies they are learning (e.g., Presslcy, Borkowski, & O'Sullivan, 1984, 1985; also, Pressley, Borkowski, & Schneider, 1987, 1989)—when and where their use will pay off. Such understanding can be developed by providing information during particular lessons about the utility of the procedures being learned and by providing multiple opportunities across the curriculum to apply the strategies being taught.

Providing Information About When and Where to Use Strategies

We have consistently observed teachers providing information about when to use strategies being learned. The following dialogue (from the SAIL program) is an illustration:

> Teacher: How did calculators help? Why was it so crucial to get right numbers?
>
> Student: We had to spend exactly $2.70.
>
> T: What if you had a range?... If you didn't need exact, but *about*, what could you do?
>
> S: Estimate.

The teacher then went on to explain how estimating might help on a similar problem, so that there were multiple references to the appropriateness of estimating when an approximate answer is required. And, of course, on other occasions it is the students who explain the value of the strategies they are using, as when they defend their choice of one strategy or another in a particular situation. In short, in strategies instruction classrooms the value of strategies plays a prominent part in dialogues.

This practice represents an overall change in the learning environment, consistent with the assumption that metacognitive knowledge about strategies is essential for their autonomous use (e.g., Pressley, Borkowski, & Schneider, 1987, 1989). General and appropriate use of strategies can only occur when learners know when and where to apply the strategic procedures they possess. Knowing that a strategy can assist a particular type of performance in a particular situation motivates the use of that strategy in that situation.

Providing Examples of Strategies Application Across the Curriculum

Teachers also explicitly attempt to link the strategies being taught to many parts of the curriculum. A case study in one classroom at the Benchmark School illustrates this point (Pressley, Gaskins, Wile, Cunicelli, & Sheridan, 1991). Over the course of a semester, students in this classroom learned mapping and webbing strategies that could be applied to the comprehension of expository text. As expected, the reading group featured many opportunities to identify cause-and-effect sequences in text, temporal relations, and descriptive analyses. So did social studies classes, in which students were taught to analyze much of the semester's social studies reading using the strategies presented in the reading group. In addition, the teachers taught their students how the text analysis strategies could be adapted to serve as methods for composing essays. They showed their students how to construct cause-and-effect outlines, temporal sequences, and coherent descriptions that then could be translated into meaningful text. In short, there were multiple opportunities to apply the strategies learned during reading across the curriculum.

The same was true in the SAIL program. One SAIL teacher frequently conducted experiments to support the concepts presented in the science text the students were reading. As part of these lessons, the students predicted the outcome of the experiments and verified their predictions through observing the experiments. This teacher pointed out to the students that they were using prediction and verification strategies learned in reading class with science texts. Another SAIL teacher explicitly used strategy vocabulary throughout the school day so that students could understand the meanings of terms in many contexts, both academic and nonacademic. For example, when the strategies instruction focus was on manipulation, the teacher said "manipulate" in a classroom management context: "You're manipulating the pages in your books when you shouldn't be. Now I need to manipulate the chalk to write something on the board."

When students in strategies instruction classrooms experience the utility of strategies across the curriculum, the multiple purposes of the strategies being learned are conveyed. Such experiences are assumed to motivate cognitive engagement in general, as well as appropriate use of particular strategies. Across-the-curriculum applications create a general environmental change, intended to produce more autonomous students, students who can apply the strategies they are learning broadly and who are motivated to use them.

Using Strategies to Process Authentic, Challenging, and Interesting Tasks

The students in the schools we have been studying are applying strategies to *authentic* academic tasks, the types of tasks that all students at their grade levels are expected to perform. This contrasts with a common response to students at risk (like those in the classrooms we have studied). Often such students are given a diet of very simple tasks. For example, primary-grade readers in special education often spend a great deal of time on skill sheets that emphasize lower-level decoding skills (e.g., Johnston & Allington, 1991).

In contrast, although there is some decoding and word attack during reading instruction at Benchmark and in the Montgomery County SAIL program, the emphasis is on getting meaning from challenging connected text, the demand put on normally achieving students; that is, these students are taught strategies such as prediction, clarification, imagery, and summarization, procedures that are unambiguously aimed at encouraging comprehension and memory of text via heightened understanding of it. Failure to decode particular words is never permitted to get in the way of seeking overall meaning. First, students are taught the problem-solving strategies for figuring out a word that was discussed earlier. Second, they learn that overall meaning can almost always be figured out even when some words are not known.

Strategies are taught in the context of the curriculum so that strategy instruction enhances, rather than displaces, time spent on academic or literary content. For example, in SAIL classrooms the youngest students read rhymes and fairy tales, intermediate students read folklore, and older elementary students read science and history texts. In addition, the content being read as part of strategies lessons can often be related to other parts of the curriculum, with teachers prompting students to notice how what is being read relates to other content that has been covered previously.

In effective classrooms of all kinds, teachers will usually provide realistic examples of how what is learned in school relates to the real world, a suggestion that dates back at least as far as Dewey (1913, 1915). This approach is also used in the strategies instruction classrooms we are examining. For example, as part of a lesson on estimation, one teacher talked about estimating the cost of her groceries to make sure she could afford them; she also used this example to explain why overestimating is often better than underestimating. The relevance of classroom materials is particularly appropriate for increasing students' autonomous use of strategies. Relevance makes the usefulness of strategies for these real-school tasks more obvious to students and in turn leads to their increased use and generalization.

Strategies instruction teachers attempt to present appropriately *challenging* tasks, tasks not so easy that no strategic engagement would be required to accomplish them nor so difficult that they cannot be accomplished even if students apply the strategies they are learning. This, of course, is consistent with a long-standing recommendation in the motivation literature that task engagement be maximized by optimal challenge and novelty (e.g., see Deci, this volume). It is also consistent with Vygotskian (Vygotsky, 1978) recommendations that instruction be directed to the "zone of proximal development," that is, just beyond what the child can now accomplish working independently, but not so far beyond the child's competence that the task cannot be accomplished with some assistance from a knowledgeable other. (See Renninger, this volume, for a discussion about how the zone of proximal development for a student varies as a function of the match between tasks and students' individual interests, with larger zones associated with tasks that are more interesting to the student. If nothing else, high interest stimulates task persistence.)

In the case of academically or economically disadvantaged students, it is especially critical that tasks be optimally challenging. On the one hand, such students are at high risk for falling behind agemates with respect to academic knowledge and skills. All too often, the public school solution is to give such students very easy tasks and content (e.g., see Johnston & Allington, 1991) relative to agemates. The result is that such students fall even farther behind their peers who are proceeding through the regular curriculum. On the other hand, these students often experience academic failure when left in the regular curriculum, with low academic motivation (e.g., learned helplessness; Dweck, 1985) being the long-term impact of cumulative failure experiences in the regular education environment.

Strategies instruction is intended to provide such students, in particular, with academic tools that will give them a fighting chance with materials and tasks that might otherwise be overwhelming to them. Even so, because of these children's great susceptibility to failure (and in some cases, histories of academic failure), great care is taken to assure that students practice the strategies they are learning on tasks so that they can experience success with a reasonable amount of effort. Challenge is provided, but not so much challenge that frustration is likely.

This instructional practice is an attempt to increase the interest and motivation of particular students by matching tasks to student abilities. By providing tasks to which strategies can be applied profitably, competence in strategy execution should increase; assigning tasks where strategy application is likely to lead to success should also increase commitment to strategies use and, thus, autonomous use of the strategies that have been learned.

The teachers we are studying present their students with *interesting* tasks. For instance, they have culled an important practice from whole language approaches to reading instruction: entertaining and interesting literature is read in class, rather than a specified sequence of stories such as those typically included in basal readers; that is, the teachers are attempting to create an interesting situation.

One common approach to selecting text is student choice. Students are given a choice, and select from several pieces of literature the one most congruent with their interests. Thus, sometimes the reading group covers content not typically encountered in elementary reading, content selected because it is intriguing to the students in the group. One example occurred at the Benchmark School when a reading group comprised of four boys covered an entire text on energy over the course of several weeks (see Pressley, Gaskins, Wile et al., 1991). It was apparent throughout that the students were definitely interested in this content area; reading strategies were practiced with important scientific content that was especially appealing to this group of students. As one editor of this volume pointed out, it is impressive that teachers attempt to both (a) create an interesting situation by offering materials believed to be interesting to most students, and (b) tap individual differences in interests by permitting student choice; that is, these teachers are adept at managing both of the dimensions of interest identified by Krapp et al. (this volume; also Hidi, 1990).

Good strategies teachers are savvy about engineering interesting classrooms and creating reading groups in which there is good reason to read and expend strategic effort, since using strategies increases understanding of content that students like.

The decision to use interesting materials is an across-the-board environmental decision. Letting students choose their own readings links assignments to the particular interests of students. It is intended to increase autonomous use of strategies by making obvious the utility of strategies for obtaining a deeper understanding of material that is personally gratifying.

ENCOURAGING STUDENT CONSTRUCTION OF KNOWLEDGE ABOUT STRATEGIES

We believe strongly that students are inherently motivated to become more competent and are especially motivated to construct new and more powerful understandings of the world (e.g., Deci, this volume; Piaget, 1987a, 1987b; White, 1959). Unfortunately, school often discourages active student construction of understandings, especially to the extent that educators either view their role as transmitting information that society expects its members to possess (see Kohlberg & Mayer, 1972), or view school as a screening mechanism for separating the talented from the untalented (see Nicholls, 1989). We suspect that one of the most powerful reasons that effective strategies instruction produces students who seem highly motivated is that, in contrast to most conventional instruction, it promotes student construction of knowledge, with the goal of bettering each student regardless of academic standing relative to peers.

For example, in all the comprehension instruction we have been watching, students are definitely actively constructing understandings about how to read better in general. Although the teacher models and explains strategies, he or she does much more. As the student attempts to apply the strategies that are being taught, the teacher diagnoses the student's understanding of the strategy and provides hints, questions, and prompts designed to encourage the student to apply the strategy even more capably. Throughout the process, it is made clear that the student's use and understanding of the strategies will not be identical to the teacher's understanding, and that by using the strategies each student will come to a personalized understanding of both the strategies and the content being strategically processed. Unique student interpretations of text, as well as applications and adaptations of strategies, are not only encouraged but embraced by the teachers we have been studying. Moreover, the teachers are accepting of all progress, rather than differentially rewarding those who "get it" faster. (For more detailed theoretical analyses of how strategy instruction promotes student construction of knowledge, see Harris and Pressley, 1991, and Pressley, Harris, and Marks, in press. For telling examples of diverse student adaptations to strategy instruction, see Pressley, Gaskins, Wile, et al., 1991.)

Presumably, the students' personalized understandings of strategies should increase competent use as well as autonomous deployment of strategies—especially in personally relevant situations; that is, student construction of strategies should lead to a deep understanding of the strategies being learned.

USING STRATEGIES TO ENCOURAGE STUDENT INTERPRETATIONS

When students in a group are encouraged to use strategies such as prediction, clarification, imagery, and summarization to understand and remember text, there is an important side effect. Rather than engaging in endless cycles of teacher-initiated questions about the text followed by student responses evaluated by teachers (see Gaskins et al., in press), the discussions in strategy instruction classrooms and reading groups are very different (e.g., Mehan, 1979): a great deal of interpretive discussion of text occurs.

Prediction encourages students to relate the text to what they already know, so that personal perspectives on the potential content of a text are a prominent part of predictive discussions. Images that students construct and describe to the group are filled with personal reactions to the meaning of the text. Clarifications often stimulate discussions about alternative meanings of text, and summaries reflect what is important to particular readers, with different parts of the text critical to different readers. Throughout the reading lessons children are encouraged to share their predictions, visualizations, and summaries. At the end of the reading, global evaluations are often solicited as well. For instance, in one of the

SAIL classrooms, the teacher always has the students rate how much they enjoyed a story after they have completed reading it.

In short, strategies instruction encourages the understanding that student reactions to text are important and that different students will have different reactions. Strategies instruction does not encourage only memory of text content (i.e., efferent reactions; Rosenblatt, 1978) but also personal and aesthetic reactions (Rosenblatt, 1978). Our strong impression is that strategy-instructed students are extremely motivated to participate in the group because the strategies-driven discussions encourage interpretive commentary by the participants. The message in these groups is clear: what you have to say as you apply strategies to text is important and interesting. Your predictions are worth considering; your visualizations are unique and valued; what you feel requires clarification is often difficult for others to understand; and your summaries often cover points that all the students should remember.

Students who might otherwise fear participation in groups in which teachers solicit "right" answers are probably more likely to communicate when it is clear that there are no right answers. Risk taking is definitely fostered in these classrooms, with the risks paying off most of the time, in that student attempts are integrated into the lesson dialogue in ways that make clear that each student's interpretations and attempts are legitimate even though others may have different outlooks.

Although encouraging interpretations affects the overall learning environment, it also associates use of strategies with the students' particular interests and points of views. By demonstrating to students the power of strategies to increase personal interpretations and understandings, commitment to strategies should increase and, thus, their autonomous use also should increase. By increasing students' autonomous use of strategies (and hence, increasing practice of strategies), competence in execution should increase. Finally, by encouraging personal reactions as part of instruction, teacher–student and student–student understandings about each other should increase. Our guess is that the many personal interpretations that occur in strategy instruction classrooms go far in creating a sense of community and relatedness in these learning environments.

COOPERATION IS FOSTERED

Cooperation is encouraged, rather than competition. Teachers continuously send the message that they are on the side of the student. Teachers in these classrooms collaborate with their students to accomplish academic tasks. For instance, reading groups in these classrooms are nothing like traditional classroom interactions that revolve around test-like questions from a teacher about text content that has been read (Cazden, 1988; Mehan, 1979). Rather, teachers coach students about how to apply the strategies they are learning to texts that are being read. When students require it, teachers provide assistance to students in using strategies with text. Student performance in these groups is taken more as an indicator about how to assist the student to accomplish the current task and master the strategies in the long-term than as something to be evaluated as right or wrong, good or bad. All of the teachers we have watched are supportive and deeply involved with their students. The result is genuinely warm interpersonal relations in the classroom that go far in increasing students' motivations to learn the strategies and content the teacher is presenting.

This general classroom policy of cooperation and support of students should increase competence by increasing the likelihood that students will figure out how to carry out instructed strategies. It should also increase autonomy in that there is a sharing of knowledge about strategies, including information about where and when they are appropriate and how they can be modified to fit new circumstances. Perhaps most important, however, is that interpersonal relatedness is enhanced by a cooperative classroom ethic. Students are not going it alone, but proceed with peers who care about them and more knowledgeable adults who make clear by their actions that they are dedicated to doing all that is possible to assure student success.

AND THERE'S MORE

Some of the most important ways that strategies teachers motivate their students to acquire and use strategies have been covered here, and there are more that could be discussed if space permitted. For example, there is a generally positive and efficient atmosphere in effective strategies instruction classrooms—we have never seen an effective strategies instruction classroom that was not in general well managed. Students are usually on-task. Discipline problems are infrequent and are handled in a minimally disruptive fashion when they do occur. There is little (if any) criticism of these in these classrooms. In short, good strategies instruction classrooms include many of the motivational elements found in effective classrooms of all kinds (e.g., Good & Brophy, 1986).

Even more impressive, however, is that there is no *one* way in which an effective classroom is facilitated. Each teacher we have studied has an individual style of teaching, including individual ways of motivating students to use the strategies being taught. Thus, some teachers talk explicitly with their students about the importance of taking responsibility for their own learning and actions. Others ask students to tell about favorite strategies and how they are using them during the school day. That is, there is no ready formula about how to motivate students to use strategies. Rather, individual teachers think about their students as individuals and concoct their own mix, although in every case the mix is rich in strategies, metacognition about strategies, nonstrategic knowledge, and motivation. Moreover, in every case there are attempts to relate instruction to the interests of the students (e.g., provide tasks that will be interesting because they are matched to the particular abilities of students) and to construct classroom environments that are generally motivating. In addition, all strategies instruction classrooms foster competence, autonomous use of intellectual abilities, and relatedness among the members of the class and especially between teacher and students.

CONCLUSIONS

Motivation as a Component of Effective Strategy Instruction

Instruction about how to execute strategies is not enough to assure their continued use. Students need to be motivated to use strategies. In particular, many authors contended in the 1980s that students should be informed about the utility of the strategies they were learning (e.g., Brown et al., 1983), with the presumption that adding utility information to strategy instruction would produce learners with both strategic skills and the will to use them (e.g., Paris, Lipson, & Wixson, 1983). Other authors (e.g., Borkowski et al., 1990; see especially Brophy & Kher, 1986) recognized that much more might be required to motivate students to learn new procedures and use them; it might be necessary to restructure the curriculum to include many motivational components not used to advantage in most classrooms. The educators who have created the effective strategies instructional environments we have been studying have created programs consistent with this perspective.

Student and Teacher Interest as Part of Effective Strategy Instruction

Interest is fostered in good strategies instruction classrooms in many ways. For example, to the extent that strategies increase learning of new content, they enlarge the academic domains in which students can develop interests—intellectual passion (or at least the motivation to read some more) cannot occur without some initial exposure to and understanding of an area.

More central here, however, is that many aspects of good strategies instruction are designed to increase interest in acquiring strategies. For instance, by scaffolding instruction and matching it so that students are learning strategies just a bit beyond their current level of functioning, the likelihood of success in strategy acquisition is increased. From a variety of perspectives (e.g., Atkinson, 1957; Bandura, Adams, & Beyer, 1977; Csikszentmihalyi, 1975; Deci, this volume; Deci & Ryan, 1985; Dweck & Gilliard, 1975; Renninger, this volume, especially Project 2), such success should increase interest in acquisition of ever more challenging and complex strategies.

In addition, the positive feedback from teachers to students for using strategies provides explicit information about what material is critical to learn in these classrooms (e.g., Rosenthal, Moore, Dorfman, & Nelson, 1971; Rosenthal & Carroll, 1972; Zimmerman, 1974). This feedback is persuasive rather than coercive, designed to interest students in strategies rather than intellectually bludgeoning them (i.e., these classrooms are informational in the Deci & Ryan, 1985, sense). An important part of making the case for strategies is highlighting the links between strategies and important increases in academic performance (see especially Clifford, 1984). Our guess is that all this information about how strategies promote competence does in fact increase student interest in strategies, for humans are greatly motivated to be more competent in general (e.g., White, 1959) and tend to be particularly interested in information that can help them as individuals (e.g., Petty & Cacioppo, 1984; Petty, Cacioppo, & Heesacker, 1981; Petty, Cacioppo, & Schumann, 1983).

The teachers we have been watching know what is interesting to their students and use this knowledge to maximize the appeal of their instruction to students. Thus, Marks and Pressley (in preparation) watched a series of strategy lessons around Mary Mapes Dodge's *Hans Brinker*, a particularly gripping book for upper-elementary students. The story was interesting enough to the students to motivate great efforts on their part to use the comprehension strategies being taught in the class.

When students experience success with strategies, greater success than they achieved with other types of instruction, teachers are reinforced for teaching strategies. In two interview studies (Pressley, Gaskins, Cunicelli et al., 1991; Pressley, Schuder et al., in preparation), teachers made it clear that their students' success with strategies was a critical factor in stimulating their interest in and commitment to strategies instruction; their interest reflected feelings of increased efficacy as teachers due to strategy instruction (e.g., Ashton, 1985). Moreover—and this brings this discussion of interest full circle—one reason teachers feel more efficacious is that since strategies instruction was implemented into the curriculum, their students are much more interested in school. They recognize that long-term academic interest and commitment to school will only occur if school is consistently interesting and fulfilling. Thus, it is no small advantage for cognitive strategy instruction that it is enjoyable and interesting.

What Next?

An hypothesis emerging from our current work is that cognitive strategies instruction might only produce important and lasting effects given a classroom environment in which (a) improvement is valued more than rank-ordering of students, (b) the individual competencies of students are considered at the same time that the teacher attempts to construct a generally motivating environment, and (c) student development of competence and autonomy is supported by positive relationships among all class members, teachers and students. This hypothesis will continue to be evaluated in our work.

And for the Time Being...

For the present, we feel the general motivational and interest literature provides enough support for our emerging hypothesis to recommend that strategies instruction teachers (a) make improvement of the strategic processing of each student in their classrooms an important goal, (b) downplay egoistic comparisons between students, (c) incorporate the changes recommended here to increase the general motivational and interest level of the classroom (e.g., reading of good literature rather than simply proceeding through each story in a basal text), (d) design instruction for particular students matched to their particular interests and abilities, and (e) develop a cooperative learning community in which teachers and students are dedicated to relating to one another to foster the development of students' academic competence and autonomy. If the instruction of effective cognitive strategies in highly motivating class-rooms should proliferate, we would expect school to be more interesting and motivating. As a result, students will be more empowered. Students will have more skill and will (Paris et al., 1983).

ACKNOWLEDGEMENTS

The University of Maryland co-authors were invited into the Benchmark School and the Montgomery County SAIL classrooms by their developers, as part of ongoing evaluations of the programs. Although the Benchmark School and the SAIL curricula are generally consistent with theoretical perspectives advanced by Pressley and his associates in previous publications, the curricula in place at these schools were developed in total by personnel at the respective institutions before they entered into working relationships with the University of Maryland team. We are deeply indebted to their faculties and staff for the opportunities to study ongoing, school-based programs involving complex strategy instruction. Those interested in Benchmark should contact Dr. Irene Gaskins, Director, Benchmark School, 2107 North Providence Rd., Media, PA 19073. Information about the SAIL program can be obtained from Dr. Janet Bergman and Mr. Ted L. Schuder, Montgomery County Public Schools, 850 Hungerford Dr., Rockville, MD 20850. We are also indebted to other schools (public schools in Carroll County, MD, Harford County, MD, and Alexandria, VA) in which we are currently making observations, all of which informed the perspectives advanced here. Many thanks to Ann Renninger for detailed commentary concerning the fit of our views with those of other authors in this volume.

REFERENCES

Ashton, P. (1985). Motivation and teacher's sense of efficacy. In C. Ames & R. Ames (Eds.), *Research on motivation in education, Vol. 2, The classroom milieu* (pp. 141–171). Orlando: Academic Press.

Atkinson, J. W. (1957). Motivational determinants of risk-taking behavior. *Psychological Review, 64,* 359–372.

Bandura, A., Adams, N. E., & Beyer, J. (1977). Cognitive processes mediating behavioral change. *Journal of Personality and Social Psychology, 35,* 125–139.

Bjorklund, D. F. (1989). *Children's thinking: Developmental function and individual differences.* Monterey, CA: Brooks/Cole.

Borkowski, J. G., Carr, M., Rellinger, E. A., & Pressley, M. (1990). Self-regulated strategy use: Interdependence of metacognition, attributions, and self-esteem. In B. F. Jones (Ed.), *Dimensions of thinking: Review of research* (pp. 53–92). Hillsdale NJ: Lawrence Erlbaum & Associates.

Brophy, J., & Kher, N. (1986). Teacher socialization as a mechanism for developing student motivation to learn. In R. Deldman (Ed.), *Social psychology applied to education* (pp. 257–288). Cambridge, England: Cambridge University Press.

Brown, A. L., Bransford, J. D., Ferrara, R. A., & Campione, J. C. (1983). Learning, remembering, and understanding. In J. H. Flavell & E. M. Markman (Eds.), *Handbook of child psychology: Vol. III. Cognitive development* (pp. 177–266). New York: Wiley.

Bruner, J. S. (1977). *The process of education.* Cambridge MA: Harvard University Press.

Cariglia–Bull, T., & Pressley, M. (1990). Short-term memory differences between children predict imagery effects when sentences are read. *Journal of Experimental Child Psychology, 49,* 384–399.

Cazden, C. B. (1988). *Classroom discourse.* Portsmouth NH: Heinemann.

Clifford, M. M. (1984). Thoughts on a theory of constructive failure. *Educational Psychologist, 19,* 108–120.

Csikszentmihalyi, M. (1975). *Beyond boredom and anxiety.* San Francisco: Jossey–Bass.

Deci, E. L., & Ryan, R. M. (1985). *Intrinsic motivation and self-determination in human behavior.* New York: Plenum Press.

Dewey, J. (1913). *Interest and effort in education.* New York: Houghton–Mifflin.

Dewey, J. (1915). *The school and society* (2nd ed.). Chicago: University of Chicago Press.

Duffy, G. G., & Roehler, L. R. (1987). Improving reading instruction through the use of responsive elaboration. *The Reading Teacher, 40,* 514–521.

Duffy, G. G., & Roehler, L. R. (1989). *Improving classroom reading instruction: A decision-making approach* (2nd ed.). New York: Random House.

Duffy, G. G., Roehler, L. R., & Rackliffe, G. (1986). How teachers' instructional talk influences students' understanding of lesson content. *Elementary School Journal, 87,* 3–16.

Dweck, C. S. (1985). Intrinsic motivation, perceived control, and self-evaluation maintenance: An achievement goal analysis. In C. Ames & R. Ames (Eds.), *Research on motivation in education, Vol. 2, The classroom milieu* (pp. 289–205). Orlando: Academic Press.

Dweck, C. S., & Gilliard, D. (1975). Expectancy statements as determinants of reactions to failure: Sex differences in persistence and expectancy change. *Journal of Personality and Social Psychology, 32,* 1077–1084.

El-Dinary, P. B., & Pressley, M. (in preparation). Manuscript in preparation. College Park MD: University of Maryland, Department of Human Development.

Gaskins, I. W., Anderson, R. C., Pressley, M., Cunicelli, E. A., & Satlow, E. (in press). Cognitive strategy instruction at Benchmark School: The instructional moves good strategy instruction teachers make. *Elementary School Journal.*

Good, T. L., & Brophy, J. E. (1986). School effects. In M. C. Wittrock (Ed.), *Handbook of research on teaching* (pp. 570–602). New York: MacMillan.

Harris, K. R., & Pressley, M. (1991). The nature of cognitive strategy instruction: Interactive strategy construction. *Exceptional Children, 57,* 392–404.

Henry, J. (1963). *Culture against man.* New York: Vintage Books.

Hidi, S. (1990). Interest and its contribution as a mental resource for learning. *Review of Educational Research, 60,* 549–571.

Holt, J. (1964). *How children fail.* New York: Deta/Seymour Lawrence.

Jenkins, J. J. (1979). Four parts to remember: A tetrahedral model of memory experiments. In L. S. Cermak & F. I. M. Craik (Eds.), *Levels of processing in human memory* (pp. 429–461). Hillsdale NJ: Erlbaum & Associates.

Johnston, P., & Allington, R. (1991). Remediation. In R. Barr, M. L. Kamil, P. B. Mosenthal, & P. D. Pearson (Eds.), *Handbook of reading research* (Vol. II, pp. 984–1012). New York: Longman.

Kohlberg, L., & Mayer, R. (1972). Development as the aim of education. *Harvard Educational Review, 42,* 449–496.

Marks, M. B., & Pressley, M. (in preparation). Manuscript in preparation. College Park, MD: University of Maryland, College of Education.

Mehan, H. (1979). *Learning lessons: Social organization in the classroom.* Cambridge, MA: Harvard University Press.

Nicholls, J. G. (1989). *The competitive ethos and democratic education.* Cambridge, MA: Harvard University Press.

O'Sullivan, J. T., & Pressley, M. (1984). Completeness of instruction and strategy transfer. *Journal of Experimental Child Psychology, 38,* 275–288.

Palincsar, A. S., & Brown, A. L. (1984). Reciprocal teaching of comprehension-fostering and comprehension-monitoring activities. *Cognition and Instruction, 1,* 117–175.

Paris, S. G., Lipson, M. Y., & Wixson, K. K. (1983). Becoming a strategic reader. *Contemporary Educational Psychology, 8,* 293–316.

Petty, R. E., & Cacioppo, J. T. (1984). The effects of involvement on responses to argument quantity and quality: Central and peripheral routes to persuasion. *Journal of Personality and Social Psychology, 46,* 69–81.

Petty, R. E., Cacioppo, J. T., & Heesacker, M. (1981). The use of rhetorical questions in persuasion: A cognitive response analysis. *Journal of Personality and Social Psychology, 40,* 432–440.

Petty, R. E., Cacioppo, J. T., & Schumann, D. (1983). Central and peripheral routes to advertising effectiveness: The moderating role of involvement. *Journal of Consumer Research, 10,* 134–148.

Piaget, J. (1987a). *Possibility & necessity* (Vol. 1). Minneapolis: University of Minnesota Press.

Piaget, J. (1987b). *Possibility & necessity* (Vol. 2). Minneapolis: University of Minnesota Press.

Pressley, M., & Associates (1990). *Cognitive strategy instruction that really improves children's academic performances.* Cambridge, MA: Brookline Books.

Pressley, M., Borkowski, J. G., & O'Sullivan, J. T. (1984). Memory strategy instruction is made of this: Metamemory and durable strategy use. *Educational Psychologist, 19,* 84–107.

Pressley, M., Borkowski, J. G., & O'Sullivan, J. T. (1985). Children's metamemory and the teaching of memory strategies. In D. L. Forrest–

Pressley, G. E. MacKinnon, & T. G. Waller (Eds.), *Metacognition, cognition, and human performance* (pp. 111–153). New York: Academic Press.

Pressley, M., Borkowski, J. G., & Schneider, W. (1987). Cognitive strategies: Good strategy users coordinate metacognition and knowledge. In R. Vasta & G. Whitehurst (Eds.), *Annals of child development*, Vol. 4 (pp. 89–129). Greenwich, CT: JAI Press.

Pressley, M., Borkowski, J. G., & Schneider, W. (1989). Good information processing: What it is and what education can do to promote it. *International Journal of Educational Research, 13*, 857–867.

Pressley, M., Cariglia–Bull, T., Deane, S., & Schneider, W. (1987). Short-term memory, verbal competence, and age as predictors of imagery instructional effectiveness. *Journal of Experimental Child Psychology, 43*, 194–211.

Pressley, M., El-Dinary, P. B., Gaskins, I., Schuder, T., Bergman, J. L., Almasi, J., & Brown, R. (in press). Direct explanation done well: Transactional instruction of reading comprehension strategies. *Elementary School Journal*.

Pressley, M., Gaskins, I. W., Cunicelli, E. A., Burdick, N. J., Schaub–Matt, M., Lee, D. S., & Powell, N. (1991). Strategy instruction at Benchmark School: A faculty interview study. *Learning Disability Quarterly, 14*, 19–48.

Pressley, M., Gaskins, I. W., Wile, D., Cunicelli, B., & Sheridan, J. (1991). Teaching literacy strategies across the curriculum: A case study at Benchmark School. In J. Zutell & S. McCormick (Eds.), *Learner factors/teacher factors: Issues in literacy research and instruction: Fortieth yearbook of the National Reading Conference* (pp. 219–228). Chicago: National Reading Conference.

Pressley, M., Goodchild, F., Fleet, J., Zajchowski, R., & Evans, E. D. (1989). The challenges of classroom strategy instruction. *Elementary School Journal, 89*, 301–342.

Pressley, M., Harris, K. R., & Marks, M. B. (in press). But good strategy instructors are constructivists!! *Educational Psychologist*.

Pressley, M., Levin, J. R., & Ghatala, E. S. (1984). Memory strategy monitoring in adults and children. *Journal of Verbal Learning and Verbal Behavior, 23*, 270–288.

Pressley, M., Schuder, Montgomery County SAIL faculty, Bergman, J., & El-Dinary, P. B. (in preparation). *The effects of comprehension strategies instruction: An interview study with Montgomery County SAIL teachers.* College Park, MD: University of Maryland, Department of Human Development.

Rosenblatt, L. M. (1978). *Reader, text, poem.* Carbondale IL: Southern Illinois Press.

Rosenthal, T. L., & Carroll, W. R. (1972). Factors in vicarious modification of complex grammatical parameters. *Journal of Educational Psychology, 63*, 174–178.

Rosenthal, T. L., Moore, W. B., Dorfman, H., & Nelson, B. (1971). Vicarious acquisition of a simple concept with experimenter as model. *Behavior Research and Therapy, 9*, 217–227.

Tobin, K. (1987). The role of wait time in high cognitive level learning. *Review of Educational Research, 57*, 69–95.

Vygotsky, L. S. (1978). *Mind in society.* Cambridge, MA: Harvard University Press.

Weiner, B. (1979). A theory of motivation for some classroom experiences. *Journal of Educational Psychology, 71,* 3–25.

White, R. W. (1959). Motivation reconsidered: The concept of competence. *Psychological Review, 66,* 297–333.

Wood, P., Bruner, J., & Ross, G. (1976). The role of tutoring in problem solving. *Journal of Child Psychology and Psychiatry, 17,* 89–100.

Zimmerman, B. J. (1974). Modification of young children's grouping strategies: The effects of modeling, verbalization, incentives, and praise. *Child Development, 45,* 1032–1041.

V DEVELOPMENTAL ASPECTS OF INDIVIDUAL INTEREST

15

Individual Interest and Development: Implications for Theory and Practice

K. Ann Renninger
Swarthmore College

Most of the time, we are reasonably accurate if we assume that student learning is influenced by interest. However, it is not so easy to say more specifically why it is that this influence occurs or to what extent this influence affects the way in which things are learned. Learning involves not only that which people assimilate and to which they accommodate as information, but it involves how individuals represent task(s) to themselves, what they do to complete a task, and how their work with that task influences the way in which they go about subsequent tasks/activities.

Although there have been numerous studies suggesting the importance of prior knowledge, informal knowledge, experience, meaningfulness, interestingness, and familiarity of task contents for the accessibility of the task and its subsequent completion (see Prawat, 1989, for a review), few studies have been designed that address the way in which the individual or idiosyncratic quality of a subject's knowledge influences his or her task performance. Rather, researchers have tended to focus on patterns typical of groups of students and as such have evaluated particular task situations or particular social settings that characterize patterns of groups of students—findings that appear intuitive to the practitioner precisely because they are applicable to teaching situations in general. While practitioners need to have an understanding of the underlying continuities of what children understand and come to know, it is my contention that they also need to have ways to talk about the individual nature of children's contributions to and involvements with learning, because these provide a framework for understanding the variation in (and possible frustrations of) ongoing classroom life.

For purposes of application in particular, knowledge about what the individual brings to the tasks with which he or she is presented is useful in remediating children's "faulty rules" (Ginsburg, 1977), mapping the range of individual variance in a variety of aspects of learning, and addressing individual variation in children's development. Focus on the particular subject–task interaction (system, or activity) that incorporates an individual's understanding of task as a function of experience— including his or her social milieu—not only permits consideration of individuals and the tasks with which they engage as independent influences on learning, but provides a lens for understanding the respective contributions of each to the other as well.

In this chapter, research on individual interest is discussed as including both the stored knowledge and the value with which individuals re-engage classes of tasks (objects, ideas, and events) in their environment. Building on the work of Vygotsky (1967) and Piaget (1940, 1981), the knowledge and value components of interest derive from what the individual brings to present action from prior experience with both objects and others. Thus, the knowledge and value components of interest can be described, on one hand, as individual in the sense that it is the individual who constructs and reconstructs the possibilities for his or her activity. The knowledge and value components of interest are also social in the sense that what come to be seen by the individual as possibilities for action are influenced by others (cf. Mead, 1934; see also Renninger, 1989, for further discussion of the knowledge and value components of interest.).

Central to this discussion is a conceptualization of interest as a psychological state. Interest is thought to be reflected in the class of objects (events, or ideas) with which an individual engages, but as referents these are interests of the child, and the features of these objects that are attractive to individuals have been discussed as the interestingness of these tasks (Hidi, 1990; Krapp, Hidi, & Renninger, this volume). Thus, whereas interest may be identified with a play object (e.g., a train) for experimental purposes, as a psychological state, interest is neither in the individual, nor in the play object/task or activity. Rather, interest is a particular relation of that individual in engagement with that play object/task, relative to the other activities with which he or she engages (see chapters by Krapp & Fink; Nenniger; Prenzel; and Schiefele, this volume, for related discussions of individual interest).

From this perspective then, interest is assumed to be reflected in the individual's perception of possibilities for action, representation of these possibilities to the self, and the setting, resolving, and resetting of challenges (see Fink, 1991; Krapp & Fink, this volume; Renninger, 1990; Renninger & Leckrone, 1991, for further discussion of interest and challenge setting). Interest is expected to vary between individuals and as such differentially influence the way in which they act. Among young children, it appears that the challenge setting and possibilities for action in which they engage are more readily identified with particular play objects (e.g., trains, playdough, dolls, etc.). With older individuals, on the other hand, interests are reflected in a particular pattern of questioning or challenge setting that may, but does not necessarily, have to be described by a specific domain (e.g., mathematics, reading, ballet).

The present discussion of interest focuses on interest as an individually varying, yet universal, psychological state. It does not address the way in which interests emerge, nor does it presume that individuals are always reflectively aware of interest as a psychological state.[1] Rather, the individual learner is understood as co-constructing his or her understanding, or theory (Karmiloff–Smith, 1974–1975) about the world, in conjunction with the objects and others that make up that world. As such, it is expected that the singular nature of the individual's understanding of the world, due to the particular content of his or her activity, contributes to individual differences in the kinds of questions with which he or she has practice, and the challenges he or she sets—in short, the way he or she understands what it is that a given task requires.

In the sections that follow, findings from two ongoing research projects designed to address the role of individual interest in learning are overviewed. Specifically, these projects were undertaken with young children (Project 1) and fifth- and sixth-grade students (Project 2) in order to evaluate the influence of individual interest on the accessibility of tasks and task completion. Following this, implications of these findings for theory and practice are discussed.

---

[1] The point about the extent to which the individual is aware of his or her interest is a critical difference between this theoretical perspective and that of others currently researching interest. The distinction has specific implications for methodology as well. If interest is not something of which an individual is necessarily reflectively aware, then identification of interest cannot be dependent on typical methods for their identification, such as interviews and questionnaires where the subject is asked to identify his or her interest(s).

PROJECT 1:
INDIVIDUAL INTEREST AND YOUNG CHILDREN'S ACTION

In order to begin mapping the role of interest in learning, studies of young children were undertaken for several reasons. First, because interest is conceptualized here as a psychological state of which the individual may not be reflectively aware, naturalistic identification of interest in the course of everyday activity was employed. Second, in order to consider how interest, regardless of its specific content, affected the activity of children relative to each other, all of the children in a nursery-school classroom were involved in the study. Finally, the nursery-school age group was appropriate because: (a) they are not able to feign interest and are not experimenter-wise, (b) they can follow directions, and (c) their actions in free play are easily videotaped and reliably coded (and, as such, do not depend on self-report).

Each of the studies reported here has focussed on one to three samples (total $N = 44$, 22M, 22F) of children between 2.9 and 4.2 years of age whose nursery school class was conducted in the same classroom.[2] Data were collected using either combined naturalistic and experimental methodologies or through independent coding of the videotapes collected for the naturalistic portion of the combined studies. Specifically, six 40-minute (or twelve 20-minute) sessions of free play in which one child was the focal child were reviewed, and the child was identified as having an interest in a particular class of objects if, over the sessions of free play, he or she: (a) returned to that object repeatedly, (b) spent more time playing with that object than with another play object, (c) would at times play with that object in solitary play, *and* (d) would at times play in other than manipulative play with that object. The child was identified as having a noninterest in a particular class of play objects if, over the videotaped play sessions, he or she: (a) did spend time with these play objects, (b) could use something other than manipulative play with the noninterest object, and (c) did not spend as much time with these play objects as with identified objects of interest, and/or (d) did not play with the object in solitary play.

---

[2] As such, the groups of children involved in these studies have all experienced the same play objects, under teachers sharing the same "whole-child" approach to education, during the second half of their nursery-school year. Thus, to the extent that it was possible in naturally occurring settings to provide them with the same types of opportunities, the children were equally familiar with the play objects and the others in the class.

For the purposes of the present discussion, results from studies designed to assess the effect of interest on young children's attention and memory, play with objects, play with others, and temperament are briefly reviewed.

Interest, Attention and Memory. In order to evaluate the role of interest in the way in which young children process information, the first study in this project focused on the effect of interest on young children's attention and memory (Renninger & Wozniak, 1985). In this study, children's behaviors in free play were first coded to identify objects of interest, and these objects were then employed as stimuli in three experimental tasks assessing attentional shift, recognition, and recall memory. In the first part of the study, videotapes of 16 children in ongoing free play were collected and individual interests were identified for each child.

Findings from the descriptive portion of this study suggested that all of the children could be identified as having two objects of interest (out of a possible 16 available objects) and that one child's identified interest was not necessarily the identified interest of the next child. In addition, objects identified as interests for boys (e.g., cars, fire engines, etc.) typically were not the same as objects identified as interests for girls (e.g., dolls, playdough, etc.).

Results from the experimental portion of this study indicate that children's interests exerted a marked influence on shifts in focal attention with respect to objects in the peripheral visual field, the likelihood that an item would be correctly recognized when encountered again, and recall. These findings suggest that individual interests reflect the knowledge/value systems that individuals bring to the task of organizing experience, memory, and activity. What this study did not address, however, was how or why interest might function in this way. Thus, the following studies were designed to evaluate the process of children's play with objects identified as interests and noninterests, their play with objects of interest and other children, and the role of interest in play under conditions that require persistence.

Interest and Children's Play with Objects. In order to evaluate the nature of the challenges undertaken by the child in free play, and the particular role of the identified objects of interest and noninterest in such challenge setting, a study of the role of interest in the structure of children's actions was undertaken (see also Renninger, 1990). Children's behaviors were first coded to identify objects of interest and noninterest;

children's behaviors in free play were then coded to identify the range and quality of individual children's actions with each of 16 discrete play objects (e.g., cars, dolls, puzzles, etc.) continuously present during their free play at nursery school. For the purposes of this study, five types of play were identified (investigative, functional, operational, transformational, and facilitative play; cf. Renninger, 1990), and then the specific actions of each of the children within each type of play with each play object were coded across the six 40-minute tapes in which that child was the focal child.

Within-child analyses revealed that: (a) Children have a wider range of types of play available to them when playing with their objects identified as interests than when playing with objects identified as noninterests; (b) children were more likely to play for longer amounts of time, repeating particular sequences of action with their identified object of interest, than when they played with objects identified as noninterests; (c) children's actions within play types were more likely to include more variations of action during play with their identified objects of interest than during play with their identified objects of noninterest; (d) children who shared the same identified object of interest did not necessarily share the same action sequences in play with their identified object of interest; (e) children in play with objects identified as noninterests were more likely either not to repeat prior actions within play types, or to repeat prior actions only, with no incorporation of changes in action sequences.

Furthermore, gender differences emerged between children suggesting that: (a) Girls were more likely than boys to reengage in investigative play (exploring the physical properties of an object) and to shift actions with their identified object of interest in investigative play. The girls' objects of interest were also more likely than the boys' to offer more possibilities for investigative activity. (b) Boys were more likely than girls to have more different types of actions in functional play (mimicking real-world use of these objects) with their identified objects of interest, and their objects of interest were also more likely to provide more possibilities for functional activity. (c) Girls are more likely than boys to have more different types of actions in operational play (exploring relations such as sequencing, balancing, etc.) with their identified objects of interest, and their objects of interest were also more likely than the boys' to provide more possibilities for exploring relations in operational play. (d) Girls were more likely than boys to have repeated engagements in transformational play (substituting something else as the "object"; maintaining an image) with their identified objects of interest, and their objects of interest were also most likely to provide more possibilities for repeated engagement in transformational play. Boys, on the other hand, were more likely than girls to shift actions in transformational play with their identified objects of interest. The boys' objects of interest also were more likely than the girls' to offer the possibility of different actions in transformational play.

Findings from this study are interpreted as indicating that children may see more possibilities for action when playing with an identified object of interest than they do in play with an identified object of noninterest. This explanation serves, in turn, to explain the increased variation in the types of play and repetition of particular action sequences in the children's play with identified objects of interest. These findings are also thought to indicate that particular play objects appear to represent possibilities for action to children that are not found in the other play objects with which they engage. That the children continue to re-engage their identified objects of interest, and to repeat particular patterns of action that incorporate systematic variations in these actions, and that these actions vary, even when children share the same identified object of interest, further suggests that the children are not only responding to the challenges that the play object affords, but that they are setting challenges for themselves with these play objects that build on their prior actions.

The finding that children who shared the same identified object of interest did not necessarily do the same things with that object supports the contention that the children's representations for actions are largely individual. The fact that there was overlap in the actions children employed also suggests that what the child represents to him or herself is probably related to the properties of the object, what others did with that play object, and/or gender. Repetition of particular patterns of action in play with identified objects of interest further suggests that the children are able to coordinate types of play in pursuit of a goal and, even when a particular goal is "unrealistic" (e.g., defying gravity in the effort to balance a block on an angle), that they can stay on task and reorganize their goals while exploring alternative possibilities for action. Moreover, that play lasted longer when the object was an identified object of interest also suggests that the child is more engaged in play, needs more time to explore and employ actions, and may even be less distractible when playing with an identified object of interest than when playing with an identified object of noninterest. Finally, the finding that children either did not repeat actions or only repeated the same actions with their identified objects of noninterest suggests that they are not representing as many possibilities for action to themselves with these objects and, as a result, are not invested in exploration.

These findings are further corroborated by Krapp and Fink (this volume), who reported that the structure of interests, or accustomed and highly preferred person–object relations, remains largely unaffected as a child moves from the family into kindergarten. Krapp and Fink found that whereas the new setting fostered the incorporation of new elements into existing person–object relations and within and among different person–object relations, it did not alter the impact of the particular person–object relation, or interest, on the child's pattern of actions.

Of particular importance to the present discussion is the role of interest in the development of children's understanding. It appears that interest as psychological state does influence children's activity. Furthermore, it appears that which play object is identified as the child's interest influences his or her activity as well.[3] That there are systematic differences that emerge between children with respect to the content of their interests, and then again when analyzed by play type with respect to the structure of play with identified interests, suggests that, at least for now, the influence of gender might be best understood as embedded in, rather than causally connected to the content of individual interests. Findings from this study do indicate that children's interests influence their representation of possibilities for action, and presumably their subsequent activity, because this activity in all likelihood will also reflect their interest.

Interest and Children's Play with Other Children. The studies described previously provide a strong argument for differences in what the child represents to him or herself as a function of an identified object of interest. However, the others in the class, who are also moving between and engaging with different play objects with their respective ideas about possibilities for action with these objects, are also an important part of the child–interest object relation. (For further discussion of social influences on children's interests, see Renninger, 1989.) Two studies that evaluate the particular relation of the child, interest object, and the other child(ren) during play have been conducted to date using different samples of children. In the first study (Renninger 1989), three coding schemes were employed.

---

[3] Whether something becomes an interest for a child because of his or her relationship with others is a question about origins that these data do not address.

First, the tapes were coded to identify objects of interest and noninterest for each child. Second, the tapes were coded to identify sustained exchanges (interactions that involved 3 or more turns) among dyads and these exchanges were then identified as synchronous or asynchronous based on the directing, rejecting, and following behaviors of each child in the interaction. Third, these tapes were coded to identify the affiliative behaviors (Blicharski & Strayer, 1985) for each child with every other child in the class.

Findings from this study that specifically relate to the effect of interest on sustained exchange around objects included: (a) children's sustained exchanges occurred most frequently around objects of interest for one but not both children; (b) children's sustained exchanges around a play object identified as an interest of one child but not the other child were most likely to be asynchronous; (c) in asynchronous exchanges around objects identified as being of interest for one but not both children, the child for whom the play object was an interest was more likely initially to direct action, to direct actions throughout the exchange, and to use nonverbal rather than verbal directives.

These findings indicate that children are making a distinction between play with identified objects of interest and noninterest, and this influenced their engagement with others. Because sustained exchanges occurred more frequently around objects of interest to one dyad member, there were significantly fewer exchanges between dyads when the object of play was of interest either to both or to neither of the children. This finding suggests that the identified object of interest exerts a powerful influence on the children's play. Presumably when an object is of interest to the child, the child has a clear idea about how the activity could and should unfold. Thus it is not surprising that these exchanges are usually asynchronous, involving more directing and rejecting behaviors on the part of the child for whom the object is an identified interest.

What is not so obvious, perhaps, is the finding that there were fewer sustained exchanges when the object was an identified interest for both of the children. However, it seems reasonable to assume that the reason there were so few of these exchanges is directly linked to the strength of the children's ideas about the possibilities for action. The strength of their ideas probably aborted potential interactions before they could be classified as such. Similarly, there might have been more instances of sustained exchanges around objects not of interest to either of the children if the children had had more of a sense of the possibilities for acting with those objects. That the identified exchanges were usually asynchronous, and as such had more directing and rejecting behaviors, suggests that the "other" child in these exchanges, the child for whom the object was not an interest, was willing to remain in the exchange because either the object or the other involved, or both, were attractions, and as such, potential interests.

Findings from this study suggest that what the children represent to themselves as potential action with objects of interest does influence how and perhaps with whom they engage in interaction. In order to evaluate how these findings might be qualified as the children develop and have more experience with both "their" objects and other children, a replication and extension of this study (Rothschild, Schwartz, & Renninger, 1989) with 10 children at both 3 and 4 years of age was conducted. Findings from this study revealed that children were likely: (a) to have the same interest at both 3 and 4 years of age, and (b) to increase the number of and to change their friends over the year. Like the findings from the previous study, these children also were more likely to have more asynchronous exchanges at age 4 than they were at age 3, and, regardless of age, sustained exchanges among friends were more likely to be more asynchronous than were those among associates.

A further analysis of the children's cooperation in play (cf. Hinde, 1979) indicated that interest for an object appeared to inversely influence the frequency of reciprocal and complementary sustained exchange at both 3 and 4 years of age, such that the children were more likely to engage in reciprocal play if the object of play was an interest of neither child, and were more likely to engage in complementary play if the object of play was an identified interest of both children. In fact, there appears to be an increased coordination of children's friendship around objects of interest at 4 years of age, suggesting that children are increasingly attentive to both the other and the object of exchange over time.

Findings from both of these studies suggest that interest fills an important role in the functioning of young children. Interest influences their actions with tasks, and the way in which they engage others around these tasks. Furthermore, these findings suggest that children have different stored knowledge and value, or interest for play objects and peer others, and that they engage the tasks these pose differently—even when the children are as familiar with all of the available play objects and peer others as is possible in a naturally occurring setting. At least among young children, it appears that interest does affect both the accessibility of tasks and the way in which the children complete these tasks.

Interest and Temperament. In order to further study the process of children's task engagement, a study of the effect of interest on young children's temperament was undertaken (Renninger & Leckrone, 1991). This study also included a contrast between interest, noninterest, and attraction—where interest is high knowledge with high value, noninterest is knowledge but little value, and attraction is low knowledge but high value. In this study, children's videotaped behaviors in free play were coded twice. Videotapes of 10 children were collected when the children were both 3 and 4 years of age. Individual interests, noninterests, and attractions were first identified for each child during each of the 2 years, and, following this, the children's play with each type of play object was rated for each of three dimensions of temperament: emotionality, sociability, and reactivity. Thus, for the purposes of this study, temperament was conceptualized as a set of concurrent responses to change in action.

Briefly, in order to study emotionality, the child's positive and negative arousal during play with an object was evaluated. Ratings of emotionality were based on the child's distractibility from play, tempo of play, attention to the flow of play, contributions to play, and immersion in play. In order to study sociability, the child's attempts to initiate interaction, the time spent with others, and reactions to being alone while playing with a given object were evaluated. Ratings of sociability were based on the child's ability to accommodate to another's actions in play, change in actions with an object to play with another, contributions made in play with another, expression of strong commitment to play with another, and initiation of a task with another. Finally, in order to study reactivity, the child's ability to reorganize actions during play in relation to either the play object or the peer other was evaluated. Ratings of reactivity were based on the child's distractibility from play, rhythm of play, attention to flow of play, return to flow of play, and immersion in play.

In summary, findings from this study suggest that children's interest and temperament are both relatively stable influences on actions at 3 and 4 years of age. All children retained at least one interest from age 3 to 4, and the levels of their emotionality, sociability, and reactivity at each age did not shift markedly. Moreover, the way in which children engaged tasks at both ages appeared to be consistently influenced by their levels of knowledge and value for the play object. Specifically, ratings for each of the dimensions of temperament and persistence were highest when the child played with an object of interest, next highest in play with a noninterest, and lowest in play with an attraction.

Within-child analyses, in which value for task was a repeated measure, indicated that under normal circumstances children's emotionality, sociability, and reactivity did not differ as a function of either value for the task (interest, noninterest, or attraction) or gender. Under conditions requiring persistence; however, value and gender did distinguish between the children's engagements. Specifically, (a) children were more likely to have higher levels of emotionality with tasks that were identified objects of interest, and girls were more likely than were boys to have higher levels of emotionality for objects identified as interest under conditions requiring persistence; (b) children were more likely to have higher levels of sociability when engaged with identified objects of interest, less with identified objects of noninterest, and least with identified objects of attraction under conditions requiring persistence; and (c) children were more likely to have higher levels of reactivity—to reorganize actions in play—when engaged with identified objects of interest, less with identified objects of noninterest, and least with identified objects of attraction under conditions requiring persistence.

These findings suggest that the information children have available to them as a function of experience is probably filtered by whether the situation in which the information was learned is stressful for them and the extent to which the information to be learned is of value. Information is more likely to be available to children if they acquire it in conjunction with their identified objects of interest because in play the child is continuously asking questions and setting challenges that center on these activities and which, presumably, invest them with value.

The differences in the emotional responses of girls and boys under conditions requiring persistence suggest further that girls may have stronger, or at least more observable, feelings about objects of interest. However, the lack of gender differences with respect to both sociability and reactivity under conditions of persistence suggest that girls are no more likely than boys to take on the challenges involved in engaging another or changing action in order to continue engagement with their identified object of interest. These findings are interpreted as suggesting that interest serves a particular cognitive function in the process of children's representation of possibilities for action. The extent to which such differences in emotion either contribute to or form the basis for children's representation of possibilities for activity remains an open question.

Implications for Theory. The findings reported here are all based on within-child comparisons: the role of each child's interest (high knowledge, high value) is directly compared to the role of his or her noninterest in (high knowledge, low value) and/or attraction (low knowledge, high value) to activity. The results from these studies indicate that children are more likely to have more attention and memory for objects identified as interests than they are for either noninterests or attractions. They are also more likely to be more systematic in their actions and to employ a wider range of play types in play with objects of interest. Furthermore, the presence of objects of interest influences children's social engagement with others as well as their persistence during play.

Using the children's own performance as the baseline of their performance (e.g., using within-child studies) and considering differences between the contexts of their activity (a play object of interest vs. a play object of noninterest) leads to a conclusion that children differ in what they chunk as information for later use and in the specific plans they generate as a function of whether the focus of their play is an identified object of interest or noninterest. Findings such as these call into question more traditional group-based evaluations of young children's learning that have led us to think, among other things, that young children are less likely than older children to chunk information for subsequent use, that they are less likely to be planful and/or strategic than are older children (cf. Folds, Footo, Guttentag, & Ornstein, 1990).

It appears that the objects with which a child plays provide a forum for pursuing learning about the properties of both those objects and the environment (including other children). A label such as *preoperational* status—suggesting that children are able to generate only one explanation for (way of understanding) an event (Piaget & Inhelder, 1969)—applies only to the limited number of objects to which they seem to be attending, and the fact that all of their hypothesizing generally has to do with their identified object of interest. At least with respect to their object of interest, children are able to entertain alternative activities and are, in fact, making choices about which object and which other(s) with whom to play. Thus, the present findings suggest that the questions and challenge setting that characterize interest engagements may well lead the child's development. These are the tasks to which children are more likely to be attentive and for which they have memory (Renninger & Wozniak, 1985), during which they repeatedly practice and develop a kind of vocabulary or repertoire of possible actions necessary to the kind of flexibility required for thinking about subsequent actions (Krapp & Fink, this volume; Renninger, 1989; Renninger & Leckrone, 1991).

In other words, children are actively involved in problem solving. They are setting and resetting challenges for themselves with their identified objects of interest. In fact, in play with an identified object of interest the child reflects the most complicated of the challenges with which he or she is currently engaged. However, an object that is of interest to one child is likely to be a noninterest for the next child, suggesting that whereas the individual object of interest of the young child can be considered a marker of his or her areas/domains of developmental strength, there are difficulties in assuming that the general use of toys in an experiment means that all children will be engaging with these similarly— thus possibly confounding experimental results—or that the provision of a couple of different play objects in a nursery/day care setting will adequately challenge the children served by that setting.

Implications for Practice. Free play appears to provide children with the opportunity to develop their basic knowledge about problem solving— the nature of relations (e.g , balance, sequence, etc.), representation, and action—through self-directed concentrated activity. Findings from the research presented here further suggest that a lot of this activity involves play with objects of interest. The use of thc same sample of children across several of these studies and replication of these studies using samples of children who also attended the same nursery school and played with the same play objects enables us to paint a rich picture of ways in which interest affects the cognitive and social development of young children.

Children in the present study had 2 hours of free play each morning that were facilitated (not directed) by teachers who used a "whole child" approach to the nursery-school environment. There was no intervention by the teachers in the play of the children, except for an occasional reminder to use words to express themselves. Furthermore, all 16 of the objects studied were available to the children every day, and in classrooms for both the 3- and the 4-year-olds there was always a novel art activity as well as at least one novel object available. In contrast, many nursery schools/day care centers limit the number of play objects available to children, the frequency of play object availability, and the chance for the child to decide what to do in "free" play. Thus, the findings from the present studies speak to what children do when they are allowed to set many of the parameters of their play/learning for themselves.

Given the powerful influence of interest across a wide variety of problem-solving contexts (e.g., play with objects; play with others; play in the face of distraction), it appears that constraining the range of objects available to children and/or directing their play may limit the development of their representational capabilities. (See Sigel, 1986, for a discussion of the importance of representational competence to young children's learning.) A child who is working on understanding a concept (e.g., balance), for example, may learn this concept (and even learn it better if he or she is able to work with/practice it across a range of play objects, instead of being limited to, say, the playdough and blocks that are the objects put out on the table on a given day. Furthermore, if a child works to understand balance using blocks on one day, and blocks are not available to him or her the next day, the child's attempts to understand this concept are not only thwarted but are only partially developed.

When given the opportunity to return to particular play objects, and to work through and develop/practice their knowledge about these objects over several weeks, all of the young children in the samples studied here appeared to be equally able to set and persist in trying to solve complex challenges for themselves with their identified objects of interest. It is in all likelihood the constraints of materials and time that cause children in classrooms with a smaller a variety of objects and more rigid time frames to falter in solidifying the attention and memory capacities (or intelligence) necessary to subsequent school success.

On the other hand, the findings from these studies further suggest that the children in the present samples might have profited from having both free play and more structured play time. Because children in free play are likely to play a great deal with their identified objects of interest, this could be considered a constraint on development. Thus it also might be useful to structure time into the day when the children are involved with objects with which they do not typically play. In this way they would also explore other objects and develop their attraction to and feelings of competence with these objects.

In addition, because children appear to learn about the possibilities for action with play objects from watching others and from developing joint goals in play with others, it might be worth thinking about when, in the child's day, alternative possibilities for activity might be introduced by simply reorganizing the others with whom they play around those play objects. Conversely, children might be helped to further their developing abilities to work with others through teacher reorganization of objects available to particular pairs/groups of children in free play.

In summary, then, it appears that children need time in their day to have a range of play objects available with which they set and reset challenges for themselves. At other points in the day, or when children encounter difficulty in their play, a teacher might consider facilitating their challenge setting through reorganizing the objects and the other children that are available. Instead of establishing an environment for children as "generic" preschoolers, the teacher might use the child's time in free play for observation, attending to his or her patterns of action and objects of apparent interest.[4] With such information, the teacher would then be in a position to adjust when and how the children's interest objects would be available in the more structured play period, and thereby to facilitate the development of each child's capabilities in light of his or her developmental strengths and weaknesses.

PROJECT 2:
INDIVIDUAL INTEREST AND FIFTH- AND SIXTH-GRADERS' READING COMPREHENSION AND MATHEMATICAL WORD PROBLEM SOLVING

In the second project, a series of studies of the role of individual interest in fifth- and sixth-graders' work with tasks involving reading comprehension and mathematical word problem solving was undertaken. The questions underlying these studies address the respective roles of interest, task difficulty, and gender in students' work with two well-articulated domains of school learning—reading and mathematics.

Briefly, the importance of further studying interest with fifth- and sixth-graders is that it permits a more specific contrast of interest and noninterest than does the work with young children's play interests and noninterests. As in the studies of the young children, identification of interest and noninterest is based on the level of each student's knowledge and value for a class of objects or activities relative to the other classes of objects/activities with which he or she is engaged. For the purposes of this

---

[4] It should be noted that the process of identifying interests for the purposes of empirical investigation is labor intensive; however, once trained, the observer knows what he or she is looking for and is able in most cases to identify interests on the basis of casual observations that are reliable with those identified by another who is coding those interests. Once trained, these individuals are in a position to use information about children's interests to adjust the questions they pose and the way they are able to individualize responses to children's frustrations, etc. Training of teachers of young children might usefully include work with identification of interest as employed in the studies described here.

study, a student's interests are those objects/activities for which he or she has both high knowledge and high value, and a student's noninterests are those objects/activities for which he or she has knowledge but low value. Thus, the contrast of interest and noninterest is not a contrast of knowledge and no knowledge but is instead a contrast of two types of prior knowledge: interest and noninterest.

There is substantial evidence that prior knowledge is useful to describe performance (e.g., Chiesi, Spilich, & Voss, 1979), to predict how information is chunked for subsequent recall (e.g., Chi, 1978), and to search material faster (Symmons & Pressley, 1990). Although it might be expected that with more prior knowledge an individual would in fact be led to better understanding and retention of material (Anderson, 1980; Entwhistle & Ramsden, 1983), the findings from the studies of young children (reported earlier in this chapter) have demonstrated a powerful influence of individual interest on young children's actions when contrast items were other play objects with which they were familiar. It seems reasonable to suggest that just because a person has knowledge of something, this does not necessarily mean that he or she has value for it— especially relative to the other things with which he or she is involved or on which he or she is being tested. Thus, the present study was designed to directly contrast individual interest and noninterest based on the assumption that there may be differences in the way in which prior knowledge is processed depending upon whether a task involves only knowledge, or both knowledge and value—or interest. In other words, whereas prior knowledge clearly informs task engagement, individual interest and noninterest may actually be an even more informative index for thinking about students' work with tasks.

Furthermore, because reading and mathematics are relatively well-articulated domains, it is possible to assess each individual student's mastery level (the level at which the student could complete the task independently) in these domains, and, similarly, an instructional level (the level at which the student would require assistance). This variable, task difficulty, was included as an independent variable in the present set of studies because it addresses the possibility raised by the studies of young children that interest leads learning. However, because there is no clear hierarchy of task performance with play objects (e.g., car, playdough, etc.), there is no way in the studies of the young children to evaluate to what extent the complexity of a task contributes to the influence of interest on a child's learning. Thus, the design of the present set of studies, which focuses specifically on domains with articulated levels of task difficulty, permits evaluation of whether students are engaging tasks (setting challenges for themselves) differently as a function of interest and task difficulty, or are experiencing the two in combination. Furthermore, whereas the use of "mastery" and "instructional" levels borrows terminology from reading instruction, together these levels are thought to describe a student's zone of proximal development (Vygotsky, 1978) for a given task. In the present set of studies, then, it was expected that these additional data would clarify links between the role of interest and students' developing capabilities with these tasks—links which were suggested by the study of the young children.

Finally, gender was included as an independent variable in the present set of studies for two reasons. First, gender differences did emerge as a function of interest among the young children with respect to the way in which they processed the possibilities for action with both objects and others. Second, previous study of interest in the research on reading has consistently demonstrated that both girls and boys do better on passages that evoke interest, but that boys are more helped by interest than are girls (cf. Asher, Hymel, & Wigfield, 1978; Asher & Markell, 1974). It seems reasonable to suspect that, together with the variables of interest and text difficulty, the extent to which gender differences are a function of interest might become clearer, whether these differences reflect the way in which the students process information, or if, in fact, there are differences in the challenges that girls and boys seem to be engaging.

General Procedures. In the studies described in this chapter (Renninger & Stavis, in preparation), the individual interests and noninterests of each student (N=222, 110M, 112F) were identified using a self-report Likert-type questionnaire that assessed the frequency of their knowledge of, value for, and activity with each of 40 items (e.g., soccer, swimming, listening to the radio, math, etc.). Interest(s) were identified as those activities with which the student did engage, and for which he or she had both more stored knowledge and more value relative to the other activities listed. Noninterests were identified as those activities with which the student engaged and for which he or she had knowledge but low value relative to other activities listed. Identification of interests (noninterests), then, like that for the young children, was based on individual actions of the students and was individually identified using the theoretical definition of interest as including both stored knowledge and value.[5]

Following identification of interests and noninterests, pretests were presented to the students in which the context of the passages and the problems were neutral. These neutral-context pretests were used to identify two levels of task difficulty (mastery—students need no assistance to complete the task successfully; instructional—students would need assistance to complete the task successfully) for each student on both the reading and the mathematics task. Following this, individualized target worksheets were developed for students that included both their identified interests and their noninterests as contexts embedded in the reading/mathematics task tailored to their individual mastery and the instructional level of problem solving in each domain.[6] The design of the worksheets in both reading and math was intended to permit consideration of the relations among value, difficulty, and gender in students' performance on these tasks. Students completed both the neutral-context pretest and the target worksheets in class as part of their ongoing classroom work.

Because the specific requirements of both reading and mathematics as domains differ, the specific methods and findings from the study of

---

[5] Nowhere during either the presentation of the questionnaire nor on the questionnaire itself were the words interest and noninterest used. In this way identification of interest and noninterest was matched as closely as possible to the theoretical definition of interest and was not necessarily reflective of a student's understanding of the words, interest or noninterest.

[6] Mastery and instructional levels were individually determined in each subject area using the following criteria. On the reading task, each student's mastery level referred to the highest "level" of reading task on which the student could both recall topic sentences and points from the passage. The student's instructional level passage was the next most difficult level passage. Passage levels were determined using a modified version of the Dale–Chall and Fry techniques for assessing readability. Passage level 1 was at the sixth-grade level. Passage level 2 was at the eighth-grade level. Passage level 3 was at the tenth-grade level. Passage level 4 was at the twelfth-grade level. On the mathematics task, each student's mastery level referred to the highest "level" of math problem solving on which the student correctly completed at least two of the three problems on the neutral worksheet. Students' instructional level was identified as that level of math problem solving on which student performance (based on type of error, e.g., set-up errors, computational errors, etc.) indicated that the student needed assistance to complete these problems. The "levels" of mathematical word problems included: level (1) one-step addition or subtraction; level (2) one-step multiplication or division; level (3) two-step addition or subtraction; and level (4) two-step multiplication or division. (Note: level here is a misnomer. It is not meant to imply that this particular sequence holds as a difficulty sequence for all children. Rather, assignment of mastery and instructional levels in mathematics followed the student's pattern of errors. As a result, a mastery level might have been 1 and the instructional level for the same student might have been 3.)

interest and reading are summarized first, followed by a summary of the methods and findings from the study of interest and mathematics.

Interest and Reading. The target reading worksheet was a modification of the reconstructive recall tasks employed by Anderson, Mason, and Shirey (1984). Students were presented with a total of four expository passages: one with a context that was an identified interest and one with a context that was an identified noninterest at the student's mastery level, and one with a context that was an identified interest and one with a context that was an identified noninterest at the student's instructional level.

The structural features of each of the passages were similar. Each passage consisted of three paragraphs. The first paragraph was a generalization that set up a comparison/contrast text structure (cf. Cook & Mayer, 1988). The second and third paragraphs were comparison/contrast in their organization. Thus, for example, the passage on fishing focused on the importance of the rod and line; the first paragraph provided basic information about fishing, the last sentence of the first paragraph set up the importance of the rod and the line to fishing. The second paragraph focused on the rod; the third paragraph focused on the line.

All of the passages contained three paragraphs, each of which had between three and five points, all were approximately the same length, and all addressed an aspect of the topic that was identified as not being common knowledge to someone who was familiar with that topic (thus, the students were in fact being asked to recall information they had just read, rather than information they already knew). The teachers directed the students to read the passage first. Then they were asked to turn the page and answer two buffer questions (e.g., name two people in your class whom you consider to be leaders). Finally, they were asked to write down as much of the passage as they could remember.

In summary, as in the findings from the studies of the young children, student responses to the questionnaire about their knowledge, value, and activity indicated that their interests and noninterests did vary and that one student's interest was likely to be another student's noninterest. A series of 2 (value: interest or noninterest) X 2 (task: mastery or instructional) X 2 (sex) MANOVAs in which both value and task were repeated measures were employed to evaluate the relation of students' value/interest for the context of the passage, level of task difficulty, gender, and reading performance. Dependent variables were: points remembered, sentences written, paragraphs represented, presence and completeness of overall gist, paragraph gists recalled, order of recall (maintained, mixed chunks, mixed, not enough written to code), and types of errors made (no errors, inclusion of extra relevant details, extraneous information, miscombined information, mislabeled information, misread information, misremembered information, misunderstood information).

Findings from these analyses indicated that students were more likely to recall more points, recall information from more paragraphs, recall more topic sentences, write more sentences, provide more detailed information about topics read, have no errors on their written recall, and provide additional topic-relevant information on passages of interest than on those of noninterest. Such findings suggest that information from the passages of interest was more easily accessed, or perhaps more efficiently chunked for subsequent recall than was information from passages of noninterest. Not surprisingly, students were also more likely to misunderstand or only recall information from one paragraph on passages of noninterest rather than on those of interest, suggesting that student inaccuracy and depressed recall was more characteristic of their work with passages of noninterest than passages of interest.

Despite the influence of value/interest on the accuracy of students' work in this task, there were no effects of task difficulty when students were accurate in their recall. In other words, if the students were accurate in their recall, they were no more likely to be accurate on the mastery than on the instructional level tasks. However, task difficulty did affect the likelihood that students would include a variety of detail and be more systematic in their recall of mastery than of instructional-level passages. Students were also more likely to be influenced by the difficulty of the passages they received, such that they were more likely to represent all three paragraphs in recall, recall the passage in mixed order or mixed chunks (or not write enough to identify the order of their recall), or to include more editorial comments on instructional-level passages than on mastery-level passages. It appears that as a result students distinguish between paragraphs based on their difficulty, that they perhaps try harder to recall more, and perhaps chunk information for recall differently for the mastery and instructional-level passages. This interpretation is supported by an increased number of editorial comments about instructional-level passages, which suggest that the students are focusing on the instructional-level passages differently than on the mastery-level passages.

On the other hand, two gender by difficulty interactions emerged that further suggest that interest and task difficulty present different types of challenges for students as a function of gender. Specifically, boys were more likely to misread and include more detailed information about mastery passages, and girls were more likely to misread and to be more detailed in their recall of instructional-level passages. In terms of what is being chunked for recall, it seems that whereas both boys and girls are presumably representing and chunking information for recall similarly, they are setting different kinds of challenges for themselves in their work with the reading task. Considering these results together with findings regarding the role of interest in the students' performance, it appears that for boys the optimal reading task may include an interesting context and be at the mastery level, whereas for girls an optimal task may include an interesting context and be at the instructional level.

In summary, it appears that students have an easier time engaging (or being distracted by) contexts of interest than contexts of noninterest. It seems that interest may actually serve to enable the student to adjust the level of the passage such that it actually becomes easier even when it is technically—with a neutral context—an instructional level passage. This interpretation provides support for Paris and Cross' (1988) notion of wider and narrower zones of proximal development. In this instance, a context of interest would support a wider zone than would a context of noninterest between the task that a student could complete independently (the mastery level) and the task that a student could complete with assistance (the instructional level).[7]

The notion that the level of the passage is adjusted by the student as a function of interest is further supported by the finding that students were more likely to be more accurate and more detailed in their recall of passages of interest than passages of noninterest. Such findings suggest that students could take on greater challenges if the context of the passage were of interest. It seems that it is the value for the context of the passage—not its difficulty level or the gender of the student—which enables students to be more accurate. Furthermore, if we look specifically at the pattern of their errors, these primarily involve misreading and lack of recall on passages of noninterest. Such findings also provide support for the notion that the students' interest and noninterest renders the passage more or less difficult for them in a way that the actual structure of the passage does not.

---

[7] It should be noted that assessment of the zone of proximal development (zpd) is generally undertaken by someone other than the individual whose zpd is being determined. In its present use, however, zpd describes differences in the way in which students represent (the same) tasks to themselves, as a function of interest, task difficulty, and/or gender.

Presumably it is the effectiveness of students' ability to chunk information as a function of their interest that leads to differing zones of proximal development despite structurally similar passages. On the other hand, the finding that girls and boys differed with respect to their attention to details (in either misreading or recalling them) suggests that this chunked information can be either a scaffold that improves performance or a distraction that hampers performance. Clearly, interest can be described as integral to students' reading performance, but its effect, depending on the variable under consideration, the difficulty level of the passage, and the gender of the student, may or may not be an asset to actual performance.

Interest and Mathematical Word Problem Solving. The mathematics task included a total of 12 word problems, 3 with interesting contexts and 3 with noninteresting contexts at the student's mastery level, and 3 with contexts that were identified interests and 3 with contexts that were identified noninterests at the student's instructional level. The structure of each of the assigned problems with contexts of identified interests matched the structure of each of the assigned problems with contexts that were identified noninterests. Only the context of the problem and the numbers used varied. Thus, for example, a problem structure that required that a student multiply 2 digits by 2 digits might be alternately posed as a problem in which the context was MTV, "One performer has 18 rock videos out. In each of the videos, there are 12 scene changes. How many scene changes are there in the videos?" or as a problem in which the context was basketball, "The basketball captain scored 24 points in each game. There were 14 games in the season. How many points did the captain score during the season?" etc.

The number of steps involved in problem solution was controlled across problems, as were sex of agent, keyword employed, number of sentences, order of information needed, vocabulary, length of words, and location of the missing value. All worksheets were formatted to look like those on which the students normally worked in their classes. The directions asked students to complete the problems on the worksheet showing all of their work.

In summary, as mentioned before, students' responses to the questionnaire about their knowledge, value, and activity indicate that students' interests and noninterests varied; one student's interest was likely to be another student's noninterest. A series of 2 (value: interest or noninterest) X2 (task: mastery or instructional) X2 (sex) MANOVAs in which both value and task were repeated measures was employed to evaluate the relation among value, task difficulty, gender, and mathematics performance. Dependent variables were: accuracy and each type of error (computation, copying, incomplete set-up, set-up, skipped parentheses) .[8]

Findings from these analyses indicate that students were more likely to be more accurate in completion of mastery than instructional problems. Where they had difficulties, these appeared to occur on instructional problems. Specifically, these errors involved setting the problem up generally, or only partially setting it up (incomplete problem set-up). Two two-way interactions of value and gender further suggest, however, that boys are more likely to have fewer set-up problems or to set the problem up only partially on interesting problems, whereas girls are more likely to have fewer set-up difficulties with noninteresting problems. No differences as a function of value, task difficulty, or gender emerged for errors involving computation, copying, or skipping the problem.

Unlike the reading task on which students' accuracy was influenced by interest and for which task difficulty was not an influence, on the mathematics task students were most able to respond accurately to mastery problems, although interest and gender did influence their approaches to these problems as well. These findings suggest that interest and gender do influence students' willingness to try to work at or to persevere in comprehending/solving mathematical word problems. The boys made more errors in setting up noninteresting problems, presumably because interest is more likely to assist in understanding these problems. The girls, on the other hand, made more errors in setting up interesting problems, presumably because interest is more likely to be a distraction than an aid on these tasks.

Interestingly enough, when the students had no difficulty with problem set-up, there were no gender differences in performance on the mathematical word problems. That the gender differences are linked specifically to problem set-up provides support for the notion that the students represent task expectations to themselves differently. Their difficulties are not in the mechanics of copying, computation, etc. It appears that, like the gender differences reported among the younger children, the gender differences in these students' problem solving reflect differences in the specific challenges they set for themselves with these

---

[8] Students typically made only one type of error. Even when students did not show their work, it was possible to determine by their answers where they had made mistakes.

problems. In other words, even though the students are presented the same (or similar) problems and presumably represent information to themselves similarly, the way in which they proceed to work on these problems (including the repertoire of strategies and questions they bring to their work) actually renders them different problems—especially when the context of the problem is an interest.

Implications for theory. In a recent paper, Hidi (1990) claims that situational interests or topics that contribute to the interestingness of text differ from what have been identified as the important elements of text in at least two ways. She reviews evidence to suggest that interest is central to determining how individuals select and persist in processing certain types of information in preference to others. In addition, she suggests that processing interesting information involves elements that are not present when processing information that lacks such interest. Findings from both the reading and mathematics portions of this study support Hidi's thesis. Furthermore, the finding that student performance varies as a function of the student's individual interest, individual level of task difficulty, and gender further suggests that interest affects not only the accessibility of tasks for students, but it results in students approaching the same task structures as radically different problems.[9] Thus it is not surprising that students make different mistakes, that at times they respond differently to tasks that are at mastery and instructional levels, and that at times they respond differently to tasks as a function of gender.

On the other hand, the student is not only engaging in a task when he or she works on a passage or a word problem. He or she is confronting the structure of a domain and a canon for its instruction. When interviewed following the completion of data collection with the students, the teachers of the fifth- and sixth-graders studied here reported that in reading instruction they typically ask students to focus on understanding the context of text (i.e., what it is about), whereas in mathematics instruction, they are more likely to direct students to the content (i.e., the numbers, operations, etc.) of the problem. Given the teachers' foci, the finding that interest is a particular influence in reading and less so in mathematics, whereas task difficulty is a particular influence in mathematics and less so in reading, appears to parallel the way in which the students are taught.

---

[9] Here "problem" is used in the broad sense to refer to task structure and requirements for task solution in both reading and mathematics.

If the focus of instruction involves questions about context, it follows that individual interest embedded in context will affect performance. If, on the other hand, the focus of instruction involves practice with content, then it follows that individual interest could influence performance, but that its effect will be connected less to instruction than to the salience of interest. As such, the finding that interest influences reading as strongly as it does is perhaps less interesting than the finding that interest influences word problem-solving performance. That any differences emerge, however, in the contrast of contexts of interest and noninterest, is significant given that both include student knowledge. Such findings suggest, much in the same vein as Mandler's (1975) discussion of affect, that interest is an even more compelling way in which to discuss student learning than is prior knowledge of the content.

Clearly, students need to be able to work with contexts that match both their individual interests and their noninterests. It is adaptive for students to learn to disembed the passages/word problems from their context, especially because schooling typically does not facilitate either the development or the maintenance of students' interest(s).[10] However, a distinction needs to be made between the role of interest in learning the vocabulary and skills of a domain and the expected performance of an expert or "good strategy user," to borrow Pressley's (1986) terminology.

From a developmental perspective, all learners start out needing to acquire vocabulary and skills and are aided by first learning these skills in contexts that match their individual interests. Once a basic understanding of concepts has been acquired (meaning that the students can ask questions and set alternative hypotheses with this information—such as the multiple dimensions of concept understanding built into the Whole Language and Language Experience approaches to reading comprehension, or Math Their Way or Bag It and Box It Mathematics), they are then in a position to disembed contexts. The issue that the present findings raise, however, is whether subsequent learning should focus on contexts that are of individual interest or noninterest, and at what levels of text difficulty.

---

[10] This is not to suggest that schools should continue this practice, but rather that it is the current state of affairs. Based on Dewey's (1963) seminal thinking in this area, it appears that in order to facilitate the development of student interest schools would need to be reorganized to: (a) provide students with time to pursue their individual curiosities; (b) encourage students to be divergent thinkers; (c) provide students with choice about which text to read and when to read it; and (d) use students' individual interests as a basis for all other learning.

In the present study, for students who made mistakes on the reading or mathematics tasks, interest appears to account for their level of willingness to engage the task and persevere on it. However, at the more "expert level," it was only in mathematics that the results indicated that students were actually able "to overcome" or attend to the content of the task such that accuracy was not as likely to be a function of interest or gender. This was not the case for reading where students were more accurate on interesting passages regardless of task difficulty or gender. The reasons for differences in the role of interest in each of these domains remain an open question, although speculation suggests that how reading is taught (not necessarily what research has suggested about teaching reading) and student performance, as well as the nature of "expertise" in each of these domains, could be useful foci for further investigation. In addition, as Hidi and Anderson (this volume) suggest in their discussion of similar differences between students' performance on reading and writing tasks, such differences may be attributed to the attentional demands of the task.

Whereas it is the student who represents information to him or herself and who articulates the challenges in the task, the range of possibilities for how a task is understood appears to be limited by the vocabulary and skills—the parameters—the student has for engaging that task. The present studies suggest that there are differences between individual students' representations of the challenges posed by these tasks that contribute to individual zone(s) of proximal development but do not obviate the possibility of identifying a zone of proximal development for a group of students: such a zone would still be individual to that group, not "generic" to all, say, fifth- and sixth-graders. Based on the present findings, the articulation of a zone for the purposes of organizing instruction cannot be understood only in terms of the task that the student does (or does not) engage, but needs to account for individual interest (for the task as well as its context), for what the student does understand of the task, as well as gender.

Like the interest of young children, which is so influential that it appears to lead their development, the interest of fifth- and sixth-graders serves as a kind of scaffold for tasks in which students' own understanding of the domain is not well developed. As students develop more expertise in these domains, it might be expected that the role of interest would change, such that the student would become more able to separate interest in the context of the passage or problem from the task requirements that the passage or problem represents.

Implications for practice. The findings from these studies suggest that interest, task difficulty, and gender are important to students' performance. Interest, in particular, has the possibilities of both aiding and distracting students' engagement in tasks. It appears that not only is there a need for teachers (parents, caretakers, clinicians, etc.) to recognize that interest informs subsequent activity, but that, together with task difficulty and gender, it makes a critical contribution to the quality of students' learning.

In order to work with individual interest and level of task understanding either individually or within a group setting, these findings suggest that where students need work on skills teachers might most profitably employ tasks with interesting contexts at students' mastery levels. Here the assumption is that no one topic will be an interest for all students, but that students would all receive practice with a task that specifically included contexts of interest to them at some point early in their work with the task.

As students become more competent with mastery-level tasks, they might then be presented with increasingly more difficult tasks. However, based on the pattern of students' performance in the studies overviewed here, two slightly different sequences of task presentation are suggested for working with students on tasks of reading comprehension and mathematical word problem solving.

If the task were reading comprehension, the teacher might move from work with students on comprehending interesting mastery-level passages to interesting instructional-level passages, before moving to noninteresting mastery-level passages, and, finally, to noninteresting instructional-level passages. If the task were mathematical word problems, on the other hand, the teacher might proceed from work with the students on mastery problems with interesting contexts to work on mastery problems with noninteresting contexts, followed by instructional problems with interesting contexts, and, finally, instructional problems with noninteresting contexts. Here the teacher would focus generally on the individual student's performance with the task, looking particularly closely at inaccurate performance on passages/problems that were of interest and noninterest as cues to the student's "faulty" rules—rules that make sense logically to the student, but that are inappropriate to the task at hand from the perspective of a more expert other (e.g., the teacher). This would provide the teacher with information about the nature of the students' present understanding of the task and suggest possibilities for ways in which the teacher could continue to work with the student.

Although both sequences for instruction emphasize the ease of mastery tasks with interesting contexts, the findings from the study of individual interest and reading suggest that interesting instructional-level reading tasks are less difficult for students than are noninteresting mastery-level reading tasks. Conversely, noninteresting mastery-level word problems are less difficult for students than are interesting instructional-level word problems. These sequences have obvious implications for thinking about adjustment of instruction to meet student needs: if student performance bears out differences between students in their understanding of the task, then the student should be asked to continue working with interesting/noninteresting contexts until he or she is ready to take on the challenge of the alternate context and begin work on disembedding the context of the task from its structure in order to successfully complete the task.

Teachers can organize the sequence of their curriculum to meet the explicit needs of weaker students and through this challenge the stronger students. In other words, it is possible for the teacher to work with students who are weak in a particular skill by using contexts and levels of problems that are individualized to those students' needs. This apparent lack of individualization for students who are "stronger" is also actually effective individualization, since the situation provides opportunities for these students to develop their abilities to work with what are for them noninteresting and increasingly difficult tasks.

Another way in which the teacher might, as a matter of course, assign students tasks with different contexts and difficulty levels would be to include cooperative learning techniques such as Aronson's (1978) jigsaw method into their work with their classes. Briefly, in reading this might involve assigning a text to students based on context and/or difficulty, having students work together to further develop their understanding of the text, and then regrouping the students to teach other students about the text. In mathematics, this might involve assigning sets of problems to students based on context and difficulty, having students work together to develop proficiency on those problem types, and then regrouping the students to share their work with and learn from other students.

As an expert, the teacher is in a position to adjust instruction to meet the needs of students. This requires that the teacher disengage from his or her interests (own way of organizing material), observe how students are interpret and complete assigned problems, and then help them acquire the strategies necessary to master the tasks or questions as they were assigned—or the challenges they were originally intended to involve. Thus the organization that the teacher may need to assume involves responding to what students appear to understand of the tasks they are assigned. In turn, this may involve adjustment of the task and/or work with students around understanding the task as presented (cf. Feurstein, 1980; Rogoff, 1990; Sigel, 1982). This further suggests that teachers should be aware that their own interests probably affect the kinds of questions they ask and the challenges they set for themselves in teaching.

CONCLUSIONS:
INDIVIDUAL INTEREST IN LEARNING AND DEVELOPMENT

Although there are probably more similarities than there are differences in the way in which individuals process information, differences that do exist between students in the way in which they understand tasks can be major stumbling blocks for both the students and those with whom they work. Rather than focusing on patterns typical of groups of students, the present chapter has focused on the individual nature of children's/students' contributions to and involvements with learning, because these can begin to provide a framework for understanding the variation in ongoing classroom life.

Briefly, findings from the studies of young children presented here indicate that: (a) all children can be identified as having individual interests and noninterests; (b) among children, objects of interest and noninterest vary; (c) interests and noninterests do affect the way in which children engage and perform on tasks, as well as the demands and potentials which they understand these tasks to include; (d) interest influences the content of information the child has for subsequent activity; and (e) interest influences the process of children's play with others, especially under conditions that require persistence. These findings are discussed as providing support for thinking about young children's learning and development as being led by the kinds of challenges they undertake, specifically challenges in relation to their identified objects of interest.

Based on findings from the two projects overviewed here, however, the role of interest appears to shift from a kind of blanket-effect in which young children are continuously engaged with and learning through their play with identified objects of interest to a more subtle, albeit pervasive influence of interest on fifth- and sixth-grade students' performance. Findings from the studies of the fifth- and sixth-grade students indicate that, like the younger children, all students could be identified as having individual interests and noninterests. In contrast to the relatively few objects (typically 2 out of 16 play objects) of interest identified for young children, however, the older students could be identified as having as many as 6 identified interests and noninterests. In other words, notwithstanding the cross-sectional comparison, it appears that over time students' interests become increasingly diversified. Interestingly enough, however, this increased diversity of interest in no way leads to similarity between children as to which activities might be identified interests and noninterests.

Like the findings from study of young children, individually identified interests and noninterests embedded in the contexts of tasks do influence the way in which the fifth- and sixth-grade students engage in and complete tasks. However, the additional variable of task difficulty and study of students' performance across two discrete domains—reading comprehension and mathematical word problem solving—further suggests that the older students engage in these tasks differently, and that the challenges they represent to themselves in these tasks differ. For these students, interest can be considered a scaffold in that it makes a task more accessible; however, it may or may not be a positive influence on the process of their completion of tasks, depending on the level of task difficulty and the students' gender. The influence of interest is particularly salient when students are in the process of developing the vocabulary and skills that are critical to understanding the bases of domains such as reading and mathematics. A long-range goal of more expert performance in each of these domains presumably includes the ability to overcome the influence of context on performance—a development that may be most effectively acquired through a teacher's adjustment of instruction that includes attention to individual interest.

The current tendency of teachers (and textbooks) to simply employ "baseball" passages or word problems as a means of engaging their students is fraught with misconceptions. It is based on the assumption that students all engage passages/problems in the same way, that they share the same interests, and that studying texts results in learning. Findings from the present studies indicate that, whereas the process of students' representation is probably similar, the specific content of these representations can vary. Students do not share the same interests; in fact, one student's interest is likely to be another student's noninterest. Finally, given differences in student interest, "interesting" text does not necessarily lead to learning—the student learns as a function of how he or she poses the challenges of that text to him or herself.

In contrast to discussions posed by both Carey (1955) and Spender (1984), who point out that baseball as a typically male avocation is an unfair topic to use for classroom purposes, the pattern of gender differences reported here suggests instead that boys who are interested in baseball would be greatly aided in their completion of these tasks, as would girls for whom baseball is a noninterest, especially if the tasks were difficult for the students. On the one hand, baseball as the sole focus of a passage or word problem is not a specifically unfair topic to select, because girls as well as boys like and play and have an interest in baseball. On the other hand, baseball would be an unfair topic to select because students have differing interest for baseball and this affects how they are able to engage in the task assigned.[11] The only way in which such a task is not "unfair" is if the teacher's purpose is to engage particular students in learning to disembed the content from the context of the passages/problems. In such a case, it is presumed that the students would have received passages/problems of interest to them on previous occasions (as part of the sequences tailored to their needs) and this set of tasks with baseball has a particular purpose related to the learning needs of the students.

Clearly, longitudinal evaluation would further knowledge about the importance of particular content and specific configurations of possibilities (Piaget, 1987) or challenges that characterize an individual's task engagement and the extent to which these could be said to vary as a function of interest. It would also permit an evaluation of shifts in interest over time and a determination of whether they are most appropriately identified with objects or perhaps more appropriately with possibilities afforded by particular engagements. On the other hand, case studies and protocol analyses of individuals engaged in tasks allowing manipulation of interest and noninterest would offer additional insights about access to and storage of information, and the depth of processing that characterizes individual performance across tasks.

The present findings provide strong support for individual interest as having a critical role in the learning and development of both younger and older students. Interest is not a variable that can be dropped from either analysis or ongoing classroom functioning—it is present whether it is accounted for or not. Instead, knowledge of individual interest is critical

---

[11] With the exception of football and ballet, no real gender stereotypes emerged across the 40 possible activities used to identify students interests and noninterests in Project 2.

to understanding the way a student is functioning, and for thinking about ways in which to work more effectively with all students.

ACKNOWLEDGMENTS

The research reported in this chapter has been supported through grants from the National Academy of Education Spencer Fellowship Program, the Eugene M. Lang Faculty Fellowship Fund, the Swarthmore College Faculty Research Fund, and four Joel Dean Fellowships for student research assistance. Portions of this chapter have been presented as parts of papers at the meetings of the Jean Piaget Society (1983, 1988, 1989, 1991), the Society for Research in Child Development (1987, 1989), and the American Educational Research Association (1988, 1989, 1990). I would like to thank Usha Balamore, Marijka Gossens, Herbert Kerns, Barbara L. Klock, Thomas G. Leckrone, Russell Marcus, Ann Morgan, Melanie Philpot, Tessa Prattos, Rachel Rothschild, Marlene Schwartz, and Jane Stavis for their research assistance on the studies presented.

REFERENCES

Anderson, J. (1980). *Cognitive psychology and its implications.* San Franscisco: Freeman.

Anderson, R. C., Mason, J., & Shirey, L. (1984). The reading group: An experimental investigation of a labyrinth. *Reading Research Quarterly, 20,* 6–37.

Aronson, E. (1978). *The jigsaw classroom.* Beverly Hills, CA: Sage.

Asher, S. R., Hymel, S., & Wigfield, A. (1978). Influence of topic interest on children's reading comprehension. *Journal of Reading Behavior, 10,* 35–47.

Asher, S. R., & Markell, R. A. (1974). Sex differences in comprehension of high- and low-interest reading material. *Journal of Educational Psychology, 66* (5), 680–687.

Blicharski, T., & Strayer, F. F. (1985). *Procedures and taxonomy for observation of preschool social ecology.* Unpublished coding manual.

Carey, G. L. (1955). Sex differences in problem solving performance as a function of attitude differences. *Journal of Abnormal and Social Psychology, 56,* 256–260.

Chi, M. T. H. (1978). Knowledge structure and memory development. In R. Siegler (Ed.), *Children's thinking: What develops?* Hillsdale, NJ: Lawrence Erlbaum Associates.

Chiesi, H. L., Spilich, G. J., & Voss, J. F. (1979). Acquisition of domain-related information in relation to high and low domain knowledge. *Journal of Verbal Learning and Verbal Behavior, 18,* 257–274.

Cook, L. K., & Mayer, R. E. (1988). Teaching readers about the structure of scientific text. *Journal of Educational Psychology, 80* (4), 448–456.

Dewey, J. (1963). *Experience and education.* New York: Collier Books.

Entwhistle, N. J., & Ramsden, P. (1983). *Understanding student learning.* London: Croom Helm.

Feurstein, R. (1980). *Instrumental enrichment: An intervention program for cognitive modifiability.* Baltimore: University Park Press.

Fink, B. (1991). Interest development as structural change in person–object relationships. In L. Oppenheimer & J. Valsiner (Eds.), *The origins of action: Interdisciplinary and international perspectives.* New York: Springer–Verlag.

Folds, T. H., Footo, M. M., Guttentag, R. E., & Ornstein, P. A. (1990). When children mean to remember: Issues of context specificity, strategy effectiveness, and intentionality in the development of memory. In D. F. Bjorklund (Ed.), *Children's strategies: Contemporary views of cognitive development* (pp. 67–92). Hillsdale, NJ: Lawrence Erlbaum Associates.

Ginsburg, H. (1977). *Children's arithmetic: How they learn it and how you teach it.* Austin, TX: Pro-ed.

Hidi, S. (1990). Interest and its contribution as a mental resource for learning. *Review of Educational Research, 60* (4), 549–571.

Hinde, R. (1979). *Towards understanding relationships.* London: Academic Press.

Karmiloff–Smith, A. (1974–1975). If you want to get ahead, get a theory. *Cognition, 3* (3), 195–212.

Mandler, G. (1975). *Mind and emotion.* New York: Wiley.

Mead, G. H. (1934). *Mind, self, and society from the standpoint of a social behaviorist.* Chicago: University of Chicago.

Paris, S. G., & Cross, D. R. (1988). The zone of proximal development: Virtues and pitfalls of a metaphorical representation of children's learning. In S. L. Golbeck & K. A. Renninger (Eds.), *Representation and learning. The Genetic Epistemologist* (XVI [1], pp. 27–37).

Piaget, J. (1940). *The mental development of the child.* In D. Elkind (Ed.), *Six psychological studies.* New York: Random House.

Piaget, J. (1981). *Intelligence and affectivity: Their relationship during child development.* Palo Alto, CA: Annual Reviews.

Piaget, J. (1987). *Possibility and necessity, Volume 1: The role of possibility in cognitive development.* Minneapolis: University of Minnesota Press.

Piaget, J., & Inhelder, B. (1969). *The psychology of the child.* New York: Basic Books.

Prawat, R. S. (1989). Promoting access to knowledge, strategy, and disposition in students: A research synthesis. *Review of Educational Research, 59* (1), 1–41.

Pressley, M. (1986). The relevance of the good strategy user model to the teaching of mathematics. *Educational Psychologist, 21,* 139–161.

Renninger, K. A. (1989). Individual patterns in children's play interests. In L. T. Winegar (Ed.), *Social interaction and the development of children's understanding* (pp.147–172). Norwood, NJ: Ablex.

Renninger, K. A. (1990). Children's play interests, representation, and activity. In R. Fivush & J. Hudson (Eds.), *Knowing and remembering in young children* (pp. 127–165). Emory Cognition Series (Vol. III). Cambridge, MA: Cambridge University Press.

Renninger, K. A., & Leckrone, T. G. (1991). Continuity in young children's actions: A consideration of interest and temperament. In L. Oppenheimer & J. Valsiner (Eds.), *The origins of action: Interdisciplinary and international perspectives* (pp. 205–238). New York: Springer–Verlag.

Renninger, K. A., & Stavis, J. (in preparation). *Individual interest as context in tasks of reading comprehension and mathematical word problem solving.*

Renninger, K. A., & Wozniak, R. H. (1985). Effect of interest on attentional shift, recognition, and recall in young children. *Developmental Psychology, 21*, 624–632.

Rogoff, B. (1990). *Apprenticeship in thinking.* New York: Oxford University Press.

Rothschild, R., Schwartz, M., & Renninger, K. A. (1989, June). *Interest and friendship in children's sustained exchanges at 3 and 4 years of age.* Paper presented at the Jean Piaget Society, Philadelphia.

Sigel, I. E. (1982). The relationship between parents' distancing strategies and the child's cognitive behavior. In L. M. Laosa & I. E. Sigel (Eds.), *Families as learning environments for children*, New York: Plenum Press.

Sigel, I. E. (1986). *Early social experience and the development of representational competence. New directions for child development* (pp. 49–65). San Francisco: Jossey Bass.

Spender, D. (1984). *Invisible women: The schooling scandal.* Writers and Readers Publishing Cooperative.

Vygotsky, L. S. (1967). Play and its role in the mental development of the child. *Soviet Psychology, 3*, 62–76.

Vygotsky, L. S. (1978). *Mind in society: The development of higher psychological processes.* Cambridge, MA: Harvard University Press.

16

The Development and Function of Interests During the Critical Transition from Home to Preschool

Andreas Krapp and Benedykt Fink
Universität der Bundeswehr – Munich

For most children, beginning school is an important developmental step. Bronfenbrenner (1979) speaks of an "environmental transition," where the child moves from a familiar world to a world that is unknown. This new world involves increased social contact with teachers and peers, new conditions in the physical environment (places, rooms, physical objects), and modified norms and role expectations. Increased contact with peers allows for new friendships. Teachers make demands on the child that require an extension or modification of the child's previous conception of his or her role. It seems reasonable that so many changes in types of interaction with the surroundings could lead to feelings of anxiety in the child. It is with good reason, then, that the terms *critical life experience* (Filipp, 1981) and *critical transition*, in the sense of the "organismic developmental approach" (Kaplan, Wapner, & Cohen, 1976), have been used to designate such a change.

In order to adapt adequately to the demands of this new setting, the child must develop coping strategies. Generally this leads to an extension of competence and determines how the child engages with his or her surroundings. This lays the foundation for a reorganization of what is called herein a child's person–object relations. Young children, however, are quite diverse in their willingness and ability to undertake such adaptation. Differences among children with respect to adaptation might be attributed to several factors. Two of the most critical factors are previous experiences with the environment, and the strategies for dealing with new situations that have developed as a result.

Research in the fields of curiosity (Voss & Keller, 1983; Keller & Schneider, in press) and attachment (Papousek, 1984) has shown that a child in an unfamiliar situation feels more comfortable and is more likely to exhibit exploratory behavior when there is a personal "security base" from which to operate (Ainsworth, Blehar, Waters, & Wall, 1978). The security base can be the presence of a trusted person, or special objects with which the child has developed a special relation (e.g., a doll, a certain toy, or a favorite blanket; Brody, 1980; Passman & Weisberg, 1975; Winnicott, 1953). The trusted person or treasured object can give the child a secure base for interaction. The child can then return to that base if the engagement with unfamiliar surroundings proves too difficult or evokes feelings of anxiety that are too strong.

In this chapter, we take the position that the child's interests often represent an anchor that helps in managing the critical transition from home life to preschool or kindergarten. The child's interests delineate the types of objects and possibilities of action with which the child is familiar and feels competent. Through these feelings of familiarity and competence, the child is able to bridge difficult social situations by commanding the attention and admiration of other children and arousing their curiosity, thereby establishing new social contacts. Childhood interests, therefore, may be described as independent variables that help to explain a more or less successful adaptation to a new life situation.

It is possible to reverse this theoretical relation. Interests might then become the dependent variables, with their form and strength being influenced by the new experiences and action possibilities found in the preschool. This approach opens important avenues of research in the fields of developmental theory and education. The question arises, for instance, whether and to what extent the modification of interests aids or hinders overall development of social behavior or cognitive abilities. Related to this is the question of how continuity or discontinuity in interest strength can be evaluated in terms of how well a child manages the critical transition. On the one hand, high stability over time may indicate successful management of the critical transition, especially when interests continue to develop and lead to increasing competence. On the other hand, stability may indicate fixation or stagnation, and might even signify an inability to profit from the stimulation of the new environment, to investigate new types of objects, and to extend personal competencies.

This chapter describes an exploratory study based on data from individual cases that attempts to shed light on the development of interests during the transition from home to preschool. Among other research questions, this study attempts to document the importance of the child's "object relations" (interests) in managing critical transitions, and to analyze how the new life situation effects the origin and early development of interests. The theoretical background for this research consists of a "person–object conception" of interest. In the following, the discussion focuses first on this conceptualization of interest, then describes the purpose, methodology, and selected findings of the exploratory study.

THEORETICAL CONSIDERATIONS

Interest as a Specific Person–Environment Relation

The present conceptualization of interest is based on theoretical consider-ations of the origin and effect of person–environment relations. The authors share the view proposed in the organismic developmental approach, a view also expressed by Bronfenbrenner (1978a, 1978b, 1979) and Wozniak (1986), that the central unit of analysis in psychology is the person–environment system. Thus, it is assumed that individual develop-ment is determined largely by the quality and course of a person's relation to the social and physical environment. Continual interaction with people, objects, events, and areas of subject matter found in the immediate environment leaves behind traces in both the person and the environment. Each experience adds to and differentiates a person's store of knowledge. The person acquires cognitive representations about the "nature of things" (declarative knowledge) and about action possibilities (procedural knowledge). Person–environment engagements thereby shape a person's cognitive structure. This includes the development of values, attitudes, motivational orientations, and other emotional components closely associated with cognitive processes.

A person experiences the environment as a structured whole. In the course of an individual's development, experiences are organized into categories and classes of categories, which are themselves subject to reorganization depending on their meaningfulness to the person. Thus, each person builds unique, subjective cognitive structures. But different individuals also acquire very similar cognitive structures simply because similar realities and interpretations occur within the cultural context. The cognitive structures reflecting these aspects of the environment are objective in the sense that they are the same across individuals. This, of course, still allows for the many idiosyncratic structures that are specific to each person (Renninger, 1990).

Regardless of the exact way a person differentiates and organizes the content of his or her surroundings, it seems safe to assume that individual categories vary in subjective importance across different situations and/or different phases of development. The person–object theory of interest assumes that, in the course of development, the person develops a special relation to certain parts of the environment, and that this relation has certain characteristics. Such pronounced person–environment relationships can be based on a wide variety of subjective experiences. The phenomenon of attachment, a common example of a special relationship with another person, can be extended to include concrete objects in early childhood (Winnicott, 1953). The special relation between a person and a material object judged to be of great personal value by the individual or by society is generally referred to as ownership (Furby, 1978a, 1978b, Stanjek, 1978, 1980).

Interest is a unique relation between a person and an object, or object domain, found in that person's environment. This relation must be of some duration and does not refer to "one-time" unrepeated forms of engagement. A more precise theoretical description of the "interest-oriented" person–object relation (P–O relation) centers around three aspects: (a) the object of interest, (b) the structural components of interest, and (c) the characteristics of the interest-oriented P–O relation.

The Interest Object

In the present theory of interest, three conceptual levels of objects are distinguished: object domains, objects of interest, and reference objects. The levels differ from one another in their degree of specificity.

The most general level involves *domains* of interest, such as "music," "sports," or "travel." School content areas, such as math, biology, or history are also interest domains.

At the next level are *interest objects*, also referred to as "objects of interest." An interest object consists of that part of an entire interest domain that a particular person at a particular time includes as an individual interest. Objects of interest are person-specific. Although two different people may enjoy the same things and action possibilities within a certain domain and therefore have very similar interest objects, each individual will have had some unique experiences, thus excluding the possibility of their interest objects being absolutely identical.

Someone who is interested in "sports," for instance, is very unlikely to be interested in or even aware of every aspect of every sport on earth. Rather, one person might be interested in performing non-team sports that require good physical condition (marathon running, cross-country skiing), whereas another person might be interested in watching professional team sports, and a third person might be interested in "outdoorsy" activities such as fishing and hunting. In each case, the totality of all the individual's choices of concrete objects, forms of activity, and possible topics, chosen from among all the possibilities in the domain "sports," represents that individual's object of interest. Thus, the interests just described all come from the same domain but represent three distinct interest objects, and, hence, three distinct P–O relations.

Finally, the third level involves the particular, concrete things used when engaging in activity with the object of interest. These are referred to as *reference objects*. Going back to the preceding examples, a person interested in non-team sports might have running shoes, cross-country skis, and a stopwatch as pertinent reference objects, whereas someone interested in watching professional team sports might have binoculars, season tickets, and subscriptions to sports magazines, and an outdoorsy type might have fishing poles, a tent, and a favorite hat. It should be noted that reference objects are not the only elements found in a person's interest object. Action possibilities and topics are found along with reference objects. The interaction among these three types of elements or structural components in the formation of an interest object is discussed more fully in the next section.

In what follows, the lone use of the terms *object*, or *interest object*, refers to the person-specific form of an interest (i.e., to the second conceptual level of objects). However, it is important to clarify some further matters relating to these interest objects. First, objects of interest are based on more than just concrete reference objects. Abstract or ideal elements, (e.g., symbolic representations of things), concepts, and events, information, and questions of a scientific nature can all be part of an object of interest. Second, insofar as they function as interaction partners, people are not regarded as objects of interest.[1] Third, even though one and the same domain can be involved in the formation of completely different P–O relations in different people, these different relations can all be described and explained in a consistent manner on the basis of general rules.

The manner in which an interest object is understood and, through repeated engagements, elaborated upon is a function of several factors. Not all of these factors are based within the experiencing person. Although subjective interpretations are of primary importance in the formation of subjective knowledge about a domain (in other words, in the formation of an interest object), an exclusively individualistic–cognitive interpretation would ignore the fact that other "outside" factors have an impact on the structure and quality of an object of interest. This becomes especially evident in the case of "cultural objects" whose meanings have evolved and become consolidated during the course of society's development (Boesch, 1982; Csikszentmihalyi & Rochberg–Halton, 1981). The cultural meanings of objects are passed from generation to generation through education and socialization, and contribute to a common understanding of the objects. In fact, tacit agreement usually exists within cultural groups about the utility, value, and meaningfulness of cultural objects (e.g., musical instruments, jewels, or most household items). Because most objects of interest are also cultural in nature, a comprehensive characterization of an object of interest must also include an analysis of its cultural meanings (Fink, 1989; Renninger, 1984, 1989).

Thus, two factors determine the structure, meaning, and environmental placement of an object of interest: (a) the individual (subjective–conative) understanding of an object's meaning; and (b) the culturally determined (objective–denotative) meaning of an object. Both

---

[1] This conceptualization of interest primarily addresses relations with non-personal objects and does not directly deal with person–person relationships. Nevertheless, knowledge about human experience and behavior can become a person's object of interest, as in the case of a psychologist who is intensively involved in the study of a particular emotional disturbance. Differentiation of personal and material units in the environment is not necessarily clear-cut in every case. On the one hand, there are situations in which physical objects can be reinterpreted as personal units, such as when children play pretend (animism). On the other hand, people are often analyzed with respect to their existence as physical objects (e.g. in the behavioral sciences). However, according to Fink (1989), this problem can be mitigated by considering the type of involvement ("personalistic" versus "nonpersonalistic"). Living beings (animals and humans), for example, are only objects of interest when involvement with them can be described as nonpersonalistic.

interpretations can be applied to the development of a person's P–O relations.

Structural Components of the Interest-Oriented P–O Relation

P–O relations may be analyzed in terms of both process and structure. These represent two theoretical perspectives and are associated with two levels of analysis. The first level deals with the internal and external interest-oriented actions related to an object. At this level, interest is understood as a state that represents the actualized relation between a person and an object in a specific situation at a certain time. The second level of analysis interprets interest as a persisting disposition (Krapp, 1989; see also Krapp, Hidi, & Renninger, this volume).

As a dispositional category, interest may manifest itself in subjective representations that are emotional, value related, or cognitive in nature. Cognitive structures would include stored memories of experiences with the object and knowledge about possibilities of action that the person has already realized or intends to realize in the future (Prenzel, 1988; Renninger, 1989, 1990).

Each interest has a more or less distinct structure. The complexity of the structure can be modified by eliminating elements (substructures, components), by adding elements, or by processes of incorporation and exclusion (Fink, 1991). This is especially true during the early developmental stages of an interest. We distinguish between simple and complex structures of an interest-oriented P–O relation. Complex P–O relations exhibit a predominantly hierarchical structure that is capable of internally integrating numerous simple P–O relations. Simple P–O relations, as well as the lowest level of a complex P–O relation, can be broken down into individual components. These basic structural components include (a) reference objects, (b) activities (i.e., action possibilities), and (c) topics.

Reference Objects. Reference objects (concrete objects) are essential elements for most P–O relations (e.g., books for the object domain "literature"; or instruments, sheet music), or records for the object domain "music"). In empirical studies, reference objects serve as landmarks for charting the boundaries and content of subjective domain perception. However, these objects are more than empirical indicators for determining the structure of individual P–O relations. In many cases, they represent the primary content of an interest (e.g., the collecting of certain things). Furthermore, the objective characteristics of an interest object often have a direct influence on a person's engagement with it. For example, an engagement may be limited by the material characteristics and/or the socioculturally determined purpose of the interest object (e.g., artistic work that involves valuable materials).

Activities. A second structural component is the type of activity associated with the object of interest. Such activities include not only observing, perceiving, manipulating, and exploring the different characteristics of an object, but also changing the object or making the imagined object real. A further important activity is acquiring and processing information about the object or activities associated with it (e.g., searching for relevant sources of information). Social contacts are also frequently included within object-related activities, particularly when the P–O relation can be realized only within a group (e.g., games involving social interaction, all forms of competition, the performance of music), or when the exchange of knowledge and experiences with others is important and pleasant.

Topics. The present and future forms of an activity that a person undertakes with an object depends, in large part, on a person's goals, topics, and questions regarding the object (Renninger, 1989, 1990). Topical categories often serve to guide interest-oriented engagement and thereby influence the specific course of events involved in an activity as well as its overall nature.[2] A teenager's interest in computers will exhibit a completely different structure for activity with a prepackaged computer game than for activity with a homemade toy robot, even though the interest involves the same reference objects (e.g., hardware, programs) and competencies (programming).

Special Characteristics of an Interest-Oriented P–O Relation

Although the basic structural components of an interest-oriented P–O relation are important landmarks for the empirical reconstruction of an interest, they give only an incomplete and approximate picture of the theoretical construct. Further characterization is possible only at the level of theoretical definition. Among other things, this would involve a description of the characteristics of the interest-oriented P–O relation.

---

[2] In later developmental stages, interests are more likely to be topical (study interests, or text-based interests, see Schiefele and Hidi Anderson, this volume) than they are to be linked to concrete objects.

The following section, therefore, involves the specific characteristics of a fully developed interest that can be determined by a person's experience and behavior. Thus, the present chapter ignores the fact that during the course of individual development new forms of interest are continually evolving from previous forms and that a precise distinction between precursor and fully developed interest is difficult.

Selective Persistence. In the present context, the term *persistence* means that interest-oriented action is not a one-time or short-term affair. Rather, it is characterized by a certain amount of stability. Strong individual interest elicits repeated engagements with the object. Thus, a child's fleeting, curious attention toward an object in the environment cannot be classified as interest unless that attention also can be observed more regularly over time.[3]

As an indicator of interest, the persistence of an action has meaning only in relation to the persistence of other actions and in terms of situational conditions. Usually it is not difficult to recognize different degrees of persistence in intraindividual comparisons of actions with respect to particular objects and topics. In empirical investigations designed to monitor the strength of an interest over time, the degree of persistence may be operationalized as the *frequency* of engagement within a particular object domain. A more precise analysis might compare the frequency of actual P–O engagement in a particular domain with the frequency of possible opportunities for engagement in that domain. Within a single incident of interest-based activity, the *duration* of engagement can serve as an indicator of persistence. Defining persistence as repeated engagement with an object and individual willingness for long-term involvement with that object implies choices. From an array of action possibilities and objects, an individual must choose those that best match his or her interests. Thus, persistence of P–O relations develops only through a selective process (see the chapter by Prenzel in this volume).

Value Orientation and Self-Intentionality. Objects, activities, and topics associated with an interest are experienced as important and meaningful because they are closely related to personal attitudes and

---

[3] This view of interest differs from research conducted in the field of interestingness (cf. Anderson, Shirey, Wilson, & Fielding, 1987; Hidi, 1989; Hidi & MacLaren, 1987), in which a child is interested in or reacts predictably to an interesting mystery or an unrepeating event such as an interestingly written text.

values. Linking personal interests to values and attitudes is common to older and more recent theories of interest (e.g., Dewey, 1913; Hidi & Baird, 1986, 1988; Kerschensteiner, 1926; Lunk, 1927; Renninger, 1989, 1990; Renninger & Leckrone, 1991; Renninger & Wozniak, 1985). This does not mean that a person is necessarily aware of personal value judgments, or that a reflective judgment is made prior to interest-based activity. However, the more advanced a person's maturational development and the more differentiated the set of values, the more inclined that person will be to develop interests on the basis of conscious value judgments.

The value orientation and the emotional components of interest can surface in diluted form, as a *preference* for particular objects, activities, and topics. Preference is a relative criterion, the strength of which can only be measured in comparison with other objects and activities. Empirically useful indicators of preference include relative desirability of the object in the eye of the individual, time spent with the object, and choice in favor of interest-relevant activities.

Another important characteristic of full-fledged interest is *self-intentionality*. This is somewhat comparable to both Csikszentmihalyi's (1975) "autotelic" behavior, which is based on the concept of "Funktionslust" (Bühler, 1918), and Deci's (1980) intrinsic motivation, both of which refer to activities that are conducted in the absence of external stimulation (e.g., sanctions or reinforcement) and thus are under subjective–internal control (Deci & Ryan, 1985a, 1985b, 1991). One can speak of an activity as self-intentional only when the person can plan and carry it out independently, as is the case with an interest-related activity. Hence, the principle of self-determination must be involved in interest (see Deci, this volume).

Self-determination differentiates the present view of interest from instrumental action models of motivation (cf. Heckhausen, 1980), which define the motivational basis of an action as a process of rational calculation. These theories presuppose that a person chooses activities on the basis of the perceived likelihood of desirable or undesirable outcomes. However, consideration of long-term "payoffs" actually plays a subordinate role in actions guided by interest. Rather, participation itself and the immediate outcomes are considered to be sufficient reasons for performing the action.

Positive Emotions. Interest-oriented engagement with an object is usually accompanied by positive or pleasant feelings. Some theories of emotion (cf. Averill, 1980; Lazarus, Kanner, & Folkman, 1980) maintain that an optimal level of arousal (somewhere between "effort" and "comfort") is experienced during elicitation and performance of the action. In extreme cases, the positive emotions that accompany activity can intensify to the point of total immersion in that activity. This results in a "flow" experience, as described by Csikszentmihalyi (1975, 1990). But positive emotion is a global evaluation that certainly cannot describe every aspect of an interest-oriented activity. During the course of such engagement, some negative feelings, such as anger and discouragement, may also occur. However, the emotional balance is presumed to be positive when the activity is considered as a whole.

Cognitive Aspects. Repeated engagement with an object of interest results in specific cognitive structures. In keeping with Renninger (1989, 1990; Renninger & Leckrone, 1991; Renninger, this volume), the authors assume that an individual tends to develop relatively differentiated knowledge about an object of interest. This includes knowledge about the object and knowledge about action possibilities (procedural knowledge). Action-oriented knowledge relates both to previous concrete experiences (Prenzel, 1988), and to object-based activities (experiences) that the person has not yet attempted but has learned about from watching others, or from other information sources (cf. the chapters by Prenzel and Renninger in this volume). In its developed form, then, interest is characterized by a high level of object-specific cognitive complexity (Norman & Rumelhart, 1978; Seiler, 1978).

As Piaget (1974, 1981) suggests, a person working in a domain of interest is exceptionally willing to assimilate that which is experienced and to adjust his or her thinking accordingly. The use of available schemata to set goals, make sense of experience, and store new information in memory (assimilation), as well as the modification of schemata and the resulting extended competence (accommodation), are based on interest to a great extent. Piaget (1974) even goes so far as to say, "Every intelligent activity is founded upon an interest" (p. 31). From the perspective of the psychology of knowledge, one could hypothesize that the origin and elaboration of cognitive structures may depend largely on the realization of short- and long-term individual interests. Empirical findings suggest that the nature and strength of interests affect primarily the qualitative aspects of acquired knowledge structures (Krapp, 1989; cf. the articles by Schiefele and by Schiefele, Krapp & Winteler in this volume).

Developmental Aspects

When viewed as an element in development, interests can be analyzed from two different research perspectives: first, the origin of interests and the modification of interest-oriented P–O relations (interests as dependent variable); second, interests as a condition of development, or, in other words, as a factor that aids in explaining changes in how things are experienced (interest as independent variable).

Origin and Modification of Interests. Interests can originate, change, or disappear entirely during any period of a person's development. Correspondingly, the structure of an interest-oriented P–O relation is in a constant state of flux. Individual substructures may grow, others may lose in importance, or a more far-reaching reorganization of the previous structure may occur. In general, all of these changes can be classified according to two fundamental principles of development: *integration* and *differentiation* (cf. Bronfenbrenner, 1979; Lewin, 1954; Oerter, 1977, 1981; Wapner, 1981, 1987b; Werner, 1957, 1959).

Fink (1991) discusses a model for describing the development of interest that distinguishes between two fundamental process components that correspond to the principles of integration and differentiation. If one assumes that an interest-oriented P–O relation consists of many integrated components within a coherent structure, then developmental changes in this structure can be described in terms of these two opposite developmental tendencies.

The first tendency corresponds to the general principal of integration and is referred to as *incorporation*. In general, incorporation involves the integration of isolated parts into an already existing whole. In the development of interest, the newly developed components or isolated simple structures of a P–O relation are incorporated into the salient preference structure of an already existing complex P–O relation. For example, one could use the term incorporation in a situation in which a child who has previously kept two activities separate (e.g., painting and animal care) begins to combine the two activities (e.g. painting pictures that show caring for animals) (see also Renninger & Leckrone, 1991).

The second developmental tendency, *exclusion*, refers to the opposite of incorporation in that it involves the elimination of parts from the whole. In the development of interest, this means that individual components of a complex P–O relation are excluded from the complete structure. In other words, certain objects or activities that have been included in a highly preferred class of activities become less important.

Going back to the last example, the preference for painting pictures of caring for animals is soon replaced by something else.

Incorporation and exclusion represent two fundamental phenomena of interest development. Both processes involve quantitative changes (e.g., number of omitted components) as well as qualitative changes (e.g., reorganization of the existing structure). A typical qualitative change might involve a change in a person's estimate of the value of a component in a complex P–O relation. New activities often introduce further new action possibilities in a P–O relation and thereby change the entire preference structure over the long term. Learning to program a computer, for instance, can completely change an existing interest in computer-related activities. Qualitative change could also involve the transformation of an unstable P–O relation into a stable structure and, thus, describe the emergence of a new interest-oriented P–O relation.

But in addition to being able to adequately describe how interest-oriented P–O relations originate and change, one would also like to be able to explain these changes. Kasten (1985) has formulated hypotheses about the origin of interests that he probed by means of case studies. His results emphasized the importance of environmental stimuli in the home, preschool and school, and of social contacts with adults and peers. Whereas Kasten's hypotheses centered around specific factors in the origin of interests, Prenzel's (1988) model for explaining the effect of interest involved more general mechanisms. According to his theoretical concept, both the cognitive and emotional effects that accompany individual engagements with the object of interest must be considered to explain selective persistence and continuity over time. Cognitive effects would include experiences that stabilize or extend the individual's interest-specific activity schemata. Emotional effects would involve experiences of optimal effort and content-related emotions, or the perception of competence, as described in theories of intrinsic motivation (deCharms, 1968; Deci, 1975; White, 1959; see Prenzel, this volume).

Interest as a Factor in Development. Interest is both commonly and scientifically regarded as an important condition for learning. Numerous studies have focused on the relation between interest, learning, and academic achievement (Krapp, 1989; see also Schiefele, Krapp, & Winteler, in this volume). These investigations often assume that interests indirectly influence emotional–motivational factors, such as motivational orientation (Lepper, 1988), or information-processing mechanisms, such as direction and intensity of attention (Csikszentmihalyi, 1988). Thus, this research relies heavily on the construct of interest to explain cognitive effects.

As discussed earlier, other studies have addressed the importance of interests for *coping* with critical life events (Filipp, 1981; e.g., the transition from home to school). An individual engaged with a personal interest may have a number of experiences that can contribute to feelings of competence and security in the new situation. Interest, therefore, presumably has a stabilizing effect when a person enters into a new social situation.

THE INTEREST GENESIS PROJECT

Objectives

The research described here is part of an exploratory longitudinal study (Interest Genesis Project). It was designed to investigate the early stages of interest development in preschool and elementary schoolchildren. To this end, the following were addressed throughout the course of data collection:

1. Assessment of the descriptive characteristics of individual structures of person–object relations during preschool and elementary school (Fink, 1991; Fink & Krapp, 1986a; Kasten, 1985).
2. Description and explanation of the developmental changes in the individual structures of interest-oriented P–O relations.
3. Description of the reciprocal influence of social factors and interest-oriented P–O relations (Fink, Schiefele, & Krapp, 1985; Krapp & Fink, 1986a).

Procedure and Methods

Data were collected continuously over a 5-year period (from 1980 to 1985) from a small group of children (n = 12), starting with their entry into preschool (Kasten, 1985). Because the preschool group stayed together over several years, the study offers a greater amount of inter-related information than would a collection of independent case studies. In order to gain the greatest variety of information and, at the same time, accurately estimate the quality of the data base, data reflecting different levels of analysis were collected. The following methods were used: interviews with parents and teachers, teacher questionnaires, and observations in the home and at kindergarten.

Parent Interviews. Twenty-four partially structured interviews were conducted at four different times: upon entry into preschool (September 1980), and at the end of 3 preschool years (June, 1981 through 1983). All of the interviews were conducted in the home with the aim of gathering information about the child's material and social relations at home during the previous time period. Although the guidelines for these interviews were changed from one year to the next, the questions consistently addressing a set of key issues such as the child's engagements in and endurance with activities in and outside the home, the desire for and the value placed on preferred activities/objects/topics, and any material and social changes.

Teacher Interviews. During the first 3 years of the project, interviews in the form of group discussions were conducted with the teachers. Teachers were asked about their perceptions of the material and social realms of the children.

Teacher Questionnaires. During the second half of the project's first year, teachers were repeatedly given a structured questionnaire over a period of 6 months. The purpose of these questionnaires was to gather continuous data about the children's preferred games, activities, and social partners.

Observations in the Home and at Kindergarten. Parallel to the first two parent interviews, unsystematic observations were also conducted in the home. The participant observer reported an impression of the living space in the family environment and observed the child's behavior in familiar surroundings. To strengthen and control the kindergarten data, participant observations were occasionally conducted in the kindergarten also.

Data Analysis

Initial data analyses focused primarily on the more strongly structured data (Kasten, 1985). Analysis was later extended to include case descriptions based on a collection of meaningful statements in the interviews (with parents and teachers) and observations. In this study qualitative content analyses (cf. Dreher, Dreher, Fink, & Hinkelmann, 1985; Mayring, 1983; Witzel, 1982) were carried out in a series of partially repetitive stages (cf. Fink, 1991). The primary goal of the data analysis was to reconstruct all of a child's P–O relations during the period of study.

The exploratory nature of this descriptive approach to research seems more conducive to hypothesis generation than to hypothesis testing. The goal was not to completely explain the particular phenomena in each individual case but to generate developmental hypotheses that could be supported by the data and preliminary results from single cases.[4]

FINDINGS AND CONSIDERATIONS ABOUT THE IMPORTANCE OF INTERESTS DURING THE TRANSITIONAL PHASE FROM HOME TO PRESCHOOL

Previous research has shown that preschool and elementary school children exhibit preliminary forms of interests consisting of repeatable interest-oriented P–O relations that become prominent in the child's structure of preferences (Fink, 1991). These preliminary interests exhibit type-specific structures and varying degrees of complexity that provide a basis for classifying different types of P–O relations. In addition, one can distinguish whether preliminary forms of interests are activity centered, object centered, or topic centered.

In the following, reconstructions of the case studies are reported. The first section focuses on the effects of the critical transition from home to preschool on the development of interests. The second section reviews the importance of interest-oriented PO relations for the management of this critical transition.

Effects of the Transition from Family to Preschool on the Development of Interests

Questions generated before beginning the study included the following: Does the transition from family to preschool have a lasting influence on the development of interests? If so, how can this influence be explained? More particularly, how do individual conditions of the critical transition, such as new social contacts, influence the development of interests? Are these influences general or specific in nature? Do they involve primarily individual P–O relations or the entire structure of P–O relations?

For purposes of illustration, two aspects of this research are presented. The first aspect refers to the general nature and direction of influence. In

---

[4] There is no formally established procedure for "inventing" such hypotheses. Frequently, the formulation of a convincing hypothesis is the result of a protracted process following the repeated study and discussion of the entire assemblage of data concerning a particular case.

this context, we discuss two hypotheses: the hypothesis of delayed effect, and the hypothesis of structural change. The second aspect refers to the influence of altered environmental conditions, especially in the realm of social relations. Here we discuss three hypotheses concerning the primacy of social versus object relations and the role of new social experiences on the structure of an individual's P–O relations.

The Hypothesis of Delayed Effects

In studying the adaptation of beginning preschool children, McGrew (1972) and Nickel (1985) found that most children exhibit receptive behavior, along with a "wait and see" attitude. This indicates that there is a delay period before any effect. The present findings confirm this. Individual behavior patterns did indeed change during the first few weeks of preschool (e.g., the new activities learned in preschool were also tried out at home). However, the established structure of accustomed and highly preferred P–O relations that existed before preschool entry remained largely unaffected. Even during the first few weeks of preschool, the children preferred to entertain themselves with familiar objects and games when given a choice.

Conspicuous changes did not occur for a number of months. Even these changes were subtle and could be confirmed only with a highly differentiated analysis. The changes involved, for example, the internal structure of a single P–O relation, and the interaction of various P–O relations.

The Hypothesis of Structural Change

Fink (1991) proposed a descriptive model for the measurement of structural and dynamic changes in interest-oriented P–O relations over time. According to this model, changes are possible on all levels of the P–O structure. These changes involve the basic components of individual P–O relations as well as the P–O relation system in its entirety. The present findings suggest that changes are possible on both levels. Generally, one finds a fairly inconspicuous, but nevertheless continuous, reorganization of existing P–O relations.

The "organismic developmental approach" (Wapner, 1981, 1987a) characterizes development as a continuous process of differentiation and integration. This also applies to changes in the structure of P–O relations, in that experiences in preschool foster the *incorporation* of new elements into already existing P–O relations and the *exclusion* of various components within and among different P–O relations. The following case study exemplifies this.

Child No. 4 (Sabine) had a rather highly preferred P–O relation, painting, upon entering preschool. Preference ratings remained at a constant high level during the first years of preschool; thus, there is no change in this regard. However, a more accurate analysis of the developing structure of this P–O relation demonstrates a number of significant changes which may be interpreted as extensions, differentiation, and tendencies toward integration:

- Extension of reference objects (e.g., painting utensils).
- Extension and differentiation of painting themes (e.g. impressions of landscapes and other subjective experiences).
- Extension of situations in which the P–O relation was realized (e.g., painting while on a trip).
- Craftwork techniques were used on painting utensils and painting products, whereas hand-crafted objects were painted originally.

Aside from changing the (internal) structure of a P–O relation, preschool entry can change the rank order and relative weight of the P–O relation, as well as its structure and its links to the system of social relations. As seen in the following example, the case-specific findings indicate that Sabine reorganized her P–O relations with an extension of her living environment. Along with this, she developed a new situation-specific preference structure.

Sabine (Child No. 4) played with dolls intensively and with great delight. In the family setting, dolls were reference objects not only for the highly popular mother–child role play, but also for other role play such as "shopping" or "visiting the doctor." Sabine would have preferred to play these games with playmates her own age, but they did not live near her. Dolls and role playing with dolls at home allegedly were a substitute for the lack of contact with peers. Upon entry into preschool, these social needs were met. Sabine rarely played alone but participated zealously in group activities and games. The opposite was true at home. Here solitary activities were gaining dominance (e.g., painting and craftwork). Doll play became less significant.

Our findings indicate that, in general, the transition from home to preschool brings about no dramatic changes in a child's P–O relations. For the most part, children maintain the P–O relations they have already developed. Any changes involve primarily only individual aspects of the child's interest structure. If one looks only at individual aspects of the new surroundings that influence the expression of interests, then one must also consider the effects of the changed social environment.

Presumably, *social influences* play an important role in the formation, change, and development of P–O relations. The type of influence, however, is very different in each case, especially because interactive processes must be taken into account. In the following, three hypotheses about social influences derived from this case material are described.

The Hypothesis of the Primacy of Social Relations

Lewis and Brooks' (1975) proposition about the primacy of social (vs. non-social) cognitions states that a child first develops cognitive categories for his or her social environment. These categories then serve as the basis for later engagements with the physical environment. One could assume, then, that a child might first seek to make and stabilize social contacts before attempting new forms of engagement or developing new P–O relations. Studies of the social contacts of beginning preschool children also indicate this. According to Schmidt–Denter (1985), such children must take the initiative in making contact. In order to be successful in their social attempts, they must observe the established forms of interaction in the preschool and adapt their repertoire for making contact accordingly. The data from our longitudinal study show that the nature of children's attempts to make contact change significantly, especially in the first half year. In addition, children initially prefer games that do not require engagement with unfamiliar objects (e.g., passive participation in group activities). Voluntary engagement in contact that involves the whole group simultaneously taking part in the same activity begins later.

During this critical phase of transition, children often retreat to familiar P–O relations, thereby avoiding new and unaccustomed activities at first, as the following case study illustrates.

Dirk (Child No. 3) was very close to his mother and suffered separation anxiety during the first few weeks. He did not succeed in developing friendships with other children during this time. He frequently withdrew and completely rejected cooperative games. After about 6 months, he gradually developed a friendship with Katrin, a girl his age. At the same time, his play behavior also changed. He participated more and more in social games and began to incorporate new activities into his repertoire of behavior (e.g., family-centered role play).

Although there is further evidence supporting the hypothesis of the primacy of "social problem solving," it should be noted that some findings seem to contradict the hypothesis. Careful investigation of the case study, however, usually unearths a plausible explanation for the absence of the expected phenomenon, for example, discovering that the child had the opportunity to become accustomed to adapting to new social situations before preschool. The following example was a case in point.

At first glance, Daniel's (Child No. 12) behavior seemed to contradict the hypothesis. As of the first day Daniel began playing without any notable reluctance, and he became especially active when his P–O relation "animals" could be converted into a game. It must be noted, however, that Daniel was an extraordinarily self-assured child who enjoyed making new contacts. Evidently the new social situation did not pose a problem for him. Because he felt secure in new social situations from the very beginning, he was able to solve the problem of social adjustment and integration. Therefore, he could profit immediately from new (objective) environmental conditions.

The Hypothesis of Catalysis

New social experiences in preschool (e.g., peer modeling) affect the extension and partial reorganization of existing P–O relations (see aforementioned hypothesis of structural change). It is also possible that entire structures of P–O relations will change dramatically during the critical transition. Our data, however, offer no indication of such structural changes due to social influences. Instead, changes usually develop slowly within the context of an already familiar P–O relation, as the next example involving Dirk shows.

After the friendship between Dirk (Child No. 3, see earlier) and Katrin stabilized, they frequently engaged in role playing (usually together), with which both were familiar. Dirk entered more and more into the kinds of games, objects, and topics stipulated by Katrin (e.g., family-related topics). He evidently later transferred this to new situations outside the preschool setting because during the second interview, his mother reported noticing a striking extension of his role-playing behavior at home.

Overall, our findings indicate that, initially, a child's successful social integration into preschool does not overwhelmingly effect his or her P–O relations (see aforementioned hypothesis of delayed effect). New social experiences may serve as a kind of catalyst to strengthen and support developmental tendencies begun at home. Furthermore, these experiences foster the child's readiness to explore new objects and become engaged in new topics of interest.

The Hypothesis of Inhibition

Not all social experiences in preschool are positive ones. For the new child, having to make contact and play with unfamiliar people, and having to adjust to new social norms can be accompanied by feelings of insecurity and anxiety. Such feelings can result in the child's isolation from social experience. Inadequate social adjustment can mean that a child and peer group may avoid contact with each other for even longer periods of time.

Most children manage to overcome problems of isolation in the first weeks of preschool by taking the initiative and successfully establishing contact with their peers (Schmidt–Denter, 1985). They are then open to new experiences in object-related fields. The difficulties of some individuals, however, last longer. Like Michael, in the next example, even though they are willing to take the initiative in making contact, they are unable to "connect" with the peer group. These children withdraw, sometimes for long periods, and thus do not profit from new preschool experiences.

Michael (Child No. 2), as the only child in the preschool group from a lower economic class, was also the only child in the group who spoke in dialect. Although at first very receptive and eager to make contact with other children, he had difficulty becoming a member of a play group. Despite his own efforts, the others rarely involved him in their games. As a result, Michael began to withdraw and increasingly came to dislike going to preschool. He began to be absent frequently and, when in the school, he usually played alone in a stereotypical manner with special playing materials.

The reports and observations, as a whole, suggest that Michael's realization and further development of object-related activities were restrained under the given conditions. Not only was he hindered in the maintenance of P–O relations for which he had developed high competence and surprising endurance at home (e.g., arts and crafts), but his increasing social isolation provided no opportunity for him to form new and longer-lasting P–O relations in the preschool setting.

THE CONTRIBUTION OF FAMILIAR P–O RELATIONS IN COPING WITH THE CRITICAL TRANSITION FROM FAMILY TO PRESCHOOL

Thus far, the P–O relations of the child have been treated largely as dependent variables. The following hypotheses assume that P–O relations can also be seen as independent variables that help to explain various phenomena of development. Of special interest are the questions of whether and how familiar P–O relations might help the child to manage the transition from home to preschool.

The Security Anchor Hypothesis

As mentioned earlier, studies with young children have shown that familiar objects (e.g., specific toys, a security blanket) can reduce fear of new situations. These objects serve as a "security anchor" and make up for the temporary absence of a primary attachment person (Brody, 1980; Fink & Krapp, 1986b; Passman & Halonen, 1979; Passman & Weisberg, 1975; Weisberg & Russel, 1971; Winnicott, 1953). Highly valued objects may even help older people overcome the problems of a critical transition (e.g., entry into a nursing home; Wapner, 1981, 1987b). This phenomenon, if applied to an older child, might be explained by viewing the object in question. An older child is familiar with a wide variety of activities involving an object of interest. The feelings that the child associates with the object are mostly positive, as the object and engagements with it are enjoyable, and the child feels secure when engaged in activity with the object, and possibly commands respect from proven competence.

The "anchor hypothesis," therefore, could support the notion of the familiar P–O relation as a secure base, with individual components or substructures comprising the externally visible "anchor point" at any given time. Our data indicate that the availability of familiar objects as well as the possibility of engaging in certain activities facilitate the successful management of problematical situations in the preschool and kindergarten. The following two examples show how concrete objects can enhance feelings of security.

When Michael (Child No. 2) felt that he had been slighted in preschool, he often turned his attention to toys with which he was familiar from home. His favorite toys in this situation were toy automobiles (especially trucks), and he played with these toys in a noticeably stereotypical fashion, continually repeating certain play behaviors.

Tobias (Child No. 10) insisted that specific building blocks be packed whenever the family took off on a long or short trip. Upon arrival, Tobias withdrew at first, and for a while played intensively with the materials he had brought along. Only after this "relaxation phase" was he prepared to investigate the new environment.

These examples show clearly that the availability of familiar objects alone cannot explain the sense of security they provide. Equally important are familiar action possibilities that can be carried out with objects found in or brought to the new environment. In many cases, the object is immaterial, as long as certain activities can be carried out with it. This is evidenced in the following example.

Following his entry into the preschool, Clements (Child No. 6) displayed a remarkable preference for games involving bodily motion. Usually this involved playing on the slide, which was often extended to include other forms of active play, such as playing with a ball, climbing, or running. Upon entering the preschool, Clemens showed little initiative in making contact with other children. He rarely accepted the offers to play made by other children and suggestions made by the teachers. He instigated most of his play himself, relying on his highly preferred games of motion, which he generally carried out alone in stereotypical fashion.

The case studies show that special knowledge and competence within an area of activity actually represent a security base. In contrast to findings from attachment research, the particular object does not seem to be of central importance. It is not necessary that a specific, beloved object be available, but rather that the child have access to an object that represents a familiar class of objects, so as to carry out a familiar object-related activity. The beloved object then becomes replaceable.

A further similarity among the examples is that the children try to deal with uncomfortable situations by turning their attention for a short time to their familiar P–O relations. They remove themselves from the demands of social interaction, and occupy themselves to their satisfaction, either alone or with close friends. In this way they increase their feelings of security. This increase, however, is a remedy for the current situation only. It does not represent a long-term solution.

P–O relations have a more encompassing function when used in initiating, maintaining, and developing social relations.

The Hypothesis of Social Contact Initiation

Common interests are an important means for establishing, maintaining, and developing social contacts at all age levels. This is true typically of people who are relative strangers but would like to learn more about one another. It is no coincidence that personal classified ads commonly indicate the interests of the writer as well as those of the partner being sought. Though they do not go to the trouble to theorize about the situation, children also use common interests as a guide when making contact with other children. This is also true at the time of the critical transition to preschool.

With only a few sporadic exceptions, teacher interviews yielded no useful data pertaining to the importance of children's interests for making social contacts in the first hours or days in preschool. Despite this, the findings of McGrew (1972) indicate that interests are very probably of great importance in this area. Also, we find in our case study material many examples of situations where children's P–O relations play an important role in the establishment, maintenance, and development of social contacts with other children. The following example illustrates how a well-defined structure of P–O relations can aid the child in mastering the social environment, in this case by relying on acquired competencies that are attractive in the eyes of peers.

Since early childhood, Daniel (Child No. 12) had been interested in animals: He was an avid reader of animal books, frequently visited the zoo and other exhibits with his parents, painted pictures of animals, and in most of his role playing mimicked animal behavior. Reconstruction of the development of his P–O relations revealed a distinctly "topic-centered" structure for the entire period in question. In preschool, Daniel acted upon his interest whenever an opportunity presented itself. His suggestions for animal role playing attracted other children to him. This form of play became his medium for making and shaping contacts to other children. From the very beginning, he was considered to be well integrated into the peer group.

In the following example, a P–O relation formed the basis for a friendship, mentioned earlier, that brought an end to one child's social isolation.

Dirk (Child No. 3) had an unusually strong attachment to his mother and, because of this, had trouble getting used to the preschool at first. He was sad when his mother left him in the morning. He closed himself off from the other children and rejected all invitations to participate in cooperative play. Instead, he sought out pastimes that required no active social partner (observing and motion activities). Partially at the urging of the teacher, he discovered that Katrin, a socially very competent girl, also liked to do animal role playing, which matched with Dirk's preferred complex P–O relation in the domain "animals." They often played with one another and had repeated contact. Over the course of the first preschool year, a very close friendship developed out of this contact. This friendship continued during the entire time in preschool. Together with his friend, Dirk extended the spectrum of his P–O relations (e.g., dolls, doctor role playing). In addition, he was able in this way to increasingly integrate himself into the peer group.

The Hypothesis of Compensation

Even children who fail to establish social relations in preschool may be able to make the situation bearable by retiring into familiar P–O relations. The engagement with these objects compensates for their lack of social integration. This can be seen in the next example.

Clemens (Child No. 6) remained an outsider for the entire first year and part of the second year. Occasionally he played with one child or another for a short time, but he never stayed in any group for long. He remained an outsider, tolerated by all of the others, while their efforts to integrate him into their play went unrewarded. Nevertheless, from the very beginning, Clemens demonstrated striking continuity in his play behavior. He was interested in a few special object areas (e.g. building blocks and picture books), toward which he directed his attention repeatedly and with extraordinary endurance. He seemed to compensate for his social isolation with the help especially of intensive and elaborate object-based engagements. It was not until the second year that the teachers were able to successfully integrate Clemens into the group.

In the final analysis, however, this attempt to cope is little more than a continuation of situation-specific withdrawal behavior (see the security anchor hypothesis aforementioned). It does not represent a solution to the problem situation and may even make it more difficult, as the following example illustrates.

Michael (Child No. 2) at first only occasionally retreated to familiar P–O relations when confronted with unpleasant situations. This behavior, however, became more and more common and interfered with his social integration. In this way, Michael remained a problem child throughout his entire time in the preschool.

SUMMARY AND SOME CONCLUSIONS

The thoughts and findings presented in this chapter are based on a theory in which interests are conceptualized as pronounced short-term or long-term person–object relations (P–O relations) that are of value to the person. During the course of development, changes occur in the pattern of a person's interests. When new experiences with the environment and increased possibilities for action open new areas of interest, areas that were previously preferred become less important. Far-reaching changes very often accompany a "critical transition" in life, such as the transition from home to preschool or kindergarten. From a developmental perspective, such changes are important in two ways. On the one hand, critical transitions can lead to an extension, modification, or reorganization of P–O relations. On the other hand, stable P–O relations represent a security base for children in overcoming transition problems.

Empirical investigation of these phenomena involves certain difficulties when one interprets interest not as a dispositional characteristic of personality, but rather as a specific relation between a person and an object from the environment which leads to a subjective representation, the structure of which constantly changes over the course of development. In general, conventional techniques for the objective recording of interests indicate only relative preferences for specific (global) interest areas. These techniques yield no information about subjective representations, and they give no insight into the effect in concert, or of the process of change, of individual components of the ideographic preference structure. To compensate for this shortcoming, the researcher must make use of other techniques. Such techniques would be based upon subjective estimation and could be used to evaluate qualitative data (see Valsiner, this volume). The research approach presented here is a first step in this direction. It is based upon various data sources and a relatively wide range of information about the development of interests in individual children. In this chapter, we have presented descriptive findings, and hypotheses derived from these findings, pertaining especially to the critical transition from home to preschool/kindergarten.

Findings from the present study indicate that the critical transition from home to school does indeed change the interests of children. In general, however, these changes are not dramatic enough to completely overturn the established system of P–O relations. Rather, changes usually take place in gradual and subtle ways. Whereas the main structure of P–O relations remains intact or changes very slowly, single components within individual P–O relations are incorporated or excluded. In addition, the nature of the connections among P–O relations and among single components changes (the hypothesis of structural change).

In keeping with the assumptions of the organismic developmental approach (Wapner, 1981, 1987b), we believe it makes sense to interpret the development of interests as the quantitative and *qualitative* modification of subjectively represented (knowledge) structures. Noticeable changes in a child's preferences for certain objects and/or activities (e.g., playing with completely new objects) does not necessarily imply a change in the existing interest structure. Frequently, such an observable change of preference involves only one component of a larger P–O relation, the basic structure of which remains unchanged. Detailed qualitative analysis of the origin of interest-oriented P–O relations supports the hypothesis (discussed elsewhere) that, already during childhood, the development of interests exhibits a high degree of "object continuity" (Fink, 1991; Renninger & Leckrone, 1991).

Social factors play a decisive role in determining whether and to what extent new interests develop or old interests are abandoned or changed during a period of critical transition. Our data seem to indicate that children, when placed in a new environment, first involve themselves in a reorganization and stabilization of their social relations, try out new friendships, overcome social anxieties, and determine their own social "rank" before developing new interests (the hypothesis of the primacy of social relations). This also explains the repeatedly recorded time delay for observable effects. It usually takes several months before the changes in the child's interest structure brought about by the new environment are obvious (the hypothesis of delayed effect). Our observations point to both the positive and negative effects of this. On the positive side, the new surroundings and the new social experiences often function as catalysts for the development of interests, by enabling components of the interest structure that are already present to "bloom" (the hypothesis of catalysis). On the negative side, some children are unable to overcome the anxieties induced by the kindergarten environment and are more likely to be inhibited in their development of interests (the hypothesis of inhibition).

The present findings confirm indirectly the educational principle that new information must be related to prior knowledge and skills if it is to be absorbed and structured for long-term retention. In terms of the development of children's interests, this means that new experiences in preschool or kindergarten will have lasting effects only if the child is able to incorporate them into an existing structure of P–O relations. These conclusions have many implications for educational practice. Preschool teachers should concentrate on acquiring a detailed picture of each child's P–O relations as soon as possible. This is especially true for children who are thought to be "difficult cases." In presenting a child with new experiences, the teacher must consider the child's existing structure of P–O relations. (See the chapter by Renninger in this volume for further discussion of this point.) From a developmental standpoint, an excessive offering may do no harm but, at first, it is probably useless.

In addition to investigating how the events associated with a critical transition can bring about changes in already existing interests, the present study also examined whether the interests acquired at home are useful in dealing with the problems of a critical transition. Beginning with the observation that many people in such transitional phases report an especially strong valuing of particular objects that belong to their "past" (Csikszentmihalyi & Rochberg–Halton, 1981; Demick, Redondo & Wapner, 1986; Wapner, 1981), we hypothesized that, in coping with the problems of a transition, a child relies heavily on already developed P–O relations. Findings from our descriptive studies confirm that a child's interests from home can facilitate this transition. Interests appear to act as a security base to which the child can return in special situations or for longer periods of time. This phenomenon has been discussed here in terms of both the anchor hypothesis and the compensation hypothesis. Stable forms of engagement with particular object domains allow a child who finds him or herself in a new, perhaps anxiety-producing environment, to search for familiar objects or to create familiar situations that correspond to his or her interests. In this way, the child can busy him or herself with familiar objects, and needs not fear that he or she will be confronted with unknown challenges.

For the anxious child, seeing that other children pursue similar activities or are interested in what that child is doing makes it possible to reduce social anxieties and/or to develop new social contacts. Interests that the child brings to the new situation appear to help build new social contacts, particularly when those interests coincide with the interests of others (initiation hypothesis).

This aspect also has implications for everyday practice. A child who will soon enter preschool should be encouraged to cultivate individual P–O relations in order to acquire some competencies. Parents, however, should bear in mind that, at this age, the concrete forms of activity involving an object of interest are at least as important as the gain in knowledge about the object that results from this activity. Knowing about different possible forms of engagement, and willingness to try out new forms of engagement, are important prerequisites for the development of personal, or individual, interests in unfamiliar situations, and in finding common elements of interest-oriented activity when interacting with strangers.

REFERENCES

Ainsworth, M. D. S., Blehar, M. C., Waters, E., & Wall, S. (1978). *Patterns of attachment: A psychological study of the strange situation.* Hillsdale, NJ: Lawrence Erlbaum Associates.

Anderson, R. C., Shirey, L. L., Wilson, P. T., & Fielding, L. G. (1987). Interestingness of children's reading material. In R. E. Snow & M. J. Farr (Eds.), *Aptitude, learning, and instruction. Vol. 3: Conative and affective process analyses* (pp. 287–299). Hillsdale, NJ: Lawrence Erlbaum Associates.

Averill, J. R. (1980). A constructivist view of emotion. In R. Plutchik & H. Kellerman (Eds.), *Emotion: Theory, research, and experience* (Vol. 1, pp. 305–339). New York: Academic Press.

Boesch, E. E. (1982). Das persönliche Objekt. In E. D. Lantermann (Ed.), *Wechselwirkungen-Psychologische Analysen der Mensch-Umwelt-Beziehung* (pp. 29–41). Göttingen: Hogrefe.

Brody, S. (1980). Transitional objects: Idealization of a phenomenon. *Psychoanalytic Quarterly, 49,* 561–605.

Bronfenbrenner, U. (1978a). Ansätze zu einer experimentellen Ökologie menschlicher Entwicklung. In R. Oerter (Ed.), *Entwicklung als lebenslanger Prozeβ* (pp. 33–65). Hamburg: Hoffmann & Campe.

Bronfenbrenner, U. (1978b). The social role of the child in ecological perspective. *Zeitschrift für Soziologie, 7,* 4–20.

Bronfenbrenner, U. (1979). *The ecology of human development.* Cambridge, MA: Harvard University Press.

Bühler, K. (1918). *Die geistige Entwicklung des Kindes.* Jena: Fischer.

Csikszentmihalyi, M. (1975). *Beyond boredom and anxiety.* San Francisco: Jossey-Bass.

Csikszentmihalyi, M. (1988). Motivation and creativity: Towards a synthesis of structural and energistic approaches to cognition. *New Ideas in Psychology, 6,* 159–176.

Czikszentmihalyi, M. (1990). *Flow: The psychology of optimal experience.* New York: Harper & Row.

Csikszentmihalyi, M., & Rochberg–Halton, E. (1981). *The meaning of things. Domestic symbols and the self.* Cambridge: Cambridge University Press.

DeCharms, R. (1968). *Personal causation.* New York: Academic Press.

Deci, E. L. (1975). *Intrinsic motivation.* New York: Plenum Press.

Deci, E. L. (1980). *The psychology of self-determination.* Lexington: Heath.

Deci, E. L., & Ryan, R. M. (1985a). *Intrinsic motivation and self-determination in human behavior.* New York: Plenum Press.

Deci, E. L., & Ryan, R. M. (1985b). The general causality orientations scale: Self-Determination in personality. *Journal of Research in Personality, 19,* 109–134.

Deci, E. L., & Ryan, R. M. (1991). A motivational aproach to self: Integration in Personality. In R. Dienstbier (Ed.), *Nebraska Symposium on Motivation: Vol. 38. Perspectives on Motivation.* Lincoln: University of Nebraska Press.

Demick, J., Redondo, J. P., & Wapner, S. (1986). *Cherished possessions and adaptation of the elderly to the nursing home environment.* Paper presented at the 9th International Conference of the International Association for the Study of People and their Physical Surroundings, Haifa, Israel.

Dewey, J. (1913). *Interest and effort in education.* Boston: Riverside Press.

Dreher, E., Dreher, M., Fink, B. & Hinkelmann, R. (1985). Dissens als methodologisches Konstrukt qualitativer Auswertung. *Entwicklungspsychologische Arbeiten und Berichte.* München: Lehrstuhl für Entwicklungspsychologie der Universität München.

Filipp, S. H. (1981). Selbstkonzept. In H. Schiefele & A. Krapp (Eds.), *Lexikon zur pädagogischen Psychologie* (pp. 331–335). München: Ehrenwirth.

Fink, B. (1989). *Das konkrete Ding als Interessengegenstand.* Frankfurt/Main: Peter Lang.

Fink, B. (1991). Interest development as structural change in person–object relationships. In L. Oppenheimer & J. Valsiner (Eds.), *The origins of action: Interdisciplinary and international perspectives* (pp. 175–204. New York: Springer.

Fink, B., & Krapp, A. (1986a, September). *Komponenten eines Modells zur Beschreibung der Interessenentwicklung als Veränderung von Person–Gegen-stands–Beziehungen: Theoretische überlegungen und empirische Befunde aus Fallanalysen* (Beitrag zur Tagung der AEPF, Fribourg, Schweiz).

Fink, B., & Krapp, A. (1986b). *Personale und nichtpersonale Bindung. Überegungen zur Anwendbarkeitbindungstheoretischer Konzepte auf gegenstündliche Person-Umwelt-Beziehungen* (Gelbe Reihe, Arbeiten zur Empirischen Pädagogik und Pädagogischen Psychologie, Nr. 10). München: Universität München und Universität der Bundeswehr.

Fink, B., Schiefele, U., & Krapp, A. (1985, September). *Zur wechselseitigen Abhängigkeit von sozialen und gegenständlichen Bezügen im Kindesalter* (Beitrag zur Arbeitstagung Pädagogische Psychologie, Trier, 25–26).

Furby, L. (1978a). Possessions: Toward a theory of their meaning and function throughout life-cycle. In P. B. Baltes (Ed.), *Life-span development and behavior* (pp. 297–336). New York: Academic Press.

Furby, L. (1978b). Possessions in humans: A developmental study of its meaning and motivation. *Social Behavior and Personality, 6,* 49–65.

Heckhausen, H. (1980). *Motivation und Handeln.* Berlin: Springer.

Hidi, S. (1990). Interest and its contribution as a mental resource for learning. *Review of Educational Research, 60* (4), 549–571.

Hidi, S., & Baird, W. (1986, March). Interestingness—A neglected variable in discourse processing. *Cognitive Science, 10,* 179–194.

Hidi, S., & Baird, W. (1988). Strategies for increasing text-based interest and students' recall of expository texts. *Reading Research Quarterly, 23,* 465–483.

Hidi, S., & McLaren, J. (1987, September). *The effect of topic and theme interestingness on the production of school expositions*. Paper presented at the Second European Conference for Research on Learning and Instruction, Tübingen.

Kaplan, B., Wapner, S., & Cohen, S. B. (1976). Exploratory applications of the organismic–developmental approach to transactions of men–in–environments. In S. Wapner, S. B. Cohen, & B. Kaplan (Eds.), *Experiencing the environment* (pp. 207–233). New York: Plenum Press.

Kasten, H. (1985). *Beiträge zu einer Theorie der Interessenentwicklung*. München: Habilitationsschrift.

Keller, A., & Schneider, K. (Eds.) (in press). *Curiosity and exploration*. New York: Springer.

Kerschensteiner, G. (1926). *Theorie der bildung*. Leipzig: Teubner.

Krapp, A. (1989). Neuere Ansätze einer pädagogisch orientierten Interessenforschung. *Empirische Pädagogik, 3,* 233–255.

Lazarus, R. S., Kanner, A. D., & Folkman, S. (1980). Emotions: A cognitive-phenomenological analysis. In R. Plutchik & H. Kellerman, (Eds.), *Emotion. Theory, research, and experience* (pp. 189–217). New York: Academic Press.

Lepper, M. R. (1988). Motivational considerations in the study of instruction. *Cognition and Instruction, 5,* 289–309.

Lewin, K. (1954). Behavior and development as a function of the total situation. In L. Carmichael (Ed.), *Manual of child psychology*. New York: Wiley.

Lewis, M., & Brooks, J. (1975). Infant's social perception: A constructivist view. In L. Cohen & P. Salapatek (Eds.), *Infant perception: From sensation to cognition* (pp. 218–243). New York: Academic Press.

Lunk, G. (1927). *Das Interesse. Bd. 2: Philosophisch-pädagogischer Teil*. Leipzig: Klinkhardt.

Mayring, P. (1983). *Qualitative Inhaltsanalyse*. Weinheim: Beltz.

McGrew, W. C. (1972). *An ethological study of children's behavior*. New York: Academic Press.

Nickel, H. (1985). *Sozialisation im Vorschulalter*. Weinheim: VCH.

Norman, D. A., & Rumelhart, D. E. (Hrsg.) (1978). *Strukturen des Wissens* (Original erschienen 1975: Explorations in cognitions). Stuttgart: Klett.

Oerter, R. (1977). *Moderne Entwicklungspsychologie*. Donauwörth: Ludwig Auer.

Oerter, R. (1981). Entwicklung. In H. Schiefele & A. Krapp (Eds.), *Handlexikon zur pädagogischen Psychologie*. München: Ehrenwirth.

Papousek, M. (1984). Wurzeln der kindlichen Bindung an Personen und Dinge: Die Rolle der integrativen Prozesse. In C. Eggers (Ed.), *Bindungen und Besitzdenken beim Kleinkind* (pp. 155–184). München: Urban & Schwarzenberg.

Passman, R. H., & Halonen, J. S. (1979). A developmental survey of young children's attachments to inanimate objects. *The Journal of Genetic Psychology, 134,* 165–178.

Passman, R. H., & Weisberg, P. (1975). Mothers and blankets as agents for promoting play and exploration by young children in a novel environment: The effects of social and nonsocial attachment objects. *Developmental Psychology, 11,* 170–177.

Piaget, J. (1974). *Theorien und methoden der modernen erziehung. Frankfurt am Main: Fischer.*

Piaget, J. (1981). *Einführung in die genetische Erkenntnistheorie.* Frankfurt am Main: Suhrkamp.

Prenzel, M. (1988). *Die Wirkungsweise von ilnteresse. Ein Erklärungsversuch aus pädagogischer Sicht.* Opladen: Westdeutscher Verlag.

Renninger, K. A. (1984). Object–child relations: Implications for both learning and teaching. *Children's Environments Quarterly, 1,* 3–6.

Renninger, K. A. (1989a, March). *Interest and noninterests as context in reading.* Paper presented at the annual meeting of the American Educational Research Association (AERA), San Francisco.

Renninger, K. A. (1989b). Individual patterns in children's play interests. In L. T. Winegar (Ed.), *Social interaction and the development of social understanding* (pp. 147–172). Norwood, NJ: Ablex.

Renninger, K. A. (1990). Children's play interests, representation, and activity. In R. Fivush & J. Hudson (Eds.), *Knowing and remembering in young children* (pp. 127–165). Vol. Emory Cognition Series (Vol. III)). Cambridge, MA: Cambridge University Press.

Renninger, K. A. & Leckrone, T. G. (1991). Continuity in young children's actions: A consideration of interest and temperament (pp. 205–238). In L. Oppenheimer & J. Valsiner (Eds.) *The origins of action: Interdisciplinary and international perspectives.* New York: Springer–Verlag.

Renninger, K. A., & Wozniak, R. H. (1985). Effect of interest on attentional shift, recognition, and recall in young children. *Developmental Psychology, 21,* 624–632.

Schmidt–Denter, U. (1985). Kurz- und langfristige Anpassungsprozesse in vorschulischen Einrichtungen und ihre Konsequenzen für die erzieherische praxis. In H. Nickel (Ed.), *Sozialisation im Vorschulalter.* Weinheim: VCH.

Seiler, T. B. (1978). Grundlegende entwicklungstätigkeiten und ihre regulative, systemerzeugende Interaktion. In G. Steiner (Ed.), *Die Psychologie des 20. Jahrhunderts, Bd. VII. Piaget und die Folgen* (pp. 628–645). Zürich: Kindler.

Stanjek, K. (1978). Das Überreichen von Gaben: Funktion und entwicklung in den ersten Lebensjahren. *Zeitschrift für Entwicklungspsychologie und Pädagogische Psychologie, 10,* 103–113.

Stanjek, K. (1980). Die Entwicklung des menschlichen Besitzverhaltens: *Materialien aus der Bildungsforschung* Max-Planck-Institut für Bildungsforschung, *16.*

Voss, H. G., & Keller, H. (1983). *Curiosity and exploration. Theories and results.* New York: Academic Press.

Wapner, S. (1981). Transactions of persons–in–environments: Some critical transitions. *Journal of Environmental Psychology, 1,* 223–239.

Wapner, S. (1987a). 1970–1972: Years of transition. *Journal of Environmental Psychology, 7,* 389–408.

Wapner, S. (1987b). A holistic, developmental, systems-oriented environmental psychology: Some beginnings. In D. Stokols & J. Altman (Eds.), *Handbook of environmental psychology* (pp. 1433–1465). New York: Wiley.

Weisberg, P., & Russell, J. E. (1971). Proximity and interactional behavior of young children to their "security" blankets. *Child Development, 42,* 1575–1579.

Werner, H. (1957). The concept of development from a comparative and organismic point of view. In D. B. Harris (Ed.), *The concept of development* (pp. 125–148). Minneapolis: University of Minnesota Press.

Werner, H. (1959). *Einführung in die Entwicklungspsychologie.* München: Barth.

White, R. W. (1959). Motivation reconsidered: The concept of competence. *Psychological Review, 66,* 297–333.

Winnicott, D. W. (1953). Transitional objects and transitional phenomena. *The International Journal of Psycho-Analysis, 34,* 89–97.

Witzel, A. (1982). *Verfahren der qualitativen Forschung.* Frankfurt/Main: Campus.

Wozniak, R. H. (1986). Notes toward a co-constructive theory of the emotion–cognition relationship. In D. J. Bearison & H. Zimiles (Eds.), *Thought and emotion* (pp. 39–63). Hillsdale, NJ: Lawrence Erlbaum Associates.

CONCLUSIONS

17 The Present State of Interest Research

Suzanne Hidi
Ontario Institutes for Research in Education

K. Ann Renninger
Swarthmore College

Andreas Krapp
Universität der Bundeswehr – Munich

At the end of Chapter 1 we suggested that there are at least three aspects of the present state of interest research that need to be addressed. The first of these involves how interest is defined. The second concerns possible strategies for researching interest. The third focuses on how existing findings might be utilized for educational purposes. Here, in our last chapter, we begin to deal with these issues by reviewing and integrating the ideas, approaches, and empirical work of the contributors to this volume.[1]

CONCEPTUALIZATION(S) OF INTEREST

In 1983, Van Dijk; and Kintsch suggested that "Interest is no more than a common-sense term—though a useful one—which needs to be defined for technical purposes" (p. 223). Ideally, the technical definition of interest might lead to a unified concept. In reality, as the chapters in this volume demonstrate, there are numerous conceptualizations of interest that emerge from both the everyday use of interest (see Valsiner's chapter for

---

[1] All references to the contributing authors' work refer to their chapters in this volume, unless otherwise noted.

further discussion of this point), and a plethora of differing research questions.

Although the authors of this book describe interest in terms of the way that individuals interact with their environment, there are differing viewpoints about what interest is and how it functions. Several authors, building on questions about motivation and school learning addressed by Herbart (1806), Dewey (1913) and, more recently, H. Schiefele (1986), focus on interest as embodied in the person–object relation, maintaining that special relations with an object (a topic, knowledge domain, or subject matter such as computers, music, etc.) lead to interest, which, in turn, serves as a motivator (see chapters by Krapp & Fink; Nenniger; Prenzel; Schiefele; and Schiefele, Krapp, & Winteler). Others, influenced by more cognitive–developmental theorists such as James (1890), Baldwin (1906, 1907), Vygotsky (1978), and Piaget (1940, 1981), discuss interest in relation to the individual's activity within a larger socio-cultural milieu that consists of both objects and others (see chapters by Deci; Pressley, El-Dinary, Marks, Brown, & Stein; Renninger; Valsiner; and Voss & Schauble). Yet another approach builds on discussions of Dewey (1913), Berlyne (1960), and Thorndike (1935,) and considers certain features of the environment to be interest-creating and centers on how and why these features might generate interest (see chapters by Garner, Brown, Sanders, & Menke; Hidi & Anderson; Iran–Nejad & Cecil; Shirey; and Wade).

Given different theoretical frameworks, it is not surprising that the authors represented in this volume also differ with respect to the focus of their analyses. Some discuss the specific relation between the individual and the task, whereas others describe that which engages people in tasks (situational interest). Those authors who study individual interest consider interest to be a relatively enduring predisposition toward a class of objects or events, which has been described by Renninger as involving high levels of both stored knowledge and value relative to the other objects and events with which the individual is involved. Krapp and Fink depict the structure of interest as consisting of the reference object, the activities with the object, and the topics/questions/challenges with which the individual engages.

From this perspective, one individual's interest relation can be thought of as differing from the next person's in such a way that two individuals interested in the same object (e.g. computers, cars, math, etc.) would not necessarily be interested in the same challenges/questions/engagement with that object (cf. Prenzel; Renninger; and Krapp & Fink;. Furthermore, what is identified as an object of interest is identified not in a vacuum, but in relation to the individual's interest for the other objects (activities, etc.) with which that individual engages. Furthermore, it is not simply knowledge that constitutes individual interest, but it is the combination of knowledge and value that contributes to individual interest and thus to individual differences in what is of interest to individuals.

Investigators of situational interest, on the other hand, do not view interest as enduring, or as based in a relation to other activity, but rather as an actualized state that is elicited by interesting features in the environment (cf. Garner et al.; Hidi & Anderson; Garner et al.; Iran–Nejad & Cecil; Wade). It is assumed that such features generate interest across subjects. As such, individual differences have not been critical variables in research on situational interest. In addition, situational interest is not necessarily associated with high knowledge and value, although Hidi and Anderson do suggest that interest generated by environmental features could also provide the basis for the development of the knowledge and value requisites of individual interest.

Interestingly enough, research into both individual and situational interest has dealt with the actualized state of interest. It is critical to an understanding of the findings of these research programs that one recognize the respective roles of the individual and the environment in these programs. Researchers who focus on individual interest tend to share the belief that interest as a psychological state involves behavioral or action tendencies which are reflected in repeated activities. Prenzel, for example, distinguishes between an individual's momentary and long-term relation with an interest object. In his view, only the latter qualify as interests; these can be further characterized by selective persistence. Similarly, Krapp and Fink argue that interest involves a special relation between person and object that cannot be based on a one-time, unrepeated form of engagement. An individual's reaction to an interesting object, text, or idea cannot be classified as interest unless it is observed more regularly over time. Renninger further suggests that individuals are not necessarily metacognitively aware of their interest(s) and its effect on learning.

In contrast, investigators of situational interest tend not to regard individual predispositions as instrumental in producing the actualized state of interest, maintaining instead that specific features of the environment can generate an actualized state of interest. Typically, this type of interest is described as evoked and as one that may have only a short duration. For example, death or sex may elicit a high level of situational interest (cf.

Schank, 1979), and their intermittent presence in text also contributes to producing the actualized state of interest. Building on Kintsch's (1980) discussion of the postdictability of text structure as significant to the creation of (cognitive) interest, research on situational interest has examined: important versus interesting text/sentence segments (Garner et al; Hidi & Anderson; Shirey; Wade); seductive details and their placement in text (Garner et al.; Wade); and the interest created by the surprise-ending story as a cause and consequence of cognitive functioning (Iran–Nejad & Cecil).

The particular relation between individual interest and situational interest remains an open question, although several authors suggest that longer lasting interests probably develop through the experience of an activity that has special significance for the individual (Deci; Pressley et al.; Valsiner; and Voss & Schauble). Hidi and Anderson specifically suggest that at some later time individuals may acquire the knowledge and value about a situational interest that then lead to its becoming an individual interest. However, the issue of how individual interests originate has not been central to the discussion of what individual interest is and how its presence affects school learning. In fact, Valsiner argues from a metatheoretical perspective that identifying the origins of interest may even be impossible. On the other hand, if, for example, the focus of one's research involves study of text organization to enhance school learning, then understanding how interests can be elicited and how they emerge is critical.

There are clearly distinctions to be made between conceptualizations of interest and their respective research questions. Across researchers of both individual and situational interest, however, there appears to be a general conceptual shift in the research questions they are posing—a shift from simply establishing the effects of interest to addressing why these effects occur. In particular, issues under discussion by researchers of both individual and situational interest include the relation between interest and attention, interest and effort, interest and physiological functioning, and interest and affect, emotion, and value.

Practically all of the chapters on individual interest, for example, refer in some way to the assumption that interest increases attention, although very few direct measurements of attention have been reported in these studies (for an exception, see Renninger, this volume; Renninger & Wozniak, 1985). Researchers examining text-based interest have traditionally measured the effect of interest on attention by comparing reading times and secondary reaction times of more and less interesting text segments (e.g., Anderson, 1982; Shirey & Reynolds, 1988; chapters by Shirey and Wade, this volume). Shirey describes differences in the way in which mature and immature readers attend to text features, arguing that differences exist in their attention to task and indicating that immature readers need to overcome interest in order to attend to the important features of text. He considers interest to be a reader-specific internal criterion. He does not distinguish between long term, individual interest that develops over time and situational interest, such as sentence interest, that may be short-term and fleeting. Further, he argues that interest is not a text or task characteristic but an internal factor that the reader brings to the reading situation.

Others also consider how interest affects attention and facilitates reading comprehension. The experimental data are confusing on this point (see chapters by Schiefele; Wade). Hidi (1990) questioned the assumption that attention should necessarily result in longer reading and reaction times, suggesting that spontaneous as opposed to voluntary attention may be involved in processing interesting information and may in fact result in faster reaction times. She further noted that the attentional consequences of interest may vary with tasks. For example, in tasks that require more complex and effortful processing or less automatized cognitive activity than reading, interest might also result in better-sustained and persistent attention. In such cases, one would expect longer duration of activity rather than faster performance.

An important and related point is how effort is influenced by the actualized state of interest. On the one hand, when they are interested, people clearly increase their efforts and persist in their activities. On the other hand, such activities seem to be more effortless; that is, one tends not to be aware of the expansion of energy. This aspect of the actualized state of interest is what has been described by Csikszentmihalyi (cf. 1988) as flow, and it is the basis of what Deci, Nenniger, Prenzel, and Pressley et al. might label an intrinsic motivator, a source of selective persistence. However, further clarification of the role of effort (and practice) as a function of interest in the development of competence needs to be articulated.

Related to the issues of attention and effort is the physiological functioning of the individual. At the present time, we do not know whether the physiological processes associated with interest have unique aspects. Krapp (1990) has suggested that arousal is a physiological phenomenon that may well be related to the state of interest, and Hidi (1990) suggested that both the psychological and the physiological aspects of interest must be integrated to explain the effect of interest on cognitive functioning.

The affective components of interest are also in the process of being further elaborated. However, discussion of interest and value should not be confused with discussions of either interest and emotion or interest and affect. Several authors describe interest as characterized by positive emotions. For example, in accordance with Izard's (1977) earlier work on emotion, Deci argues that interest is a core affect, experienced when a person's needs and desires mesh with a particular activity. Such activities usually involve some form of novelty, challenge, or aesthetic appeal. Although other authors do not equate interest with affect, several suggest that the state of interest is characterized by positive emotions (Pressley et al.; Prenzel; Schiefele; Shirey). Hidi and Anderson review this point in more detail and conclude that whereas well-developed individual interests tend to be accompanied by positive feelings, situational interests might not be as intensively and consistently associated with affect. With respect to individual interest, on the other hand, Renninger and Leckrone (1991) have suggested that interest may also involve negative emotions. They describe interest as co-occurring with positive and/or negative emotions and distinguish stored value for the particular object from the emotion experienced during the state of interest. Finally, Iran–Nejad and Cecil deny any association of interest and emotion, claiming instead that interest is the cause and consequence of intellectual functioning.

Thus, at least at the present time, at one level the discussion of interest appears to be dichotomous. Two primary sets of questions are being asked: those focusing on individual interest and those focusing on situational interests. Across these orientations, however, there are a host of questions related to understanding actualized interest. These include questions about individual(s) and tasks. They also include questions about the nature of interest in relation to value, emotions, affect, attention, effort, and physiological functioning, among other variables. Clearly, establishing the complementarity of research questions, and ways in which findings from studies of both individual and situational interest inform each other appears to be an important next step for researchers of interest.

RESEARCH METHODS FOR STUDYING INTEREST

Given that interest has been conceptualized in two somewhat different ways, it is not surprising that practically all of the investigations discussed in this volume focus on either individual or text-based interest. The specific methods for researching these questions, however, do not cluster by "content." Rather, the empirical studies reported here could generally be said to focus on the consequences of interest as a factor in how outcomes or information are processed. Typically, interest (as predisposition, actualized state or characteristic of the environment) is identified and its effects (e.g., free play, learning of information) on variable(s) (e.g., duration of activity, number of correct math problems, rating of competence) are evaluated. In these investigations, interest has been treated as an independent variable and studied as an influence on variables drawn from literature(s) as diverse as motivation, cognition, and/or text development.

Rating scales were most frequently used to identify interest, although the type of scale employed ranges from questionnaires that simply inquired about interests (Nenniger; Schiefele), to Likert-type questionnaires that identified levels of knowledge and value without using the term *interest* (Renninger), to interestingness ratings of text segments or sentences used to examine text-based interest (Garner et al.; Hidi & Anderson; Iran–Nejad & Cecil; Shirey; Wade). More naturalistic techniques for identifying interest include allowing students to select their own texts (Pressley et al.), examination of subjects' record keeping (Prenzel), observation of play activities (Krapp & Fink), and multi-level analyses of videotaped free play (Renninger). In addition, both Prenzel, and Krapp and Fink also employed interviews to verify identification of interest.

Contrasts of interest or interestingness were provided by differing levels of interest (Schiefele), or texts rated as interesting and uninteresting where uninteresting refers to lack of value (Garner et al.; Hidi & Anderson; Iran–Nejad & Cecil; Schiefele; Shirey; Wade). Alternatively, Renninger used repeated measures to systematically manipulate the knowledge and value components of each individual's engagement with tasks of interest (high knowledge, high value), noninterest (high knowledge, low value), and/or attraction (low knowledge, high value).

As a function of research questions, the dependent variables in the various investigations ranged from qualitative evaluations (e.g., qualitative analyses of ideas recalled, error analyses) to purely quantitative measures (e.g., number of ideas recalled or recognized, time spent performing activities). In addition, a number of process variables have been considered in studying the mediating effect of interest on behavior. Both Shirey and Wade used reading times to evaluate attention. Prenzel asked subjects to keep records of their feelings, competence, flow, and cognitive conflicts during activity with interest objects. Nenniger used rating scales to evaluate five dimensions of motivated academic learning. Schiefele had subjects rate the level of activation, flow and elaboration in processing texts written on individually interesting and uninteresting topics. Renninger studied the process of children's play activities with play objects identified as interests, noninterests, and attractions. Krapp and Fink used case analysis to describe change in children's activities across observations.

Several chapters called for the use of think-alouds in order to further examine the effects of interest on the process of task engagement. A few such studies are currently in process (cf. Renninger, 1991) and should greatly enhance understanding of the respective contributions of interest to both the accessibility of tasks and the depth of an individual's processing of the tasks. In addition, Rathunde (1991) recently reported use of an experimental sampling method, called the electronic paging technique, for tracking experience in natural settings, which enables him to link flow experiences and individuals' engagement with identified objects of interest.

Analyses employed a range from description and nonparametric analyses to correlation, analysis of variance, repeated measures analyses of variance, and path analyses. In addition, Schiefele et al. used meta-analysis to review literature on interest as a predictor of achievement. Some researchers have also combined quantitative and qualitative methods in their work. For example, Prenzel asked subjects to record each episode of engagement with their objects of interests, noting the details and duration of the activities; Renninger combined videotaped observation in the classroom with experimental tasks; and Krapp and Fink combined observations in the classroom over time with a series of interviews.

Combined methods have been employed in order to examine how interest influences different aspects of students' performance. It may well be that the effect of interest on behavior is more complex than it appears. If so, it may be necessary to track the interest–effect from the student's commencement of a task to its completion, integrating procedures not yet reported in interest research. As Valsiner points out, coordination of methodologies permits study of introspective processes, such as interest, precisely because it is multi-dimensional. A combination of rating scales, think-aloud protocols, and observations of activities including reading and/or activity time measures, for example, could provide a more complete picture of many aspects of both interested individuals' performance and the qualities of tasks that render them interesting.

IMPLICATIONS OF RESEARCH ON INTEREST FOR EDUCATION

Many authors in this book argue that cognitive activities such as comprehension and learning are generally facilitated by interest. The facilitative influence of interest (both individual and text-based) seems to hold across many different types of tasks, genres, and age groups. Highly interested students have more numerous and more highly developed associative structures than their less interested counterparts (Schiefele, Winteler, & Krapp, 1988), and interest influences transfer and comprehension through the activation of less specific types of learning strategies (Nenniger). Furthermore, interest has been shown to influence learning and to depend on content-specific knowledge and emotional feelings, variables that are intercorrelated with and influence academic achievement (Nenniger). On average, according to Schiefele et al., interest accounts for about 10% of the observed achievement variance, across different subject areas, types of schools, and age groups.

Evidence is also accumulating that indicates that a learning context linked to the goals or interests of the individual results in increased learning (Deci; Nenniger; Pressley et al.). For example, in their discussion of strategies instruction, Pressley et al. report that asking students to choose their own reading materials directly links assignments to the particular interests of students, in turn increasing their autonomous use of strategies. Prediction encourages students to relate the text to what they already know; images that students construct and describe to the group are filled with personal reactions to the meaning of the text; and clarifications lead to discussions about understanding and interpretation (Pressley et al.). By using interest to create facility with the use of strategies, students are led to use and become interested in using these strategies.

Study of students' understanding of text structure, for example, suggests that in narrative tasks students are particularly likely to find the important ideas interesting (Hidi & Anderson). In fact, Wade reports that among college students interest is a better predictor of recall/comprehension than is the structure of the narrative. It appears that high interest does not simply increase the quantity of learning, but it tends to change recall patterns and to result in more qualitative differences in the way in which information is comprehended (Hidi & Anderson; Schiefele). However, interest may be more accurately understood as a consequence of learning in the sense that it becomes a basis for the individual's subsequent learning (Iran–Nejad & Cecil). When a person is in a position to meet the challenges posed by a task, he or she can ask questions about what is/was understood about the task; as such, engagement in the task can concurrently create new possibilities for questioning and challenge setting (Krapp & Fink; Renninger). It is not surprising, then, that Schiefele concludes that interest is of greater importance when deeper comprehension of text content is required, and of less importance when superficial knowledge, explicitly contained in a text, is needed.

The goal for learning is not only critical in establishing the end toward which the individual is working, but it is informed by interest, in that what becomes a goal for the individual is developed in light of interest as well. Whenever goals are established for an individual by another person, such as a teacher, then the extent to which goals are shared is of particular importance. As Voss and Schauble point out, values, interests, and goals best direct and influence the amount of processing in which a student engages when they are maximally related to a given task. They also point out, however, that individuals are known to suspend processing when they believe learning has been accomplished. Establishing an optimal environment for learning entails considering not only the context of learning, but the skills to be learned, the individual's knowledge of self as learner, and facilitation by others in the form of questions, tasks, modeling, etc.

As several authors suggest, there are ways in which the structure of the school day, the materials, and the facilitation of learning can be enhanced by attention to students' interests (in particular, see chapters by Hidi & Anderson; Krapp & Fink; Prenzel; Pressley et al.; and Renninger). Specifically, in order to capitalize on interest as a facilitator of student learning, the school day needs to be organized so that students have time to work with identified interests and to explore potential interests. This may require reorganization of class time so that students can work on and return to work with tasks. It also involves recognition that students are posing different challenges to themselves, and/or are at different levels of autonomy in terms of assuming challenges, and as a consequence one student may not be on the same schedule as the next. Finally, both reconsideration and revision of materials used for instruction may be required.

In general, interest can be said to enhance learning and to have the potential to be used by those who work with others (e.g. teachers, parents, caretakers, clinicians). On the other hand, interest has also been found to interfere with learning. Interest interferes with learning in at least three ways. First, given that interest leads to student questioning and challenge setting, there needs to be a match between the individual and the environment that is optimal for the individual (cf. Hunt, 1961). Thus, where a mismatch occurs between the "task" and the activity of the learner, interest may interfere with learning. Krapp and Fink, for example, describe the transition of young children from the family to school as providing a catalyst for the further development of interest because it enables a child to engage in new questioning as a function of his or her interactions with new play objects and playmates. On the other hand, some children they studied were unable to overcome the anxieties induced by the "same" kindergarten environment and were more likely to be hindered in learning in the new setting, at least partially because of their interests. Without a match between the new sets of challenges and the child's interests, the child's interest(s) constrained learning—the child did not take on new challenges with his or her interest and what he or she did know about the play object was not incorporated into the ongoing activity of the new setting.

Interest can also interfere with learning in that it leads students to "understand" a situation as something other than it is. In other words, the information the child/student has previously chunked for subsequent recall as a function of interest influences the way in which the student interprets the demands of a task (Renninger). In this instance, the student may make assumptions based on prior experience that do not necessarily result in learning. For example, a student reading a highly interesting passage about baseball might assume that he or she understands the content of the text when in fact it is only the topic about which he or she knows something, and the specifics of that passage have been missed altogether. Such misunderstanding is at least partially the result of a mismatch in understanding what the goal of the task was in the first place, but it also involves overblown and inappropriate feelings of competence with the task due to interest. This interferes with learning.

Finally, interest can also interfere with learning because the focus of the student is disrupted by the presence of another "goal" (Voss & Schauble). Thus, although seductive details have been conventionally added to text to enhance its interestingness, their presence is likely to be counterproductive for learning because there is a good likelihood that they will be remembered (Wade). It seems that any text segment that contains traditional story elements with goal-directed activities and human interest factors is well recalled, even if it does not represent the main point of the text (Hidi & Anderson). In fact, Garner et al. maintain that it is not possible to write text that does not include seductive details. Instead, they suggest that students need to be taught to be aware of seductive details as an element of text structure that can distract them from the importance of the text.

On the other hand, especially as children get older, they are more and more frequently expected to deal with tasks that are outside their individual interests. Even though teachers and curriculum writers can aim to create situational interest and build activities around children's interests, individuals must also be able to work on and complete uninteresting tasks. Deci suggests that when individuals are aware that uninteresting activities are of personal importance or of instrumental value to them, they are willing to undertake these activities. Given minimum pressure, and with a sense of choice, these activities may eventually become internalized and more interesting. In this way, students might take on or develop new interests. Alternatively, as Prenzel suggests, future research might focus on the development of interests outside of schools in order to detail conditions conducive to interest development that might be used in classrooms.

CONCLUSIONS

Clearly, further development of the varied approaches represented in this volume should lead to a more complete picture of how and why interest influences learning and development. Both individual and situational interest explicate the varying aspects of interest. There is an obvious complementarity between understanding the interest with which an individual engages a task and the interestingness of that task. However, no attempts to assess the relation between these two types of interests have been reported. For example, would highly interested persons' reactions to interesting objects, ideas, or text segments differ from others'? Or the converse of this question could also be addressed: How does the processing of more and less interesting text segments differ as a function of individuals' personal interest in the topic(s) of these texts? Empirical work that employed a combined approach to assessing interest might result in the development of a coordinated construct, even if it did not yield a single technical definition of interest. Alternatively, research conducted on either individual or situational interest should be better informed if related questions are acknowledged and considered. Once such future research findings become available, the present discussion of interest may well need modification.

REFERENCES

Anderson, R. C. (1982). Allocation of attention during reading. In A. Flammer & W. Kintsch (Eds.), *Discourse processing* (287–299). Amsterdam: North–Holland.

Baldwin, J. M. (1906). *Thought and things: A study of the development and meaning of thought* (Vol. I). New York: Macmillan.

Baldwin, J. M. (1907). *Thought and things: A study of the development and meaning of thought* (Vol. III). New York: Macmillan.

Berlyne, D. E. (1960). *Conflict, arousel and curiosity.* New York: Grove Press.

Csikszentmihalyi, M. (1988). Motivation and creativity: Towards a synthesis of structural and energistic approaches to cognition. *New Ideas in Psychology, 6,* 159–176.

Dewey, J. (1913). *Interest and effort in education.* Boston: Riverside Press.

Herbart, J. F. (1806/1965). Allgemeine Pädagogik, aus dem Zweck der Erziehung abgeleitet. In J. F. Herbart (Ed.), *Pädagogische Schriften* (Vol. 2). Düsseldorf: Kupper.

Hidi, S. (1990). Interest and its contribution as a mental resource for learning. *Review of Educational Research, 60* (4), 549–571.

Hunt, J. McV. (1961). *Intelligence and experience.* New York: Ronald Press Co.

Izard, C. E. (1977). *Human emotions.* New York: Plenum.

James, W. (1890). *The principles of psychology.* London: Macmillan.

Kintsch, W. (1980). Learning from text, levels of comprehension, or: Why anyone would read a story anyway. *Poetics, 9,* 87–98.

Krapp, A. (1990, March). Interest and curiosity. *Paper presented at the Symposium "Curiosity and Exploration : Theoretical Perspectives, Research Fields, and Applications,"* University of Osnabrück.

Piaget, J. (1940). The mental development of the child. In D. Elkind (Ed.), *Six psychological studies.* New York: Random House.

Piaget, J. (1981). Intelligence and affectivity: Their relationship during child development. In T. A. Brown & C. E. Kaegi (Eds.), *Annual Review Monographs.* Palo Alto, CA: Annual Reviews.

Rathunde, K. (1991, April). A path with a heart: The role of interest in the development of talent. In P. Pokey (Chair). *Students' motivational beliefs: The role of interest and goal orientation.* Symposium conducted at the meeting of the American Educational Research Association.

Renninger, K. A. (1991, April). Influences of interest and text difficulty on students' strategies for reading and recall. In D. Schallert (Chair.), *Effects of interest on strategies and learning from text.* Symposium conducted at the meeting of the American Educational Research Association.

Renninger, K. A., & Leckrone, T. G. (1991). Continuity in young children's actions: A consideration of interest and temperament. In L. Oppenheimer and J. Valsiner (Eds.), *The origins of action: Interdisciplinary and international perspectives* (205–238). New York: Springer–Verlag.

Renninger, K. A., & Wozniak, R. H. (1985). Effect of interest on attentional shift, recognition, and recall in young children. *Developmental Psychology, 21,* 624–632.

Schiefele, H. (1986). Interest: New answers to an old problem. *Zeitschrift für Pädagogik, 32* (2), 153–162.

Schiefele, U., Winteler, A., & Krapp, A. (1988). Studieninteresse und fachbezogene Wissensstruktur. *Psychologie in Erziehung und Unterricht, 35,* 106–118.

Schank, R. C. (1979). Interestingness: Controlling inferences. *Artificial Intelligence, 12,* 273–297.

Shirey, L. L., & Reynolds, R. E. (1988). Effect of interest on attention and learning. *Journal of Educational Psychology, 80,* 159–166.

Thorndike, E. L. (1935). *Adult interests.* New York: Macmillan.

van Dijk, T., & Kintsch, W. (1983). *Strategies of discourse comprehension.* Orlando: Academic Press.

Vygotsky, L. S. (1978). *Mind in society: The development of higher psychological processes.* (M. Cole, V. John–Steiner, S. Scribner, & E. Souberman, Eds. & Trans.). Cambridge, MA: Harvard University Press.

Author Index

J

K

Kühn, R. 184, 210

L

Lane, D. M. 289, 295
Lang, P. J. 305, 330
Langer, E. 310, 330
Langsdorf, P. 324, 330
Larkin, A. G. 255, 276
Larson, R. 4, 23, 162, 178, 180
Lathin, D. 57, 70
Lavin, D. E. 23, 184, 188, 210
Lawler, E. E. 53, 68
Lawton, S. C. 257, 275
Lazarus, R. S. 309, 330, 407, 427
Leckrone, T. G. 5, 7, 24, 36, 40,
    78, 98, 363, 371, 374, 394, 406,
    407, 408, 423, 427, 438, 445
Lee, D. S. 338, 357
Lee, M. 183, 210
LeFevre, J. 162, 178
Leggett, E. L. 14, 21, 156, 178
Lehnert, W. G. 301, 330
Lehr, S. 230, 237
Lehrke, M. 13, 17, 23, 186, 204,
    209, 210
Lehwald, G. 127, 148
Leone, D. 60, 67
Lepper, M. R. 15, 23, 57, 66, 68,
    76, 97, 156, 158, 180, 409, 427
Leskinen, E. 186, 207, 210
Leslie, L. 171, 181
Levin, J. R. 125, 148, 333, 357
Lewin, K. 33, 40, 408, 427
Lewis, E. G. 196, 210
Lewis, M. 415, 427
Lichtenstein, E. H. 305, 328
Lin, Y. 122, 127, 148
Lind, G. 127, 148
Lindzay, G. 4, 19
Linn, M. C. 205, 210
Lipson, M. Y. 132, 351, 356
Lloyd, J. 189, 210
Loftus, E. F. 300, 328
Lomax, R. G. 184, 211
Lompscher, J. 126, 148
Lonky, E. 50, 66

Lubenow, G. C. 246, 252
Lukens, R. J. 230, 237
Lunk, G. 4, 23, 73, 78, 97, 406,
    427
Luria, A. R. 29, 33, 41
Lynch, J. 59, 69

M

Macke, G. 129, 147, 148
Maehr, M. L. 78, 97, 184, 187,
    203, 206, 212
Mahoney, M. J. 301, 330
Malone, M. R. 184, 187, 208, 246,
    252
Mandinach, E. 130, 147
Mandl, H. 3, 23, 161, 165, 178,
    180
Mandler, F. 3, 23
Mandler, G. 309, 323, 324, 325,
    330, 386, 394
Manoogian, S. T. 60, 66
Markell, R. A. 286, 294, 378, 393
Marks, M. B. 334, 348, 352, 356,
    357, 434
Maslow, A. H. 48, 68
Mason, J. 8, 19, 152, 177, 226,
    235, 245, 253, 287, 379, 393
Massad, C. E. 196, 210
Massimini, F. 173, 180
Masur, E. F. 257, 276
Mathews, S. 305, 331
Matushkin, A. M. 127, 149
Mayer, R. E. 122, 124, 149, 256,
    275, 347, 356, 380, 393
Mayor, J. D. 305, 309, 328
Mayring, P. 411, 427
McCaffrey, M. 253, 258, 275
McClintock, A. H. 152, 177, 256,
    274
McCullers, J. C. 65, 68
McDaniel, M. A. 191, 210
McGaw, B. 190, 209
McGraw, K. O. 65, 68
McGrew, W. C. 413, 420, 427
McIntyre, C. W. 257, 276
McKeachie, W. J. 122, 127, 130,
    133, 145, 148, 149

Subject Index